Semantic Web Technologies and Legal Scholarly Publishing

Law, Governance and Technology Series

VOLUME 15

For further volumes:
http://www.springer.com/series/8808

Silvio Peroni

Semantic Web Technologies and Legal Scholarly Publishing

Springer

Silvio Peroni
Department of Computer Science and Engineering
University of Bologna
Mura Anteo Zamboni 7
40126 Bologna (BO)
Italy

ISSN 2352-1902 ISSN 2352-1910 (electronic)
ISBN 978-3-319-04776-8 ISBN 978-3-319-04777-5 (eBook)
DOI 10.1007/978-3-319-04777-5
Springer Cham Heidelberg New York Dordrecht London

Library of Congress Control Number: 2014934451

Printed on acid-free paper

Springer is part of Springer Science+Business Media (www.springer.com)

Foreword

What you are holding in your hand is a multi-faceted book. From where I stand, there are at least three different points of view that can be taken to read it and enjoy its ideas and conceptual framework.

First of all, this is a book proposing innovative ideas about *Legal Publishing*. As such, positioning it within the Law, Governance and Technology Series of Springer Verlag is proper and true to its nature and aims: Peroni's work contributes new concepts and solutions for managing legal texts (doctrine as well as legislation and jurisprudence), placing them as the core cultural infrastructure upon which the universe of legal activities is based, whose workflow (from ideation to drafting, to evaluation, to publication, to evolution, to oblivion or removal) is instrumental to the correct understanding of legal processes, and whose semantic representation is a compelling and exemplary application of Semantic Web technologies that provides solid bases for innovative tools helping professionals and laymen in cataloguing, searching, and reasoning upon legal knowledge.

And yet, a second main viewpoint emerges, that of *Semantic Publishing*, constituting an explicit, confessed, and transparent focus drift, whereby legal publishing is held as but one instance of many in the larger class of publishing contexts, where similarities are more important than differences, so that they can be studied and described as one discipline.

In this sense, document publishing can be seen as the main theme of the book, and the legal domain as just the frontmost example. Several topics of great timeliness and complexity are tackled and relevant contributions are provided under one encompassing paradigm giving them integrity and uniformity: from the issue of managing multiple, reciprocally inconsistent structures over the same content (a well-known problem in the markup community since the early days of TEI) to the problem of the accurate description of the domain of scholarly publishing, to the issue of providing informative and easily understandable presentation of metadata records of publications to a lay audience, we are shown a full catalogue of tough problems whose solutions in literature are, at present, hardly satisfactory. Yet Peroni not only tackles them providing more advanced proposals and ideas than in literature, but does so by introducing to its full power just one new approach, that of Semantic Web technologies, showing how powerful and elegant they are in addressing complex issues.

Namely, multiple hierarchies are in fact managed through overlapping markup as suggested long ago in literature, but through the use of Semantic Web ontologies Peroni gives life to a fully new meta-markup language, EARMARK, that successfully and automatically replaces XML without loosing the generality and availability of its tools. Similarly, metadata for scholarly publishing are in fact managed through ontologies, as suggested in innumerable publications of the last twenty years, but Peroni suggests a unifying framework of eight different ontologies, SPAR, integrating in the same conceptualization issues as different as the FRBR-based description of the relationships between versions of the same work, the finest distinction of roles and stages in scholarly publishing, the rhetorical roles of sections and fragments in scholarly articles. Also and consequently, the familiarity of Peroni to Semantic Web technologies allows him to produce end-user tools that are immediately and concretely useful to the layman and professional alike: his documentation tool, his key concept extractor and his visualization tool for OWL ontologies are immediately useful in the publishing domain and therefore in the legal publishing domain, but they are, at heart, extremely general tools that are useful wherever OWL ontologies are employed.

But there is a third point of view in this book, a background theme connecting all foreground topics. We could call it the *time- and context-aware design pattern*, an approach to describing and formalizing complex domains by taking into account the unavoidable evolutions in time or context that sooner or later will affect the design.

For instance, traditional ontologies for publishing often consider editions as first-class concepts, fixed in time and absolute in their nature, and therefore downplay the existence of connections between subsequent versions or variants of the same publication; ontologies of organizational domain overload the description of the actors involved with the roles they hold, as if role was a persistent characteristic of an individual or an organization: is being a member of the parliament a permanent or transient characteristic of a politician? Is being a draft discussed by a specific commission a permanent or transient characteristic of a bill? Handling time and context-aware characterization of complex domains is not straightforward, and although literature of best practices for ontology design has frequently discussed the drawbacks of ignoring time in formalizations, and has proposed a number of design approaches that take care of time and contexts, the world is full of important and widespread ontologies that describe sketches of reality frozen in time, possibly not wrong now, but surely to become wrong some time in the future. Peroni's approach is systematically, sometimes painfully aware of the fact that time and contexts change and affect formalizations, and makes sure that the markup languages, the ontologies, the tools he proposes can handle in a sophisticated manner domains that evolve in time and that have different characteristics depending on contexts. From this point of view, I believe that Section 5.5 of this book, providing the ontological design pattern for handling time and context aware formalizations of domains, is the conceptual pivot of the whole book, and provides the fundamentals of an extremely mature and self-conscious scholarly approach by Peroni.

In the last five years, I witnessed Silvio Peroni's cultural evolution from the early projects as an eager master student to the full scientific maturity of this book, a rich rewriting and extension of his PhD thesis. It is with pleasure and fondness that I see many long and thought-provoking discussions with him end up in this book as fully-expressed and convincing argumentations, dutifully backed up in literature and tightly connected with practical applications and actual tools. I feel honoured to have been involved in his work and to have been collaborating with Silvio in these years.

Department of Computer Science and Engineering
University of Bologna

Prof. Fabio Vitali

Preface

This book introduces theories, formalisms and applications that permit effective interaction between legal scholarly documents and their related semantic and formal descriptions, using the semantic technologies that have been employed to create the Semantic Web and Linked Data. Such an application of Semantic Web technologies to the world of documents and publishing is here termed *Semantic Publishing*.

Research and publishing in Law have a long tradition of applying such semantic technologies to real-world scenarios. In this context, the aim of this book is to describe and propose solutions to three of the main issues faced by the application of Semantic Publishing within the context of the legal scholarly documents, namely: the need for tools to link document text to a *formal representation of its meaning*; the requirement for complete *metadata schemas/ontologies* that can be used to describe documents using the language and vocabulary of the world of publishing; and the demand for effective *user interfaces* that permit such tools and schemas to be applied in practice.

The first section of this book describes *markup theory and technology*, whereby a better comprehension of a document can be derived from a description of its structural organisation and of the formal semantics contained within it, and from clarification of how these two types of markup—structural and semantic—can overlap and interact. In digital documents, the way we say something about a text is by the addition of markup, by which is meant additional statements, not normally rendered visible for human reading, that define and delimit structural or semantic features of the text. Markup has been used for years for annotating documents at all levels of granularity, from the digital document as a whole to its sub-components. However, the most commonly used document formats employed in publishing (i.e., XML and PDF) were not developed primarily to enable semantic enhancement and overlapping markup, although in principle it is possible to use them for this purpose. To facilitate the task of integrating potentially overlapping structural and semantic markup, I have developed an OWL-based markup metalanguage called *EARMARK*. EARMARKed documents are collections of addressable text fragments associated with OWL assertions that describe the structural and semantic properties of (parts of) that content.

Digital documents and their content form the focus of Semantic Publishing, which enables their automated discovery and connection to other document-related resources and contexts, such as other articles and raw data. Unfortunately, existing Semantic Web vocabularies are too abstract and incomplete to cover the requirements of the publishing world. There is thus an acute need for new vocabularies (ontologies) that comprehensively describe the different aspects of the publishing domain. In the central section of this book, I describe a suite of orthogonal and complementary OWL 2 DL ontology modules, the *Semantic Publishing and Referencing (SPAR) Ontologies*, that enable all aspects of the publishing process to be described in machine-readable metadata statements encoded using the Resource Description Framework (RDF).

The final section of this book describes new tools and interfaces that enable users to use and interact with such semantic technologies and to create semantic data. This provision of new tools and interfaces is particularly crucial for Semantic Publishing, since its end-users are generally publishers, researchers, readers, librarians, law scholars and the like, rather than computer scientists who are experts in semantic technologies. The use of semantic languages and vocabularies such as EARMARK and the SPAR Ontologies requires simple and easy-to-use human-computer interfaces that facilitate their application to Semantic Publishing by non-experts. Here I introduce four new tools developed to support users: two (*LODE and KC-Viz*) to aid in understanding an ontology; a third (*Graffoo*) that assists in presenting such an ontology, or fragments of it, in comprehensible formalised diagrams; and a fourth (*Gaffe*) that is useful when employing such an ontology to create semantic definitions of real data.

Acknowledgements

This is a reprise of the acknowledgements I wrote for my Ph.D. thesis. It is, actually, an extended reprise, which includes more people to thank, as usual for a work like this.

As already stated in my Ph.D. thesis, I can here confirm that I have never been able to write acknowledgements. It is definitely a tautology. I always feel to forget somebody—by the way, I am quite sure it will happen again as before. Actually, I fear it is already happening. Let me begin.

First of all, I would like to thank my family, especially Tiziana, my wife, for being always patient with my work and for having always and unconditionally endured, supported and encouraged me in everything. A special thank to the newborn Giuseppe, my son, who delighted me with his yells and smiles when I was finalising this book.

A big thanks to my Ph.D. tutor—and friend, boss, proofreader, Neil Gaiman's fan—Prof. Fabio Vitali, who has involved me in his extraordinary research group, who has continuously encouraged me, my ideas and my work, and who honoured me by writing the foreword of this book. It is really a pleasure working with you.

Another thanks to the rest of my Ph.D. *commissione*, Prof. Claudio Sacerdoti Coen and, in particular, my advisor Prof. Paolo Ciancarini, for having always been ready to discuss my Ph.D. topics, even after my Ph.D. graduation.

I would also like to thank other two people, friends, who were and still are fundamental to my research: Prof. Enrico Motta and Prof. David Shotton. I am really pleased to have been part of their research groups and to carry on our prolific collaborations. And thanks again for all your help as proofreaders of both my Ph.D. thesis and, in particular, this book.

Citing proofreaders, how can I thank, in an appropriate way, the lady who helped me to correct several (really: several) grammatical mistakes, typos, Italianisms, and illogical sentences? Let me make it simple (as I said above, I have never been able to write acknowledgements): Stefania Mattei, thanks from the heart for all the time and effort you dedicated to this work.

Another big thanks goes to all my Ph.D. external referees for their precious comments and advices—namely, Dr. Jeni Tennison, Prof. Yves Marcoux, Prof. Daniel

Apollon, and in particular Prof. Pompeu Casanovas who, as editor of the Law, Governance and Technology Series, encouraged me to undertake the writing of this book—and to the anonymous reviewers of this book for their insightful remarks and suggestions. I would also like to thank the other editor of the Law, Governance and Technology Series, Prof. Giovanni Sartor, for having expressed his interest in my work, and Neil Oliveir and Diana Nijenhuijzen for having guided me, patiently and efficiently, through the publishing process.

Last but not least, I would like to thank all the other members of my research group and collaborators—in alphabetical order: Dr. Gioele Barabucci, Prof. Angelo Di Iorio, Prof. Aldo Gangemi, Andrea Giovanni Nuzzolese, Francesco Poggi, Prof. Valentina Presutti, Prof. Fabio Tamburini, Prof. Francesca Tomasi, and Jacopo Zingoni—for having supported (and still supporting) my work and for all the interesting discussions about the life, the universe, and everything.

Contents

About the Author

Silvio Peroni holds a Ph.D. degree in Computer Science and he is a post-doc at the University of Bologna. He works on document markup and semantic descriptions of bibliographic entities using OWL ontologies. He is one of the main developers of the *SPAR* (*Semantic Publishing and Referencing*) *Ontologies* that provide RDF descriptions of bibliographic entities, citations, reference collections and library catalogues, as well as the structural and rhetorical components of documents, and roles, statuses and workflows in publishing. Among his research interests are Semantic Web technologies, markup languages for complex documents, design patterns for digital documents and ontology modelling, and automatic processes of analysis and segmentation of documents. In particular, his recent works concern the empirical analysis of the nature of citations, the study of visualisation and browsing interfaces for semantic data, and the development of ontologies to manage, integrate and query bibliographic information according to temporal and contextual constraints. He maintains a personal website (`http://www.essepuntato.it`) and a blog (`http://palindrom.es/phd`) about his research.

List of Figures

List of Tables

Chapter 1
Introduction

Abstract This book describes applications in the legal domain of the increasing relationships between two distinct multidisciplinary research fields, *Semantic Web technologies* and *scholarly publishing*, that converge in the field called *Semantic Publishing*. In the spirit of the original aim of Semantic Publishing, i.e., the improvement of scholarly communication by means of semantic technologies, this book proposes theories, formalisms and applications for opening up semantic publishing (in particular, scholarly articles and legal documents) to their users, by providing an effective interaction between documents and their related semantic and formal descriptions. Indeed, the main aim of this book is to increase the users' comprehension of documents and to allow them to enrich their own documents, to automate the discovery of such documents by others, and to link to related resources such as scholarly articles, primary sources and raw data.

This book describes applications in the legal domain of the increasing relationships between two distinct multidisciplinary research fields, *Semantic Web technologies* and *scholarly publishing*, that converge in the field called *Semantic Publishing*. In the spirit of the original aim of Semantic Publishing, i.e., the improvement of scholarly communication by means of semantic technologies, this book proposes theories, formalisms and applications for opening up semantic publishing (in particular, scholarly articles and legal documents) to their users, by providing an effective interaction between documents and their related semantic and formal descriptions. Indeed, the main aim of this book is to increase the users' comprehension of documents and to allow them to enrich their own documents, to automate the discovery of such documents by others, and to link to related resources such as scholarly articles, primary sources and raw data[1].

Research in Law has a long tradition of applying such semantic technologies (Ashley and van Engers 2011), employed to create the Semantic Web and Linked Data (Breuker et al. 2009; Casanovas et al. 2013), to real-world scenarios. In this context, the aim of this book is to describe and propose solutions for three of the main issues

[1] In this way, the purposes of this book conform to the principles asserted in the Brussels Declaration on STM publishing, which states that the research data contained in journal articles should be open (International STM Publishing Community 2007).

S. Peroni, *Semantic Web Technologies and Legal Scholarly Publishing*, Law, Governance and Technology Series 15, DOI 10.1007/978-3-319-04777-5_1,

faced by Semantic Publishing within the context of the legal scholarly documents[2], namely: the need for tools to link document text to a *formal representation of its meaning*; the requirement for complete *metadata schemas/ontologies* that can be used to describe documents using the language and vocabulary of the world of publishing; and the demand for effective *user interfaces* that permit such tools and schemas to be applied in practice.

The vision of Semantic Publishing's pioneers, e.g., Shotton (2009a), Shotton et al. (2009b) and De Waard (2010), goes beyond the current interest of publishers and Semantic Web practitioners, which is focused on the mere addition of semantic markup to published articles, with the intention of categorising recognised entities (such as persons, places and proteins) by means of simple *subject-predicate-object* statements, such as "p53 is a protein", than can be encoded in RDF. Rather, the ultimate aim of Semantic Publishing is to represent, semantically, the intellectual *discourse* of a document in machine-readable form, i.e., how arguments are modelled within the text. This, of course, requires one to identify formal meanings and relations between different part of the textual content of a document (e.g., a sentence representing the main *claim*, supported by other sentences stated as its *evidences*), as well as to indicate the rhetoric functions of clearly bounded parts of the article, such as the Introduction, Background, Results, and Conclusions sections of a scholarly research article.

Moreover, in this context, additional complications are given by the need to be aware of the intrinsic provenance of the conversion and encoding of natural language texts into formal statements. Such conversion of a certain text can be made by several people, each one adopting a particular point of view on (or interpretation of) the text, and these interpretations can co-exist provided their provenance is clearly indicated. Furthermore, these different interpretations can be represented using different formalisms, and certain interpretations can be alternative and/or contrasting to others. Such multiple conversions of the same text may thus result in a complex network of semantic annotations made by different people that may actually *overlap* with one another in terms of specific textual segments. In this context, we need appropriate mechanisms that allow us without confusion to manage such overlapping annotations and their related provenance information (e.g., who made an annotation, when it was specified, and what was the original natural language source used as basis for the conversion)[3].

[2] In this volume, I make wide use of the terms *scholarly publishing* and *academic publishing* to refer to the subfield of publishing that concerns the communication of the results of endeavour in academic disciplines such as Computer Science, Philosophy and Sociology, etc. Thus, publishing the scholarly literature concerned with the discipline of Law can be described as *legal scholarly publishing*. In this book, Semantic Publishing concepts originally developed for the world of scholarly publishing generally are given concrete application within the field of legal scholarly documents.

[3] The provenance data of the conversions have particular relevance when we ask an external reader to choose which interpretations (i.e. semantic annotations) to trust. Of course, that choice can be based on the precision and completeness of a particular semantic annotation, but it may also depend on the reader's confidence in the translator, since the person making the conversion of the original natural language text into a certain formalism might either be an expert or a novice in undertaking such a task.

The practice that allows one to enrich and annotate natural language documents, associating explicit or implicit semantics to it, is that of *markup*. Markup has been used for years to describe documents at all levels of granularity, from the digital document as a whole to its sub-components (chapters, paragraphs, sentences, people, places, events, etc.). Thus, multiple and *overlapping markup* (being either *document markup* or *semantic markup*[4]) must be able to co-exist within the same textual content so as to allow one to express different—even alternative—semantics on it. However, the document formats most commonly used in publishing (i.e., XML and PDF) were not developed primarily to enable semantic enhancement and overlapping markup, although in principle it is possible to use them for this purpose.

In this book, I investigate plausible alternative paths for reaching a full and synergistic integration between document markup (usually used for describing the structural components of documents), semantic markup (used for specifying semantic annotations on textual content), and overlap markup (used for juxtaposing multiple document/semantic markup structures with others). To this end, I describe a markup metalanguage called *EARMARK* that I have developed, that allows one to instantiate the markup of a text document as an independent OWL document separated from the text strings it annotates. Through appropriate OWL characterisations, EARMARK can define structures such as trees or graphs, and can be used to verify validity constraints, including semantic constraints and co-constraints that currently cannot be expressed in most validation languages. When used in conjunction with an ontology developed to create semantics descriptions according to a semiotics model, called the *Linguistic Meta-Model* (Picca et al. 2008), EARMARK allows one to specify formal semantics for any document markup item or text content.

Of course, markup can also be used to add descriptive metadata to a document or to its sub-parts. Examples of this can be seen in all the well-known markup languages, that use appropriate elements to enclose metadata—e.g., the element *head* in HTML (Berjon et al. 2013), the element *info* in DocBook (Walsh 2010), and the elements *references*, *analysis* and *identification* in Akoma Ntoso (Barabucci et al. 2009; Barabucci et al. 2010). It is the firm intention of semantic publishing to adopt effective and complete metadata schemas. Unfortunately, existing Semantic Web vocabularies are too abstract and incomplete to cover all the requirements of the publishing world. There is thus an acute need for new vocabularies (ontologies) that comprehensively describe the different aspects of the publishing domain.

To address these needs, I have been working with professor David Shotton of the University of Oxford to develop a suite of orthogonal and complementary OWL 2

[4] Typically, a distinction is made between *document markup*(or *structural markup*), which encloses fragments of the text within markup elements (e.g., *Moby Dick*), and *semantic markup*, in which fragments of text become objects of RDF statements (e.g., *:document dcterms:title "Moby Dick"*). In my opinion, these are just two sides of the same coin. Both can be used, either interchangeable or coupled, to represent the semantics of the content of a document. I think the reason that document and semantic markup are not used in this interchangeable way, thereby acquiring two different names, is because of the different expressive powers of their most common instances, i.e., XML for document markup and RDF for semantic markup.

DL ontology modules, the *Semantic Publishing and Referencing (SPAR) Ontologies*, that enable all aspects of the publishing process to be described in machine-readable metadata statements encoded using the Resource Description Framework (RDF). In the past, several attempts have been made[5] to define general models for describing the publishing domain, but either they are too abstract, or they are not interoperable with other models, or they are very specific to particular scenarios and thus not appropriate for general use. In contrast, we have defined eight reusable SPAR ontology modules, that can be used either individually or in conjunction as need dictates, each of them precisely and coherently covering one specific aspect of the publishing domain using vocabulary terms with which publishers are familiar. Together, they provide the ability to describe bibliographic entities such as books and journal articles; citations; the organisation of bibliographic records and references into bibliographies, ordered reference lists and library catalogues; the component parts of documents; and publishing roles, publishing statuses and publishing workflows.

EARMARK and the SPAR Ontologies are plausible solutions for two of the issues mentioned above, namely the need of tools for linking document text to a formal representation of its meaning, and the need for complete metadata schemas for describing documents according to the publishers' own vocabulary. However, semantic publishing is a very multidisciplinary topic, and thus involves different kinds of users, from computer scientists and Semantic Web practitioners on the one hand, to publishers and scholars in other fields on the other. It is likely that the latter may not have experience in using ontology modelling software, and may not be expert in using formal languages, logic, inferences systems and programming languages, background knowledge of which is required for the correct use of EARMARK and the SPAR Ontologies. Nevertheless, these latter users also want to *understand* these semantic publishing ontologies, to *make sense* of them, to *adopt* them and, finally, to *produce data* using them. The final requirement is thus the development of interfaces that hide the complexity of ontology formalisms, and enable better interaction between non-experts and machine-readable datasets.

My contribution in this area has been the development of applications that simplify and clarify the interaction of users with ontologies. First of all, tools are needed to help in ontology *understanding* and *sense-making*[6]. Furthermore, an essential step in opening up the effective use of semantic publishing technologies to non-experts requires the development of *customisable user interfaces* that can be adapted quickly to particular contexts. Such interfaces must allow one to add/modify/remove semantic

[5] e.g., DC Metadata Elements (Dublin Core Metadata Initiative 2012b), DC Metadata Terms (Dublin Core Metadata Initiative 2012a), FRBR (International Federation of Library Associations and Institutions Study Group on the Functional Requirements for Bibliographic Records 2009), PRISM (International Digital Enterprise Alliance 2009) and BIBO (D'Arcus and Giasson 2009), that are introduced in detail in Chap. 2.

[6] "Sense-making" is here used to refer to a specific ontology engineering task, where the user is primarily concerned with understanding the contents and overall structure of the ontology, i.e., acquiring an overview of the concepts covered by the ontology and the way they are organised in a taxonomy, so as to comprehend what the ontology can be used for.

data correctly and intuitively, without introducing logical errors, while at the same time hiding the complexity of the underlying ontologies.

Thus, an important aspect of my work has been that of addressing these issues. Specifically, I have developed four tools:

- *LODE*, an application that automatically extracts ontological definitions from OWL ontology files, so as to render them in a human-readable HTML page designed for browsing and navigation by means of embedded links;
- *KC-Viz*, an application I have developed in collaboration with professor Enrico Motta and his research group of the Open University, that implements a novel approach for visualising and navigating ontologies, by providing concise overviews of large ontologies, and by supporting a "middle-out" ontology navigation approach, starting from the most information-rich ontological classes;
- *Graffoo*, a tool for presenting the formalisms of ontologies, or of ontology fragments, as easy-to-comprehend graphical diagrams; and
- a new version of *Gaffe*, a tool that makes it possible to build customisable editors for semantic data, and that allows users to enrich a resource with semantic descriptions (i.e., OWL assertions) according to any scheme expressed through an OWL ontology.

This book is based on my Ph.D. research thesis entitled "Semantic Publishing: issues, solutions and new trends in scholarly publishing within the Semantic Web era", that was defended at the Department of Computer Science of the University of Bologna in May 2012. In this book, I introduce these three elements, markup, ontologies and tools, emphasising their importance and innovativeness within the semantic publishing community, and explaining why previously available tools have failed to address users' needs in the same effective way. I also provide specific analysis of the potentiality of semantic publishing in the legal and legislative domain, as an aid for legal scholars and practitioners who wish to enhance the quality of the documents they produce, and to allow such documents to be fruitfully examined and used in a semantic context.

The book is thus structured as follows. Chapter 2 discusses the main issues in semantic publishing and the preceding work of others, starting by introducing the most important work on overlapping markup, on markup semantics, on markup languages for legislative documents, and on ontologies for describing the publishing domain and legal documents. Chapter 3 introduces EARMARK, the markup metalanguage that enables the definition of overlapping markup hierarchies. In Chap. 4, I then show how EARMARK may be used to enable semantic enhancement of markup structures and textual content, and I illustrate some applications of this in the legal domain, with particular reference to assessing the quality of legal drafting. Chapter 5 describes the SPAR ontologies for modelling bibliographic data, in the specific context of legal scholarly documents. Chapter 6 then focuses on the tools I have developed to help non-expert users understand ontologies and create semantic metadata using them. Final remarks and ideas for future works are then introduced in Chap. 7.

References

Ashley, K. D., and T. M. van Engers. 2011. Proceedings of the 13th International Conference on Artificial Intelligence and Law (ICAIL 2011). New York: ACM.

Barabucci, G., L. Cervone, M. Palmirani, S. Peroni, and F. Vitali. 2009. Multi-layer markup and ontological structures in Akoma Ntoso. In Proceedings of the international workshop on AI approaches to the complexity of legal systems II (AICOL-II), lecture notes in computer science 6237, ed. P. Casanovas, U. Pagallo, G. Sartor, and G. Ajani, 133–149. Berlin: Springer. DOI:10.1007/978-3-642-16524-5_9, .

Barabucci, G., L. Cervone, A. Di Iorio, M. Palmirani, S. Peroni, and F. Vitali. 2010. Managing semantics in XML vocabularies: An experience in the legal and legislative domain. Proceedings of Balisage: The markup conference 2009. Rockville: Mulberry Technologies. http://www.balisage.net/Proceedings/vol5/html/Barabucci01/BalisageVol5-Barabucci01.html. Accessed 30 July 2013.

Berjon, R., T. Leithead, E. D. Navara, E. O'Connor, and S. Pfeiffer. 2013. HTML5: A vocabulary and associated APIs for HTML and XHTML. W3C candidate recommendation, 6 August 2013. World Wide Web Consortium. http://www.w3.org/TR/html5/. Accessed 30 July 2013.

Breuker, J., P. Casanovas, M. C. A. Klein, and E. Francesconi, eds. 2009. *Law, ontologies and the semantic web*. Amsterdam: IOS.

Casanovas, P., M. Palmirani, S. Peroni, F. Vitali, and T. M van Engers. 2013. Semantic web for the legal domain. Special issue of semantic web—Interoperability, usability, applicability. Amsterdam: IOS. http://www.semantic-web-journal.net/blog/semantic-web-journal-special-issue-semantic-web-legal-domain. Accessed 30 July 2013.

D'Arcus, B., and F. Giasson. 2009. Bibliographic ontology specification. Specification document, 4 November 2009. http://bibliontology.com/specification. Accessed 30 July 2013.

De Waard, A. 2010. From proteins to fairytales: Directions in semantic publishing. *IEEE Intelligent Systems* 25 (2): 83–88. doi:10.1109/MIS.2010.49.

Dublin Core Metadata Initiative. 2012a. DCMI metadata terms. DCMI recommendation. http://dublincore.org/documents/dcmi-terms/. Accessed 30 July 2013.

Dublin Core Metadata Initiative. 2012b. Dublin core metadata element set, version 1.1. DCMI recommendation. http://dublincore.org/documents/dces/. Accessed 30 July 2013.

International Digital Enterprise Alliance. 2009. Publishing requirements for industry standard metadata specification version 2.0. Alexandria: IDEAlliance. http://www.idealliance.org/specifications/prism. Accessed 30 July 2013.

International Federation of Library Associations and Institutions Study Group on the Functional Requirements for Bibliographic Records. 2009. Functional requirements for bibliographic records final report. International federation of library associations and institutions. http://www.ifla.org/files/cataloguing/frbr/frbr_2008.pdf. Accessed 30 July 2013.

International STM Publishing Community. 2007. Brussels declaration on STM publishing. http://www.stm-assoc.org/brussels-declaration/. Accessed 30 July 2013.

Picca, D., A. Gliozzo, and A. Gangemi. 2008. LMM: An OWL-DL metamodel to represent heterogeneous lexical knowledge. Proceedings of the 6th Language Resource and Evaluation Conference (LREC 2008). Luxembourg: European Language Resources Association. http://www.lrec-conf.org/proceedings/lrec2008/pdf/608_paper.pdf. Accessed 30 July 2013.

Shotton, D. 2009. Semantic publishing: The coming revolution in scientific journal publishing. *Learned Publishing* 22 (2): 85–94. doi:10.1087/2009202.

Shotton, D., K. Portwin, G. Klyne, and A. Miles. 2009. Adventures in semantic publishing: Exemplar semantic enhancements of a research article. *PLoS Computational Biology* 5 (4): e1000361. doi:10.1371/journal.pcbi.1000361.

Walsh, N. 2010. DocBook 5: The definitive guide. Sebastopol: O'Reilly Media. Version 1.0.3. (ISBN: 0596805029).

Chapter 2
The Digital Publishing Revolution

Abstract In this Chapter I discuss the theories and technologies that take part in today's publishing revolution, a.k.a. semantic publishing. In particular, I introduce some of the most important research works on my primary fields of interest, namely markup models and languages to enhance published documents (e.g., legislative documents) semantically, and ontologies/metadata schema to describe such documents. Finally, after introducing some significant research areas in the semantic publishing domain, I conclude the chapter by listing events (i.e., projects, workshops, journal issues, competitions) that have characterised the initial development of the discipline of semantic publishing.

In this Chapter I will discuss the most relevant research areas in semantic publishing. I will focus particularly on my primary fields of interest: *markup*models, which enable the addition of *semantics* within published documents; and document *metadata schemas* and *ontologies*.

First of all, in order to appreciate the general context in which my work is set, it may be useful to describe briefly the changes that took place in digital publishing during the last decade. Scholarly authoring and publishing are undergoing a revolution due to the potential for development coming, on the one hand, from the use of Web-related technologies (e.g., transport protocols, markup languages, the Semantic Web) as a medium of communication, and, on the other hand, from the adoption of new publishing and editorial processes which seem to be converging to a fully-open accessibility of editorial contents and metadata.

The first step of this revolution was made possible by the creation of the Web, which made publishers recognise the digitalisation process and, consequently, the online publication as new effective ways of bibliographic publication. As it had been predicted (Odlyzko 2002), the social and research impact of the availability of scholarly material online is continuing to grow. One of the main reasons of this growth has been the introduction of the Open Access (OA) publishing paradigm[1]. Through it, publishers can either directly—the *gold* OA—or indirectly—the *green* OA (Harnad et al. 2004)—publish articles online and offer their complete and free-of-charge worldwide readability and accessibility at no cost.

[1] Probably, the first formal document that used the words "open access" was (Bromley 1991).

S. Peroni, *Semantic Web Technologies and Legal Scholarly Publishing*,
Law, Governance and Technology Series 15, DOI 10.1007/978-3-319-04777-5_2,

Originally, the use of OA was considered a gamble with small chance of success. However, earlier works, such as Lawrence (2001), Harnad and Brody (2004), Swan (2009), gave empirical evidence of the advantages of OA in terms of better visibility, findability and accessibility for research articles. These factors and the development of clear and established strategies (Solomon 2008; Bjork and Hedlund 2009) to change the publishers' business model from a non-OA service to an OA publishing process are some of the most important reasons of the success of the OA model—and of the (increasing) growth and consensus in digital online publication. Moreover, innovative publishing approaches have been recently proposed—e.g., the Liquid Publications Project (Simon et al. 2011) which show how to use Web technologies and OA principles to change and improve the current publication process.

Obviously, we have only covered only the first part of the long way towards a successful and widely accepted Web-oriented digitalisation and publishing of bibliographic materials. In fact, publishers have not adopted Web standards for their work yet. Rather, they still employ a variety of proprietary XML-based informational models and document type definitions (DTDs) (Beck 2010). While such independence was understandable in the pre-Web world of paper publishing, that now appears anachronistic, since publications from different sources and their metadata are incompatible, requiring hand-crafted mappings to convert from one to another. For a large community such as publishers, the lack of standard definitions that could be adopted and reused across the entire industry represents losses in terms of money, time and effort.

In contrast, modern web information management techniques employ standards such as RDF (Carroll and Klyne 2004) and OWL 2 (Motik et al. 2012) to encode information in ways that permit computers to query metadata and integrate web-based information from multiple resources in an automated manner. Since the processes of scholarly communication are central to the practice of science, it is essential that publishers now adopt such standards to permit inference over the entire corpus of scholarly communication represented in journals, books and conference proceedings. This requires the availability of appropriate ontologies and tools that are specially tailored to the requirements of authors, publishers, readers, librarians and archivists.

Some time ago, some research institutes and companies involved in publishing research started to consider whether and how Web technologies could address the issues described above. In retrospect, that moment can be marked as the beginning of what we call today *semantic publishing*.

Semantic publishing is the use of Web and Semantic Web technologies to enhance a published document such as a journal article, in order to enable the definition of formal representations of its meaning; facilitate its automatic discovery; enable its linking to semantically related articles; provide access to data within the article in actionable form; and allow integration of data between papers (Shotton et al. 2009; Shotton 2009). As confirmed by a number of recent initiatives[2], semantic publishing

[2] The various initiatives that have been involved research communities around the topics and issues of Semantic Publishing, e.g., the Elsevier Grand Challenge and the SePublica Workshops, will be introduced in Sect. 2.5.

and scholarly citation using Web standards are currently two of the most interesting topics within the scientific publishing domain. We identify some significant research areas in this domain, which include:

1. the *development of markup technologies* that facilitate the creation of complex and semantically-enhanced markup documents, which make possible to have, simultaneously, a formal semantic description of their structures (e.g., chapters, introduction, paragraphs) as well as of their content;
2. the *development of semantic models* (vocabularies, ontologies) that meet the requirements of scholarly authoring and publishing;
3. the *development of visualisation and documentation tools* that permit such ontologies to be easily understood by users who are neither experts nor technicians of particular modelling languages;
4. the *development of annotation tools* that allow these models to be used by end-users (e.g., publishers, editors, authors) for enhancing documents with relevant semantic assertions;
5. the *development of new algorithms* that can take advantages of this new semantic layer of annotations, for example when searching over large sets of on-line documents;
6. the *development of new business models* that arrange effective publishing processes for the creation, use and dissemination of semantic assertions;
7. the *study and realisation of empirical evaluations* that ascertain the benefits and/or the drawbacks of Semantic Publishing for both authors and publishers, such as understanding whether its use increases the impact factor of articles and/or the amount of visits on publishers' Web pages;
8. the *organisation of events*, such as conferences, workshops, projects, journal issues, in order to publicise and promote semantic publishing principles and advantages to a broader audience.

In the rest of this Chap. I will outline related works where solutions to the issues indicated in the first two points of the above list are presented, and that represent the research areas in which my work is set. I will address point three and four in Chap. 6. I will conclude this chapter by listing a series of events (i.e., projects, workshops, journal issues, competitions) that have characterised the initial development of the discipline of semantic publishing.

2.1 Towards Semantics-Aware Markup Languages

The original definition of markup clearly states that markup is used for saying *something* about the content of a document (Coombs et al. 1987). Understanding what "something" refers to is strictly dependant on the particular *semantics* adopted by the markup vocabulary thereby considered. However, markup languages such as XML and SGML do not provide any mechanism to define or associate a particular semantics to their markup structures. Often, the semantical characterisation of such markup lies between the human's subjective interpretation of the name given to markup items and their natural language descriptions written by the author of a particular markup schema. On the other hand, both the previous examples do not provide a formal and mathematical characterisation (e.g., by means of logic formulas) of such semantics.

Anyway, *overlapping* markup structures are needed when different agents associate multiple (even discording) semantics to the same document fragment. Note that having two different interpretations of a particular document passage is possible, in particular within a domain—i.e., Semantic Publishing—where the analysis and formalisation of the scientific discourse are encouraged. Thus, the topic of overlapping markup, that has been discussed and investigated for years, becomes extremely significant in this context.

In the following sections I will introduce previous studies about both overlapping markup and markup semantics, which are two of the most interesting topics in markup research.

2.1.1 Overlapping Markup

The need for multiple overlapping structures over documents using markup syntaxes such as XML and SGML is a long-standing issue, and a large amount of literature exists about techniques, languages and tools that allow users to create multiple entangled hierarchies over the same content. A good review can be found in DeRose (2004).

Some of this research proposes to use plain hierarchical markup (i.e., XML) and employ specially tailored elements or attributes to express the semantics of overlapping in an implicit way. The TEI Guidelines (Text Encoding Initiative Consortium 2013) present a number of different techniques that use SGML/XML constructs to force multiple hierarchies into a single one, including:

- *milestones*, through which one hierarchy is expressed using the standard hierarchical XML markup and the elements belonging to the other ones are represented through a pair of empty elements denoting the start and the end tags, and connected to each other by special attributes;
- *flat milestones*, that represents each of the hierarchy elements as a milestone, i.e., an empty element placed where the start or the end tag should be, all of them contained as children of the same root element;
- *fragmentation*, in which one hierarchy (the primary) is expressed through the standard hierarchical XML markup, while the elements of the secondary hierarchies are fragmented within the primary elements, in a way that suits the primary hierarchy and are connected to each other by special attributes;
- *twin documents*, in which each hierarchy is represented by a different document that contains the same textual content while marking up the elements according to the individual hierarchy;

- *stand-off markup*, which places all the textual content in a single structure with the possible specification of the shared hierarchy, while putting the remaining elements in other structures (e.g., files) with the positional association of each starting and ending location to the main structure, realised by using, for instance, XPointer (DeRose et al. 2001) locations[3].

Given the large number of techniques to deal with overlapping structures in XML, in Marinelli et al. (2008), Marinelli et al. present a number of algorithms to convert XML documents with overlapping structures from and to the most common approaches, as well as a prototype implementation.

In Riggs (2002), Riggs introduces a slightly different technique for fragmentation within XML structures. In this proposal, *floating elements*, i.e., those elements that do not fall in a proper or meaningful hierarchical order, are created using the name of the element followed by an index referring to its semantically-related parent element. For example, the floating element `<name.person[2]>John</name.person[2]>` means that `<name>John</name>` is semantically child of the second occurrence of the element *person*, even though the floating element is not structurally contained by its logical parent.

Other research even proposes to abandon of the theory of trees at the base of XML/SGML altogether, and use different underlying models and newly invented XML-like languages that allow the expression of overlaps through some kind of syntactical flourishing.

For instance, *GODDAG* (Sperberg-McQueen and Huitfeldt 2004) is a family of graph-theoretical data structures to handle overlapping markup. A GODDAG is a Direct Acyclic Graph whose nodes represent markup elements and text. Arcs are used to explicitly represent containment and father-child relations. Since multiple arcs can be directed to the same node, overlapping structures can be easily represented in GODDAG. Full GODDAGs cannot be linearised in any form using embedded markup, but *restricted GODDAGs*, a subset thereof, can and have been linearised into TexMecs (Huitfeldt and Sperberg-McQueen 2003; Marcoux 2008), a multi-hierarchical markup language that also allows full GODDAGs through appropriate workarounds, such as virtual elements.

LMNL (Tennison and Piez 2002) is a general data model based on the idea of *layered text fragments and ranges*, where multiple types of overlap can be modelled using concepts drawn from the mathematical theory of intervals. Multiple serialisations of LMNL are available, such as CLIX and LMNL-syntax.

XConcur (Schonefeld and Witt 2006) is a similar solution based on the representation of multiple hierarchies within the same document through *layers*. Strictly related

[3] Note that the use of standoff approaches to handle overlapping issues is not only a prerogative of the world of Computer Science and document markup: it has been in fact adopted also in several projects in Linguistics related to the processing and annotation of natural language texts, for instance the *General Architecture for Text Engineering* (*GATE*) (Cunningham 2002) and *Callisto* (Day et al. 2004).

to its predecessor CONCUR as it was included in the SGML, XConcur was developed in conjunction with the validation language XConcur-CL to handle relationships and constraints between multiple hierarchies.

The *variant graph* approach (Schmidt and Colomb 2009) is also based on graph theory. Developed to deal with textual variations—that generate multiple versions of the same document with multiple overlapping hierarchies—this theory proposes a new data model to represent literary documents and a graph linearisation (based on lists) that scales well even with a large number of versions. Schmidt et al. recently presented an extension of their theory that also allows users to merge multiple variants into one document (Schmidt 2009).

In Portier and Calabretto (2009) a detailed survey about overlapping approaches was presented, together with a discussion on the MultiX 2 data model—that uses W3C standard languages such as XInclude to link and fetch text fragments within overlapping structures—and a prototype editor for the creation of multi-structured documents.

In Tummarello et al. (2005) a proposal for using RDF as a standoff notation for overlapping structures of XML documents was proposed. By means of the open-source API *RDF Textual Encoding Framework* (*RDFTef*), Tummarello et al. demonstrate a possible way for handling overlapping markup within documents and identifying textual content of a document as a set of independent RDF resources that can be linked mutually and with other parent resources.

In addition to giving the opportunity to define multiple structural markup hierarchies over the same text content, the use of RDF as the language for encoding markup allows the user to specify semantic data on textual content as well. However, the main advantage of RDF is the possibility of using particular built-in resources that describe different kinds of containers, either ordered (rdf:Seq) or unordered (rdf:Bag), as defined in the RDF syntax specification (Carroll and Klyne 2004). Thus, RDF resources can be used to represent every printable element in the text—words, punctuation, characters, typographical symbols, and so on—while RDF containers can be used to combine such fragments and containers as well.

RDF does not provide any mechanism to define a formal vocabulary for structural markup, since it is able neither to define certain resources as classes of a particular kind (elements, attributes, comments, text nodes) nor to characterise the possible relations that such resources may have among others. However the specification of an RDFS (Brickley and Guha 2004) or of an OWL (Motik et al. 2012) layer can successfully address this issue. Hybrid solutions obtained by mixing different models, even when they are built one upon another, may seem elegant but are not necessarily the best choice. In fact, there exist well-known interoperability limits between OWL 2 DL and RDF (Krotzsch et al. 2011) that prevent the correct use of Semantic Web tools and technologies. In particular:

- any markup document made using RDF containers (e.g., to describe what the markup items contain and in which order) and OWL ontologies (e.g., to define classes of markup entities and their semantics) results in a set of axioms that make the OWL ontology completely inconsistent. This limits the applicability

of the most frequently used Semantic Web tools, that are usually built upon the (computationally-tractable) description logic underlying OWL 2 DL;
- the individual analysis of each language may be not applicable when we have to check particular properties that lay between RDF and OWL layers have to be checked. For example, to verify the validity of a markup document against a particular schema, which is one of the most common activities with markup, one needs to work with both markup item structures (that would be defined in RDF) and logical constraints about classes of markup items (e.g., elements only, attributes only, the element "p", all the element of a particular namespace, etc., all of them definable in OWL).

Being able to express everything we need directly in OWL addresses both issues in a straightforward way. The well-known absence of containers and sequences in OWL can be overcome by modelling classes in specific ways using specific design patterns such as Ciccarese et al. (2008) and Drummond et al. (2006).

2.1.2 *Markup Semantics and Semantic Markup*

The advent of the Semantic Web (and social web) has induced a shift of meaning for some terms that are traditionally associated with markup languages. Originally, the act of *marking up* was strictly associated with document markup, where the term "tag" was used to refer to *markup elements*: syntactic items representing the building blocks of a document structure. While, in the original definition, markup "tells us something about [the text or content of a *document*]" (Coombs et al. 1987), in the Semantic Web the term "markup" is sometimes used to identify any data added to a *resource* with the intention to semantically describe it (as well as "metadata" or "resource description"). Because of this recent re-drawing of the markup meaning, the term "tag" has also drastically changed its definition to "a non-hierarchical keyword or term assigned to a piece of information (such as an Internet bookmark, digital image, or computer file)"[4].

Partially because of this shift in meaning—that brought, as first consequence, the fact of having two different (and often unrelated) visions of the Web: the *Web of documents* and the *Web of data*—the Semantic Web has not considered in detail the issue of *markup semantics* (e.g., what is the meaning of a markup element *title* contained in a document *d*?), concentrating all its efforts in dealing with *semantic markup* (e.g., the resource *r* has the string "Semantic enhancement of document markup" as title) (Renear et al. 2002).

However, markup semantics is a very well-known and relevant issue for markup languages and consequently for digital libraries. Nowadays, a large amount of content stored in digital libraries is encoded with XML. XML, as any markup (meta)language,

[4] http://en.wikipedia.org/wiki/Tag_%28metadata%29

provides a machine-readable mechanism for defining document structure, by associating labels to fragments of text and/or other markup. This association has a particular meaning, since each markup element asserts something about its content. However, what is asserted by the markup is not an issue of the markup itself. One of the goals of markup metalanguages is to avoid imposing any particular semantics: they express mere syntactic labels on the text, leaving the implicit semantics of the markup to the interpretation of humans or tools programmed by humans. Of course, a lot of markup languages, such as HTML, TEI and DocBook, are accompanied by natural language descriptions of their markup, but those descriptions are not machine-readable; in other words, there is no formal mechanism to embed markup semantics within markup language schemas.

Previous works (Renear et al. 2002; Renear et al. 2003; Sperberg-McQueen et al. 2009) pointed out some clear advantages in having a mechanism to define a machine-readable semantics of markup languages: enabling parsers to perform both syntactic and *semantic validation* of document markup; *inferring facts* from documents automatically by means of inference systems and reasoners; simplifying the *federation*, *conversion* and *translation* of documents marked up with different and non-interoperable markup vocabularies; allowing users to *query* upon the structure of the document considering its semantics; creating *visualisations* of documents by considering the semantics of their structure rather than the specific vocabulary in which they are marked up; increasing the accessibility of documents' content, even in the case of *tag abuse* (Dubin 2003), i.e., "using markup languages construction in ways other than" the ones "intended by the language designer"; promoting a more flexible *software design* for those applications that use markup languages, guaranteeing a better *maintainability* even when markup language schemas evolve.

For instance, it could be interesting to query documents for specific XML structures (e.g., all data tables in a collection of scientific papers written by a specific author, regardless of the fact that they were marked up with different vocabularies), or verifying semantic constraints of XML elements regardless of their position within the document (e.g., the utterer of each instance of the speech fragments as transcribed in a parliamentary debate document is uniquely assigned to the individual that purportedly made the speech).

Although the Semantic Web could directly address XML semantics in order to gather the above-mentioned advantages, the Semantic Web community has always considered XML only as a serialisation language for RDF or OWL, or as a way to encode relational data to be subsequently extracted and expressed in RDF. However, these two usages depart from the original goal of XML, i.e., to provide a mechanism for marking up digital documents (books, papers, messages, etc.). Consequently, for example, it is often the case that relational data in XML encode both domain and document semantics; in such cases, extracting semantics from markup by means of bulk recipes generates semantic issues, because the dataset and/or ontologies obtained from that extraction will be unreliable (due to the usually conflicting data/text implicit semantics). A case study of this heterogeneity is the translation of FAO

FIGIS document management schemata[5], which generates an ontology describing real world entities as well as documents, provenance, interfaces, versioning data, etc.

There is a large literature concerning semantics applied to markup. One of the first attempts for describing formal markup semantics is introduced in Sperberg-McQueen et al. (2000). The basic idea of Sperberg-McQueen et al. is to point out how users apply markup: through it, they make inferences about the document structures and the text those structures contain. According to Sperberg-McQueen et al., "the meaning of markup is the set of inferences it licenses". The general framework they developed to associate semantics to markup and to make inferences on it needs some representation of the markup document, a *sentence skeleton* for each item of the markup language under consideration in order to associate a meaning, and a set of (categorised) predicates and rules for allowing inferences. In this work, all the examples are illustrated using Prolog both for the representation of the nodes and for defining/inferring semantics using predicates and rules.

Focusing on the best-known meta-markup language, XML, in Renear et al. (2003), Renear et al. discuss problems characterising schema languages for XML, from DTD to XMLSchema: those languages only permit a clear definition of the language syntax, and some of them (RelaxNG (Clark 2001), XML Schema (Gao et al. 2012)) allow the declaration of a simple semantics on the datatypes, and little more. Although annotations can be specified for XMLSchema structures, there is no predefined semantics associated to them. Everything else concerning semantics—the meaning of an element, the relationships among items, etc.—is not expressible in a machine-readable format through those schema languages. The Renear et al. propose the BECHAMEL Project as a possible solution to express markup semantics. As they explain in Renear et al. (2002), BECHAMEL allows one to associate semantics with markup by adding new hierarchies to the original structure of the document. Using these additional hierarchies, one can define the meaning of the elements and properties that cannot be expressed using the schema languages alone.

A different approach is used in Simons et al. (2004). Simons et al. developed a framework to associate semantics with any XML document *D* in a three-step process:

1. defining an OWL ontology *O* to express all the meanings they want to use;
2. writing a set of rules *R* in a specific XML language to associate those meanings to a set of elements *D*;
3. through a XSLT transformation, processing *D* using *O* and *R*, so obtaining a new semantically-enriched XML document.

Similarly, other works, such as Nuzzolese et al. (2010), Garcia and Celma (2005), Van Deursen et al. (2008), propose a general process that, starting from an XMLSchema *S*, an XML document *D* (written according to *S*) and an ontology *O* (that can be generated starting from *S*), allows one to convert all the data in *D*, described by XML elements and attributes, into appropriate RDF instances consistent with *O*.

[5] http://www.fao.org/fi/figis/devcon/diXionary/index.html

The approach introduced in Marcoux (2006), Marcoux and Rizkallah (2009) does not provide a formal machine-readable specification for defining markup semantics, but it is useful when human interpretation is needed in structuring a document. Marcoux et al. describe *Intertextual Semantics*, a mechanism to associate meaning with markup elements and attributes of a schema as natural language constructs; this is realised by associating a pre-text and a post-text with each of them. When the vocabulary of a schema is used correctly, the markup content is combined with the pre-text and post-text descriptions to make a correct natural language text that describes the entire information contained in a document. The difference between the common natural language documentation and Intertextual Semantics is that in the latter the meaning of a markup item is dynamically added when writing a document, and, as a consequence, can be read sequentially in the document editor itself.

Of course, eRDF[6] and RDFa (Adida et al. 2013) may be valid choices for associating—and extracting by means of GRDDL (Connolly 2007) applications—formal semantics with arbitrary text fragments, and to markup elements within documents. Although they are very helpful for annotating documents and adding semantic information about markup elements and their content, their use is possible only by adding new attributes or, even worse, new elements, therefore changing the document structure. The problem being that the need of modifying the document structure is not easily suitable for domains, for example within organisations that deal with administrative or juridical documents, which must always preserve their original structure.

2.2 Markup Languages for Legal and Legislative Documents

Markup languages to describe and define legislative documents have been an hot topic within Computer Science and Law communities for years, and they continue to attract the interests of international entities, such as countries' governments and standardisation institutes. In this section I will introduce only some of the most interesting and famous works in this area.

2.2.1 Formex

The *Formalized Exchange of Electronic Publications* (*Formex*)[7] (Guittet 1985) is a markup format released by the *Publications Office of the European Union*[8] in 1985. It was developed to enable data exchanging between the Publication Office and its contractors.

---

[6] eRDF: http://www.egeneva.ch/w3c-RDF-ResourceDescriptionFramework.

[7] Formex homepage: http://formex.publications.europa.eu.

[8] Publication Office of the European Union homepage: http://publications.europa.eu.

Originally developed as an SGML-based markup language, the current fourth version (dated May 2004) is totally based on XML technologies, as described in the introductory page of its documentation[9]:

> XML is only the starting point for the development of depending standards which allow to transform and, in particular, to present the instances (XSLT, XSLFO). Another important effort in this context was made by developing a new standard for the specification of grammars. DTDs are replaced by XML Schemas which also offers the possibility to define the contents of elements and attributes.

The current specification, called Formex 4 and written entirely in English, uses, thus, XML as base metamarkup language, XML Schema to specify the formal grammar of the language and Unicode UTF-8 to encode Formex documents. In particular the specification consists of two specific parts:

- the physical specifications which contain information on the exchange of data, the construction of filenames and, in particular, on the set of characters set;
- the grammar for the markup based on XML Schema.

2.2.2 *Norme in Rete*

The Italian project *Norme in Rete* (*NIR*, in English *Norms on the Net*) (Marchetti et al. 2002) started in 1999, was led by the Italian Ministry of Justice and financed by the *Autorità per l'Informatica nella Pubblica Amministrazione* (*AIPA*, in English *Italian Authority for the Information Technology*)[10]. The goal of this project was twofolds. Firstly, its partners aimed at creating a freely-accessible Web portal containing all the legal and legislative documents produced by the Italian Parliament, so as to have a centralised access point to all the documents having legal validity in Italy. Second, they wanted to develop an XML-based markup language to store all the legislative documents in a format that facilitated the development of search and annotation tools to easily access and browsing the huge set of normative documents produced by Italian institutions.

NIR includes two different kinds of schemas (developed in DTD and XMLSchema), one *strict* (used for the final version of norms) and the other *loose* (to define drafting rules expressed in form of *circular*). Even though they define the same set of elements, what really changes is the content model of such elements of the particular version in consideration. In particular, the loose schema relaxes several constraints introduced in the strict schema. This makes the documents written according to the strict schema still valid against the loose schema, while the vice versa does not hold.

[9] Excerpt from http://formex.publications.europa.eu/formex-4/physspec/formex-4-introduction-.htm.

[10] Note that AIPA was transformed in *Centro Nazionale per l'Informatica nella Pubblica Amministrazione* (*CNIPA*) in 2003, and then in *Ente nazionale per la Digitalizzazione della Pubblica Amministrazione* (*DigitPA*) in 2009. Its current official website is http://www.digitpa.gov.it/.

Both DTDs allow the user to define three different kinds of documents:

- articolato con preambolo, i.e., a document that includes a formalised hierarchical structure preceded by a preamble;
- articolato senza preambolo, i.e., a document like the above, but without the preamble;
- semi-articolato, i.e., a document that does not have any particular formal hierarchical structure.

In addition, both DTDs can be split in three different sub-schemas, each defining, respectively, the structure of norms, the organisation of text and all the meta-information associated to the document.

2.2.3 LexDania

LexDania XML (Petersen 2005; Lupo et al. 2007) is a joint project held by the Danish Parliament and the Danish Ministry of Justice. The aims of this project are:

- the development of an XML format to write and store legislative documents (mostly acts and rules);
- the development of tools (e.g., editors) to support the creation and editing of such legislative documents in an easy and intuitive way;
- the proposal for a process that allows a gradual transition from a digital storage of legislative documents stored as Word files to a digital storage containing such documents in the aforementioned XML format.

The LexDania XML format is based on and is currently part of the OIOXML-standard for exchanging text documents between agencies in the Danish public administration. The overall design structure of this format is split in three different and interconnected layers, each defining and increasing level of specificity of its markup vocabulary. The first level, called *meta-schema*, defines the general syntax definitions of the language and its core data types. The second level, called *omni-schema*, extends the previous schema enriching it with domain-specific terms and definitions. Finally, the schemas in the third layer, called *application schemas*, extends again the previous schema defining specific document type semantics according to the particular context they want to describe.

LexDania is already in use in several legislative processes of the Denmark Parliament, as documented in official Parliament websites[11] and Petersen (2011).

[11] E.g., http://www.ministerialtidende.dk/Forms/L0500.aspx?page=5.

2.2.4 METALex NL

One of the outputs of the projects E-POWER (IST Project 2000-28125) and e-COURT (IST Project 2000-28199) was a proposal for a Dutch Legal XML Standard (Boer et al. 2002), which was later named METALex[12] (Boer et al. 2002).

METALex is described by its authors as a "generic and easily extensible framework for the XML encoding of the structure and contents of legal and paralegal documents" (Boer et al. 2002). It is composed by several XML Schema documents which define its formal structures. The core of the language is simple. In fact, in order to achieve a sort of independence of jurisdiction, its authors chose to define only those elements that all the regulatory documents of different jurisdiction share. Of course, it is still up to the final user either to use METALex as it is or to appropriately extend it to meet specific requirements derived from specific domain or usage.

In addition to its extendibility, it is also possible to include the textual content of the document in different native languages, using the XML attribute *xml:lang*, so as to have multi-lingual versions of the same document stored within the same file. It is also possible to adapt the vocabulary of the markup language according to the particular target language simply by defining a language-specific schema extension to the neutral vocabulary of the standard document schema. The idea is that the extension should import the standard document schema and should substitute element names with the appropriate names in the target language by specifying it through the attribute *substitutionGroup* of the schema.

2.2.5 CEN MetaLex

Born as evolution of the METALex format (Boer et al. 2002) presented in Sect. 2.2.4, *CEN MetaLex*[13] (Boer et al. 2007; Boer et al. 2008) is an interchange format defined as XML-based markup language, which aims to be the minimum baseline for other standards for legal and legislative documents. In particular, it was developed not in order to replace such standards with one more format, but rather to propose standardised way of describing legal documents and facilitate their exchange and interoperability.

One of the most important innovations in CEN MetaLex compared with its oldest versions described in Sect. 2.2.4, is the adoption of the *FRBR* specification (International Federation of Library Associations and Institutions Study Group on the Functional Requirements for Bibliographic Records 2009), which I will present in more details in Sect. 2.3.5, to describe legal documents from different abstract and physical perspectives. In particular CEN MetaLex is concerned primarily with the identification of legal bibliographic entities on the basis of their content (i.e., the *Expression* level in FRBR), while it imposes an XML-based language as a mandatory format for storing documents.

[12] METALex homepage: http://www.metalex.nl.

[13] CEN MetaLex homepage: http://www.metalex.eu.

CEN MetaLex is defined through a single XML Schema file. Each XML element is characterised by a name, providing a clear meaning for the text fragment it contains, a set of attributes containing additional information about the content of the element itself, and a particular content model according to seven main types: *container* (containing a sequence of other elements and no text), *hcontainer* (as the previous, but with specific elements identifying titles and numbers), *mcontainer* (containing a sequence of other mcontainers and metas, and no text), *block* (containing a sequence of other elements and text nodes), *inline* (as the previous one, but it can be child of blocks or other inline only), *milestone* (containing no text and no elements, and it can be contained by blocks and inlines only). In addition, it is possible to specify metadata associated to the documents using the element *meta* (containing no text and no elements, and it can be contained by mcontainers only) in combination with RDFa (Adida et al. 2013).

2.2.6 *Akoma Ntoso*

Originally thought to be the standard markup language for e-Parliament services in a Pan-African context and currently primary topic of the OASIS LegalDocumentML (LegalDocML) TC[14], the *Architecture for Knowledge-Oriented Management of African Normative Texts using Open Standards and Ontologies*, a.k.a. *Akoma Ntoso*[15] (Barabucci et al. 2009, 2010), is an XML vocabulary for legal and legislative documents whose primary objective is to allow one to enrich a legal text with semantic data.

Akoma Ntoso focuses on the identification of three main aspects of legal documents:

- the structures composing the document, to be marked up according a precise XML vocabulary based on common structural patterns found in legal documents;
- the references to other related legal documents, made by using a common naming convention based on URIs;
- the storage of non-authoritative annotations, by means of other ontologically-like approaches compatible with Topic Maps (SC34/WG 2003), OWL and GRDDL (Connolly 2007).

The XML documents created according to the Akoma Ntoso specifications use a layered structure where each layer addresses a single problem. First, the *text layer* provides a faithful representation of the original content of the legal text. Then, the *structure layer* provides a hierarchical organisation of the parts present in the text

[14] OASIS LegalDocumentML (LegalDocML) TC homepage: http://www.oasisopen.org/committees/tc_home.php?wg_abbrev=legaldocml

[15] Akoma Ntoso homapage: http://www.akomantoso.org/.

layers. Finally, the *metadata layer* associates information from the underlying layers with ontological information. In addition, whenever this semantic information is the result of a subjective interpretation, Akoma Ntoso allows multiple and independent opinions to be stored in a formal way within the same document, and used alternatively, cumulatively or compared to each other.

I will describe Akoma Ntoso in Sect. 4.1 in more details.

2.2.7 HTML + RDFa and XML in gov.uk Websites

On the basis of the experience of the US government about increasing public access to datasets generated by the Executive Branch of the Federal Government[16], the UK Government's project *data.gov.uk*[17] (Sheridan and Tennison 2010) was launched in January 2010 with the aim of making datasets, containing data coming from several UK Government departments (9426, up-to-date as of May 19, 2013), freely-available. All data are non-personal (for privacy reasons) and, in principle, available in several formats such as TXT CVS, XLS, RDF and RDFa.

Each page which describes a dataset presents information about the formats used, its openness, its themes, and the temporal coverage of the dataset itself. Some of the informations is also described in embedding RDF statements within HTML pages through RDFa[18] (Adida et al. 2013). The final goal of this project is twofolds. On the one hand, it aims to make governmental data freely-accessible online to the public. On the other hand, it seeks to integrate such data within the Open Linked Data[19], which already counts several datasets coming from different UK companies and institutions (Shadbolt et al. 2012).

One of those institutions, within the legislative domain, is the London Gazette[20], which is the most important official journal of record of the British Government. The London Gazette publishes all its material as PDF files and HTML+RDFa pages[21]. The main part of the semantic assertions described through RDFa conforms to the *Gazette Ontology*[22], which defines all the classes and properties used for all the Gazette Notices.

---

16 Data.gov homepage: http://www.data.gov.

17 Data.gov.uk homepage: http://data.gov.uk.

18 Data Catalog Vocabulary/RDFa in data.gov.uk:
http://www.w3.org/egov/wiki/Data_Catalog_Vocabulary/RDFa_in_data.gov.uk.

19 An interesting description of lessons learned by the process of conforming Open Government Data with the Open Linked Data is given in Shadbolt et al. (2012).

20 London Gazette homepage: http://www.london-gazette.co.uk.

21 An example of an HTML+RDFa page in the London Gazette is available at http://www.london-gazette.co.uk/issues/58664/notices/497223/date=2008-04-10.

22 Gazette Ontology: http://www.gazettes-online.co.uk/ontology#.

A sister project of the previous one, i.e., *legislation.gov.uk*[23], managed by The National Archives[24] on behalf of Government of the United Kingdom[25], has recently released all UK Legislation from 1267 to the present in several formats[26]: HTML, XML, RDF and Atom. In particular, an XML Schema was developed[27] so as to enable users to retrieve an XML representation of legislative documents according to the *Legislation Schema*[28], which permits the specification of both metadata by means of Dublin Core (that will be introduced in Sect. 2.3.1), and the content of legislation using XHTML (W3C HTML Working Group 2002) for tables and MathML (Carlisle et al. 2010) for formulae.

2.3 Metadata Schema, Vocabularies and Ontologies for Publishing

The definition of vocabularies and ontologies that enable the description of document metadata is crucial for the Semantic Publishing. A large number of these metadata schemas appeared in the nineties, and only in recent times their Semantic Web versions were developed either as RDF/RDFS vocabularies or OWL ontologies.

Several vocabularies and/or models for the publishing domain have been developed in the past few years. In this section I will specifically list those that are usually adopted and currently defined through Semantic Web languages and technologies.

2.3.1 Dublin Core

Developed as a result of a conference held in Dublin, Ohio, USA in 1995 that involved both technicians (librarians, publishers, archivists) and academics (researches, software developers), the current versions of Dublin Core (DC) Metadata Elements (Dublin Core Metadata Initiative 2012b) and of DC Metadata Terms (Dublin Core Metadata Initiative 2012a) are the most widely used vocabularies for describing and cataloguing resources.

---

[23] Legislation.gov.uk homepage: http://www.legislation.gov.uk.

[24] The National Archives homepage: http://www.nationalarchives.gov.uk.

[25] Government of the United Kingdom homepage: https://www.gov.uk.

[26] Formats: http://www.legislation.gov.uk/developer/formats.

[27] XML format: http://www.legislation.gov.uk/developer/formats/xml.

[28] Legislation Schema: http://www.legislation.gov.uk/schema/legislation.xsd.

These vocabularies have become particularly important and relevant for sharing metadata about documents among different repositories (Koutsomitropoulos et al. 2008) and digital libraries (Montoya et al. 2005), as well as being used to describe documents in HTML (Dublin Core Metadata Initiative 2008; DocBook Walsh 2010) and other XML formats such as Open Document (OpenOffice document format) (JTC1/SC34 WG 6 2006).

While very useful for the creation of basic metadata for resource discovery, the main limitation of DC is a direct consequence of the **generic nature of its terms**. For example, using DC Terms one can identify a creator but not an author; a bibliographic resource but not a journal article; an identifier but not an ISSN, and a date but not a publication date.

2.3.2 PRISM

The *Publishing Requirements for Industry Standard Metadata* (*PRISM*) (International Digital Enterprise Alliance 2009) is a specification defining a rich set of metadata terms for describing published work. It was developed to address the need of publishers to address emerging requirements for metadata sharing and aggregation, and currently it involves some of the most important publishers and associated companies, such as *Adobe Systems*, the *McGraw-Hill Companies*, *Reader's Digest*, *Time Inc.*, the *Nature Publishing Group*, and *U.S. News and World Report*.

The PRISM metadata terms are expressible both in XML, according to a specific DTD, and in RDF (Hammond 2008). These terms are explicitly recommended for the specification of metadata of documents expressed through markup languages such as (DocBook Walsh 2010). Moreover, these terms are also included in ontologies describing the publishing domain, such as the *Bibliographic Ontology* (*BIBO*)[29] (D'Arcus and Giasson 2009), which is discussed below.

While PRISM has a much richer set of terms that describe bibliographic entities than DC, its main limitation is that it is a **flat structure,** lacking hierarchies. That prevents its use for a complete description of the characteristics of bibliographic entities. For example, while the data property *prism:volume*permits the volume number of a bibliographic reference to be represented as a string, PRISM lacks the concept of "Volume" as a distinct class among other bibliographic classes that have a hierarchical partitive relationship to one another (i.e., Journal Article > Issue > Volume > Journal), and whose members can possess other properties, such as having authors and editors.

[29] BIBO, the Bibliographic Ontology: http://purl.org/ontology/bibo/.

2.3.3 *BIBO*

BIBO, i.e., the *Bibliographic Ontology* (D'Arcus and Giasson 2009), is an OWL Full ontology that allows one to write descriptions of documents (*bibo:Document* is the core class of that model) for publication on the Semantic Web. It includes both DC terms (Dublin Core Metadata Initiative 2012a) and PRISM (International Digital Enterprise Alliance 2009) to cover common needs, and it adds other classes and properties to describe in more detail the publishing domain, such as *bibo:AcademicArticle*, *bibo:Journal*, *bibo:Collection*, *bibo:Book*, *bibo:Chapter* and *bibo:Issue*. BIBO is a good ontology that is widely used among the bibliographic community.

From a pure computational perspective, BIBO defines the range of the property *bibo:authorList* usingeither an *rdf:List* or an *rdf:Seq*, therefore making the model non-compliant with OWL 2 DL. That limits the applicability of reasoners and other Semantic Web tools that are usually built upon the (computationally-tractable) description logic underlying OWL 2 DL.

2.3.4 *MARC 21*

Another relevant work in this field, widely used in the Libraries community and developed before the introduction of the Semantic Web, is the *MARC 21 Format for Bibliographic Data* (Library of Congress - Network Development and MARK Standard Office 2010). Introduced in 1961, MARC 21 is a very complex code for describing bibliographic resources as one of seven different primary types: book, continuing resource, computer file, maps, music, visual materials and mixed materials. To each resource, there can be associated different kinds of metadata, such as titles, names, subjects, notes, publication data, etc.

In MARC21, each type of metadata is represented by a three-digit code (called a *tag* in the MARC21 specification) that identifies the main metadata category of relevance. Other characters can follow this tag in order to specify additional information. For example, let me introduce a simple bibliographic reference describing Casanovas et al. (2007):

> Pompeu Casanovas, Núria Casellas, Christoph Tempich, Denny Vrandečić, Richard Benjamins (2007). OPJK and DILIGENT: ontology modeling in a distributed environment. http://link.springer.com/content/pdf/10.1007%2Fs10506-007-9036-2.pdf.

To express these data in MARC21 I will need to use the following tags:

```
100 1#$aCasanovas, Pompeu
100 1#$aCasellas,Núria
100 1#$aTempich, Christoph
100 1#$aVrandečić, Denny
100 1#$aBenjamins, Richard
260 ##$c2007
145 10$aOPJK and DILIGENT: ontology modeling in a
   distributed environment
856 40$uhttp://link.springer.com/content/pdf/10.1007%2
   Fs10506-007-9036-2.pdf
```

where "100" identifies a personal name, "260" indicates the year of publication, "145" the title of a work, and "856" the electronic location of that entity.

With the advent of the Semantic Web, MARC21 was formalised as an RDF vocabulary (Styles et al. 2008) in order to be adopted and used in Semantic Web applications. However, many librarians now regard MARC as too complex and esoteric, and are undergoing a mind shift to more pragmatic open standards.

2.3.5 FRBR

The *Functional Requirements for Bibliographic Record* (*FRBR*) (International Federation of Library Associations and Institutions Study Group on the Functional Requirements for Bibliographic Records 2009) is a general model, proposed by the International Federation of Library Association (IFLA), for describing documents and their evolution. It works for both physical and digital resources and it has proved to be very flexible and powerful. One of the most important aspects of FRBR is the fact that it is not associated with a particular metadata schema or implementation.

The following brief description outlines FRBR's basic concepts and the way they can be applied within a publishing domain. FRBR describes all documents from four different and correlated points of view: *Work*, *Expression*, *Manifestation* and *Item*; each of which is a FRBR *Endeavour*. These can be illustrated by considering of the book *Alice's Adventures in Wonderland* by Lewis Carroll as an example:

- **Work.** A FRBR *Work* is a high-level abstract Platonic concept of the *essence* of a distinct intellectual or artistic creation, for example the ideas in Lewis Carroll's head concerning *Alice's Adventures in Wonderland*, independent of any representation of these ideas in a particular form. A Work is realised through one or more Expressions;
- **Expression.** A FRBR *Expression* is the realisation of the intellectual or artistic *content* of a Work. Thus the original text of *Alice's Adventures in Wonderland* and its Italian translation *Le Avventure di Alice nel Paese delle Meraviglie* refer to different Expressions of the same Work. An Expression is embodied in one or more Manifestations;

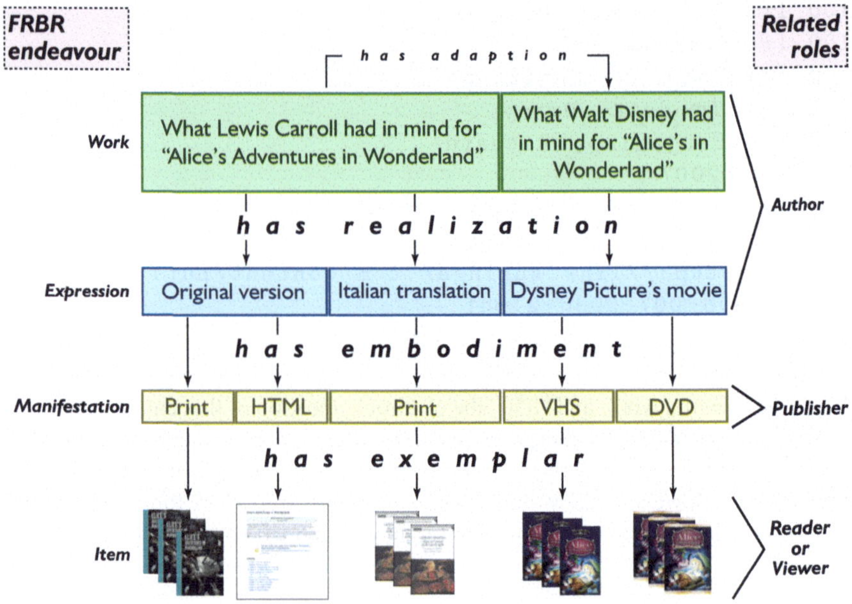

Fig. 2.1 The four FRBR layers, with a specification of roles that people may play in each layer

- **Manifestation.** A FRBR *Manifestation* of a work defines its particular physical or electronic embodiment, for example, the particular *format* in which "Alice's Adventures in Wonderland" is stored: as a printed object or in HTML, represent two quite different Manifestations. In publishing, different manifestations of a journal article will all bear the same Digital Object Identifier (DOI), which identifies the Expression of the work, not its various Manifestations. However, a paperback and a hardback version of a book will bear different International Standard Book Numbers (ISBNs), since these identifiers are assigned at the Manifestation level. A Manifestation is exemplified by one or more Items;
- **Item.** A FRBR Item is a particular physical or electronic *copy* of *Alice's Adventures in Wonderland* that a person can own, for example the printed version of the book you have in your bookcase, or the Mobipocket format copy you have downloaded to read on your e-book device. All Items that are identical to one another—for example books from the same printing, are exemplars of the same Manifestation.

In Fig. 2.1, I summarise the four distinct FRBR layers with particular reference to the publishing domain, using as example *Alice's Adventures in Wonderland,* and I indicate the most common roles (*Author*, *Publisher* and *Reader/Viewer*) that usually people have with respect to each layer.

Despite the increased expressivity enabled by these layers, the greatest limitation of FRBR with respect to the publishing domain is its lack of terms **that permit publications to be described in normal everyday language** (e.g., "research paper", "review", "book chapter", "newspaper editorial") rather than using the more abstract and esoteric FRBR-specific terms "work", "expression", "manifestation" and "item".

A further limitation that FRBR has in common with other standards—i.e., DC (Dublin Core Metadata Initiative 2012b; Dublin Core Metadata Initiative 2012a), PRISM (International Digital Enterprise Alliance 2009)—is that it has hitherto been implemented and shared **only as XML or RDF vocabularies**, rather than as OWL DL ontologies, preventing it from being used within applications that employ reasoning based on description logic models.

There now exist two different implementations of the core concepts of FRBR using standards that permit the encoding of proper formal semantics: the first, authored in 2005 by Richard Newman and Ian Davis in RDFS[30] and the second, developed from the first, created in 2010 by Paolo Ciccarese and I in OWL 2 DL[31] (Ciccarese and Peroni 2013).

In addition to being particularly adequate for the description of scholarly works, FRBR can be used also in the context of the legislative process of many different legal systems. For instance, in Civil Law legal systems, the modification in time of a legal text that has been approved in the past is a common practice, and thus it is crucial to be able to keep track of the way such text is modified. In this case, we could use an FRBR-based approach that represents the legal document as a whole through a FRBR Work, while each consecutive re-writing due to a modification of the current approved version could be specified by an FRBR Expressions explicitly linked to the other ones through a temporal relation (e.g., *is revision of* or *is successor of*).

Similarly, FRBR can be very useful within Common Law legal systems, such as the federal legislation of the United States, where it is crucial to keep track of the process of law codification, where, for instance, a certain statute is restated as positive law in the US Code. Although this topic is partially out of the scope for this book (as I mainly deal with legal scholarly publishing), I will introduce an example of such scenario in Sect. 5.6.2.

2.3.6 RDA

The *Resource Description and Access* (*RDA*)[32] is a standard released in June 2010 by the American Library Association[33], the Canadian Library Association[34], and the Chartered Institute of Library and Information Professionals (CILIP)[35] in the UK.

---

[30] The FRBR Core in RDFS: http://vocab.org/frbr/core.

[31] The FRBR Core in OWL 2 DL: http://purl.org/spar/frbr.

[32] RDA, the Resource Description and Access, standard homepage: http://www.rda-jsc.org/rda.html.

[33] American Library Association homepage: http://www.ala.org/.

[34] Canadian Library Association homepage: http://www.cla.ca/.

[35] Chartered Institute of Library and Information Professionals homepage: http://www.cilip.org.uk/.

RDA allows one to describe resources related to libraries, archives, museums, and other organisations working on information management of bibliographic entities and cultural heritage artefacts.

RDA is the the official replacement of the *Anglo-American Cataloguing Rules Second Edition* (*AACR2*)[36], and it is based on the Functional Requirements for Bibliographic Records (FRBR), introduced in Sect. 2.3.5. Essentially, RDA is a format-independent approach that standardises how metadata should be identified and structured.

RDA takes particular attention to possible ways of interaction with Semantic Web applications and the Linked Open Data. To this end, during the development of the standard, a parallel task force has been investigating how to develop formal and machine-readable representations of RDA element sets and value vocabularies so as to be used by both humans and machines. This activity resulted in the release of a set of RDF-based vocabularies (Hillmann et al. 2010) freely available online[37]. Each element set and vocabulary is available as a descriptive HTML page as well as in RDF/XML format (Beckett 2004). The element sets define the main FRBR concepts as formal OWL classes and support the relations existing between them, as well as an extended list of agent roles organised according to the FRBR layers. Additional RDA vocabularies define value sets for different applicative contexts (e.g., values for digital formats, picture colouring, text extents, etc.).

2.3.7 SWAN Citations Ontology

Another model previously used to define bibliographic resources is the *Citations Ontology*[38] included in the SWAN (Semantic Web Applications in Neuroscience) Ontologies, version 1.2 (Ciccarese et al. 2008). In this ontology, the main class *Citation*[39] is used as super-class, of which all the other resources (e.g., *JournalArticle*, *WebArticle* and *Book*) are sub-classes.

The main advantage of this ontology is that it is completely developed in OWL 2 DL. Contrary to BIBO, which defines the range of the property *bibo:authorList* using either an *rdf:List* or an *rdf:Seq* and therefore makes the model non-compliant with OWL 2 DL, the Citation Ontology uses the SWAN Collections Ontology module[40]. This is an OWL 2 DL ontology that allows one to handle lists of authors and contributors of a bibliographic object, thus enabling the specification of ordered lists while still keeping the ontology locally consistent.

---

[36] Anglo-American Cataloguing Rules Second Edition homepage: http://www.aacr2.org/.

[37] The RDA (Resource Description and Access) Vocabularies: http://rdvocab.info/.

[38] SWAN Citations Ontology Module: http://swan.mindinformatics.org/spec/1.2/citations.html.

[39] Note that in SWAN the concept "Citation" is used to represent the cited object itself, rather than the performative act of making a citation.

[40] SWAN Collections Ontology Module: http://swan.mindinformatics.org/spec/1.2/collections.html.

The main problem of the Citations Ontology is the sparseness of its vocabulary, and the difficulty of aligning it with other structurally complex models such as FRBR, because, as with BIBO, it collapses all bibliographic entity descriptions within the single class *Citation*.

2.3.8 SKOS

Publishers need to classify the documents they publish according to discipline-specific thesauri or classification schemes, for example those belonging to economics[41] or computer science[42].

The *Simple Knowledge Organization System* (*SKOS*) (Miles and Bechhofer 2009) is an RDFS model which supports the use of knowledge organisation systems (KOS) such as thesauri, classification schemes, subject heading lists and taxonomies within the framework of the Semantic Web. The reception of this language has been particularly positive: a large number of well-known thesauri and classification systems have started to convert their respective specifications into SKOS documents[43],[44],[45],[46]. This makes SKOS the *de facto* standard for encoding controlled vocabularies for the Semantic Web.

2.4 Ontologies for Legal Documents

The development of ontologies is one of the most discussed and addressed topic by several communities and players in the legal domain, from philosophers to computer scientists. Several works have been done in the past on this topic, as reviewed by Casellas in Casellas (2011).

Generally speaking, legal ontologies can be clustered according to a bipartite classification:

- core legal ontologies, which provide general definitions of general legal entities such as norm[47], legal role[48], legal process[49];

[41] The Journal of Economic Literature Classification Scheme: http://www.aeaweb.org/jel/jel_class_system.php.

[42] The Association for Computing Machinery (ACM) Computing Classification System 1998: http://www.acm.org/about/class/1998.

[43] AGROVOC: http://aims.fao.org/website/AGROVOC-Thesaurus/sub.

[44] The Medical Subject Headings (MeSH): http://www.ncbi.nlm.nih.gov/mesh.

[45] The Library of Congress Subject Headings (LCSH): http://id.loc.gov/search/.

[46] Nuovo Soggettario of the National Central Library in Florence: http://thes.bncf.firenze.sbn.it/

[47] E.g., the class *norm* in http://www.estrellaproject.org/lkif-core/norm.owl.

[48] E.g., the class *legal role* in http://www.estrellaproject.org/lkif-core/legal-role.owl.

[49] E.g., the class *process* in http://www.estrellaproject.org/lkif-core/process.owl.

- domain legal ontologies, which define concepts specific to a precise context and/or peculiar to a particular field, such as parliament[50], judge[51], etc.

Only some of the ontologies in these two sets are developed through Semantic Web technologies (i.e., OWL). For instance, as OWL-based core ontologies, we can cite the *Core Legal Ontology* (Gangemi et al. 2005), the *MetaLex Ontology* (Comité Européen de Normalisation 2010), and *Legal Knowledge Interchange Format core legal ontology* (Breuker et al. 2006). The number of ontologies in the other set (i.e., domain legal ontologies) is undoubtedly larger than the former—we can cite the *BEST ontologies* (van Laarschot et al. 2005), the *Legal Case Ontology* (Wyner and Hoekstra 2012), and the *Parliament Ontology*[52] as exemplars. We recommend interested readers to see (Casellas 2011) for a more precise discussion of ontologies of both types.

I believe it is appropriate to distinguish, within the first category of ontologies, the subset of legal core ontologies that describe aspects of legal markup languages strictly related to document metadata information—i.e., which have concepts shared among document metadata definitions by the majority of legal and legislative markup languages, such as those introduced in Sect. 2.2—from the others. I call the former subset of ontologies: *ontologies for legal documents.*

Even though the identification of the concepts emerging from the textual content of legal and legislative documents is an important issue to address within the legal domain, the purpose of this work is to discuss how *document metadata* can be represented by and/or linked to some sort of semantic characterisation of them. Thus, even though a discussion of OWL-based legal ontologies may be of interest to the reader, for the aim of this book, I will focus only on ontologies for legal documents.

On these premises, in this section I will briefly introduce some of the ontologies for legal documents (developed in OWL) referenced in Casellas (2011). In Sect. 2.4.4, I will also present an additional ontology, called ALLOT, that was developed specifically to define semantic descriptions of Akoma Ntoso documents (Barabucci et al. 2009). Some of the concepts defined in these ontologies are also used to introduce an example of use of legal markup languages and Semantic Web technologies to assess the quality of legal drafting, as discussed in Sect. 4.4.

2.4.1 *MetaLex Ontology*

CEN MetaLex (introduced in Sect. 2.2.5) defines also an OWL ontology[53] describing its core components, i.e., bibliographic elements, document metadata and citations

[50] E.g., the class *parliament* in http://reference.data.gov.uk/def/parliament.

[51] E.g., the class *judge* in http://www.wyner.info/research/case-ontology.owl.

[52] The Parliament Ontology: http://reference.data.gov.uk/def/parliament.

[53] MetaLex Ontlogy: http://justinian.leibnizcenter.org/MetaLex/metalex-cen.owl.

(Comité Européen de Normalisation 2010). Any *bibliographic object* is actually an instance of one of the classes described in FRBR (International Federation of Library Associations and Institutions Study Group on the Functional Requirements for Bibliographic Records 2009)—i.e., *work*, *expression*, *manifestation* and *item*, as introduced in Sect. 2.3.5—and it is provided with a unique identifier, which is the IRI used to refer to it. In addition, the authors added a particular class, i.e., *bibliographic citation*, to provide a mechanism to refer to a particular bibliographic object from a different context.

On the basis of the MetaLex Ontology, in 2011 Rinke Hoekstra presented an ongoing project to publish all the Dutch legislation published since 2002[54] as Open Linked Data (Hoekstra 2011). He developed and still maintains the *MetaLex Document Server* (*MDS*)[55], a store of 280619338 triples (up-to-date as of May 21, 2013) that describe Dutch national regulations (describing 33702 document versions) in CEN MetaLex XML and as RDF Linked Data. MDS exports its data as RDF triple that conforms to the MetaLex Ontology, which allows the modelling of legislative modification events in terms of time, processes and provenance information regarding the event itself by means of external ontologies such as the Simple Event Model (van Hage et al. 2011), the W3C Time Ontology (Hobbs and Pan 2006) and the Open Provenance Model Vocabulary (Zhao 2010).

Another concrete use of the CEN MetaLex ontology within actual collections of legislative documents is the *legislation.gov.uk* website, collecting all the UK Legislation since 1267. As described in the website[56], an agent can ask for the RDF/XML representation of legislative works, such as acts, and, thus, can retrieve a CEN MetaLex compliant description of such textual content.

2.4.2 Core Legal Ontology

The *Core Legal Ontology* (*CLO*)[57] (Gangemi et al. 2005) is an OWL ontology based on the "Descriptions and Situations" extension to DOLCE (Gangemi and Mika 2003), which is an OWL-based foundational ontology for domain-independent axiomatic theories.

CLO allows one to reason over constraints given by the particular context in consideration, which can be dynamically used by agents "when recognizing or classifying a state of affairs" (Gangemi et al. 2005). In addition, it was developed to address three specific kinds of legal tasks:

---

[54] The original data were retrieved from http://www.wetten.nl.

[55] MetaLex Document Server homepage: http://doc.metalex.eu.

[56] RDF/XML format: http://www.legislation.gov.uk/developer/formats/rdf.

[57] Core Legal Ontology: http://www.loa.istc.cnr.it/ontologies/CLO/CoreLegal.owl.

- *conformity checking*, which requires to link particular situations (both social and legal ones) to legal norms;
- *legal advice*, which requires to investigate the relationships that exist between legal cases and non-expected situations;
- *norm comparison*, which requires to recognise conflicts between norms according to the particular European and national legislation.

2.4.3 LKIF Core Legal Ontology

The *Legal Knowledge Interchange Format (LKIF) core legal ontology*[58] (Breuker et al. 2006) is a set of OWL ontologies which aims to describe the legal domain. It includes fifteen different ontology modules, each specialised in a specific legal topic.

Four of these modules—*top*, *place*, *mereology* and *time*—are used to describe the most abstract concepts of the model, such as: top categories, places seen as absolute (e.g., a mountain) and relative (e.g., a ship), description of part-whole relationships, and description of moments and intervals.

Other four models—*process*, *role*, *action* and *expression*—are used to describe basic level concepts, such as processes and changes, types of roles (e.g., epistemic, person, organisation roles), actions performed by particular players, and expressions of attitudes, qualifications and statements.

The aforementioned modules are then extended by three other modules—*legal action*, *legal role* and *norm*—to form the legal core of LKIF. Those modules enable the description of public acts, legal and natural people, legal professions, norms, legal sources and different types of rights and powers.

All modifications and rules are described in two separate modules—*modification* and *rule*—since they represent the two larger frameworks of the legal domain described herein, and thus deserve to be formalised as single modules.

Finally, the first eleven modules described above are integrated within LKIF core module—*lkif-core*—and all of the above modules are included in the LKIF extended module—*lkif-extended*—for a total of fifteen ontology modules.

2.4.4 A Light Legal Ontology on TLC

As briefly introduced in Sect. 2.2.6, Akoma Ntoso (Barabucci et al. 2009, 2010) prescribes the use of ontologies to describe metadata and entities that concern the particular document in consideration. However, Akoma Ntoso does not impose the use of a particular ontological model, and it suggests that ontologies should comply

[58] LKIF repository: http://github.com/RinkeHoekstra/lkif-core.

with fourteen abstract entities called *Top Level Classes* (*TLC*): *concept*, *event*, *location*, *object*, *organisation*, *person*, *process*, *reference*, *role*, *term*, and the four FRBR classes (International Federation of Library Associations and Institutions Study Group on the Functional Requirements for Bibliographic Records 2009) *work*, *expression*, *manifestation* and *item*.

ALLOT (*A Light Legal Ontology on TLC*)[59] (Barabucci et al. 2013) is a lightweight ontology that provides a vocabulary to describe Akoma Ntoso TLC as OWL classes. It can be used to describe in detail the various references that occur in Akoma Ntoso documents, and to map those references to other related entities exposed by means of other models, such as the MetaLex Ontology Sect. 2.4.1 or LKIF Sect. 2.4.3.

In addition, ALLOT is also aligned[60], when possible, with entities defined in external ontologies, such as DC Metadata Terms (Dublin Core Metadata Initiative 2012a), LKIF Time module[61], SKOS (Miles and Bechhofer 2009), FOAF (Brickley and Miller 2010), PRO (Peroni et al. 2012) and the RDF implementation of the FRBR model (introduced in Sect. 2.3.5).

2.5 Projects, Conferences and Initiatives about Semantic Publishing

Between 2010 and 2013, a large number of initiatives emerged with the precise intention of advertising Semantic Publishing to a broader audience. Each of them, from projects to workshops and journal issues, seemed to confirm that semantic publishing and scholarly citation using Web standards constitute currently two of the most interesting topics within the scientific publishing domain.

In this section I will list the most important initiatives concerning Semantic Publishing in 2010–2013, sponsored by both academia and companies. They represent proof of the increasing interest in Semantic Publishing by scientific, academic and industrial institutions.

2.5.1 JISC's Open Citation and Open Bibliography Projects

In 2010, JISC funded two sister projects: the *Open Citation project*[62] and the *Open Bibliography project*[63], held respectively by the University of Oxford and the University of Cambridge. Their broad goal was to study the feasibility, the advantages

[59] ALLOT core: http://akn.web.cs.unibo.it/allot/core.

[60] ALLOT implementation: http://akn.web.cs.unibo.it/allot/impl.

[61] LKIF time module: http://www.estrellaproject.org/lkif-core/time.owl.

[62] Open Citation project blog: http://opencitations.wordpress.com.

[63] Open Bibliography project blog: http://openbiblio.net.

and the applications at using RDF datasets and OWL ontologies when describing and publishing bibliographic data and citations.

The Open Citation project, in which I was actively involved, intended to increase the effectiveness of scientific publishing and scholarly communication, making available on the Web bibliographic information as RDF data, according to particular ontologies developed for the description of the publishing domain. In particular, the project aimed to create a semantic infrastructure to describe articles as bibliographic records and to report citations between citing articles and cited ones.

The main outcomes of this project are:

- the development of a suite of ontologies, called *Semantic Publishing And Referencing* (*SPAR*) ontologies, which I developed under the supervision of professor David Shotton when I was based at the University of Oxford. This represents an important part of my work (Chap. 5);
- the development of two tools for ontology documentation, i.e., the *Live OWL Documentation Environment* (*LODE*) (Peroni et al. 2012), and visualisation, i.e., the *Graphical Framework for OWL Ontologies* (*Graffoo*), which I developed to support users when understanding and documenting ontologies. They are introduced in detail in Sect. 6.2 and Sect. 6.4 respectively;
- a corpus of interlinked bibliographic records[64] obtained converting the whole set of reference lists contained in all the PubMed Central[65] Open Access articles into RDF data according to SPAR ontologies. The converted RDF data are published as Linked Open Data.

The Open Bibliographic project aimed at publishing a large corpus of bibliographic data as Linked Open Data, starting from four different sources: the Cambridge University Library[66], the British Library[67], the International Union of Crystallography[68], and PubMed[69]. The key strategies promoted by this project were:

- the transformation of publishers' models so as to include the open publication of bibliographic data as Linked Open Data;
- the immediate and continuing engagement of the scholarly community.

[64] It is available online at http://opencitations.net.

[65] PubMed Central: http://www.ncbi.nlm.nih.gov/pmc/.

[66] Cambridge University Library: http://www.lib.cam.ac.uk.

[67] British Library: http://www.bl.uk.

[68] International Union of Crystallography: http://www.iucr.org.

[69] PubMed: http://www.ncbi.nlm.nih.gov/pubmed/.

2.5.2 JISC's Lucero Project

The *Lucero project*[70] is another JISC project, held by the Open University, which aims to explore the use of Linked Data within the academic domain. In particular, it proposes solutions that could use the Linked Data to connect educational and research content, so that students and researches could benefit from semantic technologies.

Lucero main aims are:

- to promote the publication as Linked Open Data of bibliographic data through a tool to facilitate the creation and use of semantic data;
- to identify a process in order to integrate the Linked Data publication of bibliographic information as part of the University's workflows;
- to demonstrate the benefits derived from exposing and using educational and research data as Open Linked Data, through the development of applications that improve the access to those data.

2.5.3 SePublica and Linked Science

Two of the most important Semantic Web conferences, i.e., the *extended* and the *international* ones, began to promote explicitly Semantic Publishing through two specific workshops.

The workshop *SePublica*[71], co-located within the 8th Extended Semantic Web Conference, is the first formal event entirely dedicated to Semantic Publishing. The aim of the workshop was to investigate upon the different practices of using semantic technologies within the publishing industry. During this half-day workshop were presented seven different papers were presented, one of which was awarded best workshop paper (winning an award of $750, sponsored by Elsevier). Supported by the success of the first edition, further events followed, SePublica 2012 and SePublica 2013, co-located respectively within the 9th and the 10th Extended Semantic Web Conference.

The *Linked Science*[72] workshop, a full-day event co-located within the 10th International Semantic Web Conference, involved researchers and practitioners discussing new ways of publishing, sharing, linking and analysing scientific resources, such as articles, datasets and results. Each of the five workshop sessions related to a particular topic, from data-based applications to semantic integration of data. The event concluded with an open meeting in which the various topics of the workshop were

---

[70] Lucero project blog: http://lucero-project.info.

[71] The 1st International Workshop about Semantic Publication (SePublica 2011): http://sepublica.mywikipaper.org.

[72] The 1st International Workshop on Linked Science (LISC2011): http://data.linkedscience.org/events/lisc2011.

discussed. Similarly to SePublica, also the Linked Science workshop was followed by two other editions—Linked Science 2012 and Linked Science 2013, co-located respectively within the 11th and 12th International Semantic Web Conference –, as well as a tutorial[73] held at the 18th International Conference on Knowledge Engineering and Knowledge Management.

2.5.4 *Beyond Impact, the PDF and Research Communication*

Recently the interest in proposing and adopting new formats for the improvement of research communications appears obvious. Almost all research and industrial communities agrees that the current formats are not sufficient for the needs of Web-based research communication. The workshops entitled *Beyond the PDF*, organised at the University of California San Diego in January 2011[74] and by FORCE11[75] in Amsterdam in March 2013, went in that direction. The scope of the event was to identify a set of requirements, applications and deliverables that can be used to accelerate knowledge sharing and discovery.

Beyond the PDF was not the only event organised with the aim of exploring new research possibilities and directions in scholarly publication. The workshop *The Future of Research Communication*[76], held in Dagstuhl in August 2011, was another gathering where scientists and practitioners coming from different disciplines met to discuss the future direction in scholarly publishing. All the prominent topics of scientific communication were discussed, and, in particular, new formats were proposed, which addressed the changes in media and modes of communication, drew opportune infrastructures and outlined social challenges with the aim of showing possible directions on the future of scholarly communication.

From a broader point of view but always considering the Web as prominent medium of communication, the *Beyond Impact Workshop*[77] (held in London in May 2011) tried to establish different forms of *impact*—that is a measure of how research outcomes influence and are used by other people—in today's and in future publishing. The output of this workshop is a document[78] that introduces research collaborations and future works to be done in the next few years.

---

[73] Tutorial on Linked Science 2012 homepage: http://linkedscience.org/events/tolsci2012.

[74] The Beyond the PDF Workshop homepage: http://sites.google.com/site/beyondthepdf/.

[75] FORCE11 homepage: http://www.force11.org.

[76] The Future of Research Communication Dagstuhl Workshop: http://www.dagstuhl.de/de/programm/kalender/semhp/?semnr=11331.

[77] The Beyond Impact Workshop: http://beyond-impact.org/

[78] Beyond Impact Workshop Report: http://docs.google.com/document/d/1sH3JOW5Luki4i37Ve1mOnI2wNZJbaUOx1T42S_7txQ0/edit?hl=en_GB.

2.5.5 Special Issues of Journals on Semantic Publishing

Journals about Semantic Web technologies and digital publishing started to be actively interested in Semantic Publishing topics.

An example of that is a special issue of the *Semantic Web Journal*[79]: *New Models of Semantic Publishing in Science*[80]. The central topic addressed by this special issue was about the promotion of new forms of Web-based publications, which allow a rapid and automatic integration of research information, thus making it readily available and reproducible. Towards this goal, the issue identifies Semantic Web technologies as key tools for providing efficient ways to work with new modes of scientific publications and asks for submissions of researches in various related fields: Semantic Publishing, Computer Supported Collaborative Work, Linked Data, eScience and Workflow-driven tools, and Digital Libraries. The editors' aim is to promote and advertise all the important researches that are underway in this field.

Another example of special issue is the *Journal of Web Semantics* on *Life Science and e-Science*[81]. Its goal is to identify which role the semantic technologies play in the context of life sciences such as biology, genetics, zoology, etc. In particular, this special issue want to report on the ways in which semantic technologies can enrich research, publish and reuse data according to semantic-aware formats, increase the scholarly communication, and the like.

References

Adida, B., M. Birbeck, S. McCarron, and S. Pemberton. 2013. RDFa core 1.1. 2nd ed. Syntax and processing rules for embedding RDF through attributes. W3C recommendation 22 August 2013. World Wide Web Consortium. http://www.w3.org/TR/rdfa-syntax/. Accessed 30 July 2013.

Barabucci, G., L. Cervone, M. Palmirani, S. Peroni, and F. Vitali. 2009. Multi-layer markup and ontological structures in Akoma Ntoso. In Proceeding of the international workshop on AI approaches to the complexity of legal systems II (AICOL-II), lecture notes in computer science 6237 vols, ed. P. Casanovas, U. Pagallo, G. Sartor, and G. Ajani, 133-149. Berlin: Springer. doi:10.1007/978-3-642-16524-5_9.

Barabucci, G., L. Cervone, A. Di Iorio, M. Palmirani, S. Peroni, and F. Vitali. 2010. Managing semantics in XML vocabularies: An experience in the legal and legislative domain. Proceedings of balisage: The markup conference 2009. Rockville: Mulberry Technologies, Inc. http://www.balisage.net/Proceedings/vol5/html/Barabucci01/BalisageVol5-Barabucci01.html. Accessed 30 July 2013.

Barabucci, G., A. Di Iorio, F. Poggi, and F. Vitali. 2013. Integration of legal datasets: From meta-model to implementation. Proceedings of international conference on information integration and web-based applications and services (iiWAS2013), 585–594. New York: ACM. doi:10.1145/2539150.2539180.

[79] Semantic Web Journal: http://www.semantic-web-journal.net.

[80] New Models of Semantic Publishing in Science: http://www.semantic-web-journal.net/blog/special-issue-new-models-semantic-publishing-science.

[81] Special issue of the Journal of Web Semantics on Life Science and e-Science: http://journalofwebsemantics.blogspot.it/2013/03/cfp-special-issue-on-life-science-and-e.html.

Beck, J. 2010. Report from the field: PubMed central, an XML-based archive of life sciences journal articles. Proceedings of the international symposium on XML for the long haul: Issues in the long-term preservation of XML. doi:10.4242/BalisageVol6.Beck01.

Beckett, D. 2004. RDF/XML syntax specification (Revised). W3C recommendation, 10 February 2004. World Wide Web Consortium. http://www.w3.org/TR/rdf-syntax-grammar/. Accessed 30 July 2013.

Bjork, B., and T. Hedlund. 2009. Two scenarios for how scholarly publishers could change their business model to open access. *Journal of Electronic Publishing* 12 (1). doi:10.3998/3336451.0012.102.

Boer, A., R. Hoekstra, and R. Winkels. 2002. METALex: Legislation in XML. In Proceedings of the 15th annual conference on legal knowledge and information systems (JURIX 2002), ed. T. Bench-Capon, A. Daskalopulu, and R. Winkels, 1–10. Amsterdam: IOS Press. http://www.jurix.nl/pdf/j02-01.pdf. Accessed 30 July 2013.

Boer, A., R. Hoekstra, R. Winkels, T. Engers van, and F. Willaert. 2002. Proposal for a dutch legal XML standard. In Proceedings of the 1st international conference on Electronic Government (EGOV 2002), lecture notes in computer science. 2456 vols, ed. R. Traunmuller and K. Lenk, 142–149. Berlin: Springer. doi:10.1007/3-540-46138-8_22.

Boer, A., R. Winkels, F. Vitali. 2007. Proposed XML standards for law: MetaLex and LKIF. In Proceedings of the 12th annual conference on legal knowledge and information systems (JURIX 2007), ed. A. R. Lodder and L. Mommers, 19–28. Amsterdam: IOS Press.

Boer, A., R. Winkels, F. Vitali. 2008. MetaLex XML and the legal knowledge interchange format. Computable models of the law, languages, dialogues, games, ontologies, lecture notes in computer science. 4884 vols, ed. P. Casanovas, G. Sartor, N. Casellas, and R. Rubino, 21–41. Berlin: Springer. doi:10.1007/978-3-540-85569-9_2.

Breuker, J., A. Boer, R. Hoekstra, and K. van den Berg. 2006. Developing content for LKIF: Ontologies and frameworks for legal reasoning. Proceedings of the 19th annual conference on legal knowledge and information systems (JURIX 2006), ed. T. M. van Engers, 169–174. Amsterdam: IOS Press.

Brickley, D., and R. V. Guha. 2004. RDF vocabulary description language 1.0: RDF schema. W3C recommendation 10 February 2004. World Wide Web Consortium. http://www.w3.org/TR/rdf-schema/. Accessed 30 July 2013.

Brickley, D., and L. Miller. 2010. FOAF vocabulary specification 0.98. Namespace document, 9 August 2010—Marco polo edition. http://xmlns.com/foaf/spec/. Accessed 30 July 2013.

Bromley, A. 1991. Policy statements on data management for global change research. http://www.gcrio.org/USGCRP/DataPolicy.html. Accessed 30 July 2013.

Carlisle, D., P. Ion, and R. Miner. 2010. Mathematical markup language (MathML) version 3.0. W3C recommendation, 21 October 2010. World Wide Web Consortium. http://www.w3.org/TR/MathML3/. Accessed 30 July 2013.

Carroll, J., and G. Klyne. 2004. Resource Description Framework (RDF): Concepts and abstract syntax. W3C recommendation, 10 February 2004. World Wide Web Consortium. http://www.w3.org/TR/rdf-concepts/. Accessed 30 July 2013.

Casanovas, P., N. Casellas, C. Tempich, D. Vrandecic,and R. Benjamins. 2007. OPJK and DILIGENT: Ontology modeling in a distributed environment. *Artificial Intelligence and Law* 15 (2): 171–186. doi:10.1007/s10506-007-9036-2.

Casellas, N. 2011. Legal ontology engineering. Law, governance and technology series 3. Berlin: Springer. doi:10.1007/978-94-007-1497-7.

Ciccarese, P., and S. Peroni. 2013. The collections ontology: Creating and handling collections in OWL 2 DL frameworks. To appear in *Semantic Web—Interoperability, Usability, Applicability*. doi:10.3233/SW-130121.

Ciccarese, P., E. Wu, J. Kinoshita, G. Wong, M. Ocana, A. Ruttenberg, and T. Clark. 2008. The SWAN biomedical discourse ontology. *Journal of Biomedical Informatics* 41 (5): 739–751. doi:10.1016/j.jbi.2008.04.010.

Clark, J. 2001. RELAX NG specification. Committee specification. Committee specification 3 December 2001. Organization for the advancement of structured information standards. http://relaxng.org/spec-20011203.html. Accessed 30 July 2013.

Comité Européen de Normalisation. 2010. Metalex (Open XML interchange format for legal and legislative resources). CEN workshop agreement 15710:2010 (E). Brussels: Comité Européen de Normalisation. http://ftp.cen.eu/CEN/Sectors/List/ICT/CWAs/CWA15710-2010-Metalex2.pdf. Accessed 30 July 2013.

Connolly, D. 2007. Gleaning resource descriptions from dialects of languages (GRDDL). W3C recommendation 11 September 2007. World Wide Web Consortium. http://www.w3.org/TR/grddl/. Accessed 30 July 2013.

Coombs, J. H., A. H. Renear, and S. J DeRose. 1987. Markup systems and the future of scholarly text processing. *Communications of the ACM* 30 (11): 933–947. doi:10.1145/32206.32209.

Cunningham, H. 2002. GATE, a general architecture for text engineering. *Computers and the Humanities*, 36(2): 223–254. doi:10.1023/A:1014348124664.

D'Arcus, B., and F. Giasson. 2009. Bibliographic ontology specification. Specification document, 4 November 2009. http://bibliontology.com/specification. Accessed 30 July 2013.

Day, D. S., C. McHenry, R. Kozierok, and L. Riek. 2004. Callisto: A configurable annotation workbench. In Proceedings of the 4th international conference on Language Resources and Evaluation (LREC 2004), ed. M. T. Lino, M. F. Xavier, F. Ferreira, R. Costa, R. Silva, C. Pereira, and S. Barros, 2073–2076. Paris: European Language Resources Association. http://www.lrec-conf.org/proceedings/lrec2004/pdf/612.pdf. Accessed 30 July 2013.

DeRose, S. 2004. Markup overlap: A review and a horse. Proceedings of the extreme markup languages 2004. Rockville: Mulberry Technologies, Inc. http://conferences.idealliance.org/extreme/html/2004/DeRose01/EML2004DeRose01.html. Accessed 30 July 2013.

DeRose, S., E. Maler, and R. Daniel. 2001. XPointer xpointer scheme. W3C working draft, 19 December 2002. World Wide Web Consortium. http://www.w3.org/TR/xptr-xpointer/. Accessed 30 July 2013.

Drummond, N., A. Rector, R. Stevens, G. Moulton, M. Horridge, H. H. Wang, and J. Seidenberg. 2006. Putting OWL in order: Patterns for sequences in OWL. In Proceedings of the workshop on OWL: Experiences and directions (OWLED 2006), CEUR workshop proceedings. 216 vos, ed. B. C. Grau, P. Hitzler, C. Shankey, and E. Wallace. Aachen: CEUR-WS.org. http://ceur-ws.org/Vol-216/submission_12.pdf. Accessed 30 July 2013.

Dubin, D. 2003. Object mapping for markup semantics. Proceedings of the extreme markup languages 2003. Rockville: Mulberry Technologies, Inc. http://conferences.idealliance.org/extreme/html/2003/Dubin01/EML2003Dubin01.html. Accessed 30 July 2013.

Dublin Core Metadata Initiative. 2008. Expressing dublin core metadata using HTML/XHTML meta and link elements. DCMI recommendation. http://dublincore.org/documents/dc-html/. Accessed 30 July 2013.

Dublin Core Metadata Initiative. 2012a. DCMI metadata terms. DCMI recommendation. http://dublincore.org/documents/dcmi-terms/. Accessed 30 July 2013.

Dublin Core Metadata Initiative. 2012b. Dublin core metadata element set, Version 1.1. DCMI recommendation. http://dublincore.org/documents/dces/. Accessed 30 July 2013.

Gangemi, A., and P. Mika. 2003. Understanding the semantic web through descriptions and situations. In Proceedings of the on the move confederated international conferences, CoopIS, DOA, and ODBASE 2003 (CoopIS/DOA/ODBASE 2003), lecture notes in computer science. 2888 vols, ed. R. Meersman, Z. Tari, and D. C. Schmidt, 689–706. Berlin: Springer. doi:10.1007/978-3-540-39964-3_44.

Gangemi, A., M. T. Sagri, and D. Tiscornia. 2005. A constructive framework for legal ontologies. Law and the semantic web: Legal ontologies. Methodologies, legal information retrieval, and applications, lecture notes in computer science. 3369 vols, ed. V. R. Benjamins, P. Casanovas, J. Breuker, and A. Gangemi, 97–124. Berlin: Springer. doi:10.1007/978-3-540-32253-5_7.

Gao, S., C. M. Sperberg-McQueen, and H. S Thompson. 2012. W3C XML schema definition language (XSD) 1.1 Part 1: Structures. W3C recommendation 5 April 2012. World Wide Web Consortium. http://www.w3.org/TR/xmlschema11-1/. Accessed 30 July 2013.

Garcia, R., O. Celma. 2005. Semantic integration and retrieval of multimedia metadata. Proceedings of the 5th international workshop on knowledge markup and semantic annotation (SemAnnot 2005), CEUR workshop proceedings 185: 69–80. Aachen: CEUR-WS.org. http://ceur-ws.org/Vol-185/semAnnot05-07.pdf. Accessed 30 July 2013.

Guittet, C. 1985. Formex: Formalized exchange of electronic publications. Luxembourg: office for official publications of the European communities. (ISBN: 978-9282553992).

Hammond, T. 2008. RDF site summary 1.0 modules: PRISM. http://nurture.nature.com/rss/modules/mod_prism.html. Accessed 30 July 2013.

Harnad, S., and T. Brody. 2004. Comparing the impact of Open Access (OA) vs. Non-OA articles in the same journals. *D-Lib Magazine* 10 (6). doi:10.1045/june2004-harnad.

Harnad, S., T. Brody, F. Vallieres, L. Carr, S. Hitchcock, Y. Gingras, C. Oppenheim, H. Stamerjohanns, and E. R Hilf. 2004. The access/impact problem and the green and gold roads to open access. *Serials Review* 30 (4): 310–314. doi:10.1016/j.serrev.2004.09.013.

Hillmann, D., K. Coyle, J. Phipps, and G. Dunsire. 2010. RDA vocabularies: Process, outcome, use. *D-Lib Magazine* 16 (1/2). doi:10.1045/january2010-hillmann.

Hobbs, J. R., and F. Pan. 2006. Time ontology in OWL. W3C working draft, 27 September 2006. World Wide Web Consortium. http://www.w3.org/TR/owl-time/. Accessed 30 July 2013.

Hoekstra, R. 2011. The MetaLex document server—legal documents as versioned linked data. In Proceedings of the 10th international semantic web conference (ISCW 2011), Part II, lecture notes in computer science. 7032 vols, ed. L. Aroyo, C. Welty, H. Alani, J. Taylor, A. Bernstein, L. Kagal, N. F. Noy, and E. Blomqvist, 128–143. Berlin: Springer. doi:10.1007/978-3-642-25093-4_9.

Huitfeldt, C., and C. M Sperberg-McQueen. 2003. TexMECS: An experimental markup metalanguage for complex documents. http://decentius.aksis.uib.no/mlcd/2003/Papers/texmecs.html. Accessed 30 July 2013.

International Digital Enterprise Alliance. 2009. Publishing requirements for industry standard metadata specification version 2.0. Alexandria: IDEAlliance. http://www.idealliance.org/specifications/prism. Accessed 30 July 2013.

International Federation of Library Associations and Institutions Study Group on the Functional Requirements for Bibliographic Records. 2009. Functional requirements for bibliographic records final report. International federation of library associations and institutions. http://www.ifla.org/files/cataloguing/frbr/frbr_2008.pdf. Accessed 30 July 2013.

JTC1/SC34 WG 6. 2006. ISO/IEC 26300:2006—Information technology—open document format for office applications (OpenDocument) v1.0. Geneva: International Organization for Standardization. http://www.iso.org/iso/iso_catalogue/catalogue_tc/catalogue_detail.htm?csnumber=43485. Accessed 30 July 2013.

Koutsomitropoulos, D. A., G. D. Solomou, and T. S Papatheodorou. 2008. Semantic interoperability of dublin core metadata in digital repositories. In Proceedings of the 5th international conference on Innovations in Information Technology (IIT 2008), 233–237. Washington: IEEE Computer Society. doi:10.1109/INNOVATIONS.2008.4781709.

Krotzsch, M., F. Simancik, and I. Horrocks. 2011. A description logic primer. Ithaca: Cornell University Library. http://arxiv.org/pdf/1201.4089v1. Accessed 30 July 2013.

Lawrence, S. 2001. Free online availability substantially increases a paper's impact. *Nature* 411 (6837): 521. doi:10.1038/35079151.

Library of Congress-Network Development and MARK Standard Office. 2010. MARK 21 format for bibliographic data. 1999 edition, further updates October 2001 and October 2010. http://www.loc.gov/marc/bibliographic/. Accessed 30 July 2013.

Lupo, C., F. Vitali, E. Francesconi, M. Palmirani, R. Winkels, E. de Maat, A. Boer, and P. Mascellani. 2007. General XML format(s) for legal sources. Deliverable 3.1 of the European project for standardised transparent representation in order to extende legal accessibility (ESTRELLA). EU IST-2004-027655. http://www.estrellaproject.org/doc/D3.1-General-XML-formats-For-Legal-Sources.pdf. Accessed 30 July 2013.

Marchetti, A., F. Megale, E. Seta, and F. Vitali. 2002. Using XML as a means to access legislative documents: Italian and foreign experiences. *ACM SIGAPP Applied Computing Review* 10 (1): 54–62. doi:10.1145/568235.568246.

Marcoux, Y. 2006. A natural-language approach to modeling: Why is some XML so difficult to write? Proceedings of the extreme markup languages 2006. Rockville: Mulberry Technologies, Inc. http://conferences.idealliance.org/extreme/html/2006/Marcoux01/EML2006Marcoux01.html. Accessed 30 July 2013.

Marcoux, Y. 2008. Graph characterization of overlap-only TexMECS and other overlapping markup formalisms. Proceedings of balisage: The markup conference 2008. Rockville: Mulberry Technologies, Inc. http://www.balisage.net/Proceedings/vol1/html/Marcoux01/BalisageVol1-Marcoux01.html. Accessed 30 July 2013.

Marcoux, Y., and E. Rizkallah. 2009. Intertextual semantics: A semantics for information design. *Journal of the American Society for Information Science and Technology* 60 (9): 1895–1906. doi:10.1002/asi.21134.

Marinelli, P., F. Vitali, and S. Zacchiroli. 2008. Towards the unification of formats for overlapping markup. *New Review of Hypermedia and Multimedia* 14 (1): 57–94. doi:10.1080/13614560802316145.

Miles, A., and S. Bechhofer. 2009. SKOS simple knowledge organization system reference. W3C recommendation 18 August 2009. World Wide Web Consortium. http://www.w3.org/TR/skos-reference/. Accessed 30 July 2013.

Montoya, E., M. Ruiz, and J. Giraldo. 2005. BDNG: A dublin core-based architecture for digital libraries. Proceedings of the international conference on dublin core and metadata applications 2005. Singapore: Dublin Core Metadata Initiative. http://dcpapers.dublincore.org/pubs/article/view/802/798. Accessed 30 July 2013.

Motik, B., P. F. Patel-Schneider, and B. Parsia. 2012. OWL 2 web ontology language: Structural specification and functional-style syntax (Second edition). W3C recommendation 11 December 2012. World Wide Web Consortium. http://www.w3.org/TR/owl2-syntax/. Accessed 30 July 2013.

Nuzzolese, A. G., A. Gangemi, and V. Presutti. 2010. Gathering lexical linked data and knowledge patterns from FrameNet. Proceedings of the 6th international conference on knowledge capture (K-CAP 2011), 41–48. New York: ACM. doi:10.1145/1999676.1999685.

Odlyzko, A. 2002. The rapid evolution of scholarly communication. *Learned Publishing* 15 (1): 7–19. doi:10.1087/095315102753303634.

Peroni, S., D. Shotton, and F. Vitali. 2012. Scholarly publishing and the linked data: Describing roles, statuses, temporal and contextual extents. In Proceedings of the 8th international conference on semantic systems (I-SEMANTICS 2012), ed. H. Sack and T. Pellegrini, 9–16. New York: ACM. doi:10.1145/2362499.2362502.

Peroni, S., D. Shotton, and F. Vitali. 2012. The live OWL documentation environment: A tool for the automatic generation of ontology documentation. In Proceedings of the 18th international conference on knowledge engineering and knowledge management (EKAW 2012), lecture notes in computer science. 7603 vols, ed. A. ten Teije, J. Völker, S. Handschuh, H. Stuckenschmidt, M. d'Aquin, A. Nikolov, N. Aussenac-Gilles, and N. Hernandez, 398–412. Berlin: Springer. doi:10.1007/978-3-642-33876-2_35.

Petersen, K. E. 2005. Lex dania XML status April 2005. Proceedings of the third workshop on legislative XML: 13–19. Rome: Centro Nazionale per l'Informatica nella Pubblica Amministrazione. http://www.digitpa.gov.it/sites/default/files/Quaderno8XML_0.pdf. Accessed 30 July 2013.

Petersen, K. E. 2011. Experiences with "Lex Dania Live". From information to knowledge, frontiers in artificial intelligence and applications. 236 vols, ed. M. A. Biasiotti and S. Faro, 69–76. Amsterdam: IOS Press. doi:10.3233/978-1-60750-988-2-69.

Portier, P., and S. Calabretto. 2009. Methodology for the construction of multi-structured documents. Proceedings of balisage: The markup conference 2009. Rockville: Mulberry Technologies, Inc. http://balisage.net/Proceedings/vol3/html/Portier01/BalisageVol3-Portier01.html. Accessed 30 July 2013.

Renear, A., D. Dubin, and C. M Sperberg-McQueen. 2002. Towards a semantics for XML markup. Proceedings of the 2002 ACM symposium on Document Engineering (DocEng 2002), 119–126. New York: ACM. doi:10.1145/585058.585081.

Renear, A., D. Dubin, C. M. Sperberg-McQueen, and C. Huitfeldt. 2003. XML semantics and digital libraries. Proceedings of the 3rd ACM/IEEE-CS Joint Conference on Digital Libraries (JCDL 2003), 303–305. Washington: IEEE Computer Society. doi:10.1109/JCDL.2003.1204879.

Riggs, K.R. 2002. XML and free text. *Journal of the American Society for Information Science and Technology* 53 (6): 526–528. doi:10.1002/asi.10063.

SC34/WG3. 2003. Topic Maps. ISO 13250. Geneva: International organization for standardization. http://www.isotopicmaps.org/. Accessed 30 July 2013.

Schmidt, D. 2009. Merging multi-version texts: A generic solution to the overlap problem. Proceedings of balisage: The markup conference 2009. Rockville: Mulberry Technologies, Inc. http://balisage.net/Proceedings/vol3/html/Schmidt01/BalisageVol3-Schmidt01.html. Accessed 30 July 2013.

Schmidt, D., and R. Colomb. 2009. A data structure for representing multi-version texts online. *International Journal of Human-Computer Studies* 67 (6): 497–514. doi:10.1016/j.ijhcs.2009.02.001.

Schonefeld, O., and A. Witt. 2006. Towards validation of concurrent markup. Proceedings of the extreme markup languages 2006. Rockville: Mulberry Technologies, Inc. http://conferences.idealliance.org/extreme/html/2006/Schonefeld01/EML2006Schonefeld01.html. Accessed 30 July 2013.

Shadbolt, N., K. O'Hara, T. Berners-Lee, N. Gibbins, H. Glaser, W. Hall, and M. C. Schraefel. 2012. Linked open government data: Lessons from data.gov.uk. *IEEE Intelligent Systems* 27 (3): 16–24. doi:10.1109/MIS.2012.23.

Sheridan, J., and J. Tennison. 2010. Linking UK government data. In Proceedings of the Linked Data on the Web workshop (LDOW 2010), CEUR workshop proceedings. 628 vols, ed. C. Bizer, T. Heath, T. Berners-Lee, and M. Hausenblas. Aachen: CEUR-WS.org. http://ceur-ws.org/Vol-628/ldow2010_paper14.pdf. Accessed 30 July 2013.

Shotton, D. 2009. Semantic publishing: The coming revolution in scientific journal publishing. *Learned Publishing* 22 (2): 85–94. doi:10.1087/2009202.

Shotton, D., K. Portwin, G. Klyne, and A. Miles. 2009. Adventures in semantic publishing: Exemplar semantic enhancements of a research article. *PLoS Computational Biology* 5 (4): e1000361. doi:10.1371/journal.pcbi.1000361.

Simon, J., A. Birukou, F. Casati, R. Casati, and M. Marchese. 2011. Liquid publications green paper. http://peerevaluation.org/data/ca75910166da03ff9d4655a0338e6b09/PE_doc_28223.pdf. Accessed 30 July 2013.

Simons, G. F., W. D. Lewis, S. O. Farrar, D. T. Langendoen, B. Fitzsimons, and H. Gonzalez. 2004. The semantics of markup: Mapping legacy markup schemas to a common semantics. In Proceedings of the workshop on NLP and XML (NLPXML 2004), ed. N. Ide and L. Romary, 25–32. Stroudsburg: Association for Computational Linguistics. http://acl.ldc.upenn.edu/acl2004/nlpxml/pdf/simons-etal.pdf. Accessed 30 July 2013.

Solomon, J. S. 2008. Developing open access journals: A practical guide. Oxford: Chandos Publishing Limited. (ISBN: 1843343394).

Sperberg-McQueen, C. M., and C. Huitfeldt. 2004. GODDAG: A data structure for overlapping hierarchies. In Proceeding of the 5th international workshop on the Principles of Digital Document Processing (PODDP 2000), lecture notes in computer science 2023, ed. P. R. King and E. V. Munson, 139–160. Berlin: Springer. doi:10.1007/978-3-540-39916-2_12.

Sperberg-McQueen, C. M., C. Huitfeldt, and A. Renear. 2000. Meaning and interpretation of markup. *Markup Languages: Theory and Practice* 2 (3): 215–234. doi:10.1162/109966200750363599.

Sperberg-McQueen, C. M., Y. Marcoux, and C. Huitfeldt. 2009. Two representations of the semantics of TEI lite. Proceedings of Digital Humanities 2010 (DH 2010). http://dh2010.cch.kcl.ac.uk/academic-programme/abstracts/papers/html/ab-663.html. Accessed 30 July 2013.

Styles, R., D. Ayers, and N. Shabir. 2008. Semantic marc, MARC21 and the semantic Web. In Proceedings of the WWW 2008 workshop on Linked Data on the Web (LDOW2008), CEUR workshop proceedings. 369 vols, ed. C. Bizer, T. Heath, K. Idehen, and T. Berners-Lee. Aachen: CEUR-WS.org. http://www.ceur-ws.org/Vol-369/paper02.pdf. Accessed 30 July 2013.

Swan, A. 2009. The open access citation advantages: Studies and results to date. Technical report, School of Electronics & Computer Science, University of Southampton. http://eprints.ecs.soton.ac.uk/18516/. Accessed 30 July 2013.

Tennison, J., and W. Piez. 2002. The Layered Markup and Annotation Language (LMNL). Presented at the extreme markup languages conference 2002. 4–9 August 2002, Montreal.

Text Encoding Initiative Consortium. 2013. TEI P5: Guidelines for electronic text encoding and interchange. Charlottesville: TEI Consortium. http://www.tei-c.org/Guidelines/P5. Accessed 30 July 2013.

Tummarello, G., C. Morbidoni, and E. Pierazzo. 2005. Toward textual encoding based on RDF. In Proceedings of the 9th ICCC international conference on Electronic Publishing (ELPUB2005), ed. M. Dobreva and J. Engelen. Leuven: Peeters Publishing Leuven. http://elpub.architexturez.net/system/files/pdf/206elpub2005.content_0.pdf. Accessed 30 July 2013.

Van Deursen, D., C. Poppe, G. Martens, E. Mannens, R. Van de Walle. 2008. XML to RDF conversion: A generic approach. In Proceedings of the 4th international conference on automated solutions for cross media content and multi-channel distribution (AXMEDIS 08), ed. P. Nesi, J. Delgado, and K. Ng, 138–144. Washington: IEEE Computer Society. doi:10.1109/AXMEDIS.2008.17.

van Hage W. R., V. Malaisé, R. Segers, L. Hollink, and G. Schreiber. 2011. Design and use of the simple event model (SEM). *Journal of Web Semantics: Science, Services and Agents on the World Wide Web* 9 (2): 128–136. doi:10.1016/j.websem.2011.03.003.

van Laarschot R., W. van Steenbergen, H. Stuckenschmidt, A. R. Lodder, F. van Harmelen. 2005. The legal concepts and the Layman's terms—bridging the gap through ontology-based reasoning about liability. In Proceedings of the 18th annual conference on legal knowledge and information systems (JURIX 2005), ed. M. Moens Katholieke, P. Spyns, 115–125. Amsterdam: IOS Press. http://www.jurix.nl/pdf/j05-20.pdf. Accessed 30 July 2013.

W3C HTML Working Group. 2002. XHTML™ 1.0 The extensible hypertext markup language (Second edition). W3C recommendation, 1 August 2002. World Wide Web Consortium. http://www.w3.org/TR/xhtml1. Accessed 30 July 2013.

Walsh, N. 2010. DocBook 5: The definitive guide. Sebastopol: O'Really Media. (Version 1.0.3. ISBN: 0596805029).

Wyner, A., and R. Hoekstra. 2012. A legal case OWL ontology with an instantiation of Popov v. Hayashi. *Artificial Intelligence and Law* 20 (1): 83–107. doi:10.1007/s10506-012-9119-6.

Zhao, J. 2010. Open provenance model vocabulary specification. Revision 1. 0, 6 October 2010. http://purl.org/net/opmv/ns. Accessed 30 July 2013.

Chapter 3
Markup Beyond the Trees

Abstract The issue of enabling the coexistence of independent sets of annotations that may overlap on the same textual content has been and still is an important topic to address within the document markup community. In this chapter, I propose a solution to the problem of overlapping markup based on the use of Semantic Web technologies. In particular, I introduce EARMARK, the Extremely Annotational RDF Markup, a markup metalanguage and an OWL ontology that enable one to create documents with single hierarchies (as with XML) and also with multiple overlapping hierarchies whose textual content within the markup items belongs to some hierarchies but not to others. I show possible scenarios of application of EARMARK and, finally, I discuss how to use existing Semantic Web technologies, e.g., OWL DL reasoners, to assess the correctness properties typical of the structural markup, such as validity against a schema.

The semantic enhancement of markup documents is a crucial requirement of Semantic Publishing. It is stated in more than one important work in this field, e.g., (De Waard 2010), that a better comprehension of a document derives also from the formal semantics defined within it. The formal semantic layer, thus, becomes a vehicle to extend the amount of ways through which we practice science. Although a large amount of theoretical studies discuss the different kinds of semantics applicable to a text, it seems they miss a crucial point: the semantics of a document, such as a scientific article, must be intrinsically and explicitly tied with the textual content of the document itself.

The way we use to say something about a text is that of *markup*. In people's mind, there still exists a clear distinction between *document markup* (e.g., XML), which we commonly use to define the structure of a document, and the *semantic markup* (e.g., RDF), usually needed when we want to represent, in a particular formalism, the meaning (or, better, a subjective interpretation) of the natural language text of a document[1]. Document markup and semantic markup are, actually, two sides of the same coin. However several people see them living in two separated levels. Even if the document markup is used to structure a document in the most cases, it can also be used to characterise textual fragments as real-world entity, e.g., a person.

[1] The document structure on its own can be seen as a particular kind of semantics. In fact, when we speak about a text as structured in terms of its paragraphs, sections, chapters, etc., what we are doing is to associate a semantic role of particular parts of the text.

S. Peroni, *Semantic Web Technologies and Legal Scholarly Publishing*,
Law, Governance and Technology Series 15, DOI 10.1007/978-3-319-04777-5_3,

Within a text, the element <person>[2] and the class *foaf:Person*[3] are (commonly) used to convey the same meaning, at least from the markup author's perspective. What really differs between them is that the latter define a formal representation of their semantics (e.g., in OWL 2 Direct Semantics (Motik et al. 2012), while the former usually does not. As all the XML-like languages, the markup semantics is left to the human interpretation of a natural language definition or, in the worst case, of the name of the markup element under consideration.

Besides this difference, what XML-like languages really lack in is an appropriate expressiveness for the description of multiple and overlapping markup on the same text. Overlapping markup is a crucial feature to express multiple (even discording) semantic interpretations on the same fragment. If we agree that XML markup elements convey semantics, then our field of action is limited by the syntactic rules of XML itself that impose to structure the markup as a tree. Previous works, such as (TEI Text Encoding Initiative Consortium 2013) and RDFa (Adida et al. 2013), propose to go beyond the syntactic constraints of XML, in order to have multiple overlapping markup elements and RDF statements within the same text. The problem is that those languages are not enough to address all the possible scenarios. For example, on the one hand, XML documents with TEI-like overlap workarounds present problems when trying to validate them against a particular schema. On the other hand, RDFa uses the document content to define formal statements, but it does not allow one to link a particular piece of text, e.g., a sentence or a word, to a semantic formalisation of it.

Trying to address the aforementioned issues, in this chapter I will propose a new markup metalanguage called *EARMARK* (*Extremely Annotational RDF Markup*) defined by means of Semantic Web technologies. Along the lines of other representational frameworks for documents such as (Van Rijsbergen 1986), EARMARK is a logic-based model that tries to be a nexus between document markup and semantic markup, and aims to reach an intuitively complete equivalence between them. In the following sections I will also investigate upon issues strictly related to markup expressiveness, i.e.: handling multiple and overlapping hierarchies on the same fragment, and the validation (against a particular schema) of documents having overlapping markup—while the definition of the semantics of markup elements and textual content will be entirely discussed in Chap. 4.

---

[2] The element *person* as defined in TEI Text Encoding Initiative Consortium (2013): http://www.tei-c.org/release/doc/tei-p5-doc/en/html/ref-person.html.

[3] The class *Person* as defined in FOAF (Brickley and Miller 2010): http://xmlns.com/foaf/spec/#term_Person.

3.1 EARMARK, a Semantic Web Approach to Metamarkup

This section discusses a different approach to metamarkup, called EARMARK (Extremely Annotational RDF Markup) (Di Iorio et al. 2009; Peroni and Vitali 2009; Di Iorio et al. 2010; Di Iorio et al. 2011; Di Iorio et al. 2011; Peroni et al. 2011; Barabucci et al. 2012; Di Iorio et al. 2009) based on ontologies and Semantic Web technologies. The basic idea is to model EARMARK documents as collections of addressable text fragments, and to associate such text content with OWL assertions that describe structural features as well as semantic properties of (parts of) that content. As a result EARMARK allows not only documents with single hierarchies (as with XML) but also multiple overlapping hierarchies where the textual content within the markup items belongs to some hierarchies but not to others. Moreover EAMARK makes it possible to add semantic annotations to the content though assertions that may overlap with existing ones.

One of the advantages of using EARMARK is the capability to access and query documents by using well-known and widely supported tools for Semantic Web. EARMARK assertions are simply RDF assertions, while EARMARK documents are modelled through OWL ontologies. The consequence is that query languages (such as SPARQL 1.1 (Garlik and Seaborne 2013) and actual existing tools (such as *Jena* (Carroll et al. 2004) and *Pellet*[4] (Sirin et al. 2007) can be directly used to deal with even incredibly complicated overlapping structures. What is very difficult (or impossible) to do with traditional XML technologies becomes much easier with these technologies under the EARMARK approach.

In the rest of this section I give a brief overview of the EARMARK model and how it can be used for addressing issues of overlapping markup, validation and semantics. The model itself is defined through an OWL document[5], summarised in Fig. 3.1 on page 48[6], specifying classes and relationships. We distinguish between *ghost classes*—that define the general model—and *shell classes* - that are actually used to create EARMARK instances.

[4] Pellet: http://pellet.owldl.com.

[5] EARMARK ontology: http://www.essepuntato.it/2008/12/earmark.

[6] This and the following diagrams comply with the *Graphic framework for OWL ontologies* (*Graffoo*), introduced in Sect. 6.4. A legend for all Graffoo diagrams can be found in Fig. 6.13 on page 227.

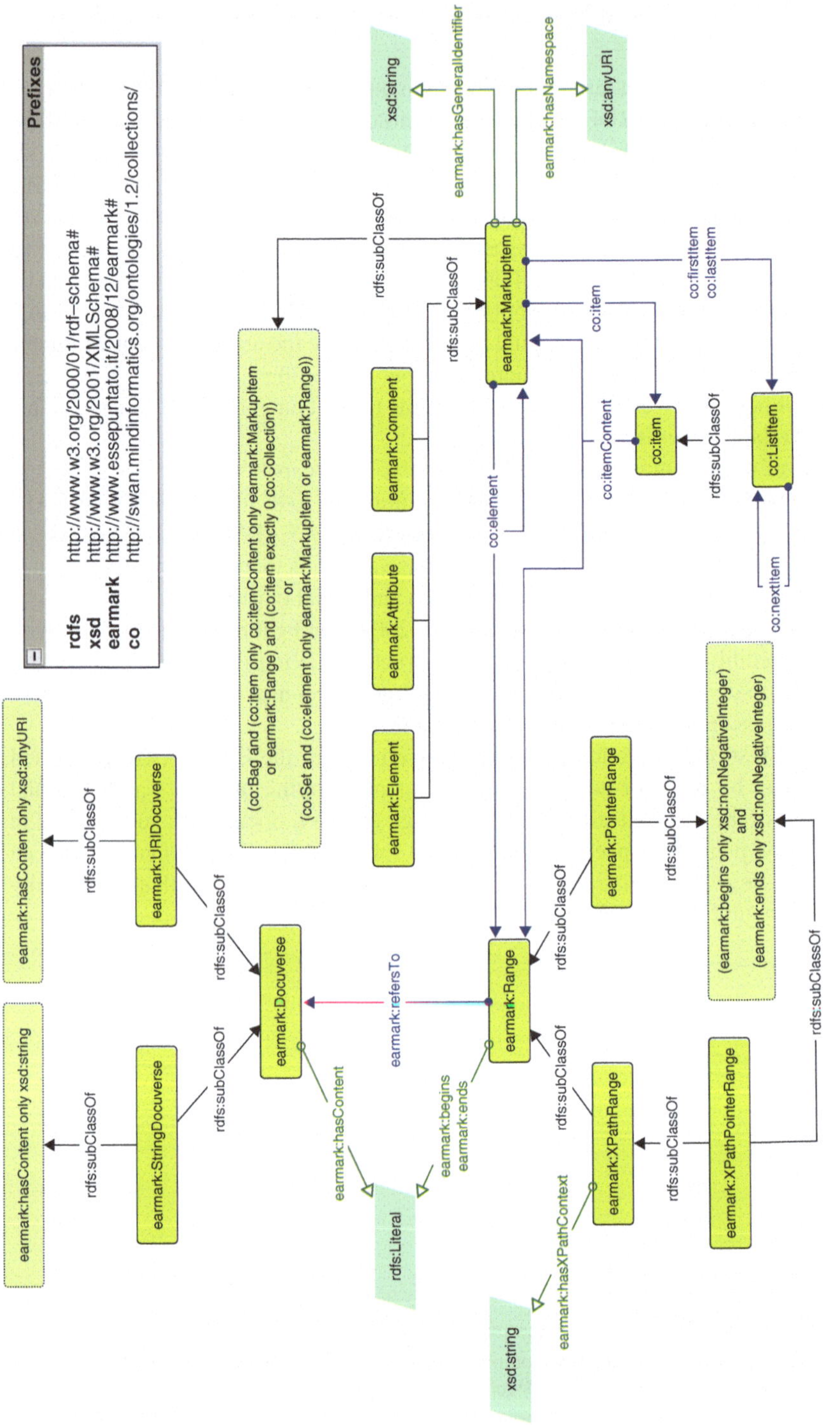

Fig. 3.1 A Graffoo (see Sect. 6.4) representation of the EARMARK ontology

3.1.1 Ghost Classes

The ghost classes describe three disjoint base concepts—*docuverses*, *ranges* and *markup items*—through three different and disjoint OWL classes[7].

The textual content of an EARMARK document is conceptually separated from its annotations, and is referred to through the *Docuverse* class[8]. The individuals of this class represent the object of discourse, i.e., all the containers of text of an EARMARK document.

```
Class: earmark:Docuverse

DatatypeProperty: earmark:hasContent
  Characteristics: FunctionalProperty
  Domain: earmark:Docuverse
  Range: rdfs:Literal
```

Any individual of the *Docuverse* class—commonly called a *docuverse* (lowercase to distinguish it from the class)—specifies its actual content with the property *hasContent*.

We then define the class *Range* for any text lying between two locations of a docuverse. A *range*, i.e., an individual of the class *Range*, is defined by a starting and an ending location (any literal) of a specific docuverse through the properties *begins*, *ends* and *refersTo* respectively.

```
Class: earmark:Range
  EquivalentTo:
    earmark:refersTo some earmark:Docuverse and
    earmark:begins some rdfs:Literal and
    earmark:ends some rdfs:Literal

ObjectProperty: earmark:refersTo
  Characteristics: FunctionalProperty
```

---

[7] All our OWL samples are presented using the Manchester Syntax (Horridge and Patel-Schneider 2012) and Turtle (Prud'hommeaux and 2013), which are two of the standard linearisation syntaxes of OWL. The prefixes *rdfs*and *xsd* refer respectively to RDF Schema and XML Schema namespaces, while the prefix *earmark* refers to the EARMARK ontology URI plus "#". Moreover, we use the prefix *co* to indicate entities taken from an imported ontology made for the SWAN project (Ciccarese et al. 2008), available at http://swan-ontology.googlecode.com/svn/tags/1.2/collections.owl.

[8] This class (and its name) is based on the concept introduced by Ted Nelson in his Xanadu Project (Nelson 1980) to refer to the collection of text fragments that can be interconnected to each other and transcluded into new documents.

```
    Domain: earmark:Range
    Range: earmark:Docuverse

  DatatypeProperty: earmark:begins
    Characteristics: FunctionalProperty
    Domain: earmark:Range
    Range: rdfs:Literal

  DatatypeProperty: earmark:ends
    Characteristics: FunctionalProperty
    Domain: earmark:Range
    Range: rdfs:Literal
```

There is no restriction on locations used for the *begins*and *ends* properties. That is very useful: it allows us to define ranges that *follow* or *reverse* the text order of the docuverse they refer to. For instance, the string "desserts" can be considered both in document order, with the *begins* location lower than the *ends* location or in the opposite one, forming "stressed"[9]. Thus, the values of properties *begins* and *ends* define the way a range must be read.

The class *MarkupItem* is the superclass defining artefacts to be interpreted as markup (such as elements and attributes).

```
Class: earmark:MarkupItem
  SubClassOf:
    (co:Set that co:element only
      (earmark:Range or earmark:MarkupItem)) or
    (co:Bag that co:item only
      (co:itemContent only
        (earmark:Range or earmark:MarkupItem))

DatatypeProperty: earmark:hasGeneralIdentifier
  Characteristics: FunctionalProperty
  Domain: earmark:MarkupItem
  Range: xsd:string

DatatypeProperty: earmark:hasNamespace
  Characteristics: FunctionalProperty
  Domain: earmark:MarkupItem
  Range: xsd:anyURI

Class: co:Collection
```

[9] http://en.wikipedia.org/wiki/Palindrome#Semordnilaps.

```
Class: co:Set
  SubClassOf: co:Collection

Class: co:Bag
  SubClassOf: co:Collection

Class: co:List
  SubClassOf: co:Bag

Class: co:Item

Class: co:ListItem
  SubClassOf: co:Item

ObjectProperty: co:element
  Domain: co:Collection

ObjectProperty: co:item
  SubPropertyOf: co:element
  Domain: co:Bag
  Range: co:Item

ObjectProperty: co:firstItem
  Characteristics: FunctionalProperty
  SubPropertyOf: co:item
  Domain: co:List

ObjectProperty: co:lastItem
  Characteristics: FunctionalProperty
  SubPropertyOf: co:item
  Domain: co:List

ObjectProperty: co:itemContent
  Characteristics: FunctionalProperty
  Domain: co:Item
  Range: not co:Item

ObjectProperty: co:nextItem
  Characteristics: FunctionalProperty
  Domain: co:ListItem
  Range: co:ListItem
```

A *markupitem* individual is a collection (co:Set, co:Bag or co:List, where the latter is a subclass of the second one and all of them are subclasses of co:Collection) of individuals belonging to the classes *MarkupItem* and *Range*. Through these collections it is possible to define a markup item as a set, a bag or a list of other markup items, using the properties *element* (for sets), *item* and *itemContent* (for bags and lists). Thus it becomes possible to define elements containing nested elements or text, or attributes containing values, as well as overlapping and complex structures. Note also that handling collections directly in OWL allows us to reason about content models for markup items, which would not be possible if we had used the corresponding constructs in RDF[10].

A *markupitem* might also have a name, specified in the functional property *hasGeneralIdentifier* (recalling the SGML term to refer to the name of elements (Goldfarb 1990), and a namespace specified using the functional property *hasNamespace*. Note that we can have *anonymous* markup items –as it is possible in LMNL (Tennison and Piez 2002) and GODDAG (Sperberg-McQueen and Huitfeldt 2004)—by simply asserting that the item belongs to the class of all those markupitems that do not have a general identifier (i.e., *earmark:hasGeneralIdentifier exactly 0*).

3.1.2 Shell Classes

The ghost classes discussed so far give us an abstract picture of the EARMARK framework. We need to specialise our model, defining a concrete description of our classes. These new *shell* subclasses apply specific restrictions to the *ghost* classes.

First of all, the class *Docuverse* is restricted to be either a *StringDocuverse* (the content is specified by a string) or an *URIDocuverse* (the actual content is located at the URI specified).

```
Class: earmark:StringDocuverse
  DisjointWith: earmark:URIDocuverse
  SubClassOf:
    earmark:Docuverse ,
    earmark:hasContent some xsd:string

Class: earmark:URIDocuverse
  SubClassOf:
    earmark:Docuverse ,
    earmark:hasContent some xsd:anyURI
```

Depending on particular scenarios or on the kind of docuverse we are dealing with—it may be plain-text, XML, LaTeX, a picture, etc.—we need to use different kinds of ranges. Therefore, the class *Range* has three different subclasses:

- *PointerRange* defines a range by counting characters. In that case, the value of the properties *begins* and *ends* must be a non-negative integer that identifies unambiguous positions in the character stream, remembering that the value *0* refers to the location immediately before the 1st character, the value *1* refers to the location after the 1st character and before the 2nd one, and so on. By using the *hasKey* OWL property, we also assert that two pointer ranges having equal docuverse, begin and end locations are the same range;

[10] A blog post by Paolo Ciccarese explaining why RDF collections cannot be used in OWL contexts: http://hcklab.blogspot.com/2008/12/moving-towards-swan-collectionshtml.

- *XPathRange* defines a range considering the whole docuverse or its particular context specifiable through an XPath expression (Berglund et al. 2011) as value of the property *hasXPathContext*. Note that, by using these ranges, we implicitly admit that the docuverse it refers to must be an XML structure. Moreover, the properties *begins* and *ends* have to be applied on the string value obtained by juxtaposing all the text nodes identified by the XPath. By using the *hasKey* OWL property, we also assert that two xpath ranges having equal docuverse, XPath context, begin and end locations are the same range;
- *XPathPointerRange* is an XPathRange in which the value of the properties begins and ends must be a non-negative integer that identifies unambiguous positions in the character stream as described for the class *PointerRange*.

```
Class: earmark:PointerRange
  HasKey: earmark:refersTo earmark:begins earmark:ends
  SubClassOf:
    earmark:Range ,
    earmark:begins some xsd:nonNegativeInteger and
    earmark:ends some xsd:nonNegativeInteger

Class: earmark:XPathRange
  SubClassOf: earmark:Range
  EquivalentTo:
    earmark:hasXPathContext some rdfs:Literal
  HasKey:
    earmark:refersTo earmark:begins
    earmark:ends earmark:hasXPathContext

Class: earmark:XPathPointerRange
  SubClassOf:
    earmark:XPathRange ,
    earmark:begins some xsd:nonNegativeInteger and
    earmark:ends some xsd:nonNegativeInteger

DatatypeProperty: earmark:hasXPathContext
  Characteristics: FunctionalProperty
  Domain: earmark:XPathRange
  Range: rdfs:Literal
```

MarkupItem is specialised in three disjointed sub-classes: *Element*, *Attribute* and *Comment*, which allow a more precise characterisation of markup items.

```
Class: earmark:Element
  SubClassOf: earmark:MarkupItem

Class: earmark:Attribute
  SubClassOf: earmark:MarkupItem

Class: earmark:Comment
  SubClassOf: earmark:MarkupItem

DisjointedClasses: earmark:Element , earmark:Attribute ,
    earmark:Comment
```

3.1.3 An Example

In order to understand how EARMARK is used to describe markup hierarchies, let me to introduce an XML excerpt, using TEI fragmentation (Text Encoding Initiative Consortium 2013) to express overlapping elements upon the string "Fabio says that overlhappens":

```
<p>
  <agent>Fabio</agent> says that
  <noun xml:id="e1" next="e2">overl</noun>
  <verb>
    h<noun xml:id="e2">ap</noun>pens
  </verb>
</p>
```

Here, the two elements *noun* represent the same element fragmented and overlapping with part of the textual content of *verb*, i.e., the characters "ap". The EARMARK translation of it is the following (linearised in Turtle (Prud'hommeaux and Carothers 2013)):

```
@prefix earmark:
      <http://www.essepuntato.it/2008/12/earmark#>.
@prefix co:
      <http://swan.mindinformatics.org/ontologies
      /1.2/collections/>.
@prefix ex: <http://www.example.com/>.

ex:doc
  earmark:hasContent "Fabio says that overlhappens" .

ex:r0-5 a earmark:PointerRange
  ; earmark:refersTo ex:doc
  ; earmark:begins "0"^^xsd:nonNegativeInteger
  ; earmark:ends "5"^^xsd:nonNegativeInteger .

ex:r5-16 a earmark:PointerRange
  ; earmark:refersTo ex:doc
  ; earmark:begins "5"^^xsd:nonNegativeInteger
  ; earmark:ends "16"^^xsd:nonNegativeInteger .

ex:r16-21 a earmark:PointerRange
  ; earmark:refersTo ex:doc
  ; earmark:begins "16"^^xsd:nonNegativeInteger
  ; earmark:ends "21"^^xsd:nonNegativeInteger .

ex:r21-28 a earmark:PointerRange
  ; earmark:refersTo ex:doc
  ; earmark:begins "21"^^xsd:nonNegativeInteger
  ; earmark:ends "28"^^xsd:nonNegativeInteger .

ex:r22-24 a earmark:PointerRange
  ; earmark:refersTo ex:doc
  ; earmark:begins "22"^^xsd:nonNegativeInteger
  ; earmark:ends "24"^^xsd:nonNegativeInteger .

ex:p a earmark:Element
  ; earmark:hasGeneralIdentifier "p"
  ; co:firstItem [ co:itemContent ex:agent
  ; co:nextItem [ co:itemContent ex:r5-16
  ; co:nextItem [ co:itemContent ex:noun
  ; co:nextItem [ co:itemContent ex:verb ]]]] .

ex:agent a earmark:Element
  ; earmark:hasGeneralIdentifier "agent"
  ; co:firstItem [ co:itemContent ex:r0-5 ] .

ex:noun a earmark:Element
  ; earmark:hasGeneralIdentifier "noun"
  ; co:firstItem [ co:itemContent ex:r16-21
  ; co:nextItem [ co:itemContent ex:r22-24 ]] .

ex:verb a earmark:Element
  ; earmark:hasGeneralIdentifier "verb"
  ; co:firstItem [ co:itemContent ex:r21-28 ] .
```

The whole EARMARK ontology has been implemented as a framework (Barabucci et al. 2013) for the creation, validation and manipulation of EARMARK documents, such as the above one, I will describe in Appendix 1. A full example of EARMARK document is available in Appendix 2.

3.2 The Issue of Overlapping Markup

There are multiple applications of EARMARK. The most interesting for this section concerns its capability of dealing with overlapping structures in an elegant and straightforward manner. Under EARMARK such structures do not need to be specified through complex workarounds as with XML, but they are explicit and can be easily described and accessed. Sophisticated searches and content manipulations become very simple when using this ontological model.

Thus, the goal of this section is to demonstrate the soundness and applicability of EARMARK by introducing theoretical aspects about overlapping markup in Sects. 3.2.1 and 3.2.2, and by discussing how some real-case scenarios are addressed (Sects. 3.2.3, 3.2.4 and 3.2.5). Notice that throughout the following sections I investigate multiple EARMARK data structures and documents, focussing on the feasibility and potentiality of such an ontological representation.

3.2.1 Range and Markup Item Overlap

The presence of overlap in EARMAK is worth discussing more in detail. Different types of overlap exist—according to the subset of items involved—and different strategies are needed to detect them. In particular, there is a clear distinction between *overlapping ranges* and *overlapping markup items*.

By definition, *overlapping ranges* are two ranges that refer to the same docuverse and so that at least one of the locations of the first range is contained in the interval described by the locations of the second range (excluding its terminal points). *Totally overlapping ranges* have the locations of the first range completely contained in the interval of the second range or vice versa, while *partially overlapping ranges*have either exactly one location inside the interval and the other outside or identical terminal points in reversed roles.

Thus, if we consider the ranges *ex:r21-28* and *ex:r24-24* of the example in Sect. 3.1.3, we can infer, through a reasoner such as Pellet (Sirin et al. 2007), that these two ranges overlap by using the following rule[11] (expressed in SWRL-like syntax (Horrocks et al. 2004):

[11] In the excerpt, the prefix *overlapping* refers to "http://www.essepuntato.it/2011/05/overlapping/".

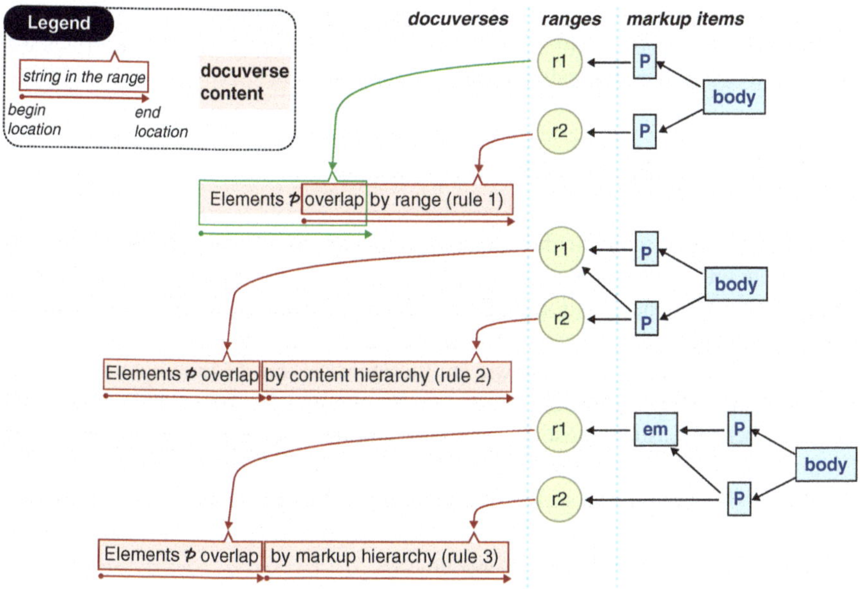

Fig. 3.2 Three EARMARK examples of overlapping between elements *p*

```
earmark:begins(x,b1) , earmark:ends(x,e1) ,
earmark:begins(y,b2) , earmark:ends(y,e2) ,
earmark:refersTo(x,d) , earmark:refersTo(y,d) ,
DifferentFrom(x,y) , P
  -> overlapping:overlapWith(x,y)
```

where *P* is one of:

- lessThan(b1,e1), greaterThan(b2,b1), lessThan(b2,e1)
- lessThan(b1,e1), greaterThan(e2,b1), lessThan(e2,e1)
- lessThan(e1,b1), greaterThan(b2,e1), lessThan(b2,b1)
- lessThan(e1,b1), greaterThan(e2,e1), lessThan(e2,b1)

The case of *overlapping markup items* is slightly more complicated. We define that two markup items *A* and *B* **overlap** when at least one of the following sentences holds:

1. **[overlap by range]** *A* contains a range that overlaps with another range contained by *B*;
2. **[overlap by content hierarchy]** *A* and *B* contain at least a range in common;
3. **[overlap by markup hierarchy]** *A* and *B* contain at least a markup item in common.

The three possible scenarios for such item overlap are summarised in Fig. 3.2[12]

[12] The EARMARK documents describing these three overlapping scenarios and all the other ones presented in the following sections are available at http://www.essepuntato.it/2011/jasist/examples.

The EARMARK ontology, in fact, is completed by another ontology[13] that models all overlapping scenarios, either for ranges or markup items, and includes rules for inferring overlaps automatically, through a reasoner.

3.2.2 *EARMARK as a Standoff Notation*

If we ignore for a moment the semantic implications of using EARMARK and concentrate only on its syntactical aspects, it is easy to observe that EARMARK is nothing but yet another standoff notation , where the markup specifications point to, rather than contain, the relevant substructure and text fragments.

Standoff notations, also known in literature as out-of-line notations (Text Encoding Initiative Consortium 2013), are hardly new, but never really caught on for a number of reasons, most having to do with their perceived fragility under the circumstances of desynchronised modification to the text. In (Georg et al. 2010; Bański, 2010) we can find a pair of recent and substantially complete analysis of their merits and demerits. In particular, according to Georg et al. (2010), "standoff annotation has [...] quite a few disadvantages:

1. very difficult to read for humans;
2. the information, although included, is difficult to access using generic methods;
3. limited software support as standard parsing or editing software cannot be employed;
4. standard document grammars can only be used for the level which contains both markup and textual data;
5. new layers require a separate interpretation;
6. layers, although separate, often depend on each other"[14].

And yet, although EARMARK *is* in practice a standoff notation, it provides a number of workarounds to most of the above-mentioned issues.

Firstly, since EARMARK is based on OWL and can be linearised in any of the large number of OWL linearisation syntaxes, it follows that '(1) readability, (2) access and (3) software support for it are exactly those existing for well-known, widespread and important W3C standards such as RDF and OWL. Being able to employ common RDF and OWL tools such as Jena and SPARQL for EARMARK documents was in fact a major motivation for it.

Issue 4 should be examined beyond the mere validation against document grammars and towards a general evaluation of the level of compliancy of the markup to some formally specified expectations. EARMARK documents, while being subject to no document grammar in the stricter XML sense, allow the specification of any number of constraints, expressed either directly in OWL, or in SWRL (Horrocks et al. 2004) or even in SPARQL (Garlik and Seaborne 2013), that trigger

[13] The EARMARK Overlapping Ontology: http://www.essepuntato.it/2011/05/overlapping.

[14] In order to individually address the issues, we edited the original bullets into a numbered list.

or generate validity evaluations. In (Di Iorio et al. 2011) we tried to show that a large number of requirements, from hierarchical well-formedness in the XML sense, to validation requirements in terms of XML DTDs, to adherence to design patterns, can be expressed satisfactorily using these technologies.

Item 5 regards the difficulty of standoff notations to provide inter-layer analysis on XML structures: separate interpretation of markup layers is easy, but identification and validation of overlapping situations is more complex: standoff markup is mainly composed of pointers to content, and does not have any direct way to determine overlap locations without some kind of pointer arithmetics to compute them. Validation of contexts allowing overlaps as describable using rabbit-duck grammars (Sperberg-McQueen 2006) is also not trivial. In this regard EARMARK provides yet again a solution that does not require special tools: although OWL does not allow direct pointer arithmetics, SWRL on the contrary does, as shown in Sect. 3.2.1 where we described a batch of (SWRL-implementable) rules that do in fact determine overlapping locations on EARMARK documents with good efficiency.

Finally, issue 6 refers to the fact that evolution of separate markup annotation layers need to take place synchronously, lest one of them become misaligned with the new state of the document. This is, in summary, the *fragility of pointers*, which can be considered the fundamental weakness of standoff, as well as of any notation that has markup separate from its content: if a modification occurs to the underlying (probably text-based) source, all standoff pointers that could not be updated at the same time of the change become outdated and possibly wrong. All standoff notations fall prey of this weakness, and there is no way to completely get rid of it.

What is possible is to identify exactly what are the conditions under which such weakness acts, and see if there is a way to reduce the mere frequency of such events. In order for a standoff pointer to become outdated, several conditions must take place at the same time:

- the standoff notation must be used as a storage format, rather than just as a processing format;
- the source document must make sense even without the additional standoff markup (i.e., the standoff notation contains no information that is necessary for at least some types of document modifications);
- the source document must be editable (and, in fact, must be edited) on its own;
- the standoff pointers must rely on positions that change when the source is edited (e.g., character-based locations);
- editing must be done in contexts and with tools that cannot or do not update the standoff pointers;
- there must be no computable way to determine the modifications of the document (e.g., via a *diff* between the old and the new version).

Of course, no standoff notation can rule out that these conditions occur on their documents. But it is worth pointing out that **all six** of them must occur, for standoff pointers to become outdated. EARMARK is not safe from these occurrences either, but, at least for some use cases, one or more of these conditions simply do not apply. For instance, when EARMARK is used as a processing format, with no need to save it on disk (conversion from the source formats, e.g., MS Word, is described in Sect. 3.2.3 and does not require special storage), the data format described is either in a very specific format (such as MS Word or ODT) that in fact already does handle internally its data changes and requires the overlapping data exactly for this purpose, or is in fact the result of a diff action on successive versions of a document (as in the case of the wiki pages, as introduced in Sect. 3.2.5).

Finally, EARMARK allows references to relatively stable fragment ids of the documents (by using XPath ranges without specifying explicitly begin and end locations), rather than the extremely fragile character locations, further reducing the chances of outdated pointers.

For this reason, without being able to completely rule out the possibility of standoff pointers to go wrong, we tend to consider it as a significantly little risk, at least for the use case here described.

3.2.3 Looking for Authorial Changes in Office Documents

Word processors such as Microsoft Word and Open Office Writer provide users with powerful tools for tracking changes, allowing each individual modification by individual authors to be identified, highlighted, and acted upon (e.g., by accepting or discarding them). The intuitiveness of the relevant interfaces actually hides the complexity of the data format and of the algorithms necessary to handle such information.

For instance, the standard ODT format (JTC1/SC34 WG 6 2006) used by Open Office, when saving change tracking information, relies on two specific constructs for insertions and deletions that may overlap with the structural markup. While adding a few words within a paragraph is not in itself complex, as it does not require the breaking of the fundamental structural hierarchy, conversely changes that affect the structure itself (e.g., the split of one paragraph in two by the insertion of a return character, or vice versa the joining of two paragraphs by the elimination of the intermediate return character) require that annotations are associated to the end of a paragraph and the beginning of the next, in an unavoidably overlapping pattern. ODT uses milestones and standoff markup for insertions and deletions respectively, and also relies on standoff markup for annotations about the authorship and date of the change.

For instance, the insertion of a return character and a few characters in a paragraph creates a structure as follows:

```
<text:tracked-changes>
  <text:changed-region text:id="S1">
    <text:insertion>
      <office:change-info>
        <dc:creator>John Smith</dc:creator>
        <dc:date>2009-10-27T18:45:00</dc:date>
      </office:change-info>
    </text:insertion>
  </text:changed-region>
  [... other changes ...]
</text:tracked-changes>
[... content ...]
<text:p>The beginning and
  <text:change-start text:change-id="S1"/></text:p>
<text:p> also<text:change-end text:change-id="S1"/> the
   end.</text:p>
```

The empty elements <text:change-start/ > and <text:change-end/ > are *milestones* marking respectively the beginning and the end of the range that constituted the insertion, while the element <text:insertion>, before the beginning of the document content, is *standoff markup* for the metadata about the change (author and date information).

Similarly, a deletion creates a structure as follows:

```
<text:tracked-changes><text:changed-region text:id="S2">
  <text:deletion><office:change-info>
    <dc:creator>John Smith</dc:creator>
    <dc:date>2009-10-27T18:46:00</dc:date>
  </office:change-info><text:p/><text:p/>
  </text:deletion></text:changed-region>
  [... other changes ...]
</text:tracked-changes>
[... content ...]
<text:p>The beginning and
  <text:change text:change-id="S2" />also the end.
</text:p>
```

The element <text:change/> represents a *milestone* of the location where the deletion took place in the content, and the corresponding *standoff markup* annotation <text:deletion> contains not only the metadata about the change, but also the text that was deleted.

The OOXML format (JTC1/SC34 WG 4 2011) (the XML-based format used by Microsoft Office 2007), on the other hand, uses a form of *fragmentation* to store change-tracking information across all previous elements involved.

```
<w:p>
  <w:pPr><w:rPr>
    <w:ins w:id="0" w:author="John Smith"
      w:date="2009-10-27T18:50:00Z"/>
  </w:rPr></w:pPr>
  <w:r><w:t>The beginning and </w:t></w:r></w:p>
<w:p>
  <w:ins w:id="1" w:author="John Smith"
    w:date="2009-10-27T18:50:00Z">
    <w:r><w:t>also </w:t></w:r></w:ins>
  <w:r><w:t>the end.</w:t></w:r></w:p>
```

This heavily simplified version of an OOXML document shows two separate changes: the first is the insertion of a return character and the second is the insertion of a word. These modifications are not considered as a single change, and therefore the segments are not connected to each other, but simply created as needed to fit the underlying structure. In fact, change tracking in OOXML is a fairly complex proposition. Although providing more complete coverage of special cases and situations than ODT, dealing with its intricacies is not for the casual programmer.

3.2.3.1 EARMARK for Processing Office Documents

At this point, it is clear that the use of complex data structures in ODT and OOXML, needed with storing overlaps generated by change-tracking functionalities, make it very difficult to search and manipulate the content when using XML languages and tools. Even very simple edits generate a rather tangled set of overlapping elements.

EARMARK, on the other hand, stores overlapping data in a direct and streamlined manner that does not require tools to rebuild information from the twists of a tree-based XML structure. The information is already available and expressed through consistent RDF and OWL statements. Figure 3.3 graphically shows the corresponding EARMARK document.

The original paragraph content and the new string "also" are now encoded as two *docuverses* over which the ranges *r1*, *r2* and *r3* are defined. The original paragraph is then composed of the (content of) ranges *r1* and *r2,* while the paragraphs resulting after the (text and carriage return) insertion now comprise respectively range *r1* and ranges *r2*, *r3*. Metadata about the author and the modification date are encoded as further RDF statements.

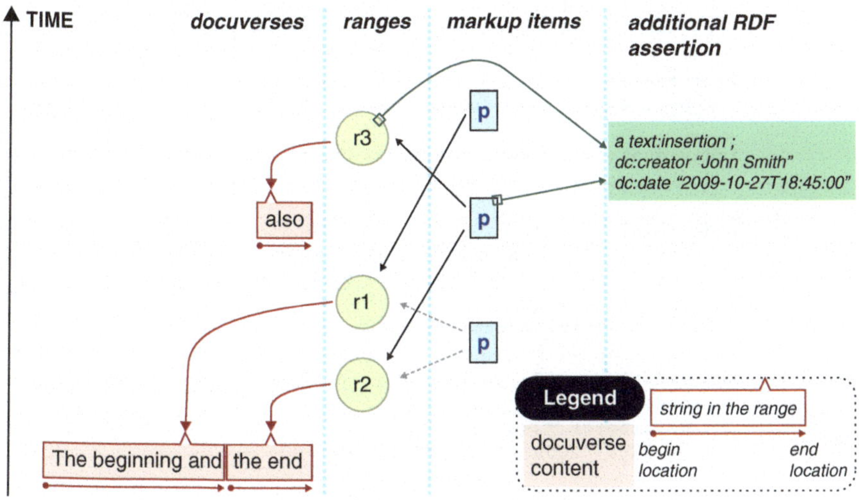

Fig. 3.3 Encoding in EARMARK the ODT change-tracking example

```
Individual: doc1 Types: earmark:StringDocuverse
  Facts: earmark:hasContent "The beginning and the end"

    Individual: doc2 Types: earmark:StringDocuverse
      Facts: earmark:hasContent " also"

    Individual: r1 Types: earmark:PointerRange
      Facts:
        earmark:refersTo doc1 ,
        earmark:begin "0"^^xsd:nonNegativeInteger ,
        earmark:end "17"^^xsd:nonNegativeInteger

    Individual: r2 Types: earmark:PointerRange
      Facts:
        earmark:refersTo doc1 ,
        earmark:begin "17"^^xsd:nonNegativeInteger ,
        earmark:end "25"^^xsd:nonNegativeInteger

    Individual: r3 Types: earmark:PointerRange , insJS
      Facts:
        earmark:refersTo doc2 ,
        earmark:begin "0"^^xsd:nonNegativeInteger ,
        earmark:end "5"^^xsd:nonNegativeInteger

    Individual: p-b Types: earmark:Element
      Facts: co:firstItem p-b-i1
```

```
Individual: p-b-i1
  Facts: co:itemContent r1 , co:nextItem p-b-i2

Individual:
  p-b-i2 Facts: co:itemContent r2

Individual: p-m Types: earmark:Element , insJS
  Facts: co:firstItem p-m-i1 , participateIn insJS

Individual: p-m-i1
  Facts: co:itemContent r3 , co:nextItem p-m-i2

Individual: p-m-i2
  Facts: co:itemContent r2

Individual: insJS Types: Insertion
  Facts:
    dc:creator "John Smith" ,
    dc:date "2009-10-27T18:45:00"

Individual: p-t Types: earmark:Element
  Facts: co:firstItem p-t-i

Individual: p-t-i
  Facts: co:itemContent r1
```

The advantages of streamlining overlaps become apparent if we consider tasks a little beyond the mere display. For instance, the query for "the textual content of all paragraphs inserted by John Smith" ends up rather entangled if we used XPath (Berglund et al. 2011) on the ODT structure. The process for finding that textual content needs to browse the current version of the document, look for all the *text:change-start/text:change-end* pairs that refer to an insertion made by John Smith involving the creation of a new paragraph (i.e., *text:change-start* is in a first paragraph while its pair, *text:change-end*, is in the following one), that are either currently present in the document body or hidden behind a subsequent deletion made by someone else. Once identified the paragraphs, I need to retrieve the content that originally was contained there, i.e., the text fragments that still are within those boundaries or that may have been deleted in subsequent versions. The following XPath represent an implementation of the above process:

```
for $cr in (//text:changed-region) , $date in ($cr/text:
  insertion//(@office:chg-date-time | dc:date)) return
  $cr[.//text:insertion[(.//@office:chg-author = 'John
  Smith' and count($cr//text:p) = 2) or (.//dc:creator
  = 'John Smith' and (//text:change-start[@text:change-
  id = $cr/@text:id]/following::text:p intersect //text
  :change-end[@text:change-id = $cr/@text:id]/(ancestor
  ::text:p)))]]/root()//((text:change-start[@text:
  change-id = $cr/@text:id]/(following::text:p//((text
  ()|(for $tc in (text:change) return //text:changed-
  region[@text:id = $tc/@text:change-id and not(text:
  insertion//(@office:chg-date-time | dc:date) > $date)
  ]//text:p[1]//text())) except ((for $tc in (text:
  change) return $tc[count(//text:changed-region[@text:
  id = $tc/@text:change-id and not(text:insertion//(
  @office:chg-date-time | dc:date) > $date)]//text:p) =
   2]/following::text()) union (//text:changed-region/
  text:deletion[.//dc:date <= $date]/text:p//text())))
  ) | (text:change[@text:change-id = $cr/@text:id]/(
  following::text()[ancestor::text:p] | (for $tc in (
  following::text:change) return //text:changed-region[
  @text:id = $tc/@text:change-id and not(text:insertion
  //(@office:chg-date-time | dc:date) > $date)]//text:p
  [1]//text())) except ((for $tc in (following::text:
  change) return $tc[count(//text:changed-region[@text:
  id = $tc/@text:change-id and not(text:insertion//(
  @office:chg-date-time | dc:date) > $date)]//text:p) =
   2]/following::text()) union (//text:changed-region/
  text:deletion[.//dc:date <= $date]/text:p//text())))
  | $cr//text:p[2]//text()) except (//(text:change|text
  :change-end)[@text:change-id = $cr/@text:id]//
  following::text:p[not((text:change-end|text:change-
  start|text:change)[1]/self::text:change-end)]/(. |
  following-sibling::element())//(text() | (for $tc in
  (text:change) return //text:changed-region[@text:id =
   $tc/@text:change-id]//text())))
```

The XML structure of a MS Word file, using segmentation rather than milestones, does simplify a bit the query, but still presents some radical complexities. The process starts by choosing all those *w:p* elements that were inserted by John Smith, as well as all their previous and contiguous *w:p* elements that were deleted before or inserted after the first ones. In OOXML, each sequence of contiguous *w:p* elements represents implicitly one paragraph. Therefore, I can now take all the text fragments contained in each *w:p* sequence that were inserted before or deleted after the paragraph defined by the sequence itself. The following is the resulting XPath for an OOXML document:

```
for $p in (//w:p[w:pPr//w:ins/@w:author = 'John Smith'])
    return for $date in ($p/w:pPr//w:ins/@w:date) return
   ($p|($p/preceding-sibling::w:p[w:pPr//w:del[@w:date <=
    $date]|w:pPr//w:ins[@w:date > $date]] except $p/
   preceding-sibling::element()[not(self::w:p) or empty(
   w:pPr//w:del[@w:date <= $date]|w:pPr//w:ins[@w:date >
    $date])]/(.|preceding-sibling::element())))//(w:t|w:
   delText)[empty(ancestor::w:ins[@w:date > $date]|
   ancestor::w:del[@w:date <= $date])]
```

The complexity of both XPath queries is due to the intrinsic complexity of the data structure the query has to work on. Although the interface of OpenOffice or MS Word may provide tools to directly deal with these queries using specific strategies on the internal data structures, applications working directly on the XML structure have very little help in disentangling the mess of the data formats.

On the other hand, since EARMARK documents are actually OWL files it is possible to access and query them with plain Semantic Web tools. Powerful searches can be then performed without using niche-specific tools or complex and long XPath expressions but simply with mainstream technologies such as SPARQL 1.1 (Garlik and Seaborne 2013).

The corresponding SPARQL query for ("the textual content of all paragraphs inserted by John Smith") can therefore be written as follows:

```
SELECT ?p ?r WHERE {
  ?r a earmark:Range .
  ?p a [ a :Insertion ; dc:creator "John Smith" ]
    ; earmark:hasGeneralIdentifier "p"
    ; earmark:hasNamespace "http://..."
    ; co:item/co:itemContent ?r . }
```

But EARMARK is useful for even more than querying: EARMARK also decreases the costs, in terms of efforts and lines of code, for manipulating documents.

Let me consider the task of generating an intermediate version (i.e., neither the first nor the last one of a version chain), from a document that includes change-tracking information about the whole document history.

The process of rebuilding these versions by working on the XML structure without specific APIs is complex and inefficient at the same time. For example a basic XSLT that returns an XML document defining the desired version requires at least to:

- define templates for all the elements actively involved in the change tracking—e.g., for ODT, *text:changed-region*, *text:change-start*, *text:change-end* and *text:change*, and similarly for OOXML—in order to understand, by looking at their creation date, whether they must be considered or ignored when building the requested version. In particular, we must exclude insertions following and deletions preceding the version we are building;
- define templates for paragraphs, in order to handle cases where the paragraph is the result of an insertion or a deletion of other paragraphs, in order to identify whether it should be considered for the result and, in such case, finding out its

real text content and remembering that, in the following versions, such content may have spread out among other paragraphs;
- define templates for handling insertions/deletions for structures such as images, sections, lists, and tables;
- define an identity template for the other elements, in order to visit the entire document.

Even the most basic and incomplete implementation of such XSLT requires hundreds of lines of complex and convoluted code and a large number of *ad hoc* decisions based on the specificities of whether we start from ODT or OOXML. Notice also that a Java-based implementation (or in any other procedural language) of the same process would be equally or even more complex.

The same result can be achieved on EARMARK documents with a few lines of Java code:

```
public EARMARKDocument getVersion(
  EARMARKDocument d, String creator, String date) {

  private final boolean RECURSIVELY = true;
  EARMARKDocument version = null;
  String query =
  "PREFIX earmark:"+
                "<http://www.essepuntato.it/2008/12/earmark#>" +
  "PREFIX co: <http://swan.mindinformatics.org/" +
            "ontologies/1.2/collections/>" +
  "PREFIX dc: <http://purl.org/dc/elements/1.1/>" +
  "PREFIX rdf: " +
                "<http://www.w3.org/1999/02/22-rdf-syntax-ns#>" +
  "SELECT ?root" +
   "WHERE {" +
   "?root a earmark:Element ; dc:creator \"" + creator +
   "\"; dc:date \"" + date + "\"." +
   "FILTER NOT EXISTS { ?mi a earmark:MarkupItem ;" +
   "co:item/co:itemContent ?root . } }";

  EARMARKElement theRoot = d.findNode(query) ;
  version = new EARMARKDocument(
    URI.create("http://www.example.com/version"));
  version.copyNode(theRoot, RECURSIVELY);
  return version;
}
```

This approach uses the EARMARK Java API that will be presented in and a single SPARQL query, runnable on any SPARQL 1.1 processor such as Jena, to identify the root node of the subtree of the version that is associated with the specified date and creator. Then, it performs a simple recursive deep-first visit in order to clone all the nodes in the tree and to combine them in the output EARMARK document.

This method heavily uses Semantic Web technologies on the structures provided by EARMARK whose characteristics are always explicit and clear. Since *all* versions coexist within the EARMARK document and each version can be encoded *explicitly* as a tree within the overall graph, this operation is straightforward and fast, as also discussed in (Peroni et al. 2013).

3.2.3.2 An Evaluation

One of the most frequent criticisms when proposing a different approach to solving a well-known problem in ICT is that the new solution may simplify the difficulties of the specific problem, but brings with it hidden costs in terms of size of the data structure, computation efforts or conversions restrictions that compensate the advantages. In our case, one of the anonymous reviewers of our paper (Di Iorio et al. 2009) wondered whether a difference in file size could weigh in on the convenience of adopting EARMARK as opposed to working with the original files.

As such, a discussion of cost functions of EARMARK versus other formats is in order. Yet, a systematic discussion of the relative costs (e.g., in byte size) of some original XML-based data structures versus their EARMARK equivalent is an open-ended undertaking that heavily depends on the original XML data structure and the specific features present in the document, and is badly defined anyway: while XML is a linearisation format immediately expressible in actual bytes, OWL (or, more precisely, RDF, the language in which OWL ontologies are expressed) is an abstract structure that allows a large number of linearisation formats (including XML itself) with corresponding huge differences in the final byte counts.

For these reasons, in order to provide at least an initial test of meaningful concepts, I selected two XML-based data formats (OOXML and ODT), and specifically a set of documents where overlapping tricks were present (i.e., where change-tracking was active). And to bypass the size discussion, I decided to test not byte-lengths (which are not meaningful and easily skewed, e.g., by reducing the string length of the element names or of the class names), but the number of nodes for XML documents and of triples for OWL documents. This comparison is again not particularly appropriate (triples are naturally numerous in OWL ontologies, and it is customary to deal with hundreds of thousands and even millions of assertions in Semantic Web applications), but closer to meaningfulness than mere byte count.

Our comparison was carried on a small set of documents in ODT and OOXML that included change-tracking information. As discussed in the previous sections, change-tracking facilities generate rather complex overlaps even for basic operations on small text fragments, which in turn are expressed as a potentially huge number of standoff and milestone markup within the XML hierarchy. The same documents were individually converted into EARMARK. I then charted how simple edits under change-tracking affect the number of nodes in XML formats and of statements in OWL files[15].

[15] The full details about each version and each format are also available at http://www.essepuntato.it/2011/jasist/discussion.

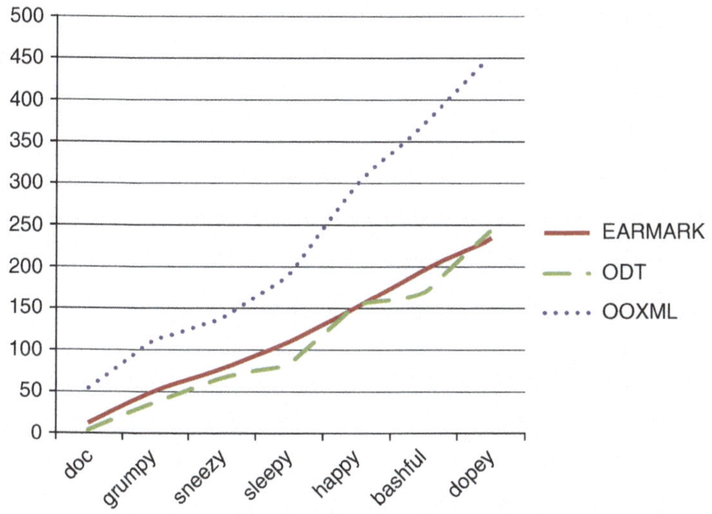

Fig. 3.4 A graph summarising the results of the first experiment

I created seven different versions, named after the Seven Dwarfs for recognisability, by applying very common edits (the insertion of few words, the deletion of some sentences, the split of a paragraph, and so on) on a small document, creating multiple overlaps. Figure 3.4 shows the results of our comparison.

The overall trend is interesting and comforting: while in simple documents with no overlap the node count of XML is lower than the assertion count of EARMARK triples, the presence of overlaps makes EARMARK and XML formats comparable. The growth of EARMARK statements is in fact very close to the growth of XML nodes when the number of overlaps increases. EARMARK is even more efficient than XML for more complex documents.

The measure for each format was done by counting only those nodes and statements instrumental to encode content and (overlapping) structures: I did not take into account neither the presentational information for ODT and OOXML (each file, for instance, includes a very long list of style definitions that are not relevant for the purposes of our analysis) nor namespace declarations (OOXML files, for instance, lists all relevant namespaces for the Office toolkit) nor ignorable white-spaces (that are only added to indent content and improve readability).

Interestingly, EARMARK and ODT show a very similar increase in size, while OOXML is much more verbose and grows faster. The content of the first version, for instance, is encoded using 4 nodes in ODT, 13 statements in EARMARK and 54 nodes in OOXML; the last one contains 241 ODT nodes, 233 EARMARK statements and 452 OOXML nodes. To return to our original enquiry, anyway, it is clear that the weight of EARMARK documents is very good compared to the other ones.

It is also worthy of note the regularity in the growth of EARMARK statements. Regardless of the actual modifications applied to the document, in fact, EARMARK

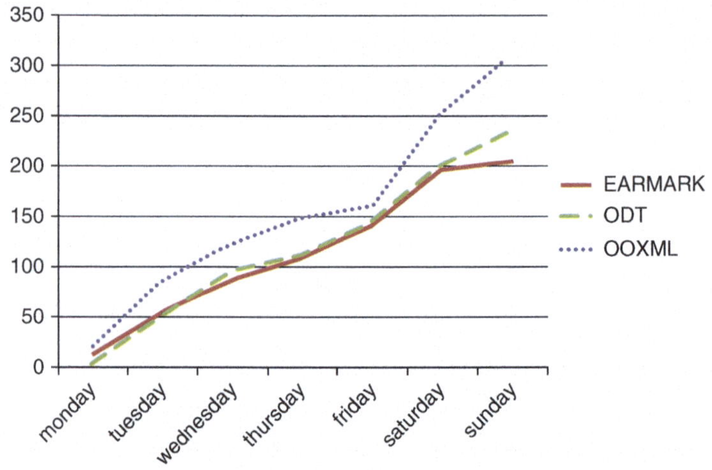

Fig. 3.5 A graph summarising the results of the second experiment

adds about 40 statements for each edit. Both OOXML and ODT, on the contrary, show a more irregular "pace". The reason is that EARMARK externalises *all* assertions, so that *all* modifications (either to leaf-nodes or to intermediate nodes in the original XML) are "flattened" onto the docuverses and do not depend on the complexity of the structure within which the edit took place.

Figure 3.5 shows the results of a similar comparison on a different set of documents and edits. We collected seven versions named after the weekdays and created by seven different authors when editing a very simple document. The overall trend does not change and shows that EARMARK and ODT have again a comparable behaviour, far better than OOXML.

In conclusion, although preliminary, this study shows clear trends of a very conservative behaviour of EARMARK with respect to document size.

3.2.4 Overlapping with Microformats and RDFa

Microformats (Allsopp 2007) add semantic markup to web documents by using common structures of the HTML language itself, in particular the *class* attribute.

The HTML code is annotated using microformats so as to provide new semantic, machine-processable assertions. In the following example, a plain HTML table is enriched with metadata about events[16] and people[17]:

[16] HCalendar: http://microformats.org/wiki/hcalendar.

[17] HCard: http://microformats.org/wiki/hcard.

```
<body>
  <p class="vevent">
    <span class="summary">WWW 2010 Conference</span>:
    <abbr class="dtstart" title="2010-04-26">April 26</abbr>
    -<abbr class="dtend" title="2010-10-30">30</abbr>,
    <span class="location">Raleigh, NC, USA</span>.</p>
  <table>
    <tr><th>Name</th><th>Role</th></tr>
    <tr class="vcard">
      <td class="fn">Juliana Freire</td>
      <td class="role">Program Committee Chair</td></tr>
    <tr class="vcard">
      <td class="fn">Michal Rappa</td>
      <td class="role">Conference Chair</td></tr>
    <tr class="vcard">
      <td class="fn">Paul Jones</td>
      <td class="role">Conference Chair</td></tr>
    <tr class="vcard">
      <td class="fv">Soumen Chakrabarti</td>
      <td class="role">Program Committee Chair</td></tr>
  </table>
<body>
```

The table was enriched by additional data declaring it to be an event (a conference) and data about the event itself—the url, summary, location—and about four relevant individuals—with their names and roles within the conference—were associated where necessary to the actual content of the table.

So far, so good, and no overlap to speak about. Things change dramatically, though, when the overall structure of the main hierarchy (the HTML table) is at odds with the intrinsic hierarchy of the microformat data, for instance if the people are organised in columns rather than rows. For instance:

```
<table>
  <tr>
    <td>Program Committee Chair</td>
    <td>Conference Chair</td>
    <td>Conference Chair</td>
    <td>Program Committee Chair</td></tr>
  <tr>
    <td>Juliana Freire</td>
    <td>Michael Rappa</td>
    <td>Paul Jones</td>
    <td>Soumen Chakrabarti</td></tr>
</table>
```

Unfortunately, vcards are a hierarchy themselves, and if the hierarchy of vcards is organised differently from the hierarchy of the HTML table, as in the latter case, it is just impossible to define the four vcards for the four people organising the conference. Thus in plain HTML the choice of one of two possible presentation models for the main hierarchy of content makes it trivial or completely impossible the existence of the second hierarchy.

A possible and partial solution to express vcard hierarchies in the latter example is RDFa (Adida et al. 2013), a W3C recommendation. It describes a mechanism to embed RDF statements into HTML documents by using some HTML attributes (*href*, *rel*, *rev*, *content*) in combination with other *ad hoc* attributes (*property*, *about*, *typeof*) proposed in the recommendation itself.

```
<table
  xmlns:vc="http://www.w3.org/2006/vcard/ns#"
  xmlns:my="http://www.essepuntato.it/2010/05/myVCard#">
  <tr>
    <td about="my:pcc" typeof="vc:Role">
      Program Committee Chair</td>
    <td about="my:cc" typeof="vc:Role">
      Conference Chair</td>
    <td about="my:cc" property="vc:hasName">
      Conference Chair</td>
    <td about="my:pcc" property="vc:hasName">
      Program Committee Chair</td></tr>
  <tr>
    <td about="my:jf" rel="vc:role" resource="my:pcc">
      <span about="my:jf" property="vc:fn">
        Juliana Freire</span></td>
    <td about="my:mr" rel="vc:role" resource="my:cc">
      <span about="my:mr" property="vc:fn">
        Michael Rappa</span></td>
    <td about="my:pj" rel="vc:role" resource="my:cc">
      <span about="my:pj" property="vc:fn">
        Paul Jones</span></td>
    <td about="my:sc" rel="vc:role" resource="my:pcc">
      <span about="my:sc" property="vc:fn">
        Soumen Chakrabarti</span></td></tr>
</table>
```

Since all attributes live in the context of elements, the price to pay is that to assert everything we want to assert we often need to add some structurally unnecessary elements to the current markup hierarchy of a document, needed only to add the RDF statements (e.g., the *span* elements emphasised above). Even if that does not represent a significant problem for strict Semantic Web theorists, document architects and markup expert see this as a kludge and an inelegant compromise.

Converting the Web document with annotations into an EARMARK document allowing both semantic and structural annotations to coexist can solve these issues. Through EARMARK, I can explicitly express both markup structures and *vcard* assertions. Figure 3.6 shows how the *vcard* example can be modelled (once again we show a graphical representation for the sake of clarity).

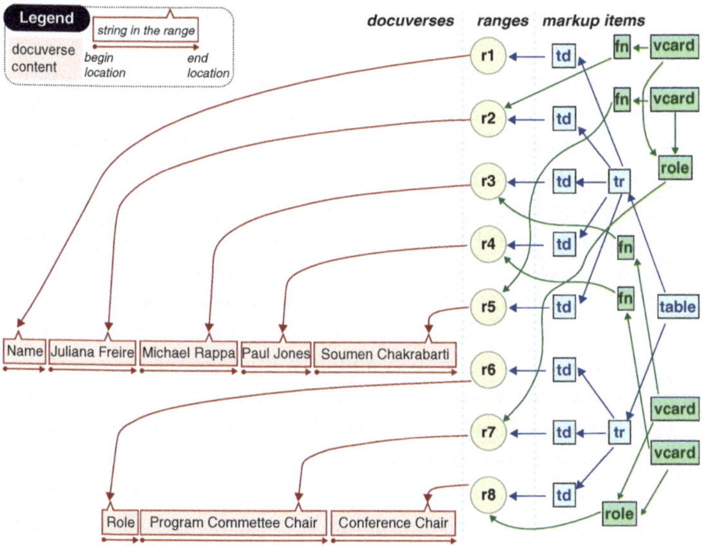

Fig. 3.6 The abstract model of the EARMARK document solving the microformats issue

The textual content of the original table cells is now encoded in two different docuverses, one for the header (with roles) and one for the body (with names of committee members). Ranges *r1*, *r2*, . . ., *r8* are then created to distinguish each role and name. Two independent and coexisting hierarchies are then built on top of the same set of ranges: the HTML table that includes one cell for each range (in blue) and the *Vcards* about each person (in green) that include only the relevant ranges and overlap the previous one. Notice also that the *Vcards* are defined in such a way that does not interfere with the structural features of the table. The full linearisation in OWL of this example can be found at http://www.essepuntato.it/2011/jasist/examples.

3.2.5 *Wikis: No Overlapping Where Some Should be*

The strength of wikis lies in their allowing users to modify content at any time. The mechanisms of change-tracking and rollback that are characteristics of all wikis, in fact, promote users' contributions and make "malicious attacks" pointless in the long run, since previous versions can be easily restored.

A number of tools exist that automatically discover "wiki vandalisms" and provide users with powerful interfaces to surf changes, *diff* subsequent versions and revert content. For instance, Huggle[18]. is an application dealing with vandalism in Wikipedia, based on a proxy architecture and .NET technologies. A straightforward

[18] Huggle: http://en.wikipediaorg/wiki/Wikipedia:Huggle.

interface allows users to access any version of a page, highlights contributions of a specific user and reverts the content to old versions.

Even client-side tools—meant to be installed as browsers extensions or bookmarklets—exist to extend the rollback mechanisms of Wikipedia, giving users more flexibility and control over (vandalistic) changes. For instance, Lupin[19] is a set of javascript scripts that check a wiki page against a list of forbidden terms so that authors can identify undesirable modifications and restore previous (good) versions without a continuous control over the full content of the page; yet again, Twinkle[20] provides users powerful rollback functions and includes a full library of batch deletion functions, automatic reporting of vandals, and users notification functions.

These tools are successful in highlighting vandalism and in identifying versions created by malicious users. However, although it is possible to revert the page to any previous version, all changes (even acceptable ones) that were subsequent to the malicious version cannot be automatically inherited by the restored page.

For instance, let me consider versions V1, V2, and V3 of a wiki page, where versions V1 contains a baseline (acceptable) content, V2 is identified as a partial vandalism and is agreed to be removed, but V3 contains (possibly, in a completely different section than the target of the malicious attack) relevant and useful content that was added before the vandalistic version V2 was declared as such. The task of removing the modifications of version V2 while maintaining (whatever is possible of) version V3 is a difficult, error-prone and time-consuming task if done manually, yet there is no tool we are aware of that automatically filters contributions from multiple versions and merges them into a new one (or, equivalently, removes only selected intermediate versions).

Yet, it is possible to characterise the interdependencies between subsequent changes to a document in a theoretical way. Literature has existed for a long time on exactly these themes (see for instance (Durand 2008; Durand 1994). Although a detailed discussion of abstract models of interconnected changes is out of scope for this paper—details and authoritative references can be found in the above mentioned works—what is relevant in this discussion is that they happen to assume a hierarchical form that is frequently at odds with the hierarchical structure of the content of the document, and as such most issues derive from the data structures in which content is stored and from the model for manipulating these structures. For instance, the fact that in the wiki perspective each version is an independent unit that shares no content (even unchanged content) with the other versions prevents considering multiple versions as overlapping structures coexisting on the same document. If we were able to make these hierarchies explicit we would be able to create models and tools to manipulate these documents in a more powerful way and to exploit the existing interconnections between the overlapping hierarchies.

EARMARK can be used to improve wiki reversion mechanisms and overcome the limitations discussed above: the automatic filtering and merging of contributions

[19] Lupin, the Anti-vandal tool: http://en.wikipedia.org/wiki/User:Lupin/Anti-vandal_tool.

[20] Twinkle: http://en.wikipedia.org/wiki/Wikipedia:Twinkle.

Table 3.1 All the versions of a wiki page modified by different authors

Version	V1	V2	V3	V4
Author	151.61.3.122	Angelo Di Iorio	Silvio Peroni	Fabio Vitali
Content	Bob was farming carrots and tomatoes	Bob was farming carrots, tomatoes *and beans*	Bob was farming carrots, tomatoes and *green* beans. *They were all tasteful.*	Bob was farming carrots, tomatoes and green beans. They were all tasteful.

from multiple versions of the same page is now still a *manual*process, but it can be fully automatised if the overlapping structures buried in the *whole* history of the page become explicit.

The role of EARMARK is to make those structures explicit and available for more sophisticated content manipulation. In order to understand to what extent EARMARK structures can be derived from wikis and how they can be exploited by the final users, we use as our example the wiki platform MediaWiki[21], i.e., the wiki engine of Wikipedia.

MediaWiki offers sophisticated functionalities for creating *diffs* of wiki content. Users can compare any two revisions in the page history and highlight changes in a friendly interface that shows modifications with a word-level granularity. *Diff* pages contain metadata about each compared version (when the version was created, who was the author or which IP address an anonymous author was connected from, etc.) and a two-column table showing the changes side-by-side. Changes are detected *a posteriori*by comparing two arbitrary versions, not even requiring them to be temporally contiguous.

The output of the MediaWiki diff engine has regularities that can be exploited to automatically build the overlapping structures of the *diff* and to express them in EARMARK. Let us consider a fictitious example summarised in Table 3.1, where an initial text is revised three times by different authors.

To display the differences between V1 and V2, Mediawiki creates a page whose HTML code is as follows[22]:

[21] MediaWiki: http://www.mediawiki.org.

[22] For the sake of clarity we removed all markup irrelevant to our discussion.

```
<table class="diff"><tbody>
  <tr valign="top">
    <td class="diff-otitle">
      <div id="mw-diff-otitle1">
        <a href="{...}oldid=413">Revision as of 15:46, 8
            November 2009</a></div>
      <div id="mw-diff-otitle2">
        <a>151.61.3.122</a></div>
    </td>
    <td class="diff-ntitle">
      <div id="mw-diff-ntitle1">
        <a href="{...}oldid=414">Revision as of 15:47, 8
            November 2009</a></div>
      <div id="mw-diff-ntitle2">Angelo Di Iorio</div>
    </td></tr>
    <tr>
      <td class="diff-marker">-</td>
      <td class="diff-deletedline">
        <div>Bob was farming carrots
          <del class="diffchange diffchange-inline">
            and </del>tomatoes.</div></td>
      <td class="diff-marker">+</td>
      <td class="diff-addedline">
        <div>Bob was farming carrots
          <ins class="diffchange diffchange-inline">
            , </ins> tomatoes
          <ins class="diffchange diffchange-inline">
            and beans</ins>.</div></td></tr>
  </tbody></table>
```

This is an HTML table of two rows, the first showing metadata (date and author of the modification) and the second the actual modifications. The first cell of the second row contains all the unmodified text and a *del* element for each inline fragment that was deleted. The second cell contains all the unmodified text and an *ins* element for each inline fragment that was inserted. Thus, these cells share *exactly* the same unmodified part(s) of the two compared versions.

When the structure itself is modified, rather than merely the text, the source code of the MediaWiki *diff* is slightly different. Thus the diff between V3 and V4 (which splits a paragraph in two) is as follows:

```
<tr>
  <td class="diff-marker">-</td>
  <td class="diff-deletedline">
    <div>Bob was farming carrots, tomatoes and green
       beans. They were all tasteful.</div></td>
  <td class="diff-marker">+</td>
  <td class="diff-addedline">
    <div>Bob was farming carrots, tomatoes and green
       beans. </div></td></tr>
<tr>
  <td colspan="2"> </td>
  <td class="diff-marker">+</td>
  <td class="diff-addedline"><div> </div></td></tr>
<tr>
  <td colspan="2"> </td>
  <td class="diff-marker">+</td>
  <td class="diff-addedline">
    <div>They were all tasteful.</div></td></tr>
```

The *diff* output is neither complete nor sophisticated, and of course it is a completely different task to re-plan such algorithm (but for a first idea of natural changes in recognising differences of XML documents, see (Di Iorio et al. 2009). Thus, limitations of that algorithm are inevitably shared by any EARMARK representation. Yet, this output is sufficiently rich to allow us to extract the overlapping information we need. For instance, the insertion of a non-breakable-space or a carriage-return generates rows according to specific rules that can be easily detected to capture the actual change by the author.

Figure 3.7 shows the above example rebuilt in EARMARK. All versions are encoded in the same document by creating overlapping assertions over the docuverses. Metadata and RDF statements are layered on top of those assertions and create a rich knowledge base about the history of the documents and, in particular, about the history of each fragment.

Due to the complexity of the example we labelled arrows with numbers indicating the position of each range within each markup item. Consider for instance version *V4*: it is composed of two DIV elements, the first one containing the concatenation of "Bob was farming carrots" + "," + "tomatoes" + "and" + "green" + "beans" + ".", and the second one contains the string "They are all tasteful".

Implementing a wiki content filtering mechanism on top of such a structure is rather simple. For instance, the removal of all the contributions of "Angelo Di Iorio", that leaves untouched all the content written (previously and subsequently) by "Silvio Peroni" and "Fabio Vitali", can be performed straightforwardly. Three steps are enough to apply such an intermediate content reversion:

1. the identification of the fragments written by "Angelo Di Iorio", which is a straightforward SPARQL query on the embedded statements;
2. the creation of a new version where references to those fragments are removed and references to fragments no longer in the document are correctly fixed;

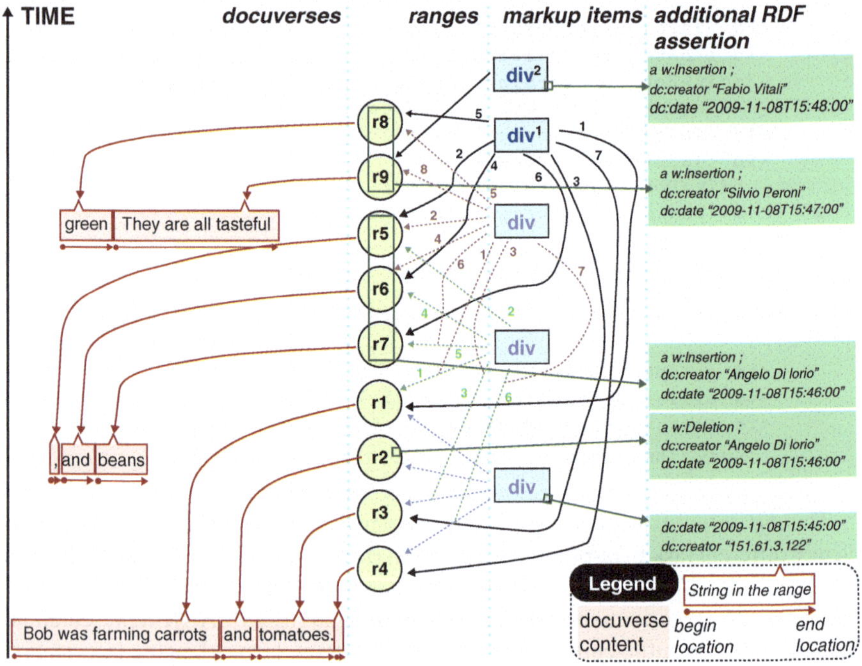

Fig. 3.7 The wiki sample versions encoded in a single EARMARK document

3. the translation of that document into an actual MediaWiki page through the serialisation process described in (Peroni and Vitali 2009).

Of course, an automatic process may generate ambiguities or even errors in the resulting content (some parts may become dangling, wrong or unclear after removing text fragments elsewhere); grammar discrepancies might also be generated by the same approach. Linguistic and semantic problems, however, become a problem once the technical issues of managing independent yet successive edits are solved. What is important is that all the information about overlaps and dependencies among fragments are available in EARMARK and can easily be searched, filtered and manipulated. Besides, foreseeing a manual intervention for checking and polishing automatically-filtered content is perfectly in line with the wiki philosophy, so that the wiki community itself can use the reversion tools wisely to revise the content and adjust any intervening minor nuisances or imperfections. Such checks would still be far simpler and faster than the manual process of partially reverting versions as we have today.

3.3 Structural Validation of Semantically-Defined Markup

One of the most important issues addressed by document markup concerns the possibility to express and verify specific syntactic properties:

- the *well-formedness*, that depends to the syntax specified for the particular markup language considered – e.g., in XML-based languages the begin and end tags which delimit elements must correctly nest without overlapping;
- the *validity* against a *vocabulary*, that (formally) restricts the set of values we can use for naming elements and attributes—definable by using schema languages such as XML Schema and RelaxNG for XML;
- the *validity* against a *content model*, that defines contexts in which a particular named element can or cannot be[23]—definable by using schema languages as well. Particularly interesting in this context is the validity of a document against a set of *patterns*, i.e., a set of recurring rules and content models.

In this section I discuss how most correctness properties typical of the structural markup, such as the *validity* against a schema, can be expressed through OWL ontologies and verified upon EARMARK documents at a semantic level by means of reasoners, such as Pellet (Sirin et al. 2007), even when dealing with multi-hierarchical structures. In order to support this claim, I also introduce two different running examples, the former based on a simple markup schema and the latter on a specific meta-level theory for document structures based on structural patterns (Dattolo 2007).

3.3.1 Defining Content-Models on EARMARK Documents

The assessment of ontological properties in the semantic domain is in a way comparable and can be made to act as validation in the XML domain, that is the process of verification of whether relevant markup items of a well-formed XML document satisfy the constraints embodied in the relevant components of a schema. In the world of XML, several schema languages have been introduced such as DTD (Bray et al. 2006), XML Schema (Gao et al. 2012; RelaxNG Clark 2001). They have different expressive power but they share the same objectives and basic principles: the validator checks the structural properties of a well-formed document by verifying all the *syntactical* constraints expressed in the schema.

Moving from a syntactic perspective to a *semantic* one—as proposed by EARMARK—opens new perspectives for a general approach to assessment as well. A key point of such approach is the translation of many markup properties from a syntactical to an ontological level. In the case of XML schema validation, for instance,

[23] More formally, for XML-based languages, a *content model* of a markup element is "a simple grammar governing the allowed types of the child elements and the order in which they are allowed to appear" (Bray et al. 2006).

this means expressing (a) schema definitions as ontology classes and properties and (b) schema documents as ontology instances and assertions, that express hierarchies as semantic relations. Starting from an ontological *TBox* representing the schema and an *ABox* representing the document, we can then conclude that the document is valid according to the schema if and only if the *ABox* is consistent with the *TBox*.

My goal is to design a framework and to implement tools that verify if an EARMARK document is compliant to any property *P* over its syntax, structure and semantics. The same approach can thus be used for common validation as well as for all the other above-mentioned constraints we want to verify on our documents. My approach—that is meant to be instantiated for each specific case—can be summarised as follows:

1. define an ontology fragment *O* that details the particular property *P* we want to verify;
2. associate the EARMARK document instances to *O*, so as to obtain an ABox for *O*;
3. use a reasoner to prove whether the ABox is consistent (i.e., that property *P* is held) or not (and *P* is not held).

In order to illustrate how to assess properties on EARMARK documents defining specific ontologies, we first take into consideration simple syntactical property definitions, such as those specifiable for the content models of markup items using schema languages such as DTD, XML schema or RelaxNG.

For instance, let us consider the following seven-sentences informal description of a schema:

1. it is only possible to use elements (e.g., no attributes are allowed anywhere);
2. no element is associated to a namespace;
3. all elements must specify a general identifier;
4. each element contains the other nodes in a specific order;
5. no element with a general identifier different from "phrase", "noun" and "verb" can be used;
6. each element with general identifier "phrase" can contain, in any order, only an unlimited number of elements with general identifier "noun" or "verb", and cannot contain text;
7. each element with general identifier "noun" or "verb" can contain only text and no other elements.

Using a RelaxNG Compact-like syntax (Clark 2002), opportunely extended to allow us to define more than one root element for our documents in the structure *start*(when applied to XML documents, RelaxNG only allows one to define one root), the previous informal schema may be formally expressed as follows:

```
start = (e.phrase | e.noun | e.verb)*
e.phrase = element phrase { (e.noun | e.verb)* }
e.noun = element noun { text }
e.verb = element verb { text }
```

As I have previously introduced, in order to understand whether an EARMARK document is written according to the previous sentences and, consequently, to the previous schema, I have to develop an OWL ontology that implements them. In this case, we can obtain implicit associations between EARMARK document instances and the above property constraints to assess by extending the EARMARK ontology itself.

First of all, I can limit the use of elements (sentence 1) simply defining all markup items equivalent to elements only, as shown in the following excerpt:

```
Class: earmark:MarkupItem
  EquivalentTo:
    earmark:Element and
    not(earmark:Attribute or earmark:Comment)
```

This sentence also results in asserting, by inference, that *Attribute* and *Comment* are subclass of the OWL class *Nothing*, which represents the empty set: no individuals can belong to it.

Then, I express sentences 2 to 4 by adding three subclass relations to the *Element* class:

```
Class: earmark:Element
  SubClassOf:
    earmark:hasNamespace exactly 0 , co:List ,
    earmark:hasGeneralIdentifier some xsd:string
```

To express sentences 5 to 7, we create a new object property to describe the parent-child relations among EARMARK nodes (i.e., markup items and ranges):

```
ObjectProperty: earmark:hasChild
  SubPropertyChain:
    co:item o co:itemContent
```

Since it is defined by a property chain between the properties *item* and *itemContent*, I can say that if an Element individual *e* has an item *i* that refers to a particular EARMARK node *m*—that is a typical parent-child relation concerning EARMARK elements expressed by bags or lists—then we can infer that *e* has *m* as child.

Then, using this property, I can easily cover the remaining sentences (4–7) by adding another subclass relation to the *Element* class:

```
(earmark:hasGeneralIdentifier value 'phrase' and
  earmark:hasChild only
    (earmark:hasGeneralIdentifier some
      {'noun' , 'verb'}))
or
((earmark:hasGeneralIdentifier some {'noun' , 'verb'})
  and
  earmark:hasChild only earmark:Range)
```

That's it: the above assertions are sufficient to assess whether an EARMARK document is valid against the schema presented[24]. For instance, when I try to verify, through a reasoner, whether the EARMARK document in Sect. 3.1.3 is consistent with the model introduced in this section, I will receive an inconsistency exception because the element *p* of the sample document is not allowed.

Property definitions through OWL ontologies can be used to define schemas for EARMARK documents. Yet, rather than discussing validation, that is addressed in other works, such as (Ferdinand et al. 2004; Rodrigues et al. 2006; Yang et al. 2007), in the following sections we will concentrate, as an extensive example, on the assessment of the properties connected to *structural patterns*, such as the ones discussed in (Dattolo et al. 2007; Di Iorio et al. 2005).

3.3.2 Structural Patterns

The idea of using patterns to produce reusable and high-quality assets is not new in the literature. Software engineers (Gamma et al. 1994), architects (as Alexander who first introduced this term (Alexander 1979) and designers very often use—or rather *reuse*—patterns to handle problems that recur over and over. Patterns have also been studied to modularise and customise web ontologies (Presutti and Gangemi 2008). They guarantee the flexibility and maintainability of concepts and solutions in several heterogeneous scenarios.

My research group has been investigating patterns for XML documents for some time (Dattolo et al. 2007; Di Iorio et al. 2005; Di Iorio et al. 2012; Di Iorio et al. 2013). The overall goal of our research is to understand how the structure of digital documents can be segmented into atomic components, which can be manipulated independently and re-flowed in different contexts. Instead of defining a large number of complex and diversified structures, a small number of *structures/patterns* has been identified, sufficient to express what most users need. The idea is that eleven patterns, shown in Table 3.2 on page 83, are enough to capture the most relevant document structures.

The two main characterising aspects of such pattern theory are:

- *orthogonality*—each pattern has a specific goal and fits a specific context. The orthogonality between patterns makes it possible to associate a single pattern to each of the most common situations in document design. Then, whenever a designer has a particular need he/she has to only select the corresponding pattern and to apply it;
- *assemblability*—each pattern can be used only in some locations (within other patterns). Although this may seem a limitation, such strictness improves the expressiveness and non-ambiguity of patterns. By limiting the possible choices,

[24] The model is available at http://www.essepuntato.it/2011/03/schemaexample.

Table 3.2 Eleven structural documents as introduced in (Di Iorio et al. 2012)

Pattern	Description	Example (DocBook)
Atom	Any simple box of text, without internal substructures (simple content) that is allowed in a mixed content structure but not in a container.	email, code
Block	Any container of text and other substructures except for (even recursively) other block elements. The pattern is meant to represent block-level elements such as paragraphs.	para, caption
Container	Any container of a sequence of other substructures and that does not directly contain text. The pattern is meant to represent higher document structures that give shape and organisation to a text document, but do not directly include the content of the document.	bibliography, preface
Field	Any simple box of text, without internal substructures (simple content) that is allowed in a container but not in a mixed content structure.	pubdate, publishername
Headed Container	Any container starting with a head of one or more block elements. The pattern is usually meant to represent nested hierarchical elements (such as sections, subsections, etc., as well as their headings).	section, chapter
Inline	Any container of text and other substructures, including (even recursively) other inline elements. The pattern is meant to represent inline-level styles such as bold, italic, etc.	emphasis
Meta	Any content-less structure (but data could be specified in attributes) that is allowed in a container but not in a mixed content structure. The pattern is meant to represent metadata elements that assert things about the document, but are disconnected to its actual text content.	imagedata, colspec
Milestone	Any content-less structure (but data could be specified in attributes) that is allowed in a mixed content structure but not in a container. The pattern is meant to represent locations within the text content that are relevant for any reason.	xref, co
Popup	Any structure that, while still not allowing text content inside itself, is nonetheless found in a mixed content context. The pattern is meant to represent complex substructures that interrupt but do not break the main flow of the text, such as footnotes.	footnote, tip
Record	Any container that does not allow substructures to repeat themselves internally. The pattern is meant to represent database records with their variety of (non-repeatable) fields.	address, revision
Table	Any container that allows a repetition of homogeneous substructures. The pattern is meant to represent a table of a database with its content of multiple similarly structured records.	tr, keywordset

Patterns prevent the creation of uncontrolled and misleading content structures. This characteristic still allows the presence of overlapping items—for example, a block that contains two different inlines that overlap upon the same segment continues to be a valid structure in terms of patterns because its content model is not violated, even though the presence of overlapping descendants.

These patterns allow authors to create unambiguous, manageable and well-structured documents. The regularity of pattern-based documents makes it possible to perform easily complex operations even when knowing very little about the documents' vocabulary. Designers can implement more reliable and efficient tools, can make hypotheses regarding the meanings of document fragments, can identify singularities and can study global properties of sets of documents.

There are two main methods to check if (and how) a document uses patterns or can be normalised into a new pattern-based resource. A procedural approach requires *ad hoc* tools—written in a procedural programming language and running on a software platform—that are difficult to write, test, maintain, and extend. A declarative approach, on the other hand, guarantees more flexibility, extensibility and portability. The ontological model adopted by EARMARK is particularly suitable for such a context: verifying that a document meets the requirements given by patterns, in fact, only requires verification using a reasoner of some properties of an OWL ontology.

In the next section I will propose an example of this approach, made even more complex by the presence of an overlapping structure that makes property verification through XML technologies much more complex, and possibly even impossible.

3.3.2.1 Assessing Structural Patterns on EARMARK Documents

The first step to verify patterns-related properties of EARMARK documents is obviously to build an ontology that describes such patterns and their relationships. We developed the ontology through a set of hierarchical class/sub-class relations, summarised in Fig. 3.8 on page 85.

We have three levels of abstraction modelling different aspects of our theory:

- the *top-level* classes describe the general features of a pattern. In particular, they characterise their content model expressing the possibility for the element to contain text (*Textual*) or not (*NonTextual*) and to contain other elements (*Structured*) or not (*NonStructured*);
- the *middle-level* classes – i.e., *Marker*, *Bucket*, *Flat* and *Mixed* – model all the combinations of top-level classes and express their disjointness;
- the *bottom-level* classes include all the "instanceable" classes, i.e., all those classes which document elements can explicitly belong to.

This ontology allows me to verify whether or not an EARMARK document follows the structural patterns. In particular, it allows me to verify if a given association between elements and patterns (that assigns one pattern to each element) is valid.

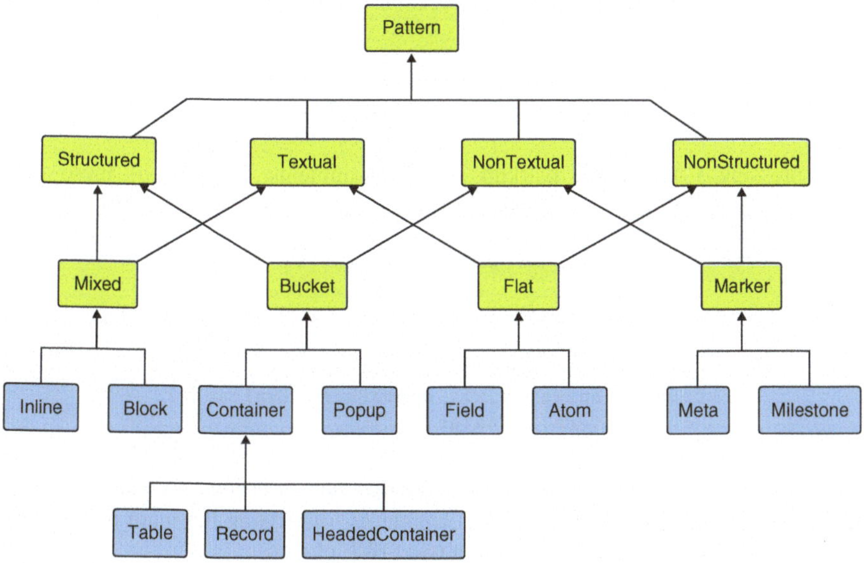

Fig. 3.8 The classes defining the hierarchical structure of the structural patterns defined in (Di Iorio et al. 2012). The arrows indicate sub-class relationships between patterns (e.g., Mixed is sub-class of Structured)

That, again, means checking whether the ontological association of each element to a particular pattern is consistent.

For assessing patterns on an EARMARK document *D*, we need to apply the following steps:

1. for each element in *D*, associate an instanceable pattern to the element;
2. for each element in *D*, assert the element belongs to the class defined by the restriction `pattern:isContainedBy exactly 0 pattern:Pattern`[25] whether it is not contained by any other element – where *isContainedBy* is a property linking a pattern-based element to the one that is actually containing it;
3. launch a reasoner to check if the pattern ontology with these added assertions is consistent (all the pattern constraints hold) or not (there are some errors when assigning patterns to elements).

Before presenting experimental results, let me show some excerpts from the pattern ontology developed, just to sketch out how we formally define those structural properties. First of all, I need to express containment relations among patterns through specific OWL object properties, as shown as follows:

[25] The prefix *pattern* refers to "http://www.essepuntato.it/2008/12/pattern#".

```
ObjectProperty: pattern:contains
  Domain: pattern:Structured
  Range: pattern:Pattern
ObjectProperty: pattern:isContainedBy
  InverseOf: pattern:contains
```

Expressing EARMARK markup item containments in terms of these two properties is straightforward by using particular rules to infer new assertions:

```
earmark:MarkupItem(x), co:Set(x),
co:element(x,y), earmark:MarkupItem(y)
  -> pattern:contains(x,y)

earmark:MarkupItem(x), co:item(x,y),
co:itemContent(y,z), earmark:MarkupItem(z)
  -> pattern:contains(x,z)
```

Taking into consideration the above properties and assertions, I illustrate, as example, the definition of *inline* and *block* patterns, discussing the main differences among them. I implement them through two OWL classes:

```
Class: pattern:Inline
  EquivalentTo:
    pattern:Mixed that
      pattern:isContainedBy only (
        pattern:Inline or pattern:Block)
  SubClassOf:
    pattern:contains only (
      pattern:Inline or pattern:Atom or
      pattern:Milestone or pattern:Popup),
    pattern:isContainedBy some (
      pattern:Inline or pattern:Block)

Class: pattern:Block
  EquivalentTo:
    pattern:Mixed that
      pattern:isContainedBy only (
        pattern:Container or pattern:Popup)
  SubClassOf:
    pattern:contains only (
      pattern:Inline or pattern:Atom or
      pattern:Milestone or pattern:Popup)
  DisjointWith: pattern:Inline
```

As shown, content models for these classes are defined by adding restrictions in form of superclasses, such as:

```
pattern:contains only (
  pattern:Inline or pattern:Atom or
  pattern:Milestone or pattern:Popup)
```

All *Textual* individuals are inferred starting from markup items containing some ranges:

```
earmark:MarkupItem(x), co:Set(x),
co:element(x,y), earmark:Range(y)
  -> pattern:Textual(x)

earmark:MarkupItem(x), co:item(x,y),
co:itemContent(y,z), earmark:Range(z)
  -> pattern:Textual(x)
```

The entire pattern ontology definition is available online[26] and uses SWRL (Horrocks et al. (2004)) as the rule language. For a detailed introduction to this ontology, please see (Di Iorio et al. (2012)).

3.3.2.2 Experimental Results

In the following I discuss an explicative example on the first three verses of the *Paradise Lost* by John Milton, which are often quoted as a standard example for enjambement in poetry:

```
Of Man's first disobedience, and the fruit
Of that forbidden tree whose mortal taste
Brought death into the World
```

I want to describe two different hierarchies, one for the verses and another one for the syntactical units giving rise to the enjambments, and we use an HTML-like syntax for the general identifiers. Figure 3.9 shows the graph representation of a corresponding EARMARK document[27].

Table 3.3 on page 88 summarises our experiments running a reasoner to verify patterns on the previous example.[28] I tried eight different combinations of patterns and—for each combination—I checked whether it generated a consistent ontology.

The fourth column of the table shows the output of the reasoner. The answer "yes" indicates that a specific combination does not violate the constraints of the relevant patterns. That combination is then valid and can be used for identifying structural roles of document's elements. Negative results are very relevant because the reasoner is able to identify that requirements are not respected, and why. For instance, the reasoner detects that an element *div* cannot be an inline, being the root of a hierarchy.

Although this example is very simple (and focuses only on a few patterns), it should give readers the idea of how a reasoner and the ontological descriptions of a set of constraints can give validity results on rules expressed over an EARMARK

[26] The Pattern Ontology: http://www.essepuntato.it/2008/12/pattern

[27] http://www.essepuntato.it/2010/04/ParadiseLost

[28] http://www.essepuntato.it/2010/04/ParadiseLost/test.

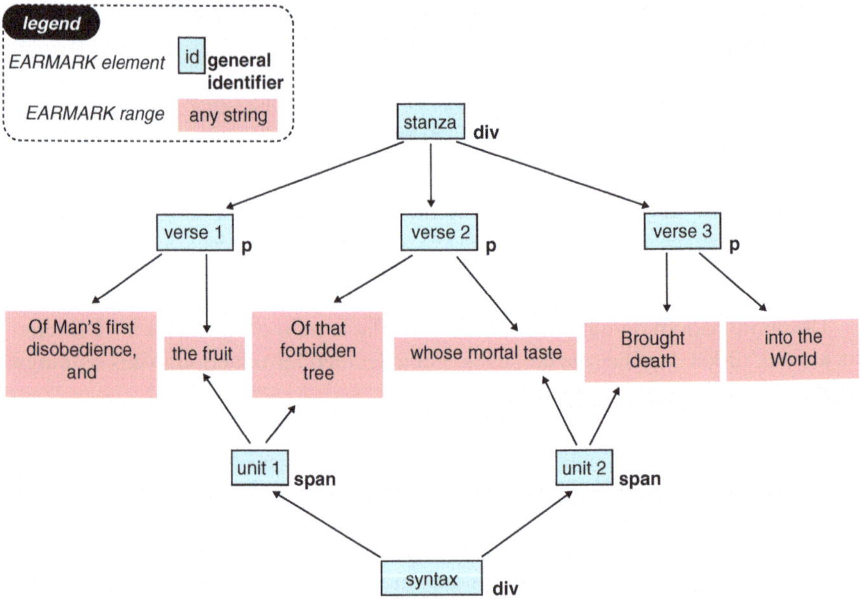

Fig. 3.9 The EARMARK document, in the form of a graph, of the first three verses of the Paradise Lost by John Milton

Table 3.3 Testing associations between elements and patterns on the "Paradise Lost" example through an OWL reasoner

Div	P	Span	Is the ontology still consistent?
Container	Block	Field	Yes
Container	Block	Inline	No: a container (syntax) cannot contain inline
Block	Block	Inline	No: a block (stanza) cannot contain at any level another block
Block	Inline	Inline	Yes
Inline	Inline	Inline	No: inlines (both stanza and syntax) cannot be the root of a hierarchy
Block	Inline	Inline for unit1 and atom for unit2	No: elements with the same general identifier (unit1 and unit2) must have the same pattern
Field	Field	Field	No: fields (both stanza and syntax) cannot contain other elements
Table	Field	Field	Yes
Record	Field	Field	No: records (stanza and syntax) can contain only elements with different general identifiers

document, and regardless of whether the document is in fact a single hierarchy (i.e., an XML document) or actually represents a multiplicity of hierarchies hard or impossible to express in XML. The fact that here I deal with patterns is just an example, and does not affect the generality and applicability of this approach: additional classes and additional SWRL rules would allow us to test other properties of the same documents.

3.3.3 Validation of Document Markup

Two particular topics are relevant to what we examine in previous sections: the ontological representation of digital document properties such as schema validity and other non-ontological approaches for validating complex overlapping structures.

After generating a well-defined document structure mapped into ontological assertions through EARMARK, we would like to verify whether it satisfies some particular properties or not – for example, validation against a document schema. Document schemas can also be good starting points for developing or reengineering ontologies, as pointed out in (Ferdinand et al. 2004). Proposing a translation mechanism from an XML document into a set of RDF assertions that describe it, Ferdinand *et al.*'s main aim is to define a way to translate an XML Schema document into an OWL ontology in order to obtain a complete TBox+ABox from a document with markup and its schema.

Similar to the previous work but following a different approach, (Rodrigues et al. 2006) introduces a framework for producing an ABox starting from an XML document, passing through an existing OWL ontology and the XML Schema document used by the original document. The *JXML2OWL*[29] framework thus generates such an ABox via some XSLT processing, made possible through handmade associations between the XML Schema declarations and the OWL classes. The result of this process is a set of OWL instances related to the OWL ontology used for the transformation. Proving the consistency of these instances with respect to the ontology means verifying the validity of the original document against the referred schema.

Another study that works similarly is (Yang et al. 2007). After introducing the main differences between XML Schema and ontologies in general, Yang *et al.* propose an ontology-based approach for representing mappings between document schema languages and ontologies. The goals of this work are round-trip translations from an XML document into ontology instances and the realisation of an ontology-mediated transformation between different XML documents, in order to allow seamless data exchange between heterogeneous XML data source.

Considering non ontological approaches, the *rabbit/duck grammars* mechanism (Sperberg-McQueen 2006) is a good technique for the validation of documents with overlaps. The basic idea of this approach is simple: to define different document schemas whose intersection describes the markup language to be validated. In each schema, each markup element is associated to one out of four classes—*normal*, *milestones*, *transparent* and *opaque*—that define how elements have to be considered in the context of the schema taken into consideration. Given a complete set of rabbit/duck grammars, each element must belong to the class *normal* in at least one schema of the set. Then, a document is considered valid against the set of rabbit/duck grammars if and only if it is valid against each schema in the set.

---

[29] JXML2OWL: http://jxml2owl.projects.semwebcentral.org.

References

Adida, B., M. Birbeck, S. McCarron, and S. Pemberton. 2013. RDFa Core 1.1 - Second edition: Syntax and processing rules for embedding RDF through attributes. W3C Recommendation 22 August 2013. World Wide Web Consortium. http://www.w3.org/TR/rdfa-syntax/. Accessed 30 July 2013.

Alexander, C. 1979. *The timeless way of building*. New York: Oxford University Press. (ISBN 0195024029)

Allsopp, J. 2007. *Microformats: Empowering your markup for web 2.0*. New York: Friends of ED Press. (ISBN: 1590598146).

Barabucci, G., A. Di Iorio, S. Peroni, F. Poggi, and F. Vitali. 2013. Annotations with EARMARK in practice: A fairy tale. Proceedings of the 2013 workshop on collaborative annotations in shared environments: Metadata, vocabularies and techniques in the digital humanities (DH-CASE 2013). New York: ACM. doi:10.1145/2517978.2517990.

Barabucci, G., S. Peroni, F. Poggi, and F. Vitali. 2012. Embedding semantic annotations within texts: The FRETTA approach. Proceedings of the 27th Symposium on Applied Computing (SAC 2012): 658–663. New York: ACM. doi:10.1145/2245276.2245403

Bański, P. 2010. Why TEI stand-off annotation doesn't quite work: And why you might want to use it nevertheless. Proceedings of balisage: The markup conference 2010. Rockville: Mulberry Technologies, Inc. http://www.balisage.net/Proceedings/vol5/html/Banski01/BalisageVol5-Banski01.html Accessed 30 July 2013.

Berglund, A., S. Boag, D. Chamberlin, M. F. Fernández, M. Kay, J. Robie, and J. Siméon. 2011. XML Path Language (XPath) 2.0 (Second edition). W3C Recommendation 14 December 2010 (Link errors corrected 3 January 2011). World Wide Web Consortium. http://www.w3.org/TR/xpath20/. Accessed 30 July 2013.

Bray, T., J. Paoli, C. M. Sperberg-McQueen, E. Maler, F. Yergeau, and J. Cowan. 2006. Extensible Markup Language (XML) 1.1 (Second edition). W3C Recommendation 16 August 2006, edited in place 29 September 2006. World Wide Web Consortium. http://www.w3.org/TR/xml11/. Accessed 30 July 2013.

Brickley, D., and L. Miller. 2010. FOAF vocabulary specification 0.98. Namespace document, 9 August 2010 - Marco Polo Edition. http://xmlns.com/foaf/spec/. Accessed 30 July 2013.

Carroll, J., I. Dickinson, C. Dollin, D. Reynolds, A. Seaborne, and K. Wilkinson. 2004. Jena: Implementing the semantic web recommendations. In Proceedings of the 13th international conference on World Wide Web - Alternate Track Papers & Posters (WWW 2004), ed. S. I. Feldman, M. Uretsky, M. Najork, and C. E. Wills, 74–83. New York: ACM. doi:10.1145/1013367.1013381.

Ciccarese, P., E. Wu, J. Kinoshita, G. Wong, M. Ocana, A. Ruttenberg, and T. Clark. 2008. The SWAN biomedical discourse ontology. *Journal of Biomedical Informatics* 41 (5): 739–751. doi:10.1016/j.jbi.2008.04.010.

Clark, J. 2001. RELAX NG specification. Committee specification. Committee specification 3 December 2001. Organization for the advancement of structured information standards. http://relaxng.org/spec-20011203.html. Accessed 30 July 2013.

Clark, J. 2002. RELAX NG Compact syntax. Committee specification. Committee specification 21 November 2002. Organization for the advancement of structured information standards. http://relaxng.org/compact-20021121.html. Accessed 30 July 2013.

Dattolo, A., A. Di Iorio, S. Duca, A.A. Feliziani, and F. Vitali. 2007. Structural documents. In Proceedings of the 7th International Conference on Web Engineering 2007 (ICWE 2007), Lecture notes in computer science 4607 Baresi, ed. L. Fraternali and P. G. Houben, 421–426. Berlin: Springer. doi:10.1007/978-3-540-73597-7_35.

De Waard, A. 2010. From proteins to fairytales: Directions in semantic publishing. *IEEE Intelligent Systems* 25 (2): 83–88. doi:10.1109/MIS.2010.49.

Di Iorio, A., D. Gubellini, and F. Vitali. 2005. Design patterns for document substructures. In Proceedings of the extreme markup languages 2005. Rockville: Mulberry Technologies, Inc. http://conferences.idealliance.org/extreme/html/2005/Vitali01/EML2005Vitali01.html. Accessed 30 July 2013.

Di Iorio, A., C. Marchetti, M. Schirinzi, and F. Vitali. 2009. Natural and multi-layered approach to detect changes in tree-based textual documents. In Proceedings of the 11th International Conference on Enterprise Information Systems (ICEIS 2009), lecture notes in business information processing 24 vols, ed. J. Cordeiro and J. Filipe, 90–101. Berlin: Springer. doi:10.1007/978-3-642-01347-8_8.

Di Iorio, A., S. Peroni, F. Poggi, and F. Vitali. 2012. A first approach to the automatic recognition of structural patterns in XML documents. Proceedings of the 2012 ACM symposium on document engineering (DocEng 2012). 85–94. New York: ACM. doi:10.1145/2361354.2361374.

Di Iorio, A., S. Peroni, F. Poggi, and F. Vitali. 2013. Dealing with structural patterns of XML documents. To appear in journal of the American society for information science and Technology. doi:10.1002/asi.23088

Di Iorio, A., S. Peroni, and F. Vitali. 2009. Towards markup support for full GODDAGs and beyond: The EARMARK approach. Proceedings of balisage: The markup conference 2009. Rockville: Mulberry Technologies, Inc. http://balisage.net/Proceedings/vol3/html/Peroni01/BalisageVol3-Peroni01.html. Accessed 30 July 2013.

Di Iorio, A., S. Peroni, and F. Vitali. 2010. Handling markup overlaps using OWL. In Proceedings of the 17th international conference on knowledge engineering and knowledge management (EKAW 2010), Lecture notes in computer science 6317 vols, ed. P. Cimiano and H. S. Pinto, 391–400. Berlin: Springer. doi:10.1007/978-3-642-16438-5_29.

Di Iorio, A., S. Peroni, and F. Vitali. 2011. A semantic web approach to everyday overlapping markup. *Journal of the American Society for Information Science and Technology* 62 (9): 1696–1716. doi:10.1002/asi.21591.

Di Iorio, A., S. Peroni, and F. Vitali. 2011. Using semantic web technologies for analysis and validation of structural markup. *International Journal of Web Engineering and Technologies* 6 (4): 375–398. doi:10.1504/IJWET.2011.043439.

Di Iorio, A., S. Peroni, F. Vitali, J. Lumley, and T. Wiley. 2009. Towards XML Transclusions. In Proceedings of the 1st workshop on new forms of xanalogical storage and function, CEUR workshop proceedings, ed. F. Vitali, A. Di Iorio, and J. Blustein, vol. 508, 23–28. Aachen: CEUR-WS.org. http://ceur-ws.org/Vol-508/paper5.pdf. Accessed 30 July 2013.

Durand, D. G. 1994. Palimpsest, a data model for revision control. Paper presented at the workshop on collaborative editing systems, co-located with the computer supported cooperative work conference (CSCW94). October 22–26, 1994, Chapel Hill.

Durand, D. G. 2008. *Palimpsest: Change-oriented concurrency control for the support of collaborative applications.* Charleston: CreateSpace.

Ferdinand, M., C. Zirpins, and D. Trastour. 2004. Lifting XML schema to OWL. In Proceedings of the 4th International Conference on Web Engineering 2004 (ICWE 2004), Lecture notes in computer science 3140, ed. N. Koch, P. Fraternali, and M. Wirsing, 354–358. Berlin: Springer. doi:10.1007/978-3-540-27834-4_44.

Gamma, E., R. Helm, R. Johnson, and J. Vlissides. 1994. Design patterns: Elements of reusable object-oriented software. Boston: Addison-Wesley. (ISBN: 0201633610).

Gao, S., C. M. Sperberg-McQueen, and H. S Thompson. 2012. W3C XML schema definition language (XSD) 1.1 Part 1: Structures. W3C Recommendation 5 April 2012. World Wide Web Consortium. http://www.w3.org/TR/xmlschema11-1/. Accessed 30 July 2013.

Garlik, S. H., and A. Seaborne. 2013. SPARQL 1.1 Query language. W3C Recommendation 21 March 2013. World Wide Web Consortium. http://www.w3.org/TR/sparql11-query/. Accessed 30 July 2013.

Georg, R., O. Schonefeld, T. Trippel, and A. Witt. 2010. Sustainability of linguistic resources revisited. Proceedings of the international symposium on XML for the long haul: Issues in the long-term preservation of XML. Rockville: Mulberry Technologies, Inc. http://www.balisage.net/Proceedings/vol6/html/Witt01/BalisageVol6-Witt01.html. Accessed 30 July 2013.

Goldfarb, C. F. 1990. *The SGML handbook.* New York: Oxford University Press. (ISBN 0198537373).

Horridge, M., and P. Patel-Schneider. 2012. OWL 2 web ontology language manchester syntax (Second edition). W3C working group note 11 December 2012. World Wide Web Consortium. http://www.w3.org/TR/owl2-manchester-syntax/. Accessed 30 July 2013.

Horrocks, I., P. F. Patel-Schneider, H. Boley, S. Tabet, B. Grosof, and M. Dean. 2004. SWRL: A semantic web rule language combining OWL and RuleML. W3C Member Submission 21 May 2004. World Wide Web Consortium. http://www.w3.org/Submission/SWRL/. Accessed 30 July 2013.

JTC1/SC34 WG 4. 2011. ISO/IEC 29500-1:2011—Information technology—document description and processing languages—office open XML file formats—Part 1: Fundamentals and markup language reference. Geneva: International Organization for Standardization. http://www.iso.org/iso/iso_catalogue/catalogue_tc/catalogue_detail.htm?csnumber=59575. Accessed 30 July 2013.

JTC1/SC34 WG 6. 2006. ISO/IEC 26300:2006—Information technology—open document format for office applications (OpenDocument) v1.0. Geneva: International Organization for Standardization. http://www.iso.org/iso/iso_catalogue/catalogue_tc/catalogue_detail.htm?csnumber=43485. Accessed 30 July 2013.

Motik, B., P. F. Patel-Schneider, and B.C. Grau. 2012. OWL 2 Web ontology language: Direct semantics (Second edition). W3C Recommendation 11 December 2012. World Wide Web Consortium. http://www.w3.org/TR/owl2-direct-semantics/. Accessed 30 July 2013.

Nelson, T. 1980. *Literary machines: The report on, and of, project Xanadu concerning word processing, electronic publishing, hypertext, thinkertoys, tomorrow's intellectual... including knowledge, education and freedom.*. Sausalito: Mindful Press.

Peroni, S., A. Gangemi, and F. Vitali. 2011. Dealing with markup semantics. In Proceedings the 7th International conference on semantic systems (I-SEMANTICS 2011), ed. C. Ghidini, A. Ngonga Ngomo, S. N. Lindstaedt, and T. Pellegrini, 111–118. New York: ACM. doi:10.1145/2063518.2063533.

Peroni, S., F. Poggi, and F. Vitali. 2013. Tracking changes through EARMARK: A theoretical perspective and an implementation. In Proceedings of 1st international workshop on (Document) changes: Modeling, detection, storage and visualization (DChanges 2013), ed. G. Barabucci, U. M. Borghoff, A. Di Iorio, and S. Maier, Aachen: CEUR-WS.org. http://ceur-ws.org/Vol-1008/paper6.pdf. Accessed 30 July 2013.

Peroni, S., and F. Vitali. 2009. Annotations with EARMARK for arbitrary, overlapping and out-of order markup. In Proceedings of the 2009 ACM Symposium on Document Engineering (DocEng 2009), ed. U. M. Borghoff and B. Chidlovskii, 171–180. New York: ACM. doi:10.1145/1600193.1600232

Presutti, V., and A. Gangemi. 2008. Content ontology design patterns as practical building blocks for web ontologies. In Proceedings of the 27th international conference on conceptual modeling (ER 2008), Lecture notes in computer science 5231 vols, ed. Q. Li, S. Spaccapietra, E. S. K. Yu, and A. Olivé, 128-141. Berlin: Springer. doi:10.1007/978-3-540-87877-3_11

Prud'hommeaux, E., and G. Carothers. 2013. Turtle, terse RDF triple language. W3C candidate recommendation 19 February 2013. World Wide Web Consortium. http://www.w3.org/TR/turtle/. Accessed 30 July 2013.

Rodrigues, T., P. Rosa, and J. Cardoso. 2006. Mapping Xml to existing owl ontologies. In Proceedings of the IADIS international conference on WWW/Internet 2006, ed. M. B. Nunes, P. Isaías, and I. J. Martínez. Lisbon: IADIS.

Sirin, E., B. Parsia, B. C. Grau, A. Kalyanpur, and Y. Katz. 2007. Pellet: A practical OWL-DL reasoner. *Journal of Web Semantics: Science, Services and Agents on the World Wide Web* 5 (2): 51–53. doi:10.1016/j.websem.2007.03.004.

Sperberg-McQueen, C. M. 2006. Rabbit/duck grammars: A validation method for overlapping structures. Proceedings of extreme markup languages conference 2006. Rockville: Mulberry Technologies, Inc. http://conferences.idealliance.org/extreme/html/2006/SperbergMcQueen01/EML2006SperbergMcQueen01.html. Accessed 30 July 2013.

Sperberg-McQueen, C. M., and C. Huitfeldt. 2004. GODDAG: A data structure for overlapping hierarchies. In Proceeding of the 5th international workshop on the Principles of Digital Document Processing (PODDP 2000), Lecture notes in computer science 2023, ed. P. R. King and E. V Munson. 139–160. Berlin: Springer. doi:10.1007/978-3-540-39916-2_12.

Tennison, J., and W. Piez. 2002. The Layered Markup and Annotation Language (LMNL). Presented at the extreme markup languages conference 2002. 4–9 August 2002, Montreal.

Text Encoding Initiative Consortium 2013. TEI P5: Guidelines for electronic text encoding and interchange. Charlottesville: TEI Consortium. http://www.tei-c.org/Guidelines/P5. Accessed 30 July 2013.

Van Rijsbergen, C. J. 1986. A new theoretical framework for information retrieval. In Proceedings of the 9th annual international ACM SIGIR conference on research and development in information retrieval (SIGIR86), ed. V. Raghavan and E. A. Fox, 23-29. New York: ACM. doi:10.1145/24634.24635.

Yang, K., R. Steele, and A. Lo. 2007. An ontology for XML schema to ontology mapping representation. In Proceedings of the 9th international conference on information integration and Web-based Applications & Services (iiWAS 2007), ed. G. Kotsis, D. Taniar, E. Pardede, and I. K. Ibrahim, 101–111. Vienna: Austrian Computer Society.

Chapter 4
Markup Semantics and Quality Evaluation of Legal Drafting

Abstract In this chapter I introduce the issue of markup semantics, i.e., formal definitions of meanings of markup elements and textual ranges, in addition to the syntactical structure of a markup document. In particular, I propose an extension of EARMARK, the OWL-based markup metalanguage introduced in the previous chapter, based on a model, the Linguistic Act Ontology, to consider more general and comprehensive theories based on shared principles and well-grounded studies on linguistics, semiology and communication theory. After a detailed introduction to Akoma Ntoso, i.e., the primarily language I use in some of markup fragments of this chapter, I show the advantages of using LA together with EARMARK (i.e., LA-EARMARK) in three different use cases: to query documents that share the same implicit semantics; to assess the quality of legal drafting; and, finally, to provide a mapping between Akoma Ntoso and CEN MetaLex.

Complementary to existing Semantic Web research work, which typically aims at studying uses and applications of *semantic markup* (i.e., defining relations among resources), in this section I address the issue of *markup semantics*: the formal definition of meanings of markup elements and textual ranges, besides the syntactical structure of a markup document (Renear et al. 2002).

EARMARK (introduced in Sect. 3.1) is suitable for expressing markup semantics straightforwardly. However, I want to associate coherent semantics to markup items following precise and theoretically-founded principles, which makes our application interoperable across different vocabularies used e.g., in digital libraries.

As a matter of fact, different existing vocabularies tackle the representation of terms vs. meanings vs. things in general, and this is not only true for XML markup languages, but also for Semantic Web ontologies such as SKOS, FRBR, CIDOC, OWL-WordNet, LIR, LMF, etc. Unfortunately, each of them has a particular approach depending on the original requirements they were designed for (thesauri encoding, media item representation, standardising digital library vocabularies, lexicon or (multi-)linguality representation, etc.), so that aligning all or part of them for a specific use is a difficult operation, specially when we consider the domain of document structures, where arbitrary representations lead to different realisations for the user, to lack of interoperability, and lock markup semantics into islands.

A viable solution to get around this problem is to align existing vocabularies to more general and comprehensive theories. The main benefit of using shared principles and well-grounded studies—e.g., patterns (e.g., documental (Dattolo et al. 2007;

S. Peroni, *Semantic Web Technologies and Legal Scholarly Publishing*,
Law, Governance and Technology Series 15, DOI 10.1007/978-3-319-04777 5_4,

Di Iorio et al. 2012), ontological (Presutti and Gangemi 2008)), linguistic theories (e.g., Pierce's semiotic triangle (Peirce 1958), Saussure's semiology (Saussure 2006), Jakobson's communication model (Jakobson 1960), Searle's linguistic acts (Searle 1970)), NLP approaches (e.g., Guthrie et al. (1996))—is that they enable the interoperability between different vocabularies.

In this work I have used EARMARK with the *linguistic act*[1] (*LA*) ontology, based on the *Linguistic Meta-Model* (*LMM*) (Picca et al. 2008), so as to model markup semantics. LA provides a semiotic-cognitive representation of linguistic knowledge. The general idea beyond it is to handle the representation of different knowledge sources developed according to different (and even implicit) semiotic theories, putting each of them in the context of the *semiotic triangle* (Peirce 1958) and some related semiotic notions.

In this chapter I will also introduce some examples that explain how it is possible to describe formal and explicit semantics upon markup items. In particular, in Sect. 4.1 I will introduce Akoma Ntoso (Barabucci et al. 2009, 2010), i.e., the primarily language I will use in some of exemplar markup excerpts of this chapter, since it offers the appropriate descriptive markup for legal documents and metadata. Then, in Sect. 4.2, I will describe the Linguistic Acts Ontology, which I will use to specify semantics to (EARMARK-defined) markup items. In the latest sections, I will show the advantages of using LA together with EARMARK (a.k.a. LA-EARMARK) in three different use cases. Firstly, I will focus on querying documents that share the same implicit semantics but that were marked up with different vocabularies Sect. 4.3. Then, I will discuss how to assess the quality of legal drafting Sect. 4.4 by using LA-EARMARK to introduce an excerpt of an Akoma Ntoso document. Finally, in Sect. 4.5, I will show how to use LA-EARMARK to allow the mapping between Akoma Ntoso and CEN MetaLex.

4.1 Akoma Ntoso for Legal and Legislative Documents

Akoma Ntoso (Barabucci et al. 2009, 2010) is an open legal XML standard for parliamentary, legislative and judiciary documents. Promoted by the Kenya Unit of the United Nations Department for Economics and Social Affairs (UN/DESA) in 2004, it means "Linked Hearts": a symbol used by the Akan people of West Africa to represent understanding and agreement. Originally meant for African Countries, it is now promoted also in Latin America, Asia and various European countries.

The role of Akoma Ntoso is to mark up legal and legislative texts so that the legal knowledge and the legal structure of the text can be *understood by* current and future computer applications. This means that legal texts form the basis on which Akoma Ntoso documents exist. Akoma Ntoso documents add information on top of the actual text (*annotate the text* in the markup lingo). The added information can itself be seen

---

[1] Linguistic Act Ontology: http://ontologydesignpatterns.org/cp/owl/semiotics.owl.

as composed of different stratified layers (text, structure, metadata, etc.) (Palmirani et al. 2009). Akoma Ntoso clearly separates the legal text from these different levels of information but still allows higher layers to reference the underlying layers, thus building knowledge on top of other knowledge, with the content of the legal text acting as the base knowledge.

This architecture allows different actors with different field experiences (e.g., experts in legal drafting, experts of document classification, experts in legal-knowledge engineering, experts in normative references, etc.) to mark up independent parts of the document. As with any technology that deals with legal resources, Akoma Ntoso has been designed to work on the original text without changing it. Words, punctuation marks and other typographical symbols are left untouched by the mark up process that transforms a plain-text legal document into an Akoma Ntoso-compliant XML document.

Additionally, Akoma Ntoso maintains a strict separation between *data* and *metadata* and provides an unambiguous definition of them as well as an operational distinction in *authoriality*: as such, data is any information that has been created or at least approved by the relevant legal author (for example, the whole of the text of an act), while metadata is any information that was not present in the original version of the document as it was approved by the relevant legal author but was added editorially in a later moment of the production process (e.g., the issue number of the official gazette or, even, the page numbers in the printed version of the same act).

The distinction between data and metadata is not only a theoretical distinction, since the actual layers of markup in Akoma Ntoso (*text*, *structure* and *metadata*) are based on it.

Textual markup identifies, within the content of the legal documents, fragments that have a precise legal or referential meaning, e.g., concepts such as "this piece of text is a date", "this piece of text is a legal reference" or "this piece of text contains the name of a party of the trial".

Structural markup identifies and organise the parts of the content that divide it into containers, and especially hierarchical containers: "this piece of text is an article" or "this piece of text is the title of an act", "this piece of text is the background section of a judgment", etc.

Metadata markup adds knowledge generated by an interpretation of the legal text performed by a human or mechanical agent: "the phrase the pre-existing Acts refers to Act 32 of 1989 and Act 2 of 1990", or "the person cited in the minutes as Mr. Gidisu is really Mr. Joe Kwashie Gisidu, the only member of the current Ghanaian parliament with that name and elected to a seat in it since 2000".

Moreover, when the typographical styles are used to represent the semantic role of a piece of text, this role is captured in the metadata section so that the specific meaning of that typographical style is not lost. There are different positions in the literature on which category is the most appropriate for structural data: textual or metadata. In our vision it belongs to a third, separate category. Actually, the structure represents the wish of the author of the legal text to organise that text in a certain order and therefore it is authoritative matter. If an annex is in the third level inside a hierarchical nested list of exhibits of an act (e.g., Table 1 of the Annex A.1) it embeds a legal message that belongs to the theory of law and in particular, a message on the hierarchy of the legal sources. What is finally voted on by a parliament in the assembly is a specific organisation of the text that incorporates, through the text structure, a precise legal message (e.g., the Article 50 is in that position because there is a certain linguistic and legal message to deploy).

The analysis of the textual and structural information is quite straightforward and its results are rarely disputed. On the contrary, the analysis of more advanced concepts found in the legal text requires some experience and it is easy for different sources to disagree on the generated interpretation. For this reason Akoma Ntoso documents have exactly one textual and one structural layer in each documents while interpretation of the advanced concepts is stored as metadata. Akoma Ntoso allows multiple metadata layers in the same document, each recording various interpretations given by different sources. Finally, each interpretation added by a specific actor can be linked to a particular ontology of legal concepts (e.g., "date of enter into force" as modelled in the LKIF core ontology (Breuker et al. 2006) or "High Court of South Africa" as modelled in an ontology about the judiciary system in Africa). This mechanism is used to connect specific ABox assertions, described in legal XML document, to more general TBox concepts, relationships, properties and axioms defined in a core or domain-specific ontology.

4.1.1 The Authorial Layers

Any Akoma Ntoso document is based on a legal resource that has been endorsed by an authority empowered by law: an act approved by a parliament, a decree issued by a ministry, a judgment entered by a court. Fidelity to the approved text is, thus, of primary importance; the data layers of Akoma Ntoso have been designed so that it is possible to markup a received legal text while preserving all the information contained in it and without changing its content. The documents Akoma Ntoso deals with are legal resources whose significance is given by the fact that they have the power to influence citizens' life. Legal texts must, thus, be handled with extreme care and all the measures should be taken to make sure that the technological tools employed to manipulate the texts do not change or interfere with their intended meaning.

In Akoma Ntoso, legal documents are created by enclosing parts of the legal text in XML tags. No pieces of the legal text are discarded, even those that could be generated by an application (e.g., the article numbers in an act). The resulting documents are thus augmented versions of the authentic text; the approved text can be retrieved by simply removing all the XML tags.

The Akoma Ntoso markup process strives to preserve the legal validity of the text as endorsed by the official authority, without adding any additional content to the text. Obviously, the mere act of marking up a sentence involves an act of interpretation or annotation and thus cannot be considered perfectly neutral.

However, the kind of markup done at the Akoma Ntoso data layers is almost objective (to the point that some automatic parsers have been developed (Palmirani and Benigni 2007)) and is rarely subject to disputes. For this reason, Akoma Ntoso documents are designed to contain only one interpretation of the text and structure layers.

4.1.1.1 Text

The *text layer*, the first of the data layers, is the XML representation of the legal text. It is the base layer on top of which all the other layers are developed. As discussed in the previous sections, the text layer only adds XML tags to the existing text.

The loose structure adopted by Akoma Ntoso, technically called mixed content, contrasts with the more rigid approach used by the first generation of XML standards for legal documents (e.g., EnAct or Formex (Lupo et al. 2007)) which favoured an organised structure where each legal text was treated like a database record. While database-oriented documents are easier to process in a computer environment, mixed content documents are a better choice when working with already-existing texts, a situation that happens with real-life legal resources and that will keep on happening in the foreseeable future. An excerpt describing the markup at the text layer in a debate of Ghana is shown as follows:

```
<speech id="sub2-spe02">
  <p>
  Mr. Opare-Hammond:
  Mr. Speaker , page 4 has a repetition of the numbers
  25 to 47. I do not know whether it
  was a typographical error or from the printing .
  It needs to be corrected.
  </p>
</speech>
```

4.1.1.2 Structure

The *structure layer*, the second of the data layers, gives roles to the blocks and fragments of the text: anonymous blocks thus become articles or clauses or simple blocks. These associations organise the text in a (often hierarchical) structure that is used to organise the content, provide a reasonable interpretation and even a base for the addresses used in the interpretation of the legal text in the metadata layer, both of the current document and of other documents.

Akoma Ntoso defines a set of common section names (for acts they include: part, chapter, tome, book, paragraph, article, clause) but does not impose a rigid structure on the way they can be combined so that they can be used differently in different law systems. An excerpt describing the markup at the structure layer in an act is shown as follows:

```
<subsection id="sec4-sub2">
  <num>(2)</num>
  <content>
    <p>The appointment of an honorary game warden-</p>
  <list id="sec4-sub2-lst1">
    <item id="sec4-sub2-itma">
      <num>(a)</num>
      <p>shall be notified in the Gazette;</p>
    </item>
    <item id="sec4-sub2-itmb">
      <num>(b)</num>
      <p>shall be effective unless sooner
       revoked by the Director, for a period
      of three years; and</p>
    </item>
    [...]
  </list>
 </content>
</subsection>
```

4.1.2 The Editorial Layer

The Akoma Ntoso *metadata layer* is a collection of pieces of legal knowledge that can be added onto a legal text as the personal interpretation of the written text, for example the analysis of the reasoning being performed by the judge while writing a judgment or the explicit consequences of the text of an amendment over an act. These pieces of legal knowledge by their nature are often subjective and dependent on one's interpretation. Instead of forcing a single interpretation for each legal document, Akoma Ntoso allows multiple, and even contrasting, interpretations to be expressed in the same document, and associates a different actor to each of them.

These interpretations of the underlying text form the groundwork upon which semantic technologies can make inferences (as discussed in Sect. 4.1.3).

Different Kinds of Information The metadata layer allows agents to provide different kinds of information over the legal text. The following are examples of the information that can be added to Akoma Ntoso.

Reference Disambiguation The references section links pieces of text to ontological entities. The usefulness of this information is twofold. First, conflicts between ambiguous phrases are resolved: for instance, in a sentence of a speech the text "Speaker" may be related to the *TLCRole* `ontology/roles/gha/speaker` while in another sentence the same text "Speaker" may refer to a specific *TLCPerson* that is in charge as speaker in the specific time when the debate was held—i.e., `/ontology/persons/gha/parliament/JohnSmith`—has shown in the following excerpt:

```
<references>
  <TLCRole id="speaker" showAs="Speaker"
    href="/ontology/roles/gha/speaker"/>
  <TLCPerson id="smith" showAs="Mr. Smith"
    href="/ontology/persons/gha/parliament/JohnSmith"/>
</references>
[...]
<speech id="sub2-spe01" by="smith" as="speaker">
  <from>Mr. Speaker</from>
  <p>Order! Order! Hon. Members, we shall
   take item 2 -- Correction of Votes and
   Proceedings. Page 1... page 4</p>
</speech>
```

Additionally, different spellings found in the text are consolidated in a single entity; in a court judgment, phrases like "Ms. Poliey", "Judge Poliey" and "Her Honour" can all be linked to the same *TLCPerson* /ontology/Person/Poliey.1954.

Legal Analysis The analysis section provides information about many legal aspects that can be inferred by a legal expert when interpreting the text. An example is the interpretation of the effects of an amendment in an amendment act, shown as follows:

```
<textualMod type="substitution" id="am5">
  <source href="# sec4-sub1-itma"/>
  <destination href="/ke/act/1997-08-22/3/main#sec34-
     sub2-itma"/>
  <old href="# mod10-qtd1"/>
  <new href="# mod10-qtd2"/>
</textualMod>
```

Another example is the identification of the role played by citations of precedents in the judgment argumentation of a judge (e.g., the application of a rule of law of a precedent, overriding a previous rule, etc.), as shown in the following excerpt:

```
<judicial>
  <result type="deny"/>
  <supports id="jdc01">
    <source href="#ref01"/>
    <destination href="/gb/judgement/1829/QB273/eng@/
       main.xml"/>
  </supports>
</judicial>
```

Work Identification The identification section classifies the document using the FRBR conceptual model (International Federation of Library Associations and Institutions Study Group on the Functional Requirements for Bibliographic Records 2009). This classification is used to inform the semantic tools that the document is the *manifestation* (in the FRBR sense) of a certain abstract *work*, so that they can distinguish between different versions of the same work. A more detailed account of

FRBR usage in Akoma Ntoso can be found in De Oliveira et al. (2008). In addition to the shown kinds of metadata, there are other types of metadata currently defined (e.g., *lifecycle* and *workflow* for tracking the events affecting the document) and other are being added as Akoma Ntoso extends to reach more and more types of analysis of the legal text.

Multiple Interpretations All the information gathered in the metadata layer is derived from the legal text (using the data layers) though subjective reasoning. Many different interpretation can arise over the same legal text from different legal experts. Take, for instance, the following sentence: "the Subsect. 3 of the Sect. 42 states a modification of the Sect. 44 of the same act". Two different actors OCSA and CIRSFID may disagree on the interpretation of that sentence: OCSA sees this modification as an authentic interpretation, CIRSFID sees it as a derogation. From a legal point of view, the two types of modification produce different effects: the authentic interpretation is applied *ex-tunc* (since the beginning), while the exception is a derogation of a norm under some conditional.

Akoma Ntoso allows both interpretations to coexist in the same document, even if they are in contrast. The Akoma Ntoso XML representation of these two different interpretations would be as shown in the following excerpt:

```
<analysis source="#ocsa">
  <activeModifications>
    <meaningMod type="authenticInterpretation" id="am1">
      <source href="# sec42-sub3"/>
      <destination href="#sec44"/>
    </meaningMod>
  </activeModifications>
</analysis>

<analysis source="#ocsa">
  <activeModifications>
    <meaningMod type="authenticInterpretation" id="am1">
      <source href="# sec42-sub3"/>
     <destination href="#sec44"/>
   </meaningMod>
  </activeModifications>
</analysis>
```

4.1.3 Semantic Technologies and Akoma Ntoso

Currently, there are interesting developments in the area of legal knowledge representation and manipulation. Akoma Ntoso documents, with their rich metadata layer, can serve as the basis upon which various tools can work on. For example, representations expressed at the metadata layer can be used to generate a legal ontology to be used by legal rule modelling technologies like RuleML[2] or the more specialised LKIF (Breuker et al. 2006).

[2] RuleML homepage: http://ruleml.org.

Akoma Ntoso documents are not tied to a particular semantic technology. The current format is very loose and permits the conversion of information into more specific models (like RDF or OWL). This strategy warrants that semantic technologies of the future decades will be able to convert Akoma Ntoso documents into their own format without going through what, by then, will be seen as ancient formats.

Semantically-Anonymous Entities Akoma Ntoso implicitly defines an ontological structure for representing metadata that is grounded in a basic set of concepts called *Top Level Classes* (*TLCs*). The word implicitly is used because, in principle, there is no implemented, exhaustive and shared ontology that defines these classes and the relation among them: what actually exists is a sort of guideline that allows users (especially producers) of Akoma Ntoso documents to develop their own ontology according to their particular needs. However, there exists so far at least one ontology, i.e., *ALLOT*, that trying to formalise all the Akoma Ntoso TLCs, as introduced in Sect. 2.4.4.

According to Akoma Ntoso, TLCs, even if represented by a clear label and a particular URI, have neither formal (logically defined) nor informal (written in natural language) semantics. The meaning beyond the text of a label of a TLC *X* does not give implicitly a meaning to *X*: it is just a label. Technically speaking, Akoma Ntoso do not define classes of a particular ontology but only a naming convention based on URIs and labels that can be used to express particular classes defined in a separate ontology. This assumption is needed to allow a great degree of flexibility in what can be expressed in the metadata layer of Akoma Ntoso documents, in order to adapt any legal document to any ontological representation of concepts. It is the duty of a third party (e.g., the document creator or the document users) to associate a clear and formal semantics to each class using a specific formalism (e.g., OWL).

This semantical anonymity is an important feature that allows Akoma Ntoso to maintain documents understandable and consumable independently from the passing of time: future toolmakers ("The 'future toolmaker' is 10 years old now"[3]) will have clues about the intended meaning of a marker even in the unfortunate case the formal ontology is no longer available. Akoma Ntoso makes ten different and disjoint TLCs available to document creators in order to identify individual entities present in the document: *Person* (`/ontology/Person`), *Organization* (/ontology/Organization), *Concept* (/ontology/Concept), *Object* (/ontology/Object), *Event* (`/ontology/Event`), *Place* (`/ontology/Place`), *Process* (`/ontology/Process`), *Role* (`/ontology/Role`), *Term* (`/ontology/Term`), *Reference* (`/ontology/Reference`).

Using these TLCs and the canonical FRBR classes *Work*, *Expression*, *Manifestation* and *Item* (International Federation of Library Associations and Institutions Study Group on the Functional Requirements for Bibliographic Records 2009), it is possible to store complex assertions in Akoma Ntoso documents and about Akoma Ntoso documents. It must be underlined that Akoma Ntoso does not aim at describing

[3] http://www.akomantoso.org/akoma-ntoso-in-detail/users.

neither objective facts nor personal opinions about such facts according to the author of the document. Rather, it allows the expression of an interpretation that is due, in a precise moment, to a particular actor who refers to statements that can be found in the published legal text.

A fundamental step towards being able to reason over an Akoma Ntoso document is to have a mechanism for describing items (actors, legal documents, properties, concepts, etc.) that are involved in the assertions (making assertions or being the subject of an assertion). Using the references mechanism described in Sect. 4.1.2 it is possible to relate each of these described items to a TLC, making it will possible to assert facts about that document, implicitly producing a data model for its semantic data.

Ontology URI Naming Convention All the items in an Akoma Ntoso document can belong to a particular TLC simply specifying an URI that must follow a particular naming convention. The following example shows a list of URI references, all pointing to the same entity representing a judge.

Even if a human may interpret some of these URIs as references to different entities, from an ontological point of view all these three URIs state the same thing: there exists a resource whose identifier is *lewanika* and that instance belongs to the top level class *Person*. Moreover, all these URI references point exactly to the same resource, regardless of the actual ontology used.

```
/ontology/Person/lewanika
/ontology/Person/judges/lewanika
/ontology/Person/za/judges/lewanika
```

The Akoma Ntoso naming convention contains few precise rules:

- The last fragment of the URI (`lewanika` in this above example) is the identifier of the instance being referred to.
- The first two fragments of the URI (`/ontology/<TLC name>`) specify the TLC the instance belongs to.
- The middle URI fragments (`za/judges/`), when they are present, provide evocative information for the human reader and for the systems that cannot access the underlying ontology used by the document. They suggest, in fact, a clear interpretation from a human perspective, e.g., that Lewanika is a South African person holding the role of judge. Since Akoma Ntoso does not force any given set of properties on the top level classes, the responsibility to choose which, and whether, additional fragments should be added lies with the author of the document.

Taking into account the implicit semantics given to each URI by the Akoma Ntoso naming convention, it is possible to query an Akoma Ntoso-compliant legal XML document using XPath (Berglund et al. 2011), without relying on external ontologies. The following excerpt shows some references to various resources:

```
<akomaNtoso xmlns="http://www.akomantoso.org/1.0">
  <references source="#cirsfid">
    <TLCOrganization id="parliament"
      showAs="Parliament of Kenya"
      href="/ontology/Organization/ke/parliament" />
    <TLCOrganization id="cirfid" showAs="CIRSFID"
      href="/ontology/Organization/cirfid" />
    <TLCPerson id="fv" showAs="Fabio Vitali"
      href="/ontology /Person/fv" />
    <TLCRole id="author" showAs="Author"
      href="/ontology/Roles/author" />
    <TLCRole id="jurist" showAs="Jurist"
      href="/ontology/Roles/jurist" />
    <TLCRole id="editor" showAs="Editor"
      href="/ontology/Roles/editor" />
  </references>
  [...]
</akomaNtoso>
```

Through XPath, it is possible to perform queries based on the semantic data that is present in the document. For example, the following queries could be performed on the data shown in the above excerpt:

- what roles have been involved in the generation of the legal document, `//references/element()[matches(@href,'/Roles/')]`;
- which Kenyan organisations are referred to in the legal document, `//references/element()[matches(@href,'/Organization/.*/?ke/')]`.

The naming convention used by Akoma Ntoso, together with the presence of additional middle URI fragments, allows the semantic data available in the document to be queried, even in sophisticated ways, without requiring access to any ontology. When the underlying ontology is available, the additional information provided by the middle URI fragments can be discarded and more complex queries, based on deductive elements such as those gathered through the use of reasoners, can be performed. The optional middle URI fragments fulfil, thus, two different tasks: on the one hand they provide clues to the human readers who do not have access to the underlying ontologies, on the other hand they allow semantic data about the referenced entities to be carried also in the document itself and not only in external knowledge bases.

4.2 Linguistic Act Ontology

Akoma Ntoso does not provide any kind of formal semantics to associate its markup to ontological entities, since it is entirely based on XML. Therefore, we need to use an external approach that allows us to provide Akoma Ntoso documents, and XML

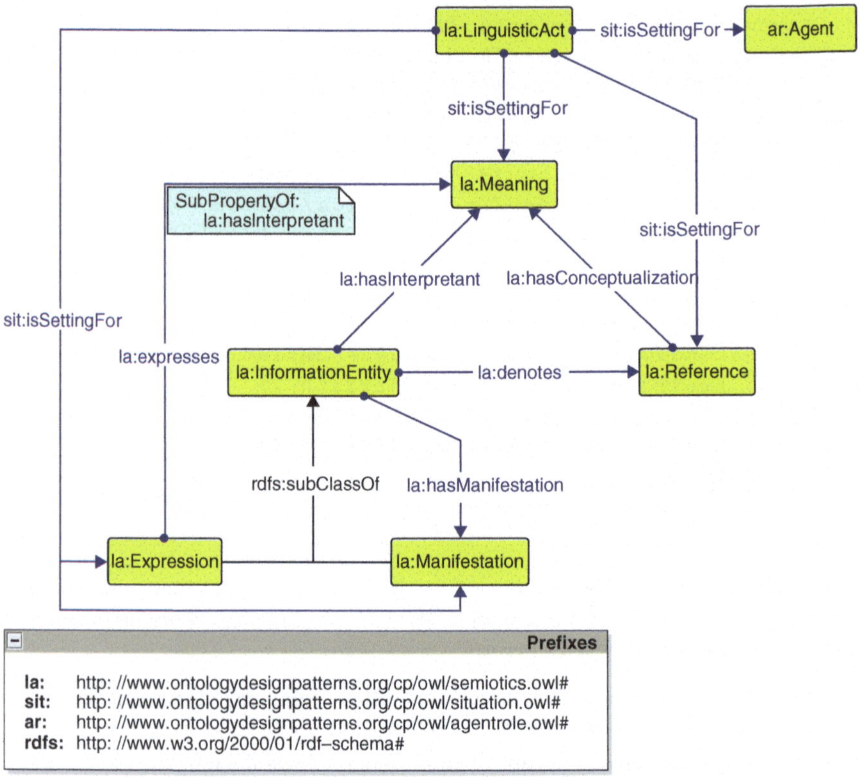

Fig. 4.1 A diagram summarising the ontology pattern *linguistic act*

documents in general, with a semantic characterisation of their components—for instance, using ALLOT (see Sect. 2.4.4) reference ontology. To this end, my proposal is to use EARMARK (presented in Chap. 3) in combination with the *Linguistic Act* (*LA*) ontology[4], based on the *Linguistic Meta-Model* (*LMM*) (Picca et al. 2008). I refer to this particular model as *LA-EARMARK*[5].

The Linguistic Act ontology provides a semiotic-cognitive representation of linguistic knowledge. The general idea beyond it is to handle the representation of different knowledge sources developed according to different (and even implicit) semiotic theories, putting each of them in the context of the *semiotic triangle* (Peirce 1958) and some related semiotic notions, as shown in Fig. 4.1.

The *linguistic act* is defined through an OWL ontology that implements the basic ideas of semiotics:

[4] Linguistic Act Ontology: http://ontologydesignpatterns.org/cp/owl/semiotics.owl.

[5] LA-EARMARK: http://essepuntato.it/2013/06/la-earmark.

- *References*: any individual, set of individuals, or fact from the world we are describing. They can have interpretations (meanings) and can be denoted by information entities. For example: *Fabio*, *the set of Fabio's relatives*, or *the fact that Fabio is a professor*;
- *Meanings*: any (meta-level) object that explains something, or is intended by something, such as linguistic definitions, topic descriptions, lexical entries, thesaurus concepts, logical concepts or relations, etc. They can be "interpretants" for information entities, and "conceptualisations" for individuals and facts. For example, concepts such as *person*, *paragraph*, *having a role*;
- *Information entities*: any symbol that has a meaning, or denotes one or more references. They can be natural language terms, sentences or texts, symbols in formal languages, icons, or whatever can be used as a vehicle for communication—for example: the string "Fabio", the markup elements *p*, *agent*, *noun* and *verb*. They have at least one meaning and can denote references. Moreover, each information entity can be an *expression*(e.g., the string "Fabio") realised in one or more *manifestations* (e.g., the string "Fabio" contained in a particular XML file stored on somebody's hard drive) having the same interpretation.
- *Linguistic acts*: *any communicative situation including information entities, agents, meanings, references, and a possible spatio-temporal context (i.e., when and/or where the act has been performed). For example, dialogs, taggings, writings.*

Considering these premises, EARMARK markup items are specific kinds of expressions expressing a particular meaning, usually assigned implicitly by the author of a schema or a markup, which are used to denote local objects (e.g., their content, according to the definition of a markup object) and/or social entities (e.g., persons, places, communication events, etc.).

For example, let me re-propose again the XML example introduced in Sect. 3.1.3:

```
<p>
  <agent>Fabio</agent> says that
  <noun xml:id="e1" next="e2">overl</noun>
  <verb>
    h<noun xml:id="e2">ap</noun>pens
  </verb>
</p>
```

In the above excerpt, there are different semantic blocks: firstly, the element *agent* expresses the meaning of "agent" (i.e., as the resource defined by DBPedia[6]) and denotes a specific person (i.e., the person, using FOAF, is known as "Fabio Vitali"), while the element *p* must be interpreted as a paragraph (i.e., a specific document structure according to the DoCO ontology, that will be introduced in Sect. 5.4) and denotes the string "Fabio says that overlhappens" (rather than the corresponding concept). This in a way differs from the XML syntactical structure in

[6] DBPedia "agent" resource: http://dbpedia.org/resource/Agent.

which the element *p* contains the elements *agent*, *noun* and *verb*—that themselves express/denote/contain the other meanings/references.

In LA-EARMARK, it is possible to describe both the rigid syntactic structure, as described in Sect. 3.1.3, as well as its semantic connotation:

```
@prefix ar: <http://www.ontologydesignpatterns.org/cp/
    owl/agentrole.owl#> .
@prefix la: <http://www.ontologydesignpatterns.org/cp/
    owl/semiotics.owl#> .
@prefix sit: <http://www.ontologydesignpatterns.org/cp/
    owl/situation.owl#> .
@prefix doco: <http://purl.org/spar/doco/> .
@prefix dbpr: <http://dbpedia.org/resource/> .
@prefix foaf: <http://xmlns.com/foaf/0.1/> .

ex:doc a earmark:StringDocuverse
  ; earmark:hasContent
    "Fabio says that overlappens."^^xsd:string .

ex:r0-28 a earmark:PointerRange # The whole sentence
  ; earmark:refersTo ex:doc
  ; earmark:begins "0"^^xsd:integer
  ; earmark:ends "28"^^xsd:integer .

ex:p la:expresses doco:Paragraph
  ; la:denotes ex:r0-28 .

ex:agent la:expresses dbpr:Agent , doco:TextChunk
  ; la:denotes ex:fv , ex:r0-5 .

ex:fv a foaf:Person
  ; foaf:givenName "Fabio"
  ; foaf:familyName "Vitali" .

ex:markupAuthor a ar:Agent
      ; ar:hasRole [ a ar:Role
                 ; rdfs:label "markup author" ] .

[] a la:LinguisticAct
  ; rdfs:comment "marking a paragraph up"
  ; sit:isSettingFor ex:p , ex:r0-28
    , doco:Paragraph , ex:markupAuthor .

[] a la:LinguisticAct ; rdfs:comment "marking text up"
  ; sit:isSettingFor ex:agent , ex:r0-5
    , doco:TextChunk , ex:markupAuthor .

[] a la:LinguisticAct
  ; rdfs:comment "markup element as instance"
  ; sit:isSettingFor ex:agent , ex:fv , dbpr:Agent .
...
```

The example introduced explains how it is possible to describe markup hierarchies—and therefore their semantics—upon those markup items. In the next sub-sections I show the advantages of using LA-EARMARK in two different use cases, previously highlighted in Renear et al. (2002): querying documents marked up with the same implicit semantics but marked up with different vocabularies that share the same implicit semantics and the semantic validation of markup items.

4.3 Searches on Heterogeneous Digital Libraries

Digital libraries about journal research articles use to actually store their documents' content using specific XML formats, e.g., the common TEI (Text Encoding Initiative Consortium 2013), DocBook (Walsh 2010), or other less common vocabularies developed expressly for a specific collection. Clearly, the more digital libraries we consider, the more non-interoperable formats we will find, although they express, more or less, the same kinds of documents and, consequently, document semantics. Paragraph, sections (implicitly or explicitly labelled as abstract, introduction, results, discussion, related works, conclusions, acknowledgements, bibliography, etc.), figures, tables, formulas are a little but important part of the elements that we will find in the markup of journal papers, regardless of the actual vocabulary used.

In this scenario of heterogeneous formats expressing homogeneous content, looking throughout a number of digital libraries for particular document fragments, such as "All the tables that are part of the results sections of articles written by Silvio Peroni", can be approached only by addressing each digital library with a query specific of the vocabulary used, and then merging the results. Obviously, the implicit (shared) semantics of the query must be implemented in each digital library in a (different) explicit way, for example by using tools for mapping the query into each specific markup structure. This means requiring a particular ad hoc and non-interoperable mechanism for each format of each digital library.

Expressing semantics of elements in a journal article by considering a shared model may help for increasing interoperability, but it is not enough, because the different formats will still be a substantial problem. For example, being a *section presenting results* in a particular research article may be expressed differently depending on the format used: `<div class="section.results">`, `<section id="results">`, `<sec class="results">`, `<results>`, etc.

Expressing journal articles in LA-EARMARK—obtained, for instance, by translating the original XML documents via GRDDL (Connolly 2007)—allows one to specify the semantics of markup elements according to some formal model, without attention to the specific markup vocabulary[7]:

[7] The prefix *deo* refers to the *Discourse Element Ontology* (*DEO*), ontology for the characterisation of the major rhetorical elements of a document (e.g., a research article), such as the introduction part, the evaluation section, the conclusions and so on. It is available at http://purl.org/spar/deo.

```
ex:div a earmark:Element
  ; earmark:hasGeneralIdentifier "div"
  ; co:firstItem [ co:itemContent ex:classAttr ]
  ; la:expresses doco:Section , deo:Results .

ex:results a earmark:Element
  ; earmark:hasGeneralIdentifier "results"
  ; la:expresses doco:Section , deo:Results .
```

As shown in the previous excerpt, both *ex:div* and *ex:results* elements express the same semantics even if their names differ: they are syntactically different (their content models differ), but semantically equivalent.

Enabling digital libraries to express each LA-EARMARK document as a named graph, with all the document metadata referring to it, allows one to query more than one digital library at the same time by using a single SPARQL 1.1 query (Garlik and Seaborne 2013). For instance, a plausible SPARQL query for the above-mentioned request—"All the tables that are part of results sections of the article written by Silvio Peroni"—is:

```
SELECT ?table WHERE {
  GRAPH ?doc {
    ?table a earmark:Element
        ; la:expresses doco:Table
      ; (^co:itemContent/^co:item)+
        [ a earmark:Element
          ; la:expresses
            doco:Section , deo:Results ] } .
    ? doc dcterms:creator "Silvio Peroni" }
```

4.4 Semantic-Aware Quality Assessment of Legal Drafting

Sometimes it is not possible to understand whether a particular markup element that is valid at the syntactic and structural level is also valid at the semantic level, i.e., the level that Bauman described as *markup sensibility*: "Does a construct make sense, e.g., a proposition or an assertion?" (Bauman 2010). A clear example of this difficulty can be found with heavily interlinked documents that make systematic references to precise concepts in their content.

For instance, as introduced in detail in Sect. 4.1, Akoma Ntoso (Barabucci et al. 2009, 2010) is an open legal XML standard for parliamentary, legislative and judiciary documents, which is defined by means of a very complex XML Schema document providing the vocabulary and the content models of markup items. Although this schema is enough to guarantee the validity of a document from a pure syntactical point of view, it does not allow us to verify the semantic connections there exists within the document, which are needed to assess the quality of legal drafting fully. Let us introduce an Akoma Ntoso excerpt to clarify the point:

```
<akomaNtoso>
  <meta>
    ...
    <references source="#fv">
      <TLCPerson id="fv"
        href="/ontology/it/person/FabioVitali" />
      <TLCPerson id="smith"
        href="/ontology/uk/person/JohnSmith" />
      <TLCRole id="mineconomy"
        href="/ontology/role/government/
           MinisterOfEconomy" />
      ...
    </references>
    ...
  </meta>
  <body>
    ...
    <speech id="sp1" by="#smith" as="#mineconomy">
      <p>Honorable Members of the Parliament, ... </p>
    </speech>
    ...
  </body>
</akomaNtoso>
```

The elements *TLCPerson* and *TLCRole*, introduced within the metadata block (element *meta*) of the document, are used for specifying the presence, in the document in which it is defined, of two particular ontological entities, respectively a person and a role, according to a specific underlying ontology. Wherever these elements are referred to by a markup element by means of its identifier (as expressed in the attribute *id*), what really is referred to are the ontological individuals that are specified by the attribute *href*. For instance, within the body of the document, the element *speech* is used to mark up the transcription of a speech performed by the person *John Smith* (attribute *by*) who is temporarily playing the particular role of *Minister of the Economy* (attribute *as*). Moreover, the attribution of all the metadata concerning the speech transcription is an editorial activity, rather than authorial, made specifically by an agent identified through the attribute *source* of the element *reference*. For self-containment, the attributes *by* and *as* do not refer directly to the ontological concepts associated to John Smith and the Minister of the Economy, but to an intermediate jumping station, i.e., the elements *TLCPerson* and *TLCRole* in the metadata block.

Although it is a fundamental requirement of the language, the syntactic validation through XML Schema of the document does not provide sufficient information to understand whether an Akoma Ntoso document is really correct and coherent, because it cannot prove the sensibleness of markup. In the preceding example, we also need to check:

- The validity of the elements *TLCPerson* and *TLCRole* as reflection of the consistence of people and role individuals within an underlying ontology, particularly by checking whether each individual can really be a person (or a role) without provoking an inconsistency with other classes the individual may belong to;
- The validity of the element *speech* as markup denoting a particular speech event that involves only and at least a person as speaker. Moreover, because it reflects a speech, it must contain some text.
- The fact that the person John Smith was, at the moment of the speech, either the Minister of Economy or acting as an authorised delegate through a track of explicit delegations starting from the current minister.

The XML Schema language is not able to express these kinds of constraints. Naive or inexpert metadata authors could very well generate documents that are syntactically and structurally valid, possibly even apparently correct from a semantic point of view, but fundamentally incoherent. For instance, a common misconception is to confuse persons and roles, as in the following (syntactically valid but ontologically incorrect) example:

```
<speech id="sp1" by="#mineconomy">
  <p>Honorable Members of
    the Parliament, ...</p>
</speech>
```

The LA-EARMARK translation of the above fragment, which also includes its semantic description according to ALLOT (see Sect. 2.4.4) and DBPedia[8], is the following[9]:

[8] DBPedia homepage: http://dbpedia.org.

[9] The prefix *akomantoso* is associated to the minimal *glue* ontology within the XML document itself that connects markup structures to legal concepts according to the model explained in Barabucci et al. (2009).

```
@prefix akomantoso: </ontology/entity/> .
@prefix allot: <http://akn.web.cs.unibo.it/allot/> .
@prefix dbpedia: <http://dbpedia.org/resource/> .
@prefix : <http://www.example.com/> .

</ontology/uk/person/JohnSmith>
  a allot:Person .

[] a la:LinguisticAct
  ; sit:isSettingFor
     <smith> , allot:Person
    , </ontology/uk/person/JohnSmith> .

:speech a earmark:Element
  ; earmark:hasGeneralIdentifier "speech"
  ; la:expresses dbpedia:Speech
  ; la:denotes :aSpeechEvent , :p .

:aSpeechEvent a akomantoso:SpeechEvent
  ; akomantoso:hasSpeaker
    </ontology/uk/person/JohnSmith> .

  :p a earmark:Element
    ; earmark:hasGeneralIdentifier "p" .

  [] a la:LinguisticAct
    ; sit:isSettingFor
       :speech , :aSpeechEvent
      , </ontology/uk/person/JohnSmith>
      , dbpedia:Speech .

  [] a la:LinguisticAct
    ; sit:isSettingFor :speech , :p
      , dbpedia:Speech .
```

LA-EARMARK allows one to check the sensibility of markup precisely, by defining semantic constraints as ontological axioms, taking into account both classes and properties defined in LA-EARMARK and in the underlying ontology behind Akoma Ntoso. Inasmuch as such semantic constraints can be defined as axioms adhering to or in contrast with axioms of the underlying ontologies, they can be directly applied to reasonings even in open world frameworks such as OWL.

For example, a plausible ontological constraint (written in Manchester Syntax) for all the markup elements *speech* is:

```
(earmark:Element that earmark:hasGeneralIdentifier
  value "speech")
SubClassOf
(sit:hasSetting only
  (la:LinguisticAct that
    sit:isSettingFor exactly 1
      (earmark:Element and la:InformationEntity)
    and
    sit:isSettingFor exactly 1
      (earmark:Range and la:Reference)
    and
    sit:isSettingFor value dbpedia:Speech)
  or
  (la:LinguisticAct that
    sit:isSettingFor exactly 1
      (earmark:Element and la:InformationEntity)
    and
    sit:isSettingFor exactly 1
      ((akomantoso:SpeechEvent and
        la:Reference) that
          akomantoso:hasSpeaker some
          allot:Person)
    and
    sit:isSettingFor
      value dbpedia:Speech))
```

This specification would be able to capture ontological errors in the actual Akoma Ntoso document such as the one presented previously, where the author of the speech is specified as a role rather than a person.

4.5 From Akoma Ntoso to CEN MetaLex Through EARMARK

As introduced in Sect. 2.2.5, CEN MetaLex (Boer et al. 2007, 2008) is an interchange format based on XML that proposes standardised way of describing legal documents and facilitate their exchange and interoperability. It is concerned primarily with the identification of legal bibliographic entities on the basis of their content (i.e., the *Expression* level in FRBR), while it imposes an XML-based language as a mandatory format for storing documents.

There exist two ways that a document expressed in a particular XML format, such as Akoma Ntoso, is made compliant with the CEN MetaLex abstract data model, which adheres to the structural patterns for markup documents introduced in Sect. 3.3.2[10]. The first way is to annotate the XML elements of an Akoma Ntoso document by means of attribute *ml:type*, specifying as value a qualified name (Bray et al.

[10] CEN MetaLex imposes that the content model of any element must be compliant with one of six main patterns: container, headed container, block, inline, milestone and meta. In addition to those content models, in CEN MetaLex there is and additional content model, called *meta container*, that requires a container to contain other meta containers or metas only.

2009) among those identifying CEN MetaLex content models: *ml:root*, *ml:container*, *ml:hcontainer*, *ml:mcontainer*, *ml:block*, *ml:inline*, *ml:milestone* and *ml:meta*. Using fixed values within attributes to assign behaviours or semantics is a well-known approach proposed in the markup language domain in the past, and, technically speaking, concerns the use of *Architectural Forms*, as proposed for SGML and HyTime (e.g., see DeRose and Durand (1994))[11]. For instance, the Akoma Ntoso excerpt introduced in the previous section could be enriched as follows:

```
<akomaNtoso
  xmlns="http://www.akomantoso.org/2.0"
  xmlns:ml="http://www.metalex.eu/metalex/1.0"
  ml:type="ml:root">
  <meta ml:type="ml:container">
    ...
    <references ml:type="ml:mcontainer" source="#fv">
      <TLCPerson ml:type="ml:meta" id="fv"
        href="/ontology/it/person/FabioVitali" />
      <TLCPerson ml:type="ml:meta" id="smith"
        href="/ontology/uk/person/JohnSmith" />
      <TLCRole ml:type="ml:meta" id="mineconomy"
        href="/ontology/role/government/
           MinisterOfEconomy" />
      ...
    </references>
    ...
  </meta>
  <body ml:type="ml:container">
    ...
    <speech ml:type="ml:container"
      id="sp1" by="#smith" as="#mineconomy">
      <p ml:type="ml:block">
        Honorable Members of the Parliament, ... </p>
    </speech>
    ...
  </body>
</akomaNtoso>
```

The above excerpt actually is already a CEN MetaLex document, and at the same time it is still an Akoma Ntoso document.

[11] Architectural Forms allow designers to express semantic information about specific instances of an element or about all elements of a given type. This is possible by extending the set of attributes and by setting some of their values appropriately. Such information does not impact the basic processing and integrity of the document but makes it possible to describe meta-structures and to define the semantic role of the elements.

The other approach to create a CEN MetaLex documents from an Akoma Ntoso one implies the full conversion of Akoma Ntoso elements into CEN MetaLex elements exemplifying the patterns described above. For instance, the previous excerpt can be converted as follows:

```
<ml:root
  xmlns="http://www.akomantoso.org/2.0"
  xmlns:ml="http://www.metalex.eu/metalex/1.0"
  ml:name="akomaNtoso">
  <ml:container ml:name="meta">
    ...
    <ml:mcontainer ml:name="references" source="#fv">
      <ml:meta ml:name="TLCPerson" id="fv"
     href="/ontology/it/person/FabioVitali" />
    <ml:meta ml:name="TLCPerson" id="smith"
      href="/ontology/uk/person/JohnSmith" />
    <ml:meta ml:name="TLCRole" id="mineconomy"
      href="/ontology/role/government/
           MinisterOfEconomy" />
      ...
    </ml:mcontainer>
    ...
  </ml:container>
  <ml:container ml:name="body">
    ...
    <ml:container ml:name="speech"
      id="sp1" by="#smith" as="#mineconomy">
      <ml:block ml:name="p">
        Honorable Members of the Parliament, ... </p>
    </ml:container>
    ...
  </ml:container>
</ml:root>
```

In this case, the original names of Akoma Ntoso elements are specified by means of the attribute *ml:name*.

The process of the adaptation of existing Akoma Ntoso documents by means of embedding additional attributes and the process of translation of such documents in new ones produces an equivalent result from an abstract point of view, even if they use two different approaches and formats. This means that the aforementioned excerpts are equivalent and, thus, express the same document. However, the former approach needs to have appropriate permissions to write the Akoma Ntoso document so as to embed CEN MetaLex information, while the latter one produces a new XML document result of some sort of transformation, a solution that has been used within the *eXistrella* XML repository proposed by Palmirani and Cervone (2009).

Expressing Akoma Ntoso documents through EARMARK would facilitate such a conversion when neither the requirement for writing permissions nor the use of a transformation framework within an XML repository are possible options. For instance, let us suppose to have an Akoma Ntoso document expressed through EARMARK, as follows:

```
:akomaNtoso a earmark:Element
  ; earmark:hasGeneralIdentifier "akomaNtoso"
  ; earmark:hasNamespace "http://www.akomantoso.org/2.0"
  ; co:firstItem [ co:itemContent :meta
  ; co:nextItem [ co:itemContent :body ] ] .

:meta a earmark:Element
  ; earmark:hasGeneralIdentifier "meta"
  ; earmark:hasNamespace "http://www.akomantoso.org/2.0"
  ; co:firstItem [ co:itemContent ...
  ; co:nextItem [
    co:itemContent :references ... ] ... ] .

...

:references a earmark:Element
  ; earmark:hasGeneralIdentifier "references"
  ; earmark:hasNamespace "http://www.akomantoso.org/2.0"
  ; co:firstItem [ co:itemContent :tlcperson-1
  ; co:nextItem [ co:itemContent :tlcperson-2 ... ] ] .

:tlcperson-1 a earmark:Element
  ; earmark:hasGeneralIdentifier "TLCPerson"
  ; earmark:hasNamespace
    "http://www.akomantoso.org/2.0" ...

...

:body a earmark:Element
  ; earmark:hasGeneralIdentifier "body"
  ; earmark:hasNamespace "http://www.akomantoso.org/2.0"
  ; co:firstItem [ co:itemContent ...
  ; co:nextItem [ co:itemContent :speech ... ] ... ] .

...

:speech a earmark:Element
  ; earmark:hasGeneralIdentifier "speech"
  ; earmark:hasNamespace "http://www.akomantoso.org/2.0"
  ; co:firstItem [ co:itemContent :attr-id
  ; co:nextItem [ co:itemContent :attr-by
  ; co:nextItem [ co:itemContent :attr-as
  ; co:nextItem [ co:itemContent :p ] ] ] ] .

:p a earmark:Element
  ; earmark:hasGeneralIdentifier "speech"
  ; earmark:hasNamespace "http://www.akomantoso.org/2.0"
  ; co:firstItem [ co:itemContent :textual-range ] .

:textual-range a earmark:PointerRange ...
```

Even if these assertions were stored within a particular read-only file or were enclosed within an RDF triplestore, one could always add information to it by providing new assertions involving the same EARMARK elements, and storing such assertions in a different file and/or triplestore. In this case, we can explicitly state the type of CEN MetaLex content model each EARMARK element relates to by means of LA-EARMARK and the structural fragments defined within the CEN MetaLex ontology[12], as follows[13]:

```
@prefix ml: <http://www.metalex.eu/metalex/2008-05-02#> .

:akomaNtoso la:expresses ml:Document .
:meta la:expresses ml:ContainerFragment .
:references la:expresses ml:MContainerFragment .
:tlcperson-1 la:expresses ml:MetaFragment .
:body la:expresses ml:ContainerFragment .
:speech la:expresses ml:ContainerFragment .
:p la:expresses ml:Block .
...
```

In this way, the alignment with the CEN MetaLex data model can be guaranteed through the definition of additional LA-EARMARK assertions accompanying the original Akoma Ntoso document expressed through EARMARK, without any need for modifying or transforming the original document.

References

Barabucci, G., L. Cervone, M. Palmirani, S. Peroni, and F. Vitali. 2009. Multi-layer markup and ontological structures in Akoma Ntoso. In Proceeding of the international workshop on AI Approaches to the Complexity of Legal Systems II (AICOL-II), lecture notes in computer science 6237 vols, ed. P. Casanovas, U. Pagallo, G. Sartor, and G. Ajani, 133–149. Berlin: Springer. doi:10.1007/978-3-642-16524-5_9.

Barabucci, G., L. Cervone, A. Di Iorio, M. Palmirani, S. Peroni, and F. Vitali. 2010. Managing semantics in XML vocabularies: An experience in the legal and legislative domain. Proceedings of Balisage: The markup conference 2009. Rockville: Mulberry Technologies, Inc. http://www.balisage.net/Proceedings/vol5/html/Barabucci01/BalisageVol5-Barabucci01.html. Accessed 30 July 2013.

Bauman, S. 2010. The 4 “Levels” of XML rectitude. Presented as poster in Balisage: The markup conference 2010. August 3–6, 2010, Montréal, Canada. http://bauman.zapto.org/~syd/temp/XML_rectitude.pdf. Accessed 30 July 2013.

Berglund, A., S. Boag, D. Chamberlin, M. F. Fernández, M. Kay, J. Robie, and J. Siméon. 2011. XML Path language (XPath) 2.0. 2nd ed. W3C recommendation 14 December 2010 (Link errors corrected 3 January 2011). World Wide Web Consortium. http://www.w3.org/TR/xpath20/. Accessed 30 July 2013.

[12] CEN MetaLex Ontology: http://justinian.leibnizcenter.org/MetaLex/metalex-cen.owl.

[13] Some of the OWL classes I use in the following excerpt—i.e., *ml:MContainerFragment* and *ml:MetaFragment*—are not declared by the CEN MetaLex Ontology explicitly. However, I have decided to adopt such classes anyway for the sake of a better understandability of the example.

Boer, A., R. Winkels, and F. Vitali. 2007. Proposed XML standards for law: MetaLex and LKIF. In Proceedings of the 12th annual conference on legal knowledge and information systems (JURIX 2007), ed. A. R. Lodder and L. Mommers, 19–28. Amsterdam: IOS Press.

Boer, A., R. Winkels, and F. Vitali. 2008. MetaLex XML and the legal knowledge interchange format. In *Computable models of the law, languages, dialogues, games, ontologies, lecture notes in computer science 4884*, ed. P. Casanovas, G. Sartor, N. Casellas, and R. Rubino, 21–41. Berlin: Springer. doi:10.1007/978-3-540-85569-9_2.

Bray, T., D. Hollander, A. Layman, R. Tobin, and H. S. Thompson. 2009. Namespaces in XML 1.0. 3rd ed. W3C recommendation 8 December 2009. World Wide Web Consortium. http://www.w3.org/TR/REC-xml-names/. Accessed 30 July 2013.

Breuker, J., A. Boer, R. Hoekstra, and K. van den Berg. 2006. Developing content for LKIF: Ontologies and frameworks for legal reasoning. In Proceedings of the 19th annual conference on legal knowledge and information systems (JURIX 2006), ed. T. M. van Engers, 169–174. Amsterdam: IOS Press.

Connolly, D. 2007. Gleaning Resource Descriptions from Dialects of Languages (GRDDL). W3C recommendation 11 September 2007. World Wide Web Consortium. http://www.w3.org/TR/grddl/. Accessed 30 July 2013.

Dattolo, A., A. Di Iorio, S. Duca, A. A. Feliziani, and F. Vitali. 2007. Structural patterns for descriptive documents. In Proceedings of the 7th International Conference on Web Engineering 2007 (ICWE 2007), lecture notes in computer science 4607, ed. L. Baresi, P. Fraternali, and G. Houben, 421–426. Berlin: Springer. doi:10.1007/978-3-540-73597-7_35.

De Oliveira Lima, A., M. Palmirani, and F. Vitali. 2008. Moving in the time: An ontology for identifying legal resources. In *Computable models of the law, languages, dialogues, games, ontologies, lecture notes in computer science 4884*, 71–85), ed. P. Casanovas, G. Sartor, N. Casellas, and R. Rubino. Berlin: Springer. doi:10.1007/978-3-540-85569-9_5.

DeRose, S. J., and D. G. Durand. 1994. *Making hypermedia work: a user's guide to HyTime*. Boston: Kluwer Academic. (ISBN 9780792394327).

Di Iorio, A. S., Peroni, F. Poggi, and F. Vitali. 2012. A first approach to the automatic recognition of structural patterns in XML documents. In Proceedings of the 2012 ACM symposium on Document Engineering (DocEng 2012), 85–94. New York: ACM. doi:10.1145/2361354.2361374.

Garlik, S. H., and A. Seaborne. 2013. SPARQL 1.1 Query language. W3C recommendation 21 March 2013. World Wide Web Consortium. http://www.w3.org/TR/sparql11-query/. Accessed 30 July 2013.

Guthrie, L., J. Pustejovsky, Y. Wilks, and B. M. Slator. 1996. The role of lexicons in natural language processing. *Communications of the ACM* 39 (1): 63–72. doi:10.1145/234173.234204.

International Federation of Library Associations and Institutions Study Group on the Functional Requirements for Bibliographic Records. 2009. Functional requirements for bibliographic records final report. International federation of library associations and institutions. http://www.ifla.org/files/cataloguing/frbr/frbr_2008.pdf. Accessed 30 July 2013.

Jakobson, R. 1960. Closing statements: Linguistics and poetics. In *Style in language*, ed. T. A. Sebeok, 351–377. Cambridge: The MIT Press. (ISBN 0262690101).

Lupo, C., F. Vitali, E. Francesconi, M. Palmirani, R. Winkels, E. de Maat, A. Boer, and P. Mascellani. 2007. General XML format(s) for legal sources. Deliverable 3.1 of the European project for standardised transparent representation in order to extend legal accessibility (ESTRELLA). EU IST-2004-027655. http://www.estrellaproject.org/doc/D3.1-General-XML-formats-For-Legal-Sources.pdf. Accessed 30 July 2013.

Palmirani, M., and F. Benigni (2007). Norma-system: A legal information system for managing time. In Proceedings of the 12th annual conference on legal knowledge and information systems (JURIX 2007), ed. A. R. Lodder and L. Mommers, 205–224. Amsterdam: IOS Press.

Palmirani, M., and L. Cervone. 2009. Legal change management with a native XML repository. In Proceedings of the 2009 conference on legal knowledge and information systems (JURIX 2009), ed. G. Governatori, 146–155. Amsterdam: IOS Press.

Palmirani, M., G. Contissa, and R. Rubino. 2009. Fill the gap in the legal knowledge modelling. In Proceedings of the 2009 international symposium on rule interchange and applications (RuleML 2009), lecture notes on computer science 5858, ed. G. Governatori, J. Hall, and A. Paschke, 305–314. Berlin: Springer. doi:10.1007/978-3-642-04985-9_28.

Peirce, C. S. 1958. Collected papers of Charles Sanders Peirce, ed. C. Hartshorne and P. Weiss. Cambridge: Harvard University Press. (ISBN: 0674138001).

Picca, D., A. Gliozzo, and A. Gangemi. 2008. LMM: an OWL-DL MetaModel to represent heterogeneous lexical knowledge. Proceedings of the 6th Language Resource and Evaluation Conference (LREC 2008). Luxembourg: European Language Resources Association. http://www.lrec-conf.org/proceedings/lrec2008/pdf/608_paper.pdf. Accessed 30 July 2013.

Presutti, V., and A. Gangemi. 2008. Content ontology design patterns as practical building blocks for web ontologies. In Proceedings of the 27th international conference on conceptual modeling (ER 2008), lecture notes in computer science 5231, ed. Q. Li, S. Spaccapietra, E. S. K. Yu, and A. Olivé, 128–141. Berlin: Springer. doi:10.1007/978-3-540-87877-3_11.

Renear, A., D. Dubin, and C. M. Sperberg-McQueen. 2002. Towards a semantics for XML markup. Proceedings of the 2002 ACM symposium on Document Engineering (DocEng 2002): 119–126. New York: ACM. doi:10.1145/585058.585081.

Saussure, F. 2006. *Writings in general linguistics*. New York: Oxford University Press. (ISBN 019926144X).

Searle, J. 1970. *Speech acts: An essay in the philosophy of language*. Cambridge: Cambridge University Press. (ISBN 052109626X).

Text Encoding Initiative Consortium. 2013. *TEI P5: Guidelines for electronic text encoding and interchange*. Charlottesville: TEI Consortium. http://www.tei-c.org/Guidelines/P5. Accessed 30 July 2013.

Walsh, N. 2010. *DocBook 5: The definitive guide*. Sebastopol: O'Really Media. Version 1.0.3. (ISBN: 0596805029).

Chapter 5
The Semantic Publishing and Referencing Ontologies

Abstract One of the main research areas in semantic publishing is the development of semantic models that fit the requirements of authors and publishers. Although several models and metadata schemas have been developed in the past, they do not fully comply with the vocabulary used by publishers or they are not adequate for describing specific topics (e.g., characterisation of bibliographic citations, definition of publishing roles, description of publishing workflows, etc.). In this chapter I introduce the Semantic Publishing and Referencing (SPAR) Ontologies, a suite of orthogonal and complementary OWL 2 DL ontology modules for the creation of comprehensive machine-readable RDF metadata for every aspect of semantic publishing and referencing. In particular, I show the characteristics and benefits of all the SPAR ontologies, and support the entire discussion with several examples of Turtle code describing a particular reference of the legal discipline, namely Casanovas et al.'s "OPJK and DILIGENT: ontology modelling in a distributed environment".

The *development of semantic models* (vocabularies and ontologies) that fit the requirements of authors and publishers is one of the main research areas in semantic publishing. As I described in Chap. 2, several recent works have proposed metadata schemas, vocabularies and ontologies to describe the publishing domain. However those models show some limitations. Some of them (e.g., Dublin Core Metadata Terms (Dublin Core Metadata Initiative 2012) define bibliographic objects by means of abstract concepts that do not fully comply with the vocabulary used by publishers. Others (e.g., the Bibliographic Ontology (D'Arcus and Giasson 2009)) have been developed to describe parts of the publishing domain, but are not adequate for describing specific topics (e.g., characterisation of bibliographic citations, definition of agent's publishing roles, description of publishing workflows) and are not interoperable with other models (e.g., FRBR (International Federation of Library Associations and Institutions Study Group on the Functional Requirements for Bibliographic Records 2009)).

It appears clear that the development of a set of models that aim to describe the main part of the publishing domain must pass through the adoption of established methodologies for ontology modularisation and development (Rector 2003; Shotton et al. 2010). These activities may be eventually supported by the use of statistical

S. Peroni, *Semantic Web Technologies and Legal Scholarly Publishing*,
Law, Governance and Technology Series 15, DOI 10.1007/978-3-319-04777-5_5,

clustering techniques, e.g., Cimiano and Volker (2005), though I did not explicitly used them in this work. Moreover, the following principles[1] should apply:

- There should be an extensive dialogue with publishers and members of academic communities to clarify their requirements.
- Any area of interest of the publishing domain (bibliographic description of documents, characterisation of citations, person's roles, etc.) should be covered by separate yet interoperable ontologies.
- Logical constraints, for example domain and range constraints on properties, should be added only where they are strictly required, to allow maximum reusability of each ontology module.
- Where well-known and widely shared vocabularies covering parts of the domain already exist, these should be properly imported and re-used.
- Alongside the development of the ontologies, tools that assist people to understand and to use each ontology with minimum effort, without having to know the specific technical language in which the ontology is implemented, should be used or opportunely developed.

In this chapter, I will describe the principles and architecture of eight ontologies, which enable the semantic description of bibliographic entities according to the publisher' language: **SPAR**, the *Semantic Publishing and Referencing Ontologies*[2], a suite of orthogonal and complementary OWL 2 DL ontology modules. These ontologies permit the creation of comprehensive machine-readable RDF metadata for every aspect of semantic publishing and referencing: document description; type of citation and related contexts; bibliographic references; document parts and status; agents' roles and workflow processes, etc.

Table 5.1 on page 123 shows briefly all the metadata schemas, vocabularies and ontologies (including SPAR)—some of which were introduced in Sect. 2.3, and others will be presented in the following sections—according to four main characteristics:

- *domain*, that indicates the main domain for which the model has been developed;
- *standard*, that indicates whether the model is acknowledged as a proper standard according to some international organisations;
- *RDF*, that indicates whether there exists an official/unofficial implementation of the model in RDF or RDFS;
- *OWL 2 DL*, that indicates whether there exits an official/unofficial implementation of the model that is compliant with OWL 2 DL.

In addition to the peculiarities introduced in Table 5.1, which sets SPAR as one of the few models developed originally for the description of bibliographic entities through OWL 2 DL, the main characteristics of SPAR, that distinguish it from previous contributions, are firstly the creation of ontologies of sufficient expressivity to

[1] All these principles are derived from my personal experience in developing ontologies for a specific domain (i.e., publishing) and for specific end-users (primarily, publishers and authors).

[2] The SPAR (Semantic Publishing and Referencing) Ontologies: http://purl.org/spar.

Table 5.1 The models, introduced in this book, that can be used for describing the publishing domain

Model	Domain	Standard	RDF	OWL 2 DL
BIBO	Bibliographic entities	No	Yes	No
Dublin core	Generic resources	Yes	Yes	no
FRBR	Bibliographic entities	Yes	Yes	Yes
MARC 21	Bibliographic entities	Yes	Yes	No
Medium-grained structure	Scientific scholarly articles	No	No	No
ORB	Scientific scholarly articles	No	Yes	Yes
PRISM	Bibliographic entities	Yes	Yes	No
RDA	Bibliographic entities	Yes	Yes	No
SRO	Scholarly articles	No	Yes	Yes
SKOS	Generic resources	Yes	Yes	Yes
SPAR	Bibliographic entities	No	Yes	Yes
SWAN	Scientific scholarly articles	No	Yes	Yes

meet the requirements of academic authors and publishers, and secondly the development of accompanying presentation technologies, *LODE* (introduced in Sect. 6.2) and *Graffoo* (presented in Sect. 6.4), that enable the ontologies to be easily understood by potential users such as academic researchers, publishers and librarians who, while expert in their own domains, lack skills in ontology modelling and knowledge formalisation.

The starting point for SPAR was version 1.6 of *CiTO*, the *Citation Typing Ontology*, described in Shotton et al. (2010). Despite the fact that this work was both preliminary and incomplete, it contained, within one single ontology, terms for handling bibliographic document descriptions, properties to enable the characterisation of citations, as well as terms which allowed the recording of the number of citations to a given article, both within the citing paper and globally.

A simple architectural diagram of the eight SPAR ontologies is shown in Fig. 5.1 on page 124. As the diagram indicates, the eight principal SPAR ontologies are supported by three other OWL 2 DL ontologies that the SPAR ontologies import as required–*FRBR* in OWL 2 DL, *DEO*, the *Discourse Elements Ontology*[3], and the *Error Ontology*[4]. They are also supported by the external *FOAF Essentials*[5] and *SWAN Collections*[6] ontologies, by three *Ontology Design Patterns* ontology modules (*Time-indexed situation*[7], *Sequence*[8], *Participation*[9]), and by the *Patterns Ontology*[10] for document structures.

[3] DEO, the Discourse Elements Ontology: http://purl.org/spar/deo.

[4] The Error Ontology: http://www.essepuntato.it/2009/10/error.

[5] FOAF essentials in OWL: http://purl.org/swan/2.0/foaf-essential.

[6] CO, the Collections Ontology: http://swan.mindinformatics.org/ontologies/1.2/collections.owl.

[7] *Time-indexed situation* pattern: http://www.ontologydesignpatterns.org/cp/owl/timeindexedsituation.owl.

[8] *Sequence* pattern: http://www.ontologydesignpatterns.org/cp/owl/sequence.owl.

[9] *Participation* pattern: http://www.ontologydesignpatterns.org/cp/owl/participation.owl.

[10] The Patterns Ontology: http://www.essepuntato.it/2008/12/pattern.

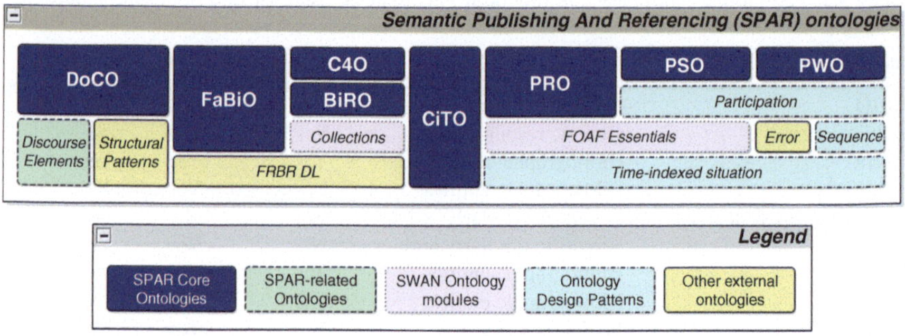

Fig. 5.1 A simple architectural diagram showing the interactions and dependencies between the component ontologies of SPAR

The characteristics and benefits of all the SPAR ontologies will be outlined in the following sections, which provide a comprehensive picture of the scope of SPAR. Where appropriate, I will also show how to integrate SPAR semantic data with documents defined through EARMARK (introduced in Chap. 3). The entire discussion will be supported by several examples of Turtle code (Prud'hommeaux and Carothers 2013) describing a particular reference of the legal discipline, i.e., Casanovas et al.'s "OPJK and DILIGENT: ontology modelling in a distributed environment" (Casanovas et al. 2007).

5.1 Representing Bibliographic Information Using FaBiO

The current well-known and commonly used vocabularies, which I described in Sect. 2.3, are either meagre in concepts or shallow, therefore preventing the description of publishing reality accurately. I will illustrate this by considering the representation of a typical bibliographic reference first using Dublin Core, then BIBO and finally FRBR. I will then show how this information can be accurately described using FaBiO, which incorporates elements of all these three vocabularies. Consider the following typical bibliographic reference describing (Casanovas et al. 2007):

> Pompeu Casanovas, Núria Casellas, Christoph Tempich, Denny Vrandečić, Richard Benjamins (2007). OPJK and DILIGENT: ontology modeling in a distributed environment. Artificial Intelligence and Law, 15 (2): 171–186. June (2007). Springer. DOI: 10.1007/s10506-007-9036-2. Print ISSN 0924-8463. Online ISSN 1572-8382. Published online (PDF) May 31, 2007.

From the previous description we can extract the following information:

1. The document is an academic research article—deducible from the journal in which it is published.
2. Pompeu Casanovas, Núria Casellas, Christoph Tempich, Denny Vrandečić, and Richard Benjamins are the authors of the article.
3. The article was published in 2007.
4. The article is entitled "OPJK and DILIGENT: ontology modeling in a distributed environment".
5. It was published in the 2nd issue of the 15th volume of *Artificial Intelligence and Law*.
6. The DOI of the article is "10.1007/s10506-007-9036-2".
7. The Print ISSN of the journal is "0924-8463".
8. The Online ISSN of the journal is "1572-8382".
9. The PDF version of the article was published online on May 31, 2007.
10. The journal issue within which the printed version of the article was published bears the publication date June 2007.
11. The page range of the article within the printed version is "171–186".
12. The publisher of the journal is Springer.

5.1.1 Bibliographic Reference Metadata Encoding Using DC Terms

In the following RDF encoding example[11], we attempt to describe all these facts using only terms from the DC Terms vocabulary (Dublin Core Metadata Initiative 2012):

[11] This and the following RDF encodings are written in Turtle (Prud'hommeaux and Carothers 2013).

```
@prefix : <http://www.example.com/> .
@prefix dcterms: <http://purl.org/dc/terms/> .
@prefix rdf: <http://www.w3.org/1999/02/22-rdf-syntax-ns#> .
@prefix xsd: <http://www.w3.org/2001/XMLSchema#> .
@prefix text: <http://purl.org/NET/mediatypes/text/> .
@prefix application: <http://purl.org/NET/mediatypes/
   application/> .

:opjk-and-diligent a dcterms:BibliographicResource
  ; dcterms:creator :casanovas , :casellas ,
    :tempich, :vrandecic, :benjamins
  ; dcterms:title "OPJK and DILIGENT: ontology modeling
     in a distributed environment"
  ; dcterms:issued "2007"^^xsd:gYear
  ; dcterms:issued "2007-06"^^xsd:gYearMonth
  ; dcterms:identifier "doi:10.1007/s10506-007-9036-2"
  ; dcterms:extent [ a dcterms:SizeOrDuration
    ; dcterms:description "171-186" ]
  ; dcterms:hasFormat :pdf
  ; dcterms:isPartOf [ dcterms:identifier "2"
    ; dcterms:description "Issue"
    ; dcterms:isPartOf [ dcterms:identifier "15"
      ; dcterms:description "Volume"
      ; dcterms:isPartOf [
        dcterms:title
          "Artificial Intelligence and Law"
        ; dcterms:publisher :springer ] ] ] .

:pdf a dcterms:BibliographicResource
  ; dcterms:format application:pdf
  ; dcterms:issued "2007-05-31"^^xsd:date .

:casanovas a dcterms:Agent
  ; dcterms:description "Pompeu Casanovas" .
:casellas a dcterms:Agent
  ; dcterms:description "Nuria Casellas" .

:tempich a dcterms:Agent
  ; dcterms:description "Christoph Tempich" .

:vrandecic a dcterms:Agent
  ; dcterms:description "Denny Vrandečić" .

:benjamins a dcterms:Agent
  ; dcterms:description "Richard Benjamins" .

:springer a dcterms:Agent
  ; dcterms:description "Springer" .
```

There are some obscure points that emerge from the preceding formalisation:

- There is *no clear characterisation* of the entities involved. We are able to speak about a general "bibliographic resource" (*dcterms:BibliographicResource*) and an "agent" (*dcterms:Agent*), but not about a journal article, a journal, a volume, or an issue of a journal, nor about persons, authors, etc.
- Some of the statements are *too generic*. E.g., the property *dcterms:issued* that is used to represent the various dates associated with the publication of this article, is also employed in conjunction with three different date formats, e.g., `"2007-05-31"^^xsd:date`, `"2007-06"^^xsd:gYearMonth`, and `"2007"^^xsd:gYear`.
- Some of the statements *hide the semantics within the textual content* of the statement. E.g., the statement *dcterms:identifier "doi:10.1007/s10506-007-9036-2"* implicitly says that the character string "10.1007/s10506-007-9036-2" is a Digital Object Identifier, i.e., a special type of identifier used to identify journal articles. Similarly `"171–186"` implicitly says that the *printed version* (**only**) of the article starts at page "171" and ends at page "186". While these implied facts are understandable to human readers, they are not available to computational agents processing the metadata.
- The relationships between the various formats of the article are not clear. For example, the manner in which the resource "*:opjk-and-diligent*" relates to the resource "*:pdf*" is not specified. Do the latter represents the content of the former in a different format, or there is something more to it?

5.1.2 Bibliographic Reference Metadata Encoding Using BIBO

Some of these points are addressed by BIBO (D'Arcus and Giasson 2009). BIBO is the first OWL ontology specifically designed to address the domain under discussion, and expands the DC Terms vocabulary with terms which are specific for bibliographic metadata, with particular regards to legal documents, and for various types of event. It also includes PRISM (Hammond 2008) and FOAF (Brickley and Miller 2010) terms.

In the following RDF encoding example, the information given in the bibliographic reference cited above is encoded using BIBO:

```
@prefix bibo: <http://purl.org/ontology/bibo/> .
@prefix foaf: <http://xmlns.com/foaf/0.1/> .

:opjk-and-diligent a bibo:AcademicArticle
  ; bibo:authorList ( :casanovas :casellas
    :tempich :vrandecic :benjamins )
  ; dcterms:title "OPJK and DILIGENT: ontology modeling
     in a distributed environment"
  ; dcterms:issued "2007"^^xsd:gYear
  ; dcterms:issued "2007-06 "^^xsd:gYearMonth
  ; bibo:doi "10.1007/s10506-007-9036-2"
  ; bibo:pageStart "171"
  ; bibo:pageEnd "186"
  ; dcterms:hasFormat :pdf
  ; dcterms:isPartOf [ a bibo:Issue
    ; bibo:issue "2"
    ; bibo:volume "15"
    ; dcterms:isPartOf [ a bibo:Journal
      ; dcterms:title
        "Artificial Intelligence and Law"
      ; dcterms:publisher :springer ] ] .

:pdf a bibo:AcademicArticle
  ; dcterms:format application:pdf
  ; dcterms:issued "2007-05-31 "^^xsd:date .

:casanovas a foaf:Person
  ; foaf:givenName "Pompeu"
  ; foaf:familyName "Casanovas" .

:casellas a foaf:Person
  ; foaf:givenName "Nuria"
  ; foaf:familyName "Casellas" .

:tempich a foaf:Person
   ; foaf:givenName "Christoph"
   ; foaf:familyName "Tempich" .

:vrandecic a foaf:Person
   ; foaf:givenName "Denny"
   ; foaf:familyName "Vrandécic" .

:benjamins a foaf:Person
   ; foaf:givenName "Richard"
   ; foaf:familyName "Benjamins" .

:springer a foaf:Organization
   ; foaf:name "Springer" .
```

As this example shows, BIBO resolves many of the semantic ambiguities present in the DC version–the DOI is specifiable through the specific data property *bibo:doi*; the article is identified as a *bibo:AcademicArticle*; the authors and the publisher are respectively *foaf:Persons* and *foaf:Organization*, etc. However, other ambiguities are still unresolved. The relationships between the various formats are still not clear, and the date properties continue to be too generic. In addition, new issues emerge:

- BIBO specifies that the property for listing authors (*bibo:authorList*) must have, as its range, either an *rdf:List* or an *rdf:Seq*. Since these RDF classes are not supported by OWL 2, this has the disadvantage of making that model non-compliant with the decidable and computable OWL 2 DL, and thus preventing OWL 2 DL reasoners from inferring new axioms from a current knowledge base encoded using BIBO[12].
- BIBO can record a volume number through the data property *bibo:volume*, but, although BIBO has the classes *bibo:AcademicArticle*, *bibo:Issue* and *bibo:Journal*, it lacks the concept of "Volume" as a distinct class among other bibliographic classes that have a hierarchical partitive relationship to one another (e.g., Journal Article > Issue > Volume > Journal).
- Furthermore, because it lacks the layered structure of FRBR (International Federation of Library Associations and Institutions Study Group on the Functional Requirements for Bibliographic Records 2009), it does not have the flexibility to distinguish between concepts at these various levels, for example an academic paper (a FRBR Work) and the various possible Expressions of that paper as a journal article, a conference paper or a book chapter. The class *bibo:AcademicArticle* is in fact a conflation of the concepts "academic paper" and "journal article".

5.1.3 Bibliographic Reference Metadata Encoding Using FRBR

It is possible to resolve the third of the issues raised above by adopting the more structured FRBR model (International Federation of Library Associations and Institutions Study Group on the Functional Requirements for Bibliographic Records 2009), as expressed in the FRBR Core ontology, together with DC terms for textual statements (i.e., those statements having a literal string as their object). This is illustrated in the following example:

[12] For a more detailed explanation of why RDF collections and containers are neither usable nor interpreted correctly by OWL 2 DL, consult http://hcklab.blogspot.com/2008/12/moving-towards-swan-collections.html.

```
@prefix frbr: <http://purl.org/vocab/frbr/core#> .

:opjk-and-diligent a frbr:Work
  ; frbr:creator :casanovas , :casellas,
    :tempich, :vrandecic, :benjamins
  ; dcterms:title "OPJK and DILIGENT: ontology modeling
     in a distributed environment"
  ; frbr:realization :version-of-record .

:version-of-record a frbr:Expression
  ; dcterms:issued "2007"^^xsd:gYear
  ; dcterms:identifier "doi:10.1007/s10506-007-9036-2"
  ; frbr:embodiment :printed , :pdf
  ; frbr:partOf [ a frbr:Expression
    ; dcterms:identifier "2"
    ; dcterms:description "Issue"
    ; frbr:embodiment :printed-issue
    ; frbr:partOf [ a frbr:Expression
      ; dcterms:identifier "15"
      ; dcterms:description "Volume"
      frbr:partOf [ a frbr:Expression
        ; dcterms:title
          "Artificial Intelligence and Law" ] ] ] .

:printed-issue a frbr:Manifestation
  ; frbr:producer :springer
  ; dcterms:issued "2007-06"^^xsd:gYearMonth
  ; frbr:part :printed .

:printed a frbr:Manifestation
  ; frbr:producer :springer
  ; dcterms:issued "2007-06"^^xsd:gYearMonth
  ; dcterms:extent [ a dcterms:SizeOrDuration
    ; dcterms:description "171-186" ] .
:pdf a frbr:Manifestation
  ; frbr:producer :springer
  ; dcterms:format application:pdf
  ; dcterms:issued "2007-05-31"^^xsd:date .

:casanovas a frbr:Person
  ; dcterms:description "Pompeu Casanovas" .

:casellas a frbr:Person
  ; dcterms:description "Nuria Casellas" .

:tempich a frbr:Person
  ; dcterms:description "Christoph Tempich" .
```

```
:vrandecic a frbr:Person
  ; dcterms:description "Denny Vrandečić" .

:benjamins a frbr:Person
  ; dcterms:description "Richard Benjamins" .

:springer a frbr:CorporateBody
  ; dcterms:description "Springer" .
```

Although it is possible to use FRBR in this manner to give a structured and unambiguous description of all the bibliographic entities, the example makes it clear the severe limitations of FRBR. These are caused by the lack of terms in the FRBR Core ontology which allow publications to be described in normal everyday language.

5.1.4 Bibliographic Reference Metadata Encoding Using FaBiO

FaBiO, the *FRBR-aligned Bibliographic Ontology*[13] (Peroni and Shotton 2012), was developed precisely to address all the issues raised by the previous examples, while re-using the previous fundamental work in this domain (so as not to re-invent the wheel). In particular, DC Terms, PRISM, FRBR and SKOS terms are all included in FaBiO.

Considering again the previous bibliographic reference example, a possible FaBiO formalisation would be:

[13] FaBiO, the FRBR-aligned Bibliographic Ontology: http://purl.org/spar/fabio.

```
@prefix fabio: <http://purl.org/spar/fabio> .
@prefix prism: <http://prismstandard.org/namespaces/
   basic/2.0/> .
@prefix rdf: <http://www.w3.org/1999/02/22-rdf-syntax-ns#> .
@prefix rdfs: <http://www.w3.org/2000/01/rdf-schema#> .
@prefix xsd: <http://www.w3.org/2001/XMLSchema#> .
@prefix dcterms: <http://purl.org/dc/terms/> .
@prefix foaf: <http://xmlns.com/foaf/0.1/> .

:opjk-and-diligent a fabio:ResearchPaper
  ; dcterms:creator :casanovas , :casellas,
    :tempich, :vrandecic, :benjamins
  ; dcterms:title "OPJK and DILIGENT: ontology modeling
     in a distributed environment"
  ; frbr:realization :version-of-record .

:version-of-record a fabio:JournalArticle
  ; fabio:hasPublicationYear "2007"^^xsd:gYear
  ; prism:doi "10.1007/s10506-007-9036-2"
  ; frbr:embodiment :printed , :pdf
  ; frbr:partOf [ a fabio:JournalIssue
    ; prism:issueIdentifier "2"
    ; frbr:embodiment :printed-issue
    ; frbr:partOf [ a fabio:JournalVolume
      ; prism:volume "15"
      frbr:partOf [ a fabio:Journal
        ; dcterms:title
          "Artificial Intelligence and Law" ] ] ] .

:printed-issue a fabio:Paperback
  ; dcterms:publisher :springer
  ; prism:publicationDate "2007-06"^^xsd:gYearMonth
  ; frbr:part :printed .

:printed a fabio:PrintObject
  ; dcterms:publisher :springer
  ; prism:publicationDate "2007-06"^^xsd:gYearMonth
  ; prism:startingPage "171"
  ; prism:endingPage "186" .

:pdf a fabio:DigitalManifestation
  ; dcterms:publisher :springer
  ; dcterms:format application:pdf
  ; prism:publicationDate "2007-05-31"^^xsd:date .
```

```
:casanovas a foaf:Person
  ; foaf:givenName "Pompeu"
  ; foaf:familyName "Casanovas" .

:casellas a foaf:Person
  ; foaf:givenName "Nuria"
  ; foaf:familyName "Casellas" .

:tempich a foaf:Person
  ; foaf:givenName "Christoph"
  ; foaf:familyName "Tempich" .

:vrandecic a foaf:Person
  ; foaf:givenName "Denny"
  ; foaf:familyName "Vrandečić" .

:benjamins a foaf:Person
  ; foaf:givenName "Richard"
  ; foaf:familyName "Benjamins" .

:springer a foaf:Organization
  ; foaf:name "Springer" .
```

With FaBiO, it thus becomes possible:

- To write semantic descriptions of a wide variety of bibliographic objects, including research articles, journal articles and journal volumes, using terms that closely resemble the language used in everyday speech by academics and publishers[14].
- To employ FRBR categories to define clear separations between each part of the publishing process, which involves different people (authors, publishers, readers), depending on which aspect of the bibliographic entity we are considering: the high-level conceptualisation of the research paper, the version of record of that paper forming a journal article: the publication of the article in various formats, and the individual physical or electronic exemplars of the published article that people may read and own.
- To include with ease elements from other vocabularies which describe particular entities involved in the publishing process that are not specified by FaBiO itself, such as those from FOAF for persons and organisations.

Other advantages of FaBiO will be outlined in the following sections.

[14] This has been achieved through many meetings with a number of academics and publishers that we have undertaken in order to understand their working practices and requirements.

5.1.4.1 Using External Models

As already mentioned, FaBiO has been developed so to limit any restriction to its classes as well as the domains and ranges of its properties. This flexibility has the great advantage of allowing FaBiO to be used together with other models. We have already seen how FOAF can be used to describe agents. Another common requirement would be to specify the order of components in a list, e.g., authors in an author list. This can be achieved in a manner that is compliant with the decidable and computable OWL 2 DL, unlike the *bibo:authorList* as described above, by combining FaBiO with the *Collections Ontology* (*CO*)[15] (Ciccarese and Peroni 2013), an OWL 2 DL ontology specifically designed for defining orders among items. In particular:

```
@prefix co: <http://purl.org/co/> .

:opjk-and-diligent a fabio:ResearchPaper
  ; dcterms:creator :listOfAuthors .

:listOfAuthors a co:List
  ; co:firstItem [ co:itemContent :casanovas
  ; co:nextItem [ co:itemContent :casellas
  ; co:nextItem [ co:itemContent :tempich
  ; co:nextItem [ co:itemContent :vrandecic
  ; co:nextItem [ co:itemContent :benjamins ] ] ] ] ] .

:casanovas a foaf:Person
  ; foaf:givenName "Pompeu"
  ; foaf:familyName "Casanovas" .

:casellas a foaf:Person
  ; foaf:givenName "Nuria"
  ; foaf:familyName "Casellas" .

:tempich a foaf:Person
  ; foaf:givenName "Christoph"
  ; foaf:familyName "Tempich" .

:vrandecic a foaf:Person
  ; foaf:givenName "Denny"
  ; foaf:familyName "Vrandečić" .

:benjamins a foaf:Person
  ; foaf:givenName "Richard"
  ; foaf:familyName "Benjamins" .
```

In this way we can still keep the model in OWL 2 DL. Additionally, because the ranges of *dcterms:creator* and other properties within FaBiO have intentionally been left unspecified, FaBiO guarantees a level of interoperation with other models without incurring in any undesirable side effects, such as ontology inconsistencies or generation of undesired inferences.

[15] CO, the Collections Ontology: http://purl.org/co.

5.1.4.2 Extending FRBR Within FaBiO

One of the explicit requests from publishers and end-users was to be able to create shortcuts between FRBR endeavours (work, expression, manifestation, item) that were not part of the original FRBR model. Let me introduce an example to illustrate this requirement, by marginally changing the bibliographic reference we introduced earlier:

> Pompeu Casanovas, Núria Casellas, Christoph Tempich, Denny Vrandečić, Richard Benjamins (2007). OPJK and DILIGENT: ontology modeling in a distributed environment. http://link.springer.com/content/pdf/10.1007%2Fs10506-007-9036-2.pdf.

In this reference, we have one FRBR work—the paper by Casanovas et al.—and the URL for a specific FRBR item that portrays that work—the PDF version of the paper on the publishers' website. If I wished to link these concepts using the FRBR OWL ontology terms I have employed so far, I would be obliged to specify each intermediate FRBR endeavour, namely the expression and manifestation of that paper, even if we were not interested in doing that:

```
@prefix springer: <http://link.springer.com/content/pdf/> .
:opjk-and-diligent a frbr:Work
  ; frbr:creator :casanovas , :casellas,
    :tempich, :vrandecic, :benjamins
  ; dcterms:title "OPJK and DILIGENT: ontology modeling
     in a distributed environment"
  ; frbr:realization [ a frbr:Expression
    ; frbr:embodiment [ a frbr:Manifestation
      ; frbr:exemplar springer:10.1007%2Fs10506
         -007-9036-2.pdf ] ] .
```

To avoid this long-windedness, it is possible to use the new FaBiO properties, shown in Fig. 5.2[16], to link a work directly to its manifestations (*fabio:hasManifestation*) or to its items (*fabio:hasPortrayal*), or to link an expression directly to its items (*fabio:hasRepresentation*).

Evidently, these added properties allows us to treat these cases quite easily and in a less verbose way:

```
@prefix springer: <http://link.springer.com/content/pdf/> .
:opjk-and-diligent a frbr:Work
  ; frbr:creator :casanovas , :casellas,
    :tempich, :vrandecic, :benjamins
  ; dcterms:title "OPJK and DILIGENT: ontology modeling
     in a distributed environment"
  ; fabio:hasPortrayal springer:10.1007%2Fs10506
     -007-9036-2.pdf .
```

[16] This and the following diagrams comply with the *Graphic framework for OWL ontologies* (*Graffoo*), introduced in Sect. 6.4. A legend for all Graffoo diagrams can be found in Fig. 6.13 on page 227.

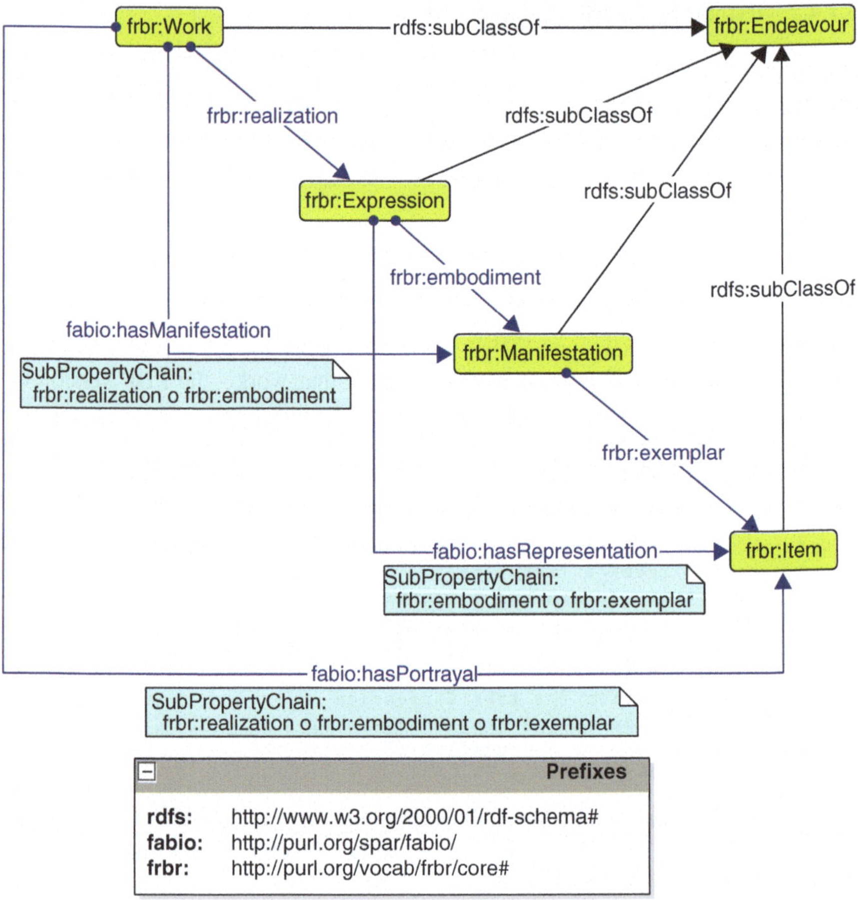

Fig. 5.2 The main FRBR object properties relating FRBR endeavours (work, expression, manifestation, item), and the related new object properties introduced by FaBiO (fabio:hasManifestation, fabio:hasRepresentation, fabio:hasPortrayal) to provide shortcuts between Work and Manifestation, Work and Item, and Expression and Item, respectively

5.1.4.3 Categorising Bibliographic Resources with SKOS

One of the most important needs for a publisher is to categorise each bibliographic entity it produces by adding free-text keywords and/or specific terms structured according to recognised classification systems and/or thesauri developed for specific academic disciplines. While through FaBiO the definition of keywords is possible using the PRISM property *prism:keyword*, terms from thesauri, structured vocabularies and classification systems are described using SKOS (Miles and Bechhofer 2009).

To facilitate this, FaBiO extends some classes and properties of SKOS as shown in Fig. 5.3.

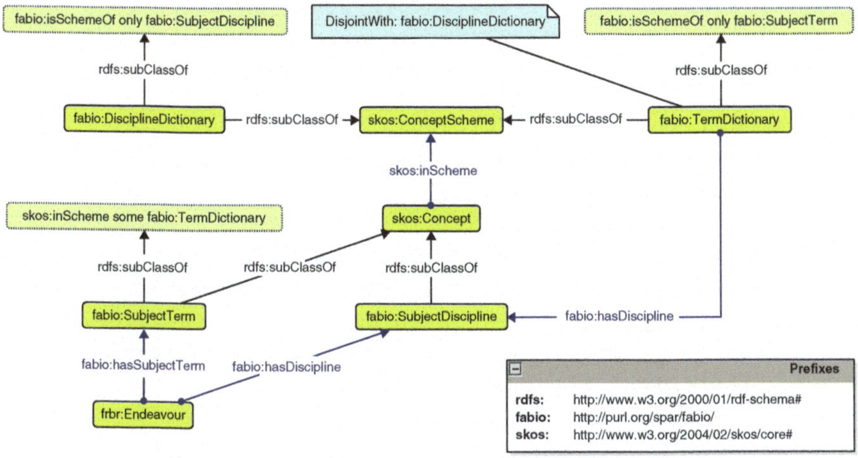

Fig. 5.3 The extension to the common SKOS classes and relations implemented in FaBiO

As shown, any FRBR endeavour can be associated (*fabio:hasSubjectTerm*) with one or more descriptive terms (*fabio:SubjectTerm*, a sub-class of*skos:Concept*) found in a specific dictionary (*fabio:TermDictionary*, a sub-class of *skos:ConceptScheme*) that is relevant to (*fabio:hasDiscipline*) particular disciplines (*fabio:SubjectDiscipline*, also a sub-class of*skos:Concept*) describing a field of knowledge or human activity such as computer science, biology, economics, cookery or swimming. At the same time, the subject disciplines can be grouped by an opportune vocabulary (i.e., *fabio:DisciplineDictionary*).

For instance, the previous example can be enriched in this way:

```
@prefix skos: <http://www.w3.org/2004/02/skos/core#> .
@prefix facet: <http://link.springer.com/facet/> .
@prefix dbpedia: <http://dbpedia.org/resource/> .

:opjk-and-diligent a fabio:ResearchPaper
  ; fabio:hasSubjectTerm facet:air-and-space-law ,
    facet:computational-linguistics ,
    facet:philosophy-of-law ,
    facet:legal-aspects-of-computing ,
    facet:artificial-intelligence-incl-robotics
  ; prism:keywords "legal ontologies" , "methodology" ,
    "ontology modeling" , "professional knowledge" ,
    "rhetorical structure theory" .

<http://link.springer.com/facet> a fabio:TermDictionary
  ; skos:prefLabel "Facet dictionary used in Springer
     library"
  ; fabio:hasDiscipline dbpedia:Computer_science ,
     dbpedia:Law .

facet:air-and-space-law a fabio:SubjectTerm
  ; skos:prefLabel "Air and Space Law"
  ; skos:inScheme <http://link.springer.com/facet> .

computational-linguistics a fabio:SubjectTerm
  ; skos:prefLabel "Computational Linguistics"
  ; skos:inScheme <http://link.springer.com/facet> .
...
```

5.2 Characterising Citations with CiTO

Bibliographic citation, i.e., the act of referring from a citing entity to the cited one, is one of the most important activities of an author in the production of any bibliographic work, since the acknowledgement of the sources used by the author stands at the very core of the scholarly enterprise. The network of citations created by combining citation information from many academic articles and books, is a source of rich information for scholars, and can be used by publishers to create new and interesting ways of browsing their material, as well as for calculating metrics which reflect the relative importance of a journal (i.e., the *impact factor*) or an author (i.e., the *h-index*).

The reasons why an author cites other publications are varied. Usually, it is because the author has gained assistance of some sort, perhaps in the form of background information, ideas, methods or data, from a previously published work, and they wish to acknowledge this. More rarely, citations may be made to review, critique or refute previous work. Most citations are direct and explicit (as in the reference list of a journal article). However, they can also be indirect (for example, by means of a citation to a more recent paper by the same research group on the same topic), or implicit (as in artistic quotations or parodies, or *in extremis*in cases of plagiarism).

Traditionally, scholars had well-developed methods for citing individual sections, paragraphs or verses of referenced works. In addition, it was not uncommon for the citing author to reproduce entire sections of the cited work in their own document, so that the reader could understand exactly the relationship of the earlier document to the present one, since the author could not be sure the reader would have ready access to the works of the cited authority (for example, Aristotle). In contrast, modern scientific practice takes the other extreme–a citation is made to the previously published paper as a whole, with little or no indication given as to why this paper has been cited or what portions of it are relevant to the discussion in hand, except for what the reader can glean from the citation context.

Previously developed models for describing bibliographic objects would normally allow for the existence of citations among bibliographic entities to be recorded. For instance, considering again the example of the article "OPJK and DILIGENT: ontology modeling in a distributed environment", using BIBO (D'Arcus and Giasson 2009) it is possible to declare citations as follows:

```
@prefix bibo: <http://purl.org/ontology/bibo/> .

:opjk-and-diligent bibo:cites
    :principles-design-ontologies
  , :ontological-engineering
  , :ontology-integration ...
```

Alternatively, it is possible to use the Discourse Relationships Module[17] in SWAN v1.2 (Ciccarese et al. 2008) in the same way:

```
@prefix disrel: <http://swan.mindinformatics.org/
   ontologies/1.2/discourse-relationships/> .

:version-of-record disrel:cites
    :principles-design-ontologies
  , :ontological-engineering
  , :ontology-integration ...
```

However, while the *cites* properties in these two ontologies, as well as the more generic property *dcterms:relation* in DC Terms, permit the bald **existence** of a citation to be recorded, they do not permit the author to invest the citation with any specific

[17] The Discourse Relationships Ontology: http://swan.mindinformatics.org/spec/1.2/discourserelationships.html.

factual and/or rhetorical meanings that would describe the **reasons** why the author decided to create such citation.

CiTO, the *Citation Typing Ontology* [18] version 2.0 (Peroni and Shotton 2012), seeks to improve upon this situation by making it possible for authors (or others) to capture their intent when citing a particular publication, as it allows them to create metadata describing citations that are distinct from metadata describing the cited works themselves. CiTO thus permits the motives of an author when referring to another document to be captured. The previous example would therefore be written using CiTO as follows:

```
@prefix cito: <http://purl.org/spar/cito/> .
:version-of-record
  cito:includesQuotationFrom
     :principles-design-ontologies
; cito:usesMethodIn :ontological-engineering
; cito:citesAsRelated :ontology-integration ...
```

The current version of CiTO, version 2.6.2, contains and extends the citation-specific object properties that were originally contained in CiTO version 1.6 (Shotton 2010), to the exclusion of those other original classes and properties within CiTO v1.6, which, as part of the modularisation we have undertaken, have been moved into FaBiO (Sect. 5.1) or into C4O (Sect. 5.3.2) and PSO (Sect. 5.5.7).

CiTO now contains just two main object properties, *cito:cites* and its inverse *cito:isCitedBy*, each of which has 41 sub-properties, plus four additional generic object properties–i.e. *cito:shareAuthorsWith*, *cito:sharesAuthorInstitutionWith*, *cito:sharesFundingAgencyWith* and *cito:likes*–that may be used even outside a citation act. As defined in *Functions of Citations* ontology[19], all these properties (and, consequently, their inverses) may be classified as rhetorical and/or factual, with the rhetorical properties being grouped in three sets depending on their connotation: *positive*, *informative* (or *neutral*) or *negative*.

When developing CiTO v2.6.2 from CiTO v1.6, we intentionally removed the domain and range constraints from the object properties, so that this ontology could be easily integrated with other models. Obviously, it can be successfully used in conjunction with FaBiO, so that descriptions of a bibliographic entity and its citations can be mixed within a single RDF graph:

[18] CiTO, the Citation Typing Ontology: http://purl.org/spar/cito.

[19] Functions of Citations ontology: http://www.essepuntato.it/2013/03/cito-functions.

```
:version-of-record a fabio:JournalArticle
  ; frbr:realizationOf :opjk-and-diligent
  ; cito:includesQuotationFrom
    :principles-design-ontologies
  ; cito:usesMethodIn :ontological-engineering
  ; cito:citesAsRelated :ontology-integration ...

:principles-design-ontologies a fabio:JournalArticle
  ; frbr:realizationOf [ a fabio:ResearchPaper
    ; dcterms:title "Toward principles for the design of
        ontologies used for knowledge sharing"
    ; dcterms:creator :gruber ]
  ; cito:providesQuotationFor :version-of-record .

:ontological-engineering a fabio:Book
  ; frbr:realizationOf [ a fabio:ReferenceWork
    ; dcterms:title "Ontological Engineering"
    ; dcterms:creator :gomez-perez , :fernandez-lopez ,
        :corcho ]
  ; cito:providesMethodFor :version-of-record .

:ontology-integration a fabio:ConferencePaper
  ; frbr:realizationOf [ a fabio:ResearchPaper
    ; dcterms:title "Ontology integration: Experiences
        with medical terminologies"
    ; dcterms:creator :gangemi , :pisanelli , :steve ]
  ; cito:isCitedAsRelatedBy :version-of-record .
...
```

5.3 Documents and Their Bibliographic References

The word "citation" is often subject of misinterpretations and misuse. The reason being that the word can be used to identify objects which have different purposes, at least in scientific literature. For instance, we often identify as "citation" the *act of citing* another work, a *bibliographic reference* put at the end of a paper (usually in a list), as well as particular *pointers* (e.g., "[3]") denoting that bibliographic reference.

In order to expand more on this topic, let we consider the following text from the article "OPJK and DILIGENT: ontology modeling in a distributed environment" (Casanovas et al. 2007) used in the previous examples:

> **DILIGENT Methodology**
>
> ...
>
> an ontology is defined as 'a shared specification of a conceptualization' (Gruber 1995). Although 'shared' is an essential feature, it is often neglected. In DILIGENT, experts exchange arguments while building the initial shared ontology in order to reach consensus;
>
> ...
>
> **References**
>
> ...

Gruber (1995). Toward principles for the design of ontologies used for knowledge sharing, International Journal of Human Computer Studies, 43(5–6): 907–928.

The above excerpt contains a particular paragraph from the section "DILIGENT Methodology" of the paper and a list item from the final "References" section. We can clearly identify six different kinds of objects that relate to this citation, all of them having different purposes:

1. The *citing article*, i.e., the article that contains such a text.
2. The *cited article*, i.e., the article that is being referred to by the text.
3. The *in-text reference pointer* which refers to a particular bibliographic reference (usually contained in the section "References"), e.g., the text "(Gruber 1995)". In scientific literature this can be presented in different forms—as an in-square-brackets number (e.g., "[3]"); as an in-square-brackets string with the first letter of each (at most three) authors' surname plus the last two digits of the publication year (e.g., "[RDS02]"); or as an in-round-brackets string with the first author's surname followed by "et al.," and the publication year (e.g., "(Renear et al. 2002)");
4. The *citation context*, the unit of the paper (sentence, paragraph, section, chapter, etc.) in which the in-text reference pointer appears.
5. The *bibliographic reference*, i.e., the list item at the end of the above excerpt that briefly summarises some metadata of a particular paper. It is explicitly denoted (by an in-text reference pointer) somewhere in the text.
6. The *act of citing*, i.e., a statement that connects two different articles (more precisely, the *citing document* and the *cited document*) for a particular reason, as described in Sect. 5.2.

Ontologies that aim to describe such elements should be provided with appropriate entities (classes and properties) in order to prevent or minimise any ambiguity when modelling citing acts in documents.

Having a clear and unambiguous description of elements used in citations is particularly relevant for those applications that extract citation contexts in an automatic and semi-automatic ways. For instance, the *Citation-Sensitive In-Browser Summariser* (*CSIBS*) (Wan et al. 2010) is a tool for presenting a preview of possible excerpts from the cited document that are relevant to a particular in-text reference pointer in the citing document. One of this tool's expected future development would be to enable RDF-based descriptions of these elements.

In Sect. 5.2 I introduced the SPAR ontology for the description of factual and rhetorical aspects of citations. In the next section I will present two models which focus on the remaining aspects of the citing acts: the *Bibliographic Reference Ontology* (*BiRO*) and the *Citation Counting and Context Characterisation Ontology*(*C4O*). They are two SPAR ontologies developed for describing bibliographic lists, bibliographic references, in-text reference pointers, citation contexts and a mechanism for counting locally (within an article) or globally (by means of particular platforms, such as Google Scholar[20]) document citations.

[20] Google Scholar: http://scholar.google.com.

5.3.1 Describing the Bibliographic Reference Lists of Articles with BiRO

According to Shotton (2009), one of the rules that digital publishers should follow to participate actively to Semantic Publishing is at least to make available reference lists of articles in a machine-readable form. In principle, reference lists are the platform from where citation networks should be built. In order to accomplish this aim, ontologies which model article references and reference lists are needed. Besides offering flexible mechanisms for the description of references, these ontologies should also allow the user to link the reference to the particular semantic representation of the document being *referenced*.

This is an important point to understand: the reference in the reference list of a particular article **is not** the cited document. Rather, it is a compact description considered (usually) sufficient to make the reader aware of what document has been cited. Therefore, having references expressed in a machine-readable form should allow machines to make the inference step, i.e., to link automatically the article containing the reference (i.e., the citing document) to the article referenced by the reference itself (i.e., the cited document).

I have developed the *Bibliographic Reference Ontology*[21] (*BiRO*) to offer a standard model for the description of reference lists and references according to (machine-readable) Semantic Web standards. In particular, BiRO is an ontology structured according to the FRBR model Sect. 2.3.5 to define bibliographic records (as subclasses of FRBR Work) in relation to bibliographic references (as subclasses of FRBR Expression), and their compilation into bibliographic collections and ordered bibliographic lists, respectively (as shown in Fig. 5.4).

An individual bibliographic reference, such as one in the reference list of a published journal article, may exhibit varying degrees of incompleteness, depending on the formatting rules of the journal. For example, it may lack the title of the cited article, the full names of the listed authors, or indeed a full listing of all the authors. It will also lack other information that one would expect to find in the complete bibliographic description for that article.

BiRO provides a logical system for relating such an incomplete bibliographic reference:

- To the full bibliographic record for that cited article, which, in addition to any author and title fields missing from the reference, may also be expected to include the name of the publisher, and the ISSN or ISBN of the publication.
- To collections of bibliographic records, such as library catalogues.
- To ordered bibliographic lists, such as reference lists.

In order to understand how to use BiRO to describe reference lists, let use again the reference introduced above which refers to (Gruber 1995):

[21] BiRO, the Bibliographic Reference Ontology: http://purl.org/spar/biro.

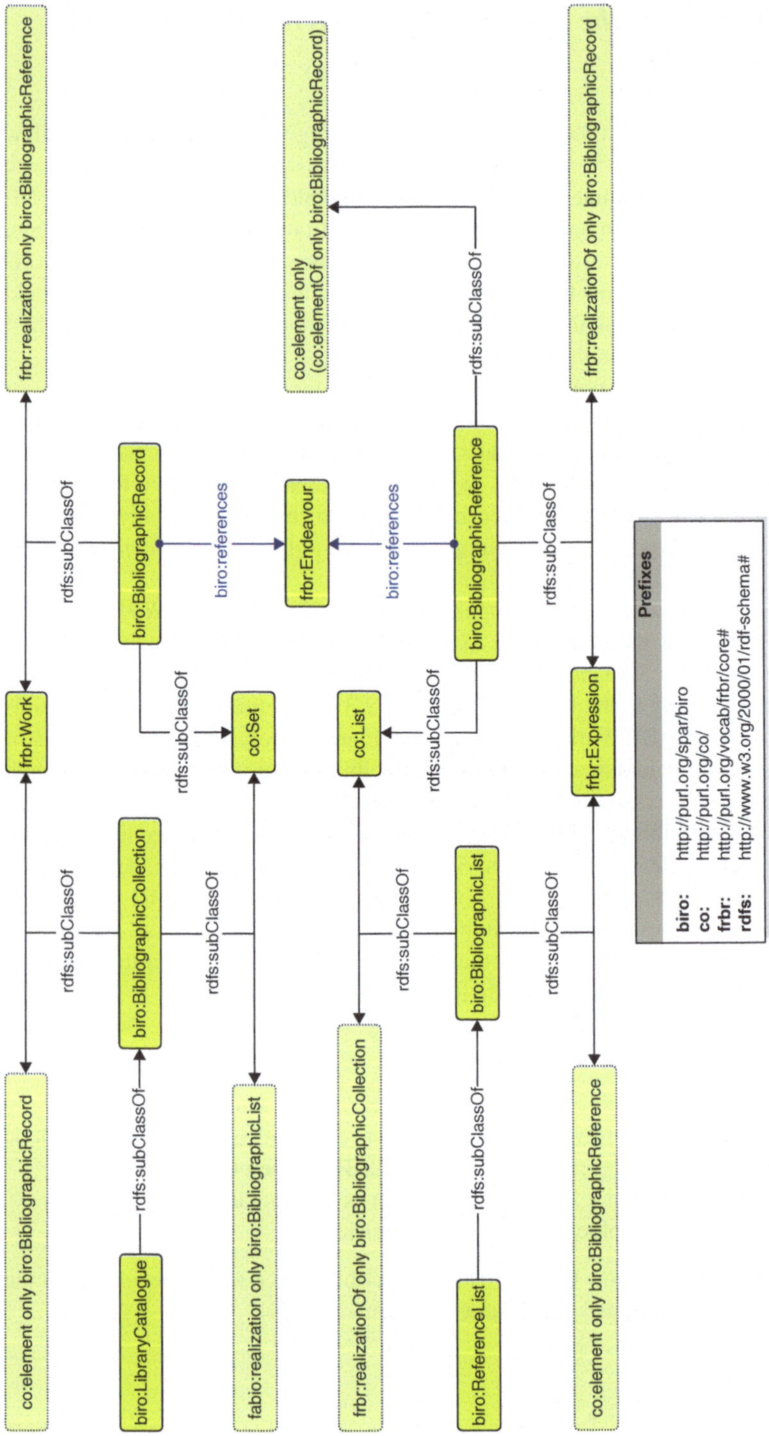

Fig. 5.4 Graffoo diagram summarising the Bibliographic Reference Ontology (*BiRO*)

Gruber (1995). Toward principles for the design of ontologies used for knowledge sharing, International Journal of Human Computer Studies, 43(5–6): 907–928.

5.3.1.1 An URI for the Reference

A first, very quick, way for defining a simple machine-readable representation of that reference using BiRO is as follows[22]:

```
:version-of-record frbr:part :reference-list .

:reference-list a biro:ReferenceList
  ; co:firstItem [ co:itemContent :ayuso03
  ; co:nextItem [ co:itemContent :benjamins04 ...
  ; co:nextItem [
    co:itemContent :gruber95 ... ] ... ] ] .
:gruber95 a biro:BibliographicReference
  ; biro:references :principles-design-ontologies
  ; dcterms:bibliographicCitation "Gruber, T. R. (1995).
      Toward principles for the design of ontologies
      used for knowledge sharing, International Journal
      of Human Computer Studies, 43(5-6): 907-928." .
```

Evidently, this formal description does not achieve a substantial improvement, as I only assigned an URL to the reference list and to each of its references. The semantics beyond the string representing the reference is still obscure. For instance, at this stage I do make clear that the strings "Gruber", "T. R.", "1995", "Toward principles for the design of ontologies used for knowledge sharing" are, respectively, the surname of one of the authors, the first letters of his names, the year of publication and the title of the article.

5.3.1.2 Semantic Enhancement of Literal Elements in References

A way to enable the semantic enhancement of strings is to use literals as subjects of statements and assertions, which is not allowed by Semantic Web standards such as RDF and OWL. Recently, within the Semantic Web community, this topic, i.e., whether and how to allow literals to be subjects of RDF statements[23], has been actively discussed. However, this discussion has still failed to provide a unique and clear indication of how to proceed in that regard.

Although one of the suggestions coming out of the discussion was to explicitly include the proposal in a (future) specification of RDF, this idea is not in fact new,

---

[22] The prefix *swan* refers to entities defined in the old version of the Collection Ontology (SWAN Collection Ontology 1.2), currently imported in BiRO. The SWAN Collection Ontology is available at http://swan.mindinformatics.org/ontologies/1.2/collections.owl.

[23] Literals as subjects: http://www.w3.org/2001/sw/wiki/Literals_as_Subjects.

particularly in ontology modelling. The need to describe "typical" literals (especially strings) as individuals of a particular class has been addressed by many models in past, such as Common Tag[24] (through the class *Tag*), SIOC (Bojars and Breslin 2010) (through the classes *Category* and *Tag*), SKOS-XL (Miles and Bechhofer 2009) (through the class *Label*), and LMM (Picca et al. 2008) (through the class *Expression*). After considering the above-mentioned models, among others, I have developed–in collaboration with Aldo Gangemi and Fabio Vitali–a pattern called *literal reification*to address this issue. It allows one to express literal values as proper ontological individuals so that they can be used as subject/object of any assertion within OWL models.

By extending the pattern *region*[25] (Gangemi 2010b), the pattern *literal reification*[26] (Gangemi et al. 2010) promotes any literal as "first class object" in OWL by reifying it as a proper individual of the class *litre:Literal*. Individuals of this class express literal values through the functional data property *litre:hasLiteralValue* and can be connected to other individuals that share the same literal value by using the property *litre:hasSameLiteralValueAs*. Moreover, a literal may refer to, and may be referred by, any OWL individual through *litre:isLiteralOf* and *litre:hasLiteral* respectively.

It is to be noted that the pattern defines also a SWRL rule (Horrocks et al. 2004) that allows one to infer the (not explicitly asserted) literal value of a particular literal individual when it is connected to another literal individual via *litre:hasSameLiteralValueAs*:

```
litre:hasSameLiteralValueAs(x,y) ,
litre:hasLiteralValue(y,v)
  -> litre:hasLiteralValue(x,v)
```

This pattern allows one to use each reified literal as subject or object of any assertion, and it is able to address scenarios described, for example, by the following competency questions:

- What is the context in which entities refer to a particular literal value?
- What is the meaning of a particular value considering the context in which it is used?

Plausible scenarios of its application include:

- Modelling domains concerning descriptive tags, in which each tag may have more than one meaning depending on the context in which it is used.

[24] Common Tag: http://www.commontag.org.

[25] Region pattern: http://ontologydesignpatterns.org/cp/owl/region.owl. The prefix *region* refers to entities defined in it.

[26] Literal reification pattern: http://www.essepuntato.it/2010/06/literalreification. The prefix *literal* refers to entities defined in it.

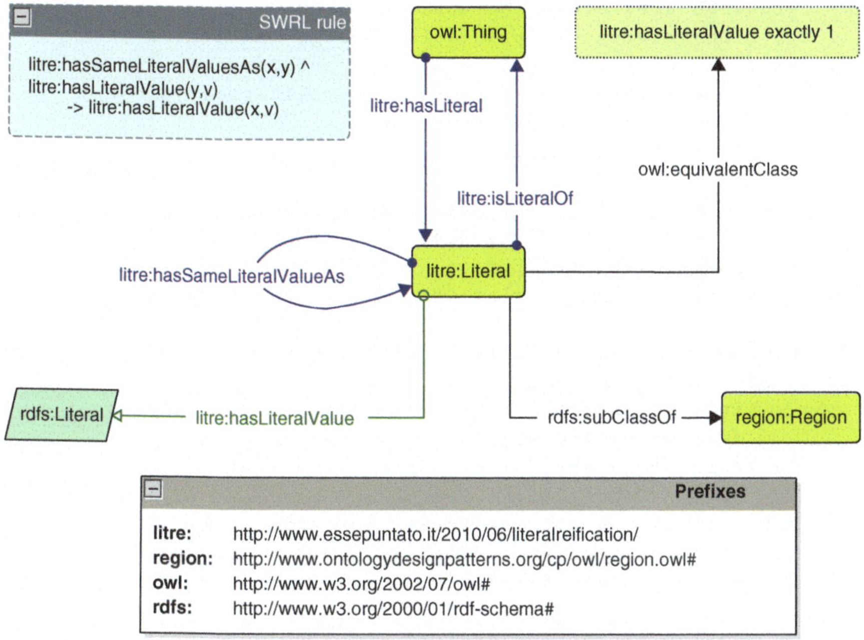

Fig. 5.5 Graffoo diagram summarising the *Literal Reification* pattern

- Extending the capabilities of a model by adding the possibility to make assertions on values, previously referred through data properties, without modifying it.

As briefly introduced above and also shown in Fig. 5.5, the pattern *literal reification* is composed by a class, a data property and three object properties, which are described as follows:

- class *litre:Literal*. It describes reified literals, where the literal value they represent is specified through the property *litre:hasLiteralValue*. Each individual of this class must always have a specified value;
- data property *litre:hasLiteralValue*. It is used to specify the literal value that an individual of *litre:Literal* represents;
- object property *litre:hasSameLiteralValueAs*. It relates the reified literal to another one that has the same literal value;
- object property *litre:hasLiteral*. It connects individuals of any class to a reified literal;
- object property *litre:isLiteralOf*. It connects the reified literal to the individuals that are using it.

By means of this pattern and of the OWL 2 capabilities in meta-modelling, it becomes possible to link specific strings in the references and to enhance them through semantic assertions according to specific vocabularies, as shown in the following excerpt:

```
:gruber95 a biro:BibliographicReference
  ; biro:references :principles-design-ontologies
  ; co:firstItem [ co:itemContent :author-name
  ; co:nextItem [ co:itemContent :publication-year
  ; co:nextItem [ co:itemContent
    :article-title ... ] ] ] .

:author-name a litre:Literal , foaf:name
  ; litre:isLiteralOf :gruber  # it is the URL
     identifying the person
  ; litre:hasLiteralValue "Gruber, T. R."^^xsd:string .

:publication-year a litre:Literal , fabio:
   hasPublicationYear
  ; litre:isLiteralOf [ frbr:realization :principles-
     design-ontologies ]
  ; litre:hasLiteralValue "1995"^^xsd:gYear .

:article-title a litre:Literal , dcterms:title
  ; litre:isLiteralOf [ frbr:realization :principles-
     design-ontologies ]
  ; litre:hasLiteralValue "Toward principles for the
     design of ontologies used for knowledge sharing"^^
     xsd:string .

...
```

As shown above, now the bibliographic reference under consideration is described as a list of literals, each of them having a particular semantic connotation.

5.3.1.3 EARMARK Ranges for Describing References

Another approach to deal with the semantic enhancement of bibliographic references would be to use LA-EARMARK ranges for associating appropriate semantic statements to textual fragments, as illustrated in Chap. 4. For instance, let us consider the article by Casanovas et al.'s "OPJK and DILIGENT: ontology modeling in a distributed environment" (Casanovas et al. 2007) implemented as an EARMARK document. In this case, I will have a particular docuverse containing the text of the reference used previously, for example:

```
:gruber95 a biro:BibliographicReference
  ; biro:references :principles-design-ontologies
  ; dcterms:bibliographicCitation "Gruber, T. R. (1995).
     Toward principles for the design of ontologies
     used for knowledge sharing, International Journal
     of Human Computer Studies, 43(5-6): 907-928." .
```

From this docuverse, I can define ranges for each string I want to use in order to describe the bibliographic reference according to BiRO. These ranges, that cover the same literal values used in the previous example can be defined as follows:

```
:gruber95 a biro:BibliographicReference
  ; biro:references :principles-design-ontologies
  ; co:firstItem [ co:itemContent :author-familyname
  ; co:nextItem [
    co:itemContent :author-firstlettersname
  ; co:nextItem [ co:itemContent :publication-year
  ; co:nextItem [ co:itemContent
    :article-title ... ] ] ] ] .

# the string "Gruber"
:first-author-surname a earmark:PointerRange
  ; earmark:refersTo :gruber95-reference
  ; earmark:begins "0"^^xsd:nonNegativeInteger
  ; earmark:ends "6"^^xsd:nonNegativeInteger .

# the string "T. R."
:author-firstlettersname a earmark:PointerRange
  ; earmark:refersTo :gruber95-reference
  ; earmark:begins "8"^^xsd:nonNegativeInteger
  ; earmark:ends "13"^^xsd:nonNegativeInteger .

# the string "1995"
:publication-year a earmark:PointerRange
  ; earmark:refersTo :gruber95-reference
  ; earmark:begins "15"^^xsd:nonNegativeInteger
  ; earmark:ends "19"^^xsd:nonNegativeInteger .

# the string "Toward principles for..."
:paper-title a earmark:PointerRange
  ; earmark:refersTo :gruber95-reference
  ; earmark:begins "22"^^xsd:nonNegativeInteger
  ; earmark:ends "95"^^xsd:nonNegativeInteger .

...
```

Furthermore, using the Linguistic Act ontology introduced in Chap. 4, it is possible to link EARMARK ranges to their formal meaning and to their particular references, i.e., literals. For instance, considering the range *:author-firstlettersname*, I can say that:

1. This range denotes a particular literal (e.g., "Thomas Robert") that is owned by the first author.
2. This range express a particular meaning, e.g., the fact of having a given name.
3. This meaning is a conceptualisation of the literal hereby introduced.

Thus, according to LA-EARMARK, I will have:

```
# string "T. R."
:author-firstlettersname a la:Expression
  ; la:expresses foaf:givenName
  ; la:denotes :gruber-given-name .

:gruber-given-name a litre:Literal
  ; litre:hasLiteralValue "Thomas Robert"
  ; litre:isLiteralOf :gruber
  : la:hasConceptualization foaf:givenName .

[] a la:LinguisticAct
  ; sit:isSettingFor
    # myself, as author of this interpretation
      <http://www.essepuntato.it/me>
    # as the person having a certain name
    , :gruber
    # The letter identifying the name
    , :author-firstlettersname
    # The full version of the name
    , :gruber-given-name
    # The meaning associated to such a string
    , foaf:givenName .
```

5.3.2 C4O: How Much, Where and what Someone is Citing

Besides defining reference lists and bibliographic references in a machine-readable form, I will also focus on how these references are used in the citing paper. In particular, I would need entities that describe:

- in-text reference pointers within the citing paper;
- links to the bibliographic references denoted by in-text reference pointers;
- how much a particular document is locally cited by the citing document–i.e., the total amount of in-text reference pointers within the citing paper denoting the same bibliographic reference;
- how much an article is globally cited (according to particular bibliographic citation service);
- the contexts involved in a citation–i.e., the part P_{citing} of the citing article containing a particular in-text reference pointer and the part P_{cited} of the cited article that is relevant to P_{citing}.

The *Citation Counting and Context Characterization Ontology*[27] (*C4O*) has been developed to allow the description of the above entities. This ontology enables the characterisation of bibliographic citations in terms of their presence in an article by means of the following classes (shown in Fig. 5.6):

[27] C4O, the Citation Counting and Context Characterization Ontology: http://purl.org/spar/c4o. The prefix *c4o* refers to entities defined in it.

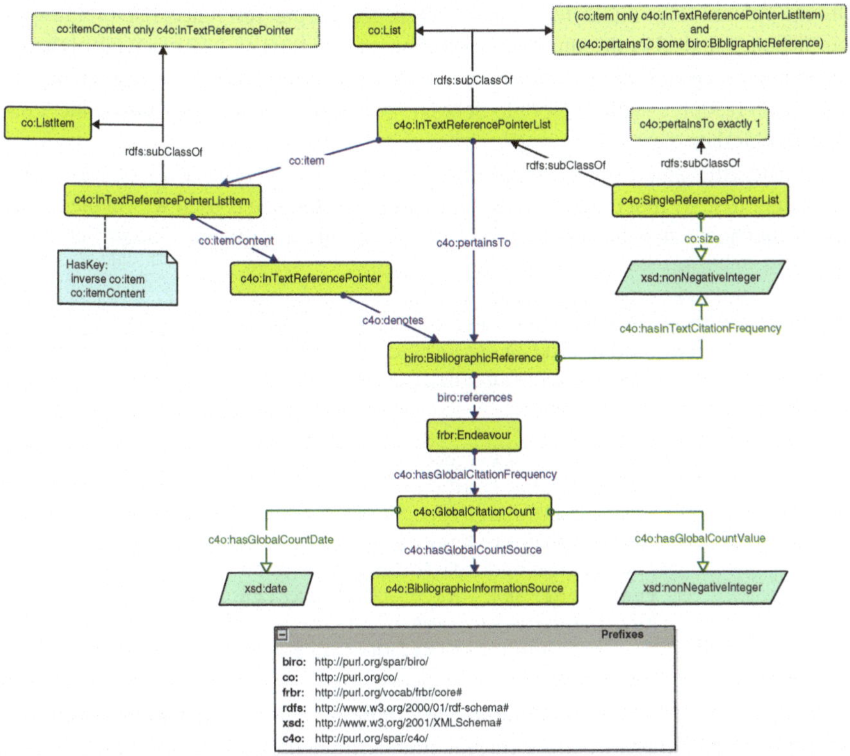

Fig. 5.6 Graffoo diagram summarising the C4O entities used for counting citations and references

- class *c4o:InTextReferencePointer*. An in-text reference pointer is a textual device denoting (property *c4o:denotes*) a single bibliographic reference that is embedded in the text of a document within the context of a particular sentence;
- class *c4o:InTextReferencePointerList*. A list containing (through the chain *co:item* and *co:itemContent*) only in-text reference pointers denoting the specific bibliographic references to which the list pertains (property *c4o:pertains*). Such a list cannot contain more than one item containing the same in-text reference pointer;
- class *c4o:SingleReferencePointerList*. Defined as subclass of the previous class, it is an in-text reference pointer list that pertains to exactly one bibliographic reference;
- class *c4o:GlobalCitationCount*. The number of times a work has been cited globally (property *c4o:hasGlobalCountValue*), as determined from a particular bibliographic information source (property *c4o:hasGlobalCountSource*) on a particular date (property *c4o:hasGlobalCountDate*).

C4O provides the ontological structures which allow one to record the number of in-text citations (property *c4o:hasInTextCitationFrequency*, i.e., the number of in-text reference pointers to a single reference in the reference list of the citing article), and also the number of citations a cited entity has received globally (property *c4o:hasGlobalCitationFrequency*), as determined by a bibliographic information resource such as Google Scholar[28], Scopus[29] or Web of Knowledge[30] on a particular date.

Considering again the example in Sect. 5.3.1, I can write a set of assertions according to C4O that describe how many times a reference is used within the citing article and how much the cited article is globally cited (according to Google Scholar):

```
:gruber95 a biro:BibliographicReference
  ; biro:references :principles-design-ontologies
  ; c4o:hasInTextCitationFrequency
    "1"^^xsd:nonNegativeInteger .

:principles-design-ontologies
   c4o:hasGlobalCitationFrequency [
   a c4o:GlobalCitationCount
  ; c4o:hasGlobalCountDate "2013-06-09"^^xsd:date
  ; c4o:hasGlobalCountSource [
    a c4o:BibliographicInformationSource
      ; foaf:homepage <http://scholar.google.com> ]
  ; c4o:hasGlobalCountValue
    "6559"^^xsd:nonNegativeInteger ] .
```

Moreover, C4O enables ontological descriptions of the context where an in-text reference pointer appears in the citing document (modelled as shown in Fig. 5.7), and allows one to relate that context to relevant textual passages in the cited document.

Considering the previous bibliographic reference example, a possible C4O formalisation of the contexts involved by that citing act is:

[28] Google Scholar: http://scholar.google.it.

[29] Scopus: http://www.info.sciverse.com/scopus/.

[30] Web of Knowledge: http://apps.isiknowledge.com.

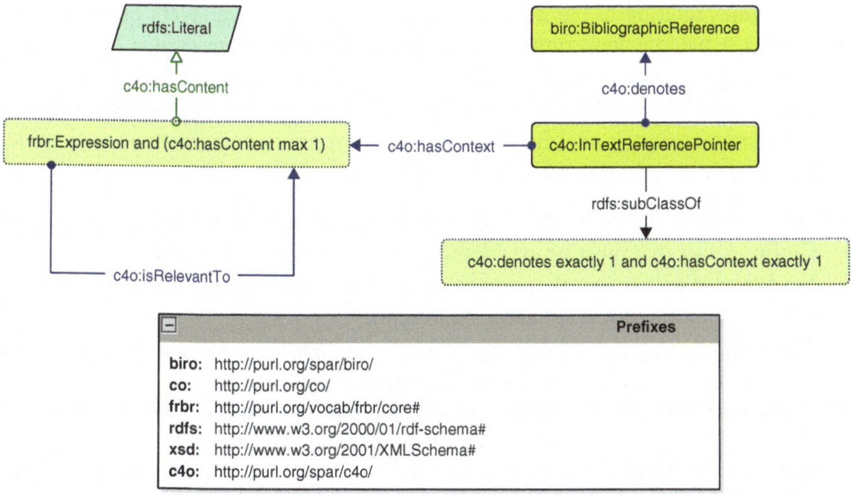

Fig. 5.7 Graffoo diagram summarising the C4O entities used for describing citation contexts

```
:version-of-record frbr:part :in-text-gruber95 .

:in-text-gruber95 a c4o:InTextReferencePointer
  ; c4o:denotes :gruber95
  ; c4o:hasContext :paragraph-in-version-of-record .

:paragraph-in-version-of-record a frbr:Expression
  ; c4o:hasContent "an ontology is defined as 'a shared
    specification of a conceptualization' (Gruber 1995)
    . Although 'shared' is an essential ..." .

:sentence-in-principles-design-ontologies a frbr:Expression

  ; frbr:partOf :principles-design-ontologies
  ; c4o:hasContent "An ontology is an explicit
    specification of a conceptualization."
  ; c4o:isRelevantTo :paragraph-in-version-of-record .
```

5.4 Characterising Document Parts with DoCO

A large amount of literature exists about models and theories for the description of structural, rhetorical and argumentative functions of texts through the adoption of Semantic Web technologies, as summarised in Schneider et al. (2011). The description of these different document layers is crucial for Semantic Publishing. As stated in De Waard (2010a), to improve substantially the users' comprehension of a document, a formalisation of the document *discourse* (e.g., the *scientific discourse* in scholarly articles) should be explicitly represented in machine-readable form within the document itself.

The issues relating to the rhetorical and the argumentative layers in documents have been debated a long time, e.g., Kircz (1991) and Groza et al. (2011), even in communities outside Computer Science, such as Philosophy and Publishing. For example, in his influential work (Toulmin 1959), the British philosopher Stephen Toulmin introduces a model for the explanation of arguments (including scientific arguments). In this model, each argument is composed of statements belonging to one of the following six roles:

- **Claim.** A fact that must be established–"This is a scientific article".
- **Evidence.** Another fact that represents a foundation for the claim–"The article has been submitted to a scientific conference".
- **Warrant.** A statement bridging from the evidence to the claim–"An article submitted to a scientific conference is a scientific article".
- **Backing (optional).** Credentials that certify the warrant–the Call for Papers of the particular conference where the article was submitted.
- **Rebuttal (optional).** Restrictions that may be applied to the claim–"Unless the conference reviewers reject it, judging it altogether non-scientific".
- **Qualifier (optional).** It asserts the degree of certainty in relation to the claim via words or phrases such as "certainly", "possible", "probably", etc.

Similarly, in the field of Publishing there exist specific constraints that authors have to follow when writing a paper. For example, some scientific journals, such as the Journal of Web Semantics[31], impose that their articles to follow a particular rhetorical segmentation, in order to identify explicitly what the meaningful parts are from a scientific point of view–e.g., *introduction, background, evaluation, materials, methods, conclusion*, etc. Although these parts usually (but do not necessarily) correspond to the structural parts of the article, i.e. the sections, they carry a specific semantics that characterises all the text they contain. From this perspective, this text means more than "being within a section".

During the development of the SPAR ontologies, these aspects were analysed in detail. Particularly, I studied carefully the previous works that had tried to address the description of structural and rhetorical components of a document. With regards to the rhetorical aspect, I found three models that dealt with document segmentation: the *Ontology of Rhetorical Blocks* (*ORB*) (Ciccarese and Groza 2011), the *SALT Rhetorical Ontology* (Groza et al. 2007a, 2007b) and the *Medium-Grained structure* (De Waard 2010b). The first and the second models offer a coarse-grained description (header, introduction, methods, claims, etc.) and, the third one, a medium-grained description (hypothesis, objects of study, direct representation of measurements, etc.) of the rhetorical components of a document.

Although all those models are currently in use, they do not deal satisfactorily with all the compositional aspects of a document. As well as not allowing the user to express all the rhetorical functions that SPAR needs, those models do not enable

[31] Journal of Web Semantics, Guide for Authors: http://www.elsevier.com/wps/find/journaldescription.cws_home/671322/authorinstructions.

rich descriptions of the document structure. One of the requirements of publishers is to have a model that enables the description of the several sub-parts of a document according to its structural components and their rhetorical characterisations. To this end, I developed the *Document Components Ontology*[32] (*DoCO*), which provides a structured vocabulary of document components. These components are structural (e.g., block, inline, container), rhetorical (e.g., introduction, discussion, acknowledgements, reference list, figure, appendix) and mixed (e.g., paragraph, section, chapter), and the ontology allows them, and the documents which are composed by them, to be described in RDF.

In particular, DoCO imports the *Patterns Ontology* presented in Sect. 3.3.2 and the *Discourse Elements Ontology*[33] (*DEO*) to describe, respectively, structural and rhetorical components of documents. Moreover, the latter ontology uses seven rhetorical block elements (*background*, *conclusion*, *contribution*, *discussion*, *evaluation*, *motivation* and *scenario*) abstracted from the *SALT Rhetorical Ontology*[34]. In the following subsections I will analyse in detail the structural and rhetorical functions which can be expressed through DoCO entities.

5.4.1 Building Blocks for Structuring Documents

A brief introduction to the theory of structural patterns for documents was illustrated in Sect. 3.3.2 and in the cited works (Dattolo et al. 2007; Di Iorio et al. 2005, 2012). In this section I will list the instanceable patterns again and give more precise definitions, using HTML examples[35].

The first patterns I will introduce are *milestone* and *meta*. They are defined as empty elements that can have zero or more attributes. In addition:

- The distinctive characteristic of the pattern *milestone* is the *position* that it assumes in the document. This pattern typically describes elements that change the aspect of a document, depending on where they are inserted. Moreover, this pattern is usually followed by elements that are used to define the actual content of a document. In HTML, the element *img* is a perfect example of this pattern.

---

[32] DoCO, the Document Components Ontology: http://purl.org/spar/doco. The prefix *doco* refers to entities defined in it.

[33] DEO, the Discourse Elements Ontology: http://purl.org/spar/deo. The prefix *deo* refers to entities defined in it.

[34] SRO, the SALT Rhetorical Ontology: http://salt.semanticauthoring.org/ontologies/sro.rdfs.

[35] Note that it is possible to create valid HTML documents that are not compliant with the presented structural pattern theory hereby presented. For that reason, in the examples that follow I will use HTML elements and consider their (informal) semantics as a strong requirement to make a *correct* document. Indeed, there are other markup formats that fit the structural pattern theory better than HTML, such as Akoma Ntoso (Barabucci et al. 2009). However, I have chosen to use HTML because it is a well-known and easily understandable markup format.

- The main feature of the pattern *meta* is its *existence*, independently from the position that it takes within the document. All the elements following this pattern are commonly used to define metadata which relate to the document itself or part of it, independently of where they are. In HTML, the elements *meta* and *link* are good examples that comply with this pattern.

The patterns *atom* and *field* define elements that can contain text only. In HTML, the element *title* (inside the element *head*) is an example of the pattern *field*, while there is no particular representative for the pattern *atom*.

The following HTML code summarises the patterns introduced so far:

```
<html>
  <head>
    <title>S.'s home</title>
    <link href="layout.css"
      rel="stylesheet" type="text/css" />
    <meta http-equiv="Content-Type"
      content="text/html; charset=UTF-8" />
  </head>
  <body>
    <img src="profile/thumbnail.jpg" />
  </body>
</html>
```

The next two patterns I am going to illustrate, i.e., *inline* and *block*, are followed by elements that are commonly used for the specification of the document content. They can both contain text and have the same content model that enable the definition of hierarchical structures: they can contain other *inline*, *atom* and *milestone* elements and items that comply with the pattern *popup*–which I will introduce further below. Elements which are compliant with the patterns *inline* and *block* differ for two aspects:

- Although inline elements can contain other inlines, block elements cannot contains other blocks.
- Inline elements cannot be used as root element of documents, but they must always be contained by block elements.

In HTML, there are many elements that comply with these two patterns. For example, *p* and *h1* follow the pattern block, while *em* and *a* comply with the pattern inline.

The pattern *container* concerns the structural organisation of a document. All the elements following this pattern do not contain any non-empty text. However, they can contain elements compliant with the following patterns: meta, atom, block and all the subtypes of container, but excluding popup.

While the content model of container elements (e.g., HTML *body*) is allowed to contain all optional and repeatable elements, particular restrictions are applied to the subtypes of the pattern container in terms of element repeatability. In particular:

- The pattern *table* contains homogeneous and repeatable elements. In HTML, elements that comply with this pattern are *ul* and *table*.
- The pattern *record* contains no repeatable elements (e.g., HTML element *html*).

- The pattern *headed container* contains always an header at the beginning that must be formed by block elements only. In HTML, the element *section* (when containing always an *h1* as first child) is a good example of this pattern.

Finally, the pattern *popup* is a particular structure that does not contain text and that can be contained by block and inline elements only. It is often used for the inclusion of complex quotations or other complex structures. In HTML, the element *math* is a primal example of this pattern.

The following HTML code summarises the set of patterns described above:

```
<html>
  <head><title>The formula</title></head>
  <body>
    <section>
      <h1>The <em>magic</em> mathematical formula</h1>
      <p>In this section I would like to introduce two
         things:</p>
      <ul>
        <li><p>the magic mathematical formula;</p></li>
        <li><p>the <a href="http://dev.w3.org/html5">
           website</a> that inspired me.</p></li>
      </ul>
      <p>And now the <em>magic</em> mathematical formula
         , that is
        <math>
          <mi>x</mi>
          <mo>=</mo>
          <mfrac>
            <mrow>
              <moform="prefix">-</mo>
                     <mi>3</mi>
                     <mo>*</mo>
                     <msqrt>
                       <msup>
                         <mi>y</mi>
                         <mn>2</mn>
                       </msup>
                     </msqrt>
                   </mrow>
                   <mrow>
                     <mn>2</mn>
                   </mrow>
                 </mfrac>
               </math>.
             Isn'titterrific?</p>
           </section>
         </body>
       </html>
```

The ontology introduced in Sect. 3.3.2 implements the whole theory I presented so far. As highlighted in that section, a document compliant with this theory results less ambiguous, more manageable and better-structured according to defined and shared principles of document engineering.

I have chosen to use this theory as one of the building blocks of DoCO (by importing the related ontology) for two reasons. On the one hand, it allows one to understand whether a document described in terms of DoCO entities is valid against the pattern theory, by simply checking whether the ABox which describes that document is consistent or not. On the other hand, by following specific and precise instructions, one can model a new document according to the pattern theory from scratch.

5.4.2 Mixing Rhetorical Characterisation and Structural Components

Documents such as a scientific research articles are characterised by precise rhetorical organisations, sometimes in a way that is in some measure independent from their structural components. As stated beforehand, there exist models—e.g., Ciccarese and Groza (2011), Groza et al. (2011), Groza et al. (2007a), Groza et al. (2007b), De Waard (2010b)–that try to describe rhetorical characterisations of documents from different perspectives. Although these ontologies can be used for the description of rhetorical aspects of documents, some of them do not link explicitly and correctly pure structural behaviours to rhetorical aspects. Probably, one of the principal causes of this deficiency should be attributed to the intrinsic complexity of defining some components as purely rhetorical or purely structural.

In order to clarify this point, let me consider as example a well-known document component: the *paragraph*. The structural behaviour of a document component can be described by the syntactic structures that it enables and not by relating it to its rhetoric nature. From this perspective, a paragraph cannot be considered a pure structural component–i.e., a component which carries only a syntactic function–since it carries *de facto* a meaning through its natural language sentences. Thus, paragraphs have more than a syntactic character. At the same time, the aforementioned models for the rhetorical characterisation of documents do not include the concept *paragraph* as part of them. Are thus paragraphs neither structural components nor rhetorical elements?

Of course, the truth must lie somewhere in between. Let me recall the two definitions that take an important part in this discussion. The definition of *rhetoric* as "the art of discourse, an art that aims to improve the facility of speakers or writers who attempt to inform, persuade, or motivate particular audiences in specific situations"[36], and the definition of *paragraph* as "a self-contained unit of a discourse in writing

[36] Wikipedia article "Rhetoric": http://en.wikipedia.org/wiki/Rhetoric.

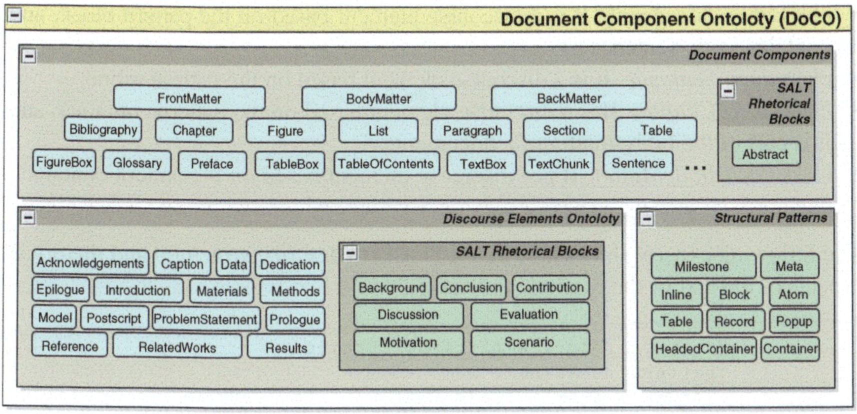

Fig. 5.8 Diagram describing the composition and the classes of the Document Components Ontology (*DoCO*)

dealing with a particular point or idea"[37]. From these definitions I can deduce that: the fact that a paragraph is a unit of *discourse* implies that it must have a rhetorical connotation, since the rhetoric is the art of *discourse*. Therefore, a textual fragment of a document is a paragraph when it is more than a mere syntactic structure: it should express some ideas and should carry some meanings.

On the other hand, document markup languages such as HTML and DocBook define a paragraph as a pure structural component, without any reference to its rhetoric function:

- "A paragraph is typically a run of phrasing content that forms a block of text with one or more sentences" (Berjon et al. 2013).
- "Paragraphs in DocBook may contain almost all inlines and most block elements" (Walsh 2010).[38]

Here the term "block of text" and the verb "contains" emphasise the structural connotation of the paragraph, which is amplified by our direct experience as readers. Our experience implicitly tells us that a particular textual fragment shown in a book or in an HTML page is a paragraph rather than a chapter or a table.

The *Document Components Ontology* (*DoCO*), shown in Fig. 5.8, has been developed to fill the gap between the pure structural characterisation of document elements and their the pure rhetorical connotation. Besides including the Pattern Ontology (describing structural components) and the Discourse Element Ontology (describing rhetorical components), DoCO defines also some other hybrid classes which describe elements that are structural and rhetorical at the same time. For instance:

[37] Wikipedia article "Paragraph": http://en.wikipedia.org/wiki/Paragraph.

[38] The words *inline* and *block* in these list items do not refer to the structural pattern theory introduced earlier, although some sort of overlapping exist.

- class *doco:Paragraph*. It is a discourse element based on the pattern block, and contains some sentences;
- class *doco:Sentence*. It is a discourse element based on the pattern inline;
- class *doco:Chapter*. It is a discourse element based on the pattern container, and it is part of the body-matter of a document;
- class *doco:BodyMatter*. It is a discourse element based on the pattern container, etc.

The following excerpt shows how to use DoCO to describe structural and rhetorical aspects of the text of the example in Sect. 5.3:

```
:version-of-record a pattern:Container
  ; pattern:contains
    :front-matter , :body-matter , :back-matter .

...

:body-matter a doco:BodyMatter
  ; pattern:contains :introduction , :related-works ,
    ...

:related-works a doco:Section , deo:RelatedWork
  ; pattern:contains :first-paragraph , ...
    , :paragraph-in-version-of-record , ...

:paragraph-in-version-of-record a doco:Paragraph
  ; pattern:contains :sentence1 , :sentence2, ...

:sentence1 a doco:Sentence
  ; pattern:contains :in-text-renear02 .

:in-text-renear02 a deo:Reference , pattern:Inline .

...

:back-matter a doco:BackMatter
  ; pattern:contains [ a doco:Section
    ; pattern:contains :reference-list ] .

:reference-list a doco:ListOfReferences
  ; pattern:contains
    :barwise83 ,:black37 ... , :renear02 , ...

:renear02 a
  deo:BibliographicReference , pattern:Inline .

...
```

Moreover, as shown for BiRO (Sect. 5.3.1.3) and as illustrated in Sect. 4.3, DoCO can be used in combination with LA-EARMARK to enhance the document markup with axioms related to its structural and rhetorical aspects.

5.5 In the Past you were it, Now you are not it

When modelling a domain, we often need to describe scenarios in which an *entity* has some *value* only within a specific temporal interval and/or contextual (e.g., social, cultural, physical) environment, and a different one (or none at all) otherwise. For instance, in the publishing domain, we may want to describe the *status* of a document at any given moment (e.g., *draft*, *under review*, *accepted*, *published*), the institution of which the author is a member, or the *role* held by different people in the publishing process. All these scenarios involve an *entity*, a *value* and, in particular, a *time* and a *context* within which the entity is associated to the value.

Most ontologies are unable to model such scenarios effectively, for different reasons. Three techniques in particular have been used in attempting to address this modelling issue–*class subsumptions*, *property links* and *inter-linked classes*, but each fell short in some aspect[39].

5.5.1 Using Class Subsumptions

To clarify this design technique and the issues that arise from it, let me consider the agent/role relations as described in the Portal Ontology[40] of the AKT Reference Ontology. This ontology defines the class *Student* as a person (class *portal:Person*) who studies at (property *portal:studies-at*) some institution (class *portal:EducationalOrganization*), as follows (in Turtle (Prud'hommeaux and Carothers 2013)):

```
portal:Student a owl:Class
  ; rdfs:subClassOf [ owl:intersectionOf (
    portal:Person
    [ a owl:Restriction
      ; owl:onProperty portal:studies-at
      ; owl:someValuesFrom
        portal:EducationalOrganization ] ) ] .
```

The fact of being a person is *time-independent*–Silvio Peroni is a living person while Kurt Vonnegut is a dead person, but we still describe both as persons. On the contrary, the fact of being a student is strictly *time-dependent*–Silvio Peroni was recently a graduate student, but he is one no longer.

[39] Contrarily to the paper used as examplar in the previous sections, i.e., Casanovas et al. (2007), here I have decided to use other two papers, i.e., Peroni et al. (2008) , which I co-authored. This is totally necessary because in Sects. 5.5 and 5.6 I will describe in detail how bibliographic entities and related resources are perceived over time. Thus, it is preferable to use a context I am well versed in rather than inventing possible (or even fake) scenarios related to Casanovas et al. (2007).

[40] Portal Ontology: http://www.aktors.org/ontology/portal. The prefix *portal* refers to entities defined in it.

Thus the subsumption model shows a clear design problem: a class having time-dependent characteristics, namely *portal:Student*, has been placed in the same *is-a* hierarchy (i.e., defined through a *rdfs:subClassOf* relation) as a class having time-independent characteristics, namely *portal:Person*. As suggested in Guarino and Welty (2002), which calls them respectively *anti-rigid* and *rigid* classes, I believe they should be part of two separated hierarchies, and I conclude that descriptions of time-dependant entities cannot be satisfactorily achieved using plain subsumption.

5.5.2 *Using Property Links*

A solution that takes into proper account anti-rigid characteristics is the use of a specific property for defining each time-dependent *value* that an entity has (e.g., the role of a person), while continuing to express the *entity* itself as an individual of a particular class (e.g., a document). Many ontologies for describing bibliographic resources, such as DCTerms (Dublin Core Metadata Initiative 2012) and BIBO (D'Arcus and Giasson 2009), use object properties to model this, linking the document to the persons who are its authors by the use of a specific property (namely, *dcterms:creator*and *bibo:authorList*, respectively), as shown here:

```
# Using DCTerms
:paper1 a dcterms:BibliographicResource
  ; dcterms:creator :peroni , :vitali .
:paper2 a dcterms:BibliographicResource
  ; dcterms:creator
    :peroni , :motta , :daquin .
# Using BIBO
:paper1 a bibo:Article
  ; bibo:authorList ( :peroni , :vitali ) .
:paper2 a bibo:Article
  ; bibo:authorList
    ( :peroni , :motta , :daquin ) .
```

This approach presents at least two problems. The first is that we need as many properties as there are roles. Thus if the requirements are not fully known in advance or change over time, the TBox of the ontology will require extensions to include new properties on a case-by-case basis, and will require continuous maintenance, with the increasing risk of inconsistencies. For instance, the number of roles in the publishing domain (author, editor, publisher, etc.) has been increasing in recent times (see, for example, the list of MARC relators[41] dated 7th December 2010), and the current technological and cultural evolution will surely lead to the creation of new ones (for instance, very soon now, that of *linked-data manager*).

Alternatively, one could use data properties rather than object properties. For instance, the W3C specification of the ontology for describing vCard objects in

[41] MARC Code List for Relators: http://www.loc.gov/marc/relators/relaterm.html.

RDF (Iannella 2013) prescribes the use of a (very general) data property, *vcard:role*, for an individual's roles. But while this allows easy extensions to the ontology by adding arbitrary literals to represent new roles, it also lacks a clear and well-defined vocabulary for existing ones, causing potential ambiguities (e.g., with the literals "Graduate student" and "Ph.D. student" being used to refer to the same role but being formally different within the model).

A second problem, that affects the scenario regardless of whether we use object properties or data properties, is the difficulty of discerning the context in which an *entity-value* association holds. For instance, consider an author having different institutional affiliations in the context of different publications (e.g., because he/she moved from one to the other). Using the *Semantic Web Conference Ontology*[42] (Moller et al. 2009), we can define affiliations for *:peroni* as follows:

```
:peroni swrc:affiliation :cs-unibo . # Paper 1
:cs-unibo a foaf:Organization
  ; dcterms:description
    "CS Dept., University of Bologna" .
:peroni swrc:affiliation :kmi . # Paper 2
:kmi a foaf:Organization
  ; dcterms:description
    "KMi, Open University" .
```

This specification, although straightforward, does not differentiate between associations. Namely, in OWL author *:peroni*, is associated indifferently to both *:cs-unibo* and *:kmi*, and it is not possible to determine the affiliation of an author within the context of a particular paper–e.g., "give me the institutional affiliation of the person *:peroni* as author of paper 2" (although in Masolo et al. (2004), Masolo et al. propose an approach to deal with this issue by using *qua-individuals*). Finally, the approach proposed in CIDOC CRM allows one to use the meta-property *P14.1 in the role of* Crofts et al. (2011) (a sub-property of property *P14 carried out by*) in order to specify the role that an agent has in the context of a particular event (such as being affiliated to an institution) through an instance of the class *E55 Type*. However, the official RDFS ontology of CIDOC CRM[43] does not implement any meta-property, and in practice RDF lacks the expressive power needed to define meta-properties.

5.5.3 *Using Inter-Linked Classes*

A different way to address the time-dependent association of entities to values is to consider both as classes (with no declared or inferable subsumption), and to link

---

[42] The Semantic Web Conference Ontology: http://data.semanticweb.org/ns/swc/ontology. The prefixes *swc* and *swrc* refer to entities defined in it.

[43] RDFS ontology of CIDOC CRM: http://www.cidoc-crm.org/rdfs/cidoc-crm-english-label.

them through object properties. For instance, the *Semantic Web Conference Ontology* (Moller et al. 2009) implements this method through two classes, *foaf:Person* and *swc:Role*, and the property *swc:holdsRole* linking them.

The extensibility of the ontology is thus guaranteed, reducing the possibility of undesirable inferential side effects. In fact, adding new roles simply involves adding new individuals to the class *swc:Role,* requiring no modification to the TBox. However, as before, this method is still unable to describe the context or time frame in which the person holds the particular role. For instance, Silvio Peroni was an undergraduate student at the University of Bologna between 2005 and 2008, a graduate student at the same university between 2009 and 2012, and also an intern at the University of Oxford in 2010

The SWC ontology, used together with FOAF (Brickley and Miller 2010), gives only a partial description of this, as shown by the following excerpt:

```
:undergraduateStudent a swc:Role .
:graduateStudent a swc:Role .
:intern a swc:Role .
:peroni a foaf:Person
  ; swc:holdsRole :undergraduateStudent
    , :graduateStudent , :intern .
```

This description cannot answer the question "Was *:peroni* a graduate student in 2008?", because it lacks information about time. By adding a specific model, such as the Time ontology[44] (Hobbs and Pan 2006), we manage to capture this information as follows:

```
:atTime a owl:ObjectPropery
  ; rdfs:domain swc:Role
  ; rdfs:range time:TemporalEntity .
:undergraduateStudent :atTime [
a time:TemporalEntity
; time:hasBeginning [ a time:Instant
  ; time:inDateTime [
  ; time:year "2005" ] ]
; time:hasEnd [ a time:Instant
  ; time:inDateTime [
  ; time:year "2008" ] ] ] . ...
```

The problem here is that the time-related information is associated to the roles, rather than to the person holding them. Being an undergraduate student is associated to the 2005–2008 time interval. This of course creates problems once we add another person with the same role, since it will become impossible to reuse the same role unless he/she also happens to have been an undergraduate in the same period. Things becomes even more complicated if we need also to describe the social or cultural *context* within which the agent-role relation holds, for example, by specifying in

[44] The Time Ontology: http://www.w3.org/2006/time. The prefix *time* refers to entities defined in it.

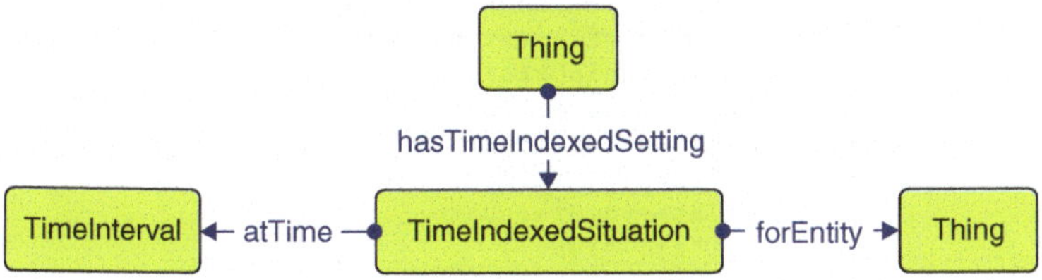

Fig. 5.9 A graphical representation of the *time-indexed situation* ontological pattern

which institution *:peroni* was an intern on a given date. It would require one to multiply the instances of role by the number of contexts and time intervals for which the different roles are relevant.

5.5.4 Using N-ary Class Modelling

Some ontological patterns that partially address these issues have been developed (Presutti and Gangemi 2008; Hayes and Welty 2006; Aranguren et al. 2008). For example, through the *time-indexed situation* pattern[45], shown in Fig. 5.9[46], it becomes possible to link a subject to a time-dependant description of a situation[47].

Using this pattern, the scenario presented in Sect. 5.5.3 can be defined as follows:

```
# University of Bologna
:unibo a foaf:Organization .
# University of Oxford
:oxac a foaf:Organization .
```

---

[45] Time-indexed situation pattern: http://ontologydesignpatterns.org/cp/owl/timeindexedsituation.owl. The prefixes *tisit*, *sit* and *ti* refer to entities defined in it.

[46] This and all the following graphical representations of ontologies are drawn using Graffoo, the Graphical Framework for OWL Ontologies, available at http://www.essepuntato.it/graffoo. *Yellow rectangles* represent classes (*solid border*) and restrictions (*dotted border*), *green parallelograms* represent datatypes, *arrows* starting out of a *filled circle* refer to object property definitions, *arrows* starting out of an *open circle* refer to data property definitions, while other arrows represent assertions between resources.

[47] In this context, a *situation* is defined as a view on a set of entities. It can be seen as a "relational context", reifying a relation.

```
:peroni tisit:hasTimeIndexedSetting
  :peroniAsGraduateStudentInUnibo
  , :peroniAsIndernInOxAc .
:peroniAsGraduateStudentInUnibo
  a tisit:TimeIndexedSituation
  ; tisit:atTime [ a ti:TimeInterval
    ; ti:hasIntervalStartDate
      "2009"^^xsd:gYear ]
  ; tisit:forEntity :unibo , :graduateStudent .
:peroniAsInternInOxAc a
  tisit:TimeIndexedSituation
  ; tisit:atTime [ a ti:TimeInterval
    ; ti:hasIntervalStartDate
      "2010-06"^^xsd:gYearMonth
    ; ti:hasIntervalEndDate
      "2010-12"^^xsd:gYearMonth ]
  ; tisit:forEntity :oxac , :intern .
```

Although this pattern correctly describes our scenario, it is still too abstract, both as a model and in terms of its terminology. In particular, the *tisit:forEntity* object property provides little or no guidance as to the interpretation of the relation with the entity. In fact, for instance in *:peroniAsInternInOxAc*, the way the various entities were involved in the situation is not clear, and we do not know what are the relations linking *:peroni*, *:oxac* and *:intern*. Given that, we could come to different conclusions just permuting the entities involved, e.g., a) the person *:peroni* was associated to the institution *:oxac* in a particular period, during which the latter had the role of *:intern* (definitely incorrect), or b) that the person *:peroni* worked for a particular period with somebody having the role of *:intern* within the institution *:oxac* (still incorrect), or c) that the person *:peroni* has the role *:intern* within the institution *:oxac* during a particular period (as intended, finally). Thus, using this pattern we would need to apply additional (unwarranted and "smart") steps to infer the correct interpretation of the situation.

To resolve this ambiguity, I decided to extend this pattern so as to specify the relations held by individuals in a situation involving a time-indexed value in a context.

5.5.5 A General Pattern for Roles and Statuses

What emerges from the preceding argument is the need for a model to describe time-dependant and contextualised entities. In particular, I identified four different items involved in these types of scenarios:

1. the *entity* having some value, e.g., a person or a document possessing a role or a status;
2. the *value* had by someone, e.g., a role or a status;
3. the *time period* during which the entity *has* that value, e.g., from April 2008 to September 2008;
4. the particular *context* that characterises the act of *having that value*, e.g., being a member of an institution or the editor of a particular journal.

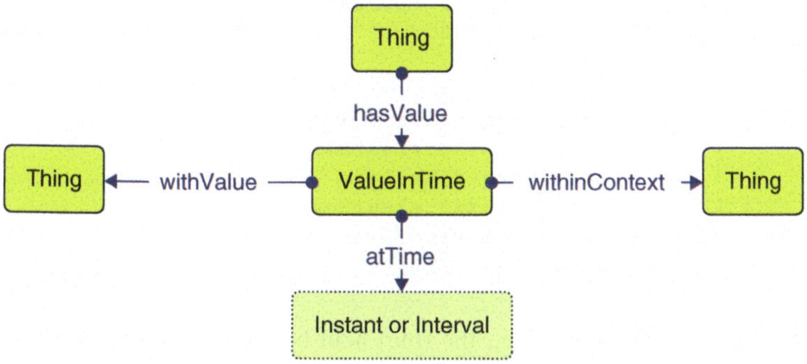

Fig. 5.10 The Graffoo diagram of the *time-indexed value in context* ontological pattern

In Sect. 5.5.4 I introduced a pattern that is able to describe this scenario at an abstract level but that it lacks a mechanism to describe the reciprocal relations of the entities involved. Using that as a starting point, we now wish to define a new ontological pattern called *time-indexed value in context* (*TVC*), summarised in Fig. 5.10 and available as an OWL ontology[48].

This pattern is composed by of different classes and four object properties:

- The class *ValueInTime* is a particular kind of time-indexed situation (i.e., a subclass of *tisit:TimeIndexedSituation*) as shown in Sect. 5.5.4 that represents a hub linking the *entity* having a particular value, the *value* itself and the *temporal and contextual extents* on which the entity-value relationship depends.
- The object property *hasValue* (sub-property of *tisit:hasTimeIndexedSetting*) links an entity (e.g., a Person) to a particular *ValueInTime* situation.
- The object property *withValue* (sub-property of *tisit:forEntity*) gives the value held by the entity taking part inthe situation.
- The classes *Instant* and *Interval* are used, respectively, to specify the particular temporal instant or time period in which the situation takes place. This is done through the object property *atTime*, which is not defined as a sub-property of *tisit:atTime* since it can be used to describe instants as well as intervals.
- The object property *withinContext* (sub-property of *tisit:forEntity*) links to the specific social, cultural or physical context within which the fact of the entityhaving the valueis relevant.

Using the TVC ontology, the *:peroniAsInternInOxAc*excerpt introduced in the previous section can be re-written as follows.

[48] *Time-indexed value in context* pattern: http://www.essepuntato.it/2012/04/tvc. The prefix *tvc* refers to entities defined in it.

```
:peroni tvc:hasValue :peroniAsInternInOxAC .
:peroniAsInternInOxAc
  a tvc:ValueInTime
  ; tvc:atTime [ a ti:TimeInterval
    ; ti:hasIntervalStartDate
      "2010-06"^^xsd:gYearMonth
    ; ti:hasIntervalEndDate
      "2010-12"^^xsd:gYearMonth ]
  ; tvc:withinContext :oxac
  ; tvc:withValue :intern .
```

where *:intern* is the value (i.e., the role) held by *:peroni* during that particular time period, and *:oxac* is the context. In the following sections I will expand these concepts, introducing use cases and explaining the benefits of using TVC.

5.5.5.1 Querying a TVC-Based Model via SPARQL

In principle, the TVC pattern allows a large number of SPARQL 1.1 queries (Garlik and Seaborne 2013) to return intuitively correct answers. In this section, I will discuss as examples three queries of increasing difficulty.

For instance, we can ask for all the values assigned to a person (e.g., the roles held by *:peroni*):

```
SELECT DISTINCT ?value WHERE {
  :peroni a foaf:Person
    ; tvc:hasValue/tvc:withValue ?value }
```

This query can be refined to consider, for instance, only those values that are defined in a particular context, e.g., the University of Bologna (entity *:unibo*):

```
SELECT DISTINCT ?value WHERE {
  :peroni a foaf:Person
    ; tvc:hasValue [ a tvc:ValueInTime
      ; tvc:withValue ?value
      ; tvc:withinContext :unibo ] }
```

This will return both the undergraduate and the graduate student roles of *:peroni*. We can further filter the previous results to return just those roles that are applicable at a particular date such as 24 August 2010:

```
SELECT DISTINCT ?value WHERE {
  :peroni a foaf:Person
    ; tvc:hasValue [ a tvc:ValueInTime
      ; tvc:withValue ?value
      ; tvc:withinContext :unibo
      ; tvc:atTime [ a ti:TimeInterval
        ; ti:hasIntervalStartDate ?start
        ; ti:hasIntervalEndDate ?end ] ]
  FILTER(
    xsd:dateTime(?start)
      <= "2010-08-24T00:00:00Z" &&
    xsd:dateTime(?end) > "2010-08-25T00:00:00Z"
  ) }
```

This will return just the role of graduate student. If the condition *tvc:withinContext:unibo* was omitted, the query would return both *:peroni*'s role as a graduate student at the University of Bologna, and his concurrent role on that date as an intern at the University of Oxford. More complicated and domain-specific queries are introduced in Sect. 5.5.6.

5.5.5.2 Reusing External Classes as Values

It is possible, by means of the meta-modelling features of OWL 2 (i.e., OWL punning), to define classes of external ontologies as objects of *tvc:withValue* assertions. In this way, we can use them interchangeably either as instances, when we want to associate them directly with some entity, or as classes when we want to understand hierarchical relationships between them. In addition to opening up the TVC ontology for reuse, this method may be very useful for inferring new data for specific categories, even when, in a query, we use their more abstract generalisations (i.e., superclasses).

Consider for example the following dataset defined according to TVC and including entities from the Portal Ontology:

```
:person1 tvc:hasValue [ a tvc:ValueInTime
  ; tvc:withValue portal:Affiliated-Person ] .
:person2 tvc:hasValue [ a tvc:ValueInTime
  ; tvc:withValue portal:Student ] .
:person3 tvc:hasValue [ a tvc:ValueInTime
  ; tvc:withValue portal: PhD-Student ] .
# Statements defined in the Portal Ontology
portal:Student rdfs:subClassOf
  portal:Affiliated-Person .
portal:PhD-Student rdfs:subClassOf
  portal:Student .
```

In this way, it is possible to query the dataset through SPARQL, asking for all the people affiliated with the University of Bologna (the entity *:unibo*), independently from the roles they may hold as a student, a Ph.D. student, or other subclass of *portal:Affiliated-Person*:

```
SELECT DISTINCT ?person WHERE {
  ?person tvc:hasValue [ a tvc:ValueInTime
    ; tvc:withValue ?aff
    ; tvc:withinContext :unibo ] .
  { SELECT ?aff WHERE {
    { ?aff a owl:Class .
      FILTER(?aff = portal:Affiliated-Person) }
            UNION
            { ?aff rdfs:subClassOf+
              portal:Affiliated-Person } } } }
```

TVC makes it possible and useful to reuse specific parts of other ontologies which describe categories in the form of classes, thus taking advantages of the OWL 2 punning.

5.5.5.3 Constructing Second-Order Inferences

Of course, it is sometimes desirable to reuse ontologies that specify categories (e.g., roles) through properties rather than classes, as introduced in Sect. 5.5.2. Consider, for example, BIBO (D'Arcus and Giasson 2009), that associates agent roles with documents through particular sub-properties (e.g., *bibo:translator*, *bibo:director*, *bibo:editor*) of the general property *dcterms:contributor*. Using the BIBO ontology with TVC, these object properties can be used as objects of *tvc:withValue* assertions, by means of OWL 2 punning. Moreover, it is possible to construct second-order inferences using the objects of *tvc:withValue* assertions as properties:

```
CONSTRUCT { ?doc ?property ?person } WHERE {
  ?person a foaf:Person
    ; tvc:hasValue [ a tvc:ValueInTime
      ; tvc:withValue ?property
      ; tvc:withinContext ?doc ]
  { SELECT ?property WHERE {
    { ?property a owl:ObjectProperty .
     FILTER(?aff = dcterms:contributor) } UNION
    { ?property rdfs:subPropertyOf+
      dcterms:contributor } } } }
```

Through a model that combines TVC and an ontology which defines categories as property links, such as BIBO, it becomes feasible to infer second-order logical statements. More generally, TVC can be used as an intermediate model for the conversion of entity-value relationships from one ontology into another, independent of the particular design technique used by each ontology (e.g., class subsumptions, property links, inter-linked classes or n-ary relationships).

5.5.6 *Identifying a Person's Roles with PRO*

The ability to define publishing roles in SPAR was crucial for the completeness of this suite of ontologies. The problems associated with the adoption of external ontologies to handle this particular requirement has been discussed above. None of those ontologies were able to satisfy the modelling requirements imposed by SPAR in full, in particular the need for an ease of *extendibility* and for the simultaneous representation of *time periods* and *contexts*.

Using TVC as the basis, I implemented *PRO*, the *Publishing Roles Ontology*[49]. This ontology, shown in Fig. 5.11, permits the characterisation of the roles of agents–people, corporate bodies and computational agents–in the publication process. Furthermore, it allows one to specify the role an agent has in relation to a particular bibliographic entity (as author, editor, reviewer, etc.) or to a specific institution (as publisher, librarian, etc.), and the period during which each role is held.

Using PRO and its TVC-compliant structure as illustrated in Table 5.2 on page 173, it is possible to describe all the scenarios discussed in Sects. 5.5.2 and 5.5.3, as follows:

[49] PRO, the Publishing Roles Ontology: http://purl.org/spar/pro. The prefix *pro* refers to entities defined in it.

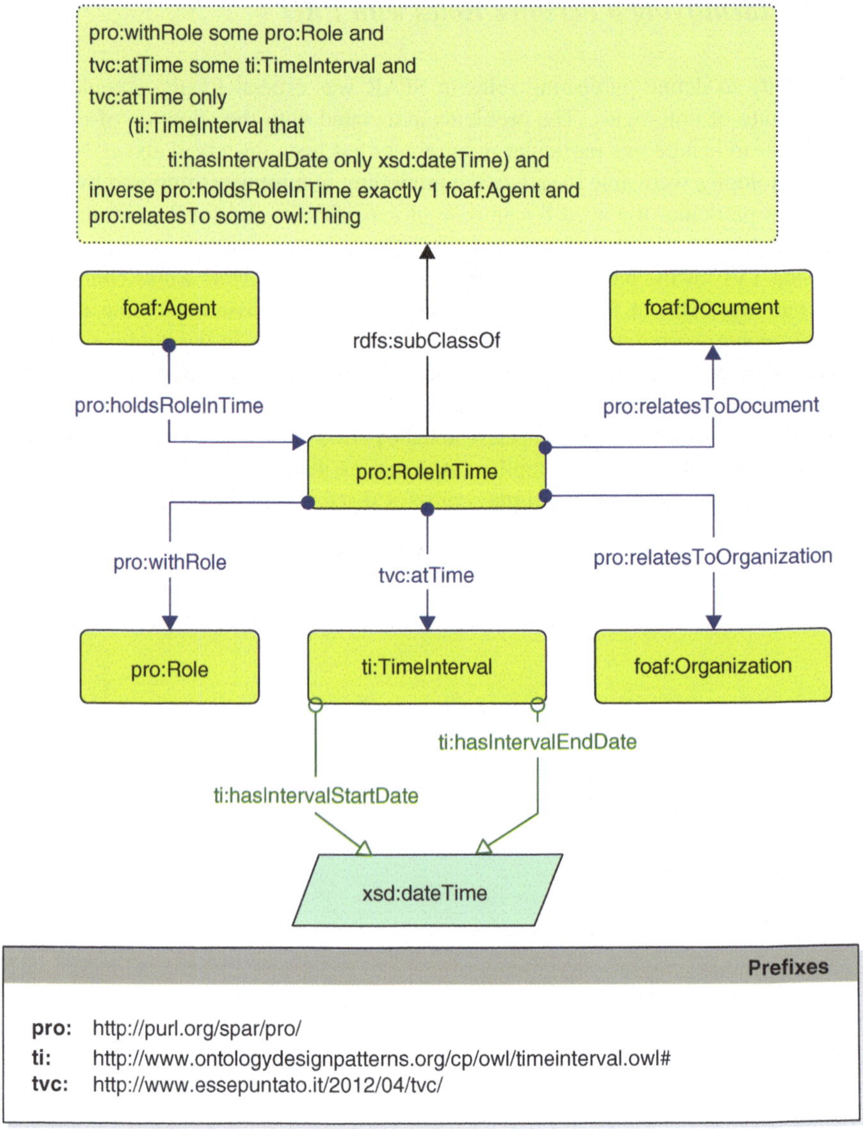

Fig. 5.11 Graffoo representation of the Publishing Roles Ontology (*PRO*)

Table 5.2 Alignments between TVC and PRO

TVC entity	PRO entity	Description
ValueInTime	RoleInTime	The class of the particular situation that describes the role an agent has within a particular time interval
hasValue	holdsRoleInTime	The object property linking any *foaf:Agent* (e.g., a person, a group, an organisation or a software agent), to a *pro:RoleInTime* situation
withValue	withRole	The object property linking the situation to the role the agent has. Currently, 31 roles are defined in the PRO ontology as individuals of the class *pro:Role*
Instant or Interval	TimeInterval	Two (starting and ending) points in time that define a particular period related to (object property *tvc:atTime*) a *pro:RoleInTime* situation
withinContext	relatesToDocument and relatesToOrganization	Object properties linking any kind of bibliographic work (*foaf:Document*) or publishing organisation (*foaf:Organization*) taking part in a *pro:RoleInTime* as contextual extent

```
:peroni pro:holdsRoleInTime
  # as author of two different papers
  [ a pro:RoleInTime
    ; pro:withRole pro:author
    ; pro:relatesToDocument
      :earmark-paper , :kce-paper ]
  # as affiliate of UniBo CS Dept
  , [ a pro:RoleInTime
    ; pro:withRole pro:affiliate
    ; pro:relatesToDocument :earmark-paper
    ; pro:relatesToOrganization :cs-unibo ]
  # as affiliate of OU KMi
  , [ a pro:RoleInTime
    ; pro:withRole pro:affiliate
    ; pro:relatesToDocument :kce-paper
    ; pro:relatesToOrganization :kmi ] .
```

As we can see, through PRO one can model very rich scenarios, and thus answer complex queries, such as the previously introduced "give me the institutional affiliation of the person *:peroni* as author of the paper *:earmark-paper*":

```
SELECT ?aff WHERE { :peroni pro:holdsRoleInTime
  [ a pro:RoleInTime ; pro:withRole pro:author
    ; pro:relatesToDocument :earmark-paper ]
     , [ a pro:RoleInTime
       ; pro:withRole pro:affiliate
       ; pro:relatesToDocument :earmark-paper
       ; pro:relatesToOrganization ?aff ] }
```

5.5.7 *Specifying Document Statuses with PSO*

The *status* of a document is the second subdomain of publishing handled in SPAR and based on the TVC pattern. In this case, the entity is a document holding a particular status at a certain time as a direct consequence of a particular event. For instance, a document is under review until all reviewers send in their comments and the editor decides whether to accept or reject the paper. After the acceptance/rejection decision is made, the status "under review" is no longer valid: this should be formally describable using an appropriate ontology. Moreover, it is sometimes useful to link documents to the decisions or events that cause the acquisition or loss of a particular status.

Preexisting ontologies describing the status of documents (e.g., BIBO (D'Arcus and Giasson 2009), the *Project Documents Ontology*[50] (Varma 2010) and the *Document Status Ontology*[51]), rely for this on specific property links. As discussed in Sect. 5.5.2, this approach prevents a proper description of scenarios that require a temporal duration for each status. With the exception of the Document Status Ontology, which describes status changes as events, the other ontologies do not allow time-dependent data, or can do so only partially.

In order to address these issues in a more satisfactory manner, I developed *PSO*, the *Publishing Status Ontology*[52]. This ontology (shown in Fig. 5.12) characterises the publication status of a document or any other publication entity at each of the different stages in the publishing process (e.g., draft, submitted, under review, rejected for publication, accepted for publication, version of record, peer reviewed, open access, etc.). As with PRO, PSO was developed following the TVC pattern, as shown in Table 5.3 on page 176. Using PSO, it is possible to describe the statuses of a document and how they change over time. For instance, consider the following description:

> The paper *:earmark-paper* was submitted to DocEng 2009 on 24 April 2009 at 13:18. At noon on 26 April, when the authors received acknowledgement of safe receipt of the paper from the conference editorial committee, the paper was considered "under review" until 27 May at 17:38.

PSO can be used to represent this description, as follows:

[50] Project Documents Ontology:http://ontologies.smile.deri.ie/pdo#.

[51] Document Status Ontology: http://ontologi.es/status#.

[52] PSO, the Publishing Status Ontology: http://purl.org/spar/pso. The prefix *pso* and *part* refer to entities defined in it.

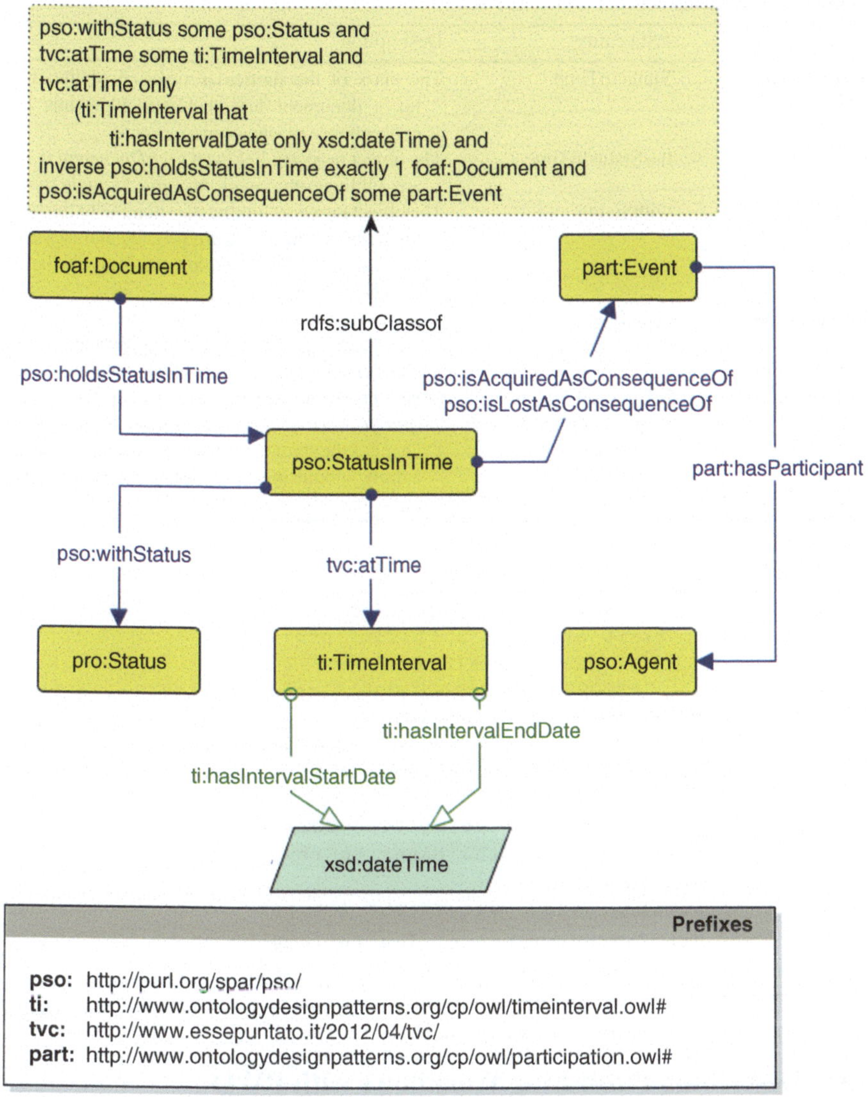

Fig. 5.12 Graffoo representation of the Publishing Status Ontology (*PSO*)

```
.earmark-paper
  pso:holdsStatusInTime [ a pso:StatusInTime
    ; pso:withStatus pso:submitted
    ; tisit:atTime [ a ti:TimeInterval
      ; ti:hasIntervalStartDate
        "2009-04-24T13:18:21Z"^^xsd:dateTime ]
    ; pso:isAcquiredAsConsequenceOf [
      a part:Event
      ; dcterms:description "An author
      submitted the paper through the online
      conference submission system."] ]
```

Table 5.3 Alignments between TVC and PSO

TVC entity	PSO entity	Description
ValueInTime	StatusInTime	The class of the particular situation of the status a document has at a particular time as consequence of one or more events.
hasValue	hasStatusInTime	The object property linking a *foaf:Document* (i.e., any bibliographic work) to a *pro:StatusInTime*.
withValue	withStatus	The object property linking the situation to the status a document has. Currently, 26 statuses are defined in the PSO ontology as individuals of the class *pro:Status*.
Instant or Interval	TimeInterval	Two (starting and ending) points in time that define a particular period related to (object property *tisit:atTime*) a *pso:StatusInTime* situation.
withinContext	isAcquiredAsConsequenceOf and isLostAsConsequenceOf	Object properties linking a situation to the events (*part:Event*) of any publishing process that changes the status of the document (e.g., writing a draft, submitting a preprint for publication, or publishing the final paper).

```
      , [ a pso:StatusInTime
        ; pso:withStatus pso:under-review
        ; tisit:atTime [ a ti:TimeInterval
          ; ti:hasIntervalStartDate
            "2009-04-26T12:00:00Z"^^xsd:dateTime
        ; ti:hasIntervalEndDate
          "2009-05-27T17:38:01Z"^^xsd:dateTime ]
      ; pso:isAcquiredAsConsequenceOf [
        a part:Event
        ; dcterms:description "The editorial
        committee sent the paper to reviewers for
        consideration." ]
      ; pso:isLostAsConsequenceOf [ a part:Event
      ; dcterms:description "The reviewers
        completed their reviews of the paper." ].
```

5.6 Describing Publishing Workflows with PWO

Keeping track of the publication processes is a crucial task for publishers. This activity allows them to produce statistics on their goods (e.g., books, authors, editors) and to understand whether and how their production changes over time. Organisers of particular events, such as academic conference, have similar needs. Tracking the number of submissions in the current edition of the conference, the number of accepted papers, the review process, and etc., are important statistics that can be used to improve the review process in future edition of the conference itself.

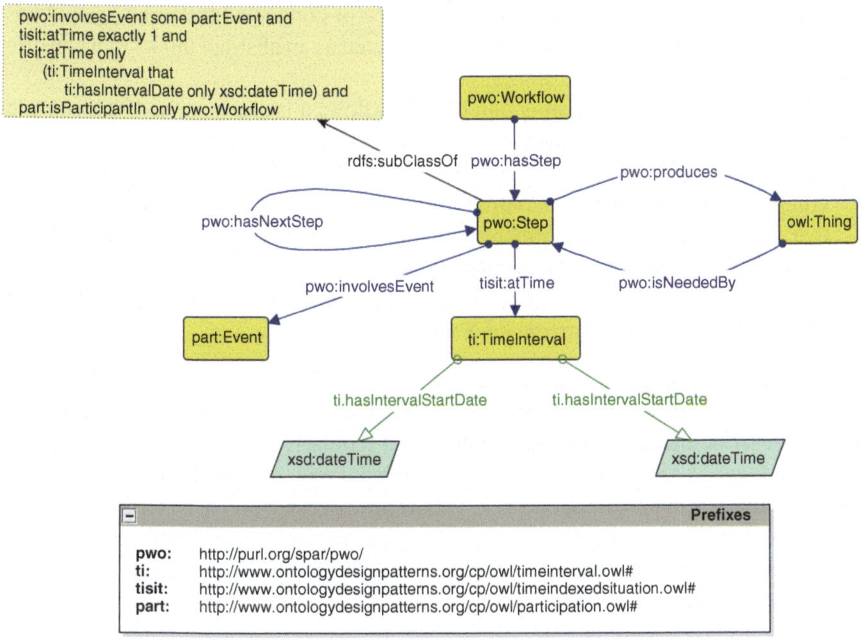

Fig. 5.13 Graffoo representation of the Publishing Workflow Ontology (*PWO*)

Some communities have started to publish[53] data which describes those events as RDF statements in the Linked Data, in order to allow software agents and applications to check and reason on them and to infer new information. However, the description of processes, for instance the peer-review process or the publishing process, is something that is not currently handled—although sources of related raw data exist. Furthermore, having these types of data publicly available would increase the transparency of the aforementioned processes and allow their use for statistical analysis. Of course, a model for describing these data is needed. Moreover, the model should be easy to integrate and adapt according to the needs and constraints of different domains (publishing, academic conferences, research funding, etc.).

In order to accommodate these requirements, I developed the *Publishing Workflow Ontology*[54] (*PWO*). This ontology allows one to describe the logical steps in a workflow, as for example the process of publication of a document. Each step may involve one or more events that take place to a particular phase of the workflow (e.g., authors are writing the article, the article is under review, reviewer suggests to revise the article, the article is in printing, the article has been published, etc.).

As shown in Fig. 5.13, PWO is based on two main classes, which are:

---

[53] Semantic Web Dog Food: http://data.semanticweb.org.

[54] PWO, the Publishing Workflow Ontology: http://purl.org/spar/pwo. The prefix *pwo* refers to entities defined in it.

- class *pwo:Workflow*. It represents a sequence of connected tasks (i.e., steps) undertaken by the agents. A workflow may be seen as an abstract model of a real-life work;
- class *pwo:Step*. It is an atomic unit of a workflow; it is characterised by a starting time and an ending time, and it is associated with one or more events. A workflow step usually involves some input information, material or energy needed to complete the step, and some output information, material or energy produced by that step. In the case of a publishing workflow, a step typically results in the creation of a publication entity, usually by the modification of another pre-existing publication entity, e.g., the creation of an edited paper from a rough draft, or of an HTML representation from an XML document.

In the following sections I introduce two example of application of PWO for the description of workflow processes in two different domain. First, in Sect. 5.6.1, I show how to describe the process of publication of a scholarly article and I also introduce the main features and ontological component that PWO includes for modelling these kinds of scenario. Then, in Sect. 5.6.2, I show how to use PWO to describe workflow scenarios that are not directly connected to the scholarly publishing domain, such as the description of the process of codification of statutes according to the United States legislation.

5.6.1 An Example of Workflow in Scholarly Publishing

The following excerpt presents the PWO description of the workflow which describes the publication of an article (i.e., the resource *:earmark-paper*) introduced in the example in Sect. 5.5:

```
:workflow a pwo:Workflow
  ; pwo:hasFirstStep :stepOne
  ; pwo:hasStep :stepTwo , :stepThree , :stepFour .

:stepOne a pwo:Step # Authors write the paper
  ; pwo:involvesEvent [ a part:Event
    ; dcterms:description "Authors write the paper" ]
  ; tisit:atTime [ a ti:TimeInterval
    ; ti:hasIntervalStartDate
      "2009-02-14T00:00:00Z"^^xsd:dateTime
    ; ti:hasIntervalEndDate
      "2009-03-25T00:00:00Z"^^xsd:dateTime ]
  ; pwo:produces :earmark-paper
  ; pwo:hasNextStep :stepTwo .

:stepTwo a pwo:Step # Paper submitted
  ; pwo:involvesEvent :author-submits-paper
  ; tisit:atTime [ a ti:TimeInterval
    ; ti:hasIntervalStartDate
      "2009-04-24T13:18:21Z"^^xsd:dateTime
    ; ti:hasIntervalEndDate
      "2009-04-24T13:18:21Z"^^xsd:dateTime ]
  ; pwo:needs :earmark-paper
  # New status in time for the paper
  ; pwo:produces :submitted
  ; pwo:hasNextStep :stepThree .

:stepThree a pwo:Step # Paper reviewed
  ; pwo:involvesEvent
    :reviewers-working , :reviewers-finish
  ; tisit:atTime [ a ti:TimeInterval
    ; ti:hasIntervalStartDate
      "2009-04-26T12:00:00Z"^^xsd:dateTime
    ; ti:hasIntervalEndDate
      "2009-05-26T12:00:00Z"^^xsd:dateTime ]
  ; pwo:needs :earmark-paper
  ; pwo:produces :review1 , :review2 , review3 .
  ; pwo:hasNextStep :stepFour .

:review1 a fabio:Comment # Review 1
  ; frbr:realizationOf [ a fabio:Review ]
  ; cito:reviews :earmark-paper
  ; pro:isDocumentContextFor [ a pro:RoleInTime
    ; pro:withRole pro:author
    # First anonymous reviewer
    ; pro:isRoleHeldBy [ a foaf:Person
      ; pro:hasRoleInTime [ a pro:RoleInTime
        ; pro:withRole pro:reviewer
        ; pro:relatesToDocument :earmark-paper ] ] .
```

```
:review2 a fabio:Comment ...

:stepFour a pwo:Step # Notification of acceptance
  ; pwo:involvesEvent
    :committee-accepts , :committee-notifies-to-authors
  ; tisit:atTime [ a ti:TimeInterval
    ; ti:hasIntervalStartDate
      "2009-04-26T12:00:00Z"^^xsd:dateTime
    ; ti:hasIntervalEndDate
      "2009-05-27T17:38:01Z"^^xsd:dateTime ]
  ; pwo:needs :review1 , :review2 , :review3
  ; pwo:produces
     :reviewed-and-accepted-for-publication
    , :acceptance-notification .

# The e-mail notifying the acceptance
:acceptance-notification a fabio:Email
  ; frbr:realizationOf [ a fabio:Opinion ]
  ; pro:isDocumentContextFor [ a pro:RoleInTime
    ; pro:withRole pro:author
    # The committee
    ; pro:isRoleHeldBy [ a foaf:Group ] .
```

PWO was implemented according to three particular ontology patterns:

- The *time-indexed situation pattern* (Gangemi 2010d) to describe workflow steps as entities that involve a duration and that are characterised by events and objects (needed for and produced by the step).
- The *sequence pattern*[55] (Gangemi 2010c) to define the order in which steps appear within a workflow.
- The *participation pattern*[56] (Gangemi 2010a) to describe events (and eventually agents involved) taking part in the steps.

In order to be consistent, PWO implements strong constraints on the steps by means of a particular model: the *Error Ontology*[57]. This ontology is a unit test that produces an inconsistent model if a particular (and incorrect) situation happens. It works by means of a data property, *error:hasError*, that denies its usage for any resource, as shown as below (in Manchester Syntax (Horridge and Patel-Schneider 2012)):

[55] The sequence pattern: http://www.ontologydesignpatterns.org/cp/owl/sequence.owl. The prefix *seq* refers to entities defined in it.

[56] The participation pattern: http://www.ontologydesignpatterns.org/cp/owl/participation.owl. The prefix *part*refers to entities defined in it.

[57] The Error Ontology: http://www.essepuntato.it/2009/10/error. The prefix *error* refers to entities defined in it.

```
DataProperty: error:hasError
  Domain: error:hasError exactly 0
  Range: xsd:string
```

A resource that asserts to have an error makes the ontology inconsistent, since its domain is defined as "all those resources that do not have any *error:hasError* assertion".

By means of the Error Ontology, I can generate an inconsistency every time the steps of a workflow are not arranged in a correct temporal order. In particular, an error is raised when a step requires (property *pwo:needs*) to use a particular object that will be produced (property *pwo:produces*) as consequence of another sequent step. The following excerpt shows the implementation of this constraint through a SWRL rule (Horrocks et al. 2004):

```
step(?step1) , step(?step2) ,
needs(?step1,?resource) ,
produces(?step2,?resource) ,
sequence:precedes(?step1,?step2)
  -> error:hasError(?step1,"A step cannot need a
        resource that will be produced by a following
        step"^^xsd:string)
```

5.6.2 *An Example of Workflow in the Legislative Domain*

Although PWO had been thought in principle to describe workflows related with the publishing domain, it has been developed on purpose as an ontology for the description of generic workflows. To this end, in this section I show how to use PWO to describe a workflow that concerns the process of codification of a particular law of the United States legislation, i.e. the codification of Title 51 of the United States Code, as described in an introductory webpage of the Office of the Law Revision Counsel[58].

The first step of such a workflow was the introduction of the codification bill "H.R. 3237" by the Office of the Law Revision Counsel on July 16, 2009. The result of the first step was the production of a first version of such bill, which was accompanied by an explicative document, the *bill explanation*, which documented the modifications that should be done on the Title 51 of the Code. The step is rendered through PWO as follows[59]:

[58] Positive law codification of title 51 of the United States Code: http://uscode.house.gov/codification/t51/index.html.

[59] The RDF representation of the agents involved in this and in the following examples are taken from DBpedia, where the prefix *dbpedia* stands for http://dbpedia.org/resource/.

```
:workflow a pwo:Workflow
  ; pwo:hasFirstStep :step-one .

# introduction of the codification bill
:step-one a pwo:Step
  ; pwo:involvesEvent [ a part:Event
    ; dcterms:description "Drafting the codification
       bill H.R. 3237"
    ; part:hasParticipant
       dbpedia:Office_of_the_Law_Revision_Counsel ]
  ; tisit:atTime [ a ti:TimeInterval
    ; ti:hasIntervalEndDate
      "2009-06-16T00:00:00Z"^^xsd:dateTime ]
  ; pwo:produces
    :hr-3237-bill-first-version , :hr-3237-explanation .

:hr-3237-bill a fabio:Work
  ; frbr:realization :hr-3237-bill-first-version .

:hr-3237-bill-first-version a fabio:Expression
  ; frbr:realizer dbpedia:
     Office_of_the_Law_Revision_Counsel .

:hr-3237-explanation a fabio:Expression
  ; frbr:realizer
     dbpedia:Office_of_the_Law_Revision_Counsel
  ; frbr:supplementOf :hr-3237-bill-first-version .
```

The second step of the process involved the Committee on the Judiciary of the House of Representatives, that referred the codification bill. In particular, the Committee considered the bill in full committee markup on October 21, 2009, and ordered the bill to be reported. The (amended version of the) bill was then reported by the Committee on November 2, 2009. The amended version of the bill was also accompanied by a written report based on the bill explanation produced in the previous step. The step is rendered through PWO as follows:

```
:workflow pwo:hasStep :step-two .

:step-one pwo:hasNextStep :step-two .

# the bill was reported by the C.J.H.
:step-two a pwo:Step
  ; pwo:involvesEvent :referring-bill-committee-judiciary-house
  ; tisit:atTime [ a ti:TimeInterval
    ; ti:hasIntervalStartDate
      "2009-10-21T00:00:00Z"^^xsd:dateTime
    ; ti:hasIntervalEndDate
      "2009-11-02T00:00:00Z"^^xsd:dateTime ]
  ; pwo:needs
    :hr-3237-bill-first-version , :hr-3237-explanation
  ; pwo:produces
    :hr-3237-bill-amended , :hr-3237-report-document ,
    :hr-3237-bill-reported-by-committee-judiciary-house .

:referring-bill-committee-judiciary-house a part:Event
  ; dcterms:description
    "Referring the codification bill H.R. 3237"
  ; part:hasParticipant
    dbpedia:
      United_States_House_Committee_on_the_Judiciary .

:hr-3237-bill-amended a fabio:Expression
  ; frbr:realizationOf :hr-3237-bill
  ; frbr:realizer
    dbpedia:
      United_States_House_Committee on the Judiciary
  ; frbr:revisionOf :hr-3237-bill-first-version
  ; pso:holdsStatusInTime
    :hr-3237-bill-reported-by-committee-judiciary-house .

:hr-3237-report-document a fabio:ReportDocument
  ; frbr:realizer dbpedia:
     United_States_House_Committee_on_the_Judiciary
  ; frbr:adaptionOf :hr-3237-explanation
  ; frbr:supplementOf :hr-3237-bill-amended .

:hr-3237-bill-reported-by-committee-judiciary-house
    a pso:StatusInTime
  ; pwo:withStatus :reported
  ; tvc:atTime [ a ti:TimeInterval
    ; ti:hasIntervalStartDate
      "2009-11-02T00:00:00Z"^^xsd:dateTime ]
  ; pso:isAcquiredAsConsequenceOf
    :referring-bill-committee-judiciary-house .

:reported a pso:Status .
```

In third step of the process, the bill was passed by the House of Representatives on January 13, 2010. On January 20, 2010, the bill was received by the Senate and referred to the Committee on the Judiciary of the Senate. The Committee considered the bill in full committee markup on May 6, 2010, and ordered the bill to be reported. The bill was reported by the Committee on May 10, 2010. The step is rendered through PWO as follows:

```
:workflow pwo:hasStep :step-three .

:step-two pwo:hasNextStep :step-three .

# the bill was reported by the C.J.S.
:step-three a pwo:Step
  ; pwo:involvesEvent
    [ a part:Event
      ; dcterms:description "Passing the codification
         bill H.R. 3237 by the House of Representatives"
      ; part:hasParticipant
        dbpedia:United_States_House_of_Representatives ] ,
    [ a part:Event
      ; dcterms:description "Receiving the codification
         bill H.R. 3237"
      ; part:hasParticipant dbpedia:United_States_Senate ] ,
    :referring-bill-committee-judiciary-senate
  ; tisit:atTime [ a ti:TimeInterval
    ; ti:hasIntervalStartDate
      "2010-01-13T00:00:00Z"^^xsd:dateTime
    ; ti:hasIntervalEndDate
      "2010-05-10T00:00:00Z"^^xsd:dateTime ]
  ; pwo:needs
    :hr-3237-bill-amended , :hr-3237-report ,
    :hr-3237-status-reported-by-committee-judiciary-
       house
  ; pwo:produces
    :hr-3237-status-reported-by-committee-judiciary-
       senate .

:referring-bill-committee-judiciary-senate a part:Event
  ; dcterms:description "Referring the codification bill
     H.R. 3237"
  ; part:hasParticipant
    dbpedia:
       United_States_Senate_Committee_on_the_Judiciary .

:hr-3237-bill-reported-by-committee-judiciary-senate
    a pso:StatusInTime
  ; pwo:withStatus :reported
  ; tvc:atTime [ a ti:TimeInterval
    ; ti:hasIntervalStartDate
      "2010-05-10T00:00:00Z"^^xsd:dateTime ]
  ; pso:isAcquiredAsConsequenceOf
    :referring-bill-committee-judiciary-senate .
```

Finally, in the latest step of the process, the bill was passed by the Senate on December 3, 2010. On December 18, 2010, the bill became Public Law 111–314, which was codified in Title 51 of the United States Code.

```
:workflow pwo:hasStep :step-four .

:step-three pwo:hasNextStep :step-four .

# the bill became Public Law 111-314
:step-four a pwo:Step
  ; pwo:involvesEvent
    [ a part:Event
      ; dcterms:description "Passing the codification
        bill H.R. 3237 by the Senate"
    ; part:hasParticipant dbpedia:United_States_Senate ]
; tisit:atTime [ a ti:TimeInterval
  ; ti:hasIntervalStartDate
    "2010-12-03T00:00:00Z"^^xsd:dateTime
  ; ti:hasIntervalEndDate
    "2010-12-18T00:00:00Z"^^xsd:dateTime ]
; pwo:needs
  :hr-3237-bill-amended ,
  :hr-3237-status-reported-by-committee-judiciary-
     senate
; pwo:produces
  :public-law-111-314 ,
  :title-51-enacted-by-public-law-111-314 .

:public-law-111-314 a fabio:Work ;
  frbr:adaptationOf :hr-3237-bill ;
  frbr:realization [ a fabio:Expression
    ; cito:providesExcerptFor
      :title-51-enacted-by-public-law-111-314 ] .

:title-51 a fabio:Work ;
  frbr:realization
    :title-51-negative-law ,
    :title-51-enacted-by-public-law-111-314 .

:title-51-enacted-by-public-law-111-314
  a fabio:Expression
  ; frbr:revisionOf :title-51-negative-law .
```

The aim of this section was twofold. On the one hand, the above excerpts have provided a running example of the use of PWO to describe processes of codification of laws of US legislation. On the other hand, as promised in Sect. 2.3.5, the excerpts have also showed how FRBR can be used in the context of the legislative process of the federal legislation of the United States.

5.7 How Communities Uptake SPAR

The SPAR ontologies are now being used or are under consideration in a variety of academic and publishing environments. The adoption of these models by different communities can be ascribed, at least in part, to the fact that we have adopted the following strategies during the development of the ontologies:

- Frequent and ongoing interactions between the authors of SPAR, and publishers, service developers and other end-users, that have allowed us to understand their various needs and interests.
- The minimisation of the constraints applied to the ontological entities, so that the ontologies can be applied in a wide variety of situations.

The following sections will briefly describe how SPAR ontologies are now being used in various communities.

5.7.1 SWAN Ontology

The most recent version (v2.0) of the *SWAN ontology ecosystem* (Ciccarese et al. 2008), introduced above in Sect. 2.3.7, has recently been harmonised to include FaBiO and it now works seamlessly with CiTO (Ciccarese et al. 2011). David Shotton and I undertook this harmonisation collaboratively, while developing version 1.6 of CiTO (Shotton 2010) into CiTO v2.0 and FaBiO v1.0, and by Paolo Ciccarese and Tim Clark (Harvard University), authors of the SWAN Ontologies. The resulting CiTO/FaBiO + SWAN model is specified in OWL 2 DL, it is fully modular, and it inherently supports agent-based searching and mash-ups.

The principles adopted for its activity, which resulted in the harmonisation described in Fig. 5.14, involved:

- The renaming of classes (concepts) or properties (relationships) in one or both set of ontologies to avoid any apparent overlap.
- The re-definition of classes or properties to resolve actual overlap between concepts.
- The deprecation of elements of individual ontologies, or even whole ontologies, in favour of others that would more effectively serve the domain of knowledge under consideration, having greater granularity or a more effective structure.

In summary, the SWAN Citations ontology module was deprecated in favour of FaBiO, certain classes in the SWAN Discourse Relationship were renamed and redefined, the property *discourse-relationships:cites* in that module was deprecated, and CiTO was linked to that module by making *cito:cites* a sub-property of *discourse-relationships:refersTo.*Full details are given in Ciccarese et al. (2011).

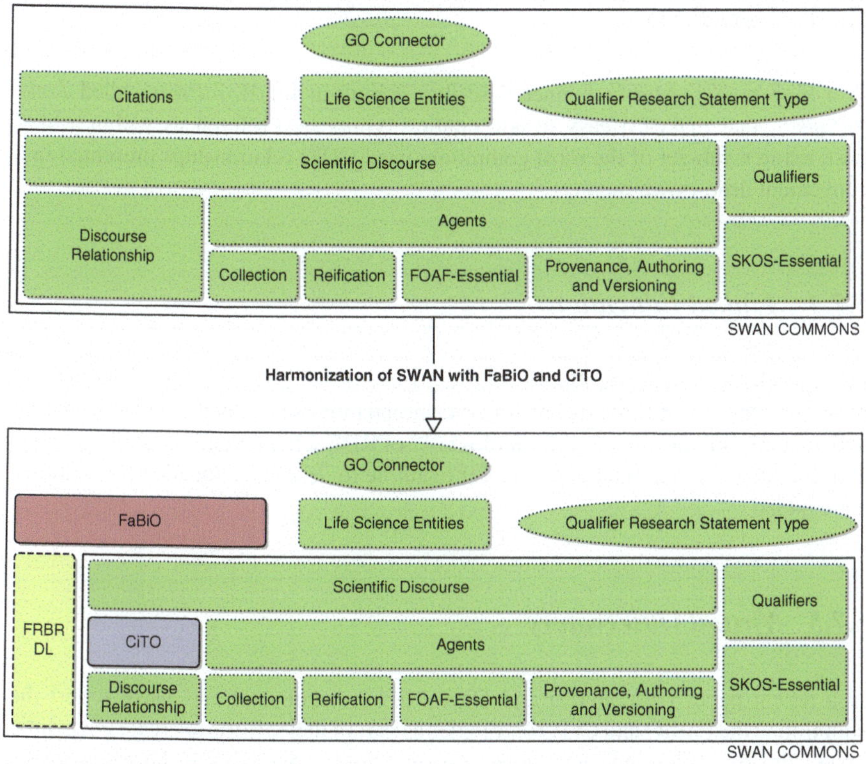

Fig. 5.14 The SWAN ontology ecosystem before (*above*) and after (*below*) the harmonisation activity that resulted in the inclusion of FaBiO and CiTO in the SWAN Commons set of ontologies

5.7.2 CiteULike

Egon Willighagen of Uppsala University has pioneered the use of CiTO[60] to characterise bibliographic citations within *CiteULike*[61], the free service for managing and discovering scholarly references. A user can add a CiTO relationship between articles via the CiteULike interface, provided that both the citing and the cited articles are in the user's library.

[60] http://chem-bla-ics.blogspot.com/2010/10/citeulike-cito-use-case-1-wordles.html.

[61] CiteULike: http://www.citeulike.org/.

5.7.3 WordPress

In a blog post[62], Martin Fenner describes a plug-in for *WordPress* called *Link-to-Link*[63], that makes it easy to add citation typing into references within a blog post, using a sub-set of the most commonly used CiTO relationships presented in a convenient drop-down menu.

5.7.4 Linked Education

Few months ago, the open platform *Linked Education*[64], which aims at sharing and promoting the use of Linked Data for educational purposes, added CiTO to its listing and, recently, all the other SPAR ontologies[65] of RDF schemas and vocabularies suitable for use in educational contexts, for example to describe educational resources, were added.

5.7.5 Virtual Observatory

In a recent paper (Accomazzi and Dave 2011), Accomazzi and Dave report the adoption of the FaBiO and CiTO ontologies as part of their efforts to create a semantic knowledge base allowing easier integration and linking of the body of heterogeneous astronomical resources into what they term a Virtual Observatory.

5.7.6 Open Citations Corpus

The Open Citations Corpus[66] is a database of approximately 6.3 million biomedical literature citations, harvested from the reference lists of all open access articles in PubMed Central. These contain references to approx. 3.4 million papers, which represent ~20 % of all PubMed-listed papers published between 1950 and 2010, including all of the most highly cited papers in every biomedical field. The Open

[62] Blog post by Martin Fenner entitled "How to use citation typing ontology (CiTO) in your blog post": http://blogs.plos.org/mfenner/2011/02/14/how-to-use-citation-typing-ontology-cito-in-your-blog-posts/.

[63] Link to link: http://wordpress.org/extend/plugins/link-to-link/.

[64] Linked Education: http://linkededucation.org/.

[65] Linked Education–Schemas and vocabularies: http://linkededucation.wordpress.com/data-models/schemas/.

[66] The Open Citations Corpus: http://opencitations.net/.

Citations Corpus website allows one to browse these bibliographic records and citations, to select an individual article, and to visualise its citation network in a variety of displays. Details of each selected reference, and the data and diagrams for its citation network, may be downloaded in a variety of formats, while the entire Open Citations Corpus can be downloaded in several formats including RDF and BibJSON. SPAR ontologies have been used to encode this information in RDF. Further information is given on the Open Citations Blog[67].

5.7.7 WebTracks

WebTracks[68] is an open source project funded by the JISC Managing Research Data Programme[69] that is developing a peer-to-peer protocol to enable web-scale link tracking.

Established techniques such as OAI-PMH and the emerging Linked Web of Data provide tools to publish data for linking. WebTracks focuses on actually making these connections, particularly between research datasets and related publications. It provides a mechanism for informing the target of a hyperlink that a link has been made to that target, so that it can reciprocally link back–for example, by including the correct DOI of a published paper in the metadata of a previously published dataset to which the paper refers. WebTracks creates semantically annotated links between data resources using CiTO, yielding a graph of citation and provenance to enable web-scaled data management by exposing links between related objects.

5.7.8 Società editrice il Mulino

The Italian scholarly publishing house *Società editrice il Mulino*[70] is collaborating with the Department of Computer Science of the University of Bologna, to explore how best to benefit from Semantic Web technologies can be used for the digital publication and sharing of bibliographic objects such as books and articles, and their related metadata.

This has led to the recent prototyping of an application called *Folksauro* (the name comes from the concatenation of the words *folksonomy* and *thesaurus*). Using FaBiO and DoCO as its main ontologies, and one or more discipline-specific thesauri developed in SKOS, Folksauro allows a user to associate terms from the thesauri and/or

[67] The Open Citations Blog: http://opencitations.wordpress.com/.

[68] WebTracks: http://webtracks.jiscinvolve.org/wp/about/.

[69] JISC Managing Research Data Programme: http://www.jisc.ac.uk/whatwedo/programmes/mrd.aspx.

[70] Il Mulino: http://www.mulino.it.

free-text keywords with the whole document, and/or with its sub-parts (chapters, sections, paragraphs, etc.), by means of an intuitive interface that hides the complexity of models and languages used.

5.7.9 Utopia

Utopia Documents[71] (Attwood et al. 2010) is a novel PDF reader that semantically integrates visualisation and data-analysis tools with published research articles. It brings PDF documents to life by linking to live resources on the web and by turning static data into live interactive content, and is now being regularly used by the editors of the Biochemical Journal[72] to transform static document features into objects that can be linked, annotated, visualised and analysed interactively.

Utopia has a mechanism that deconstructs a PDF document into its constituent parts, which are then annotated using DoCO. This is useful for a number of reasons: generating bibliometric metadata; improving "mouse selection" in multi-column documents; and identifying the correct flow of text in the document, by allowing intruding text such as running headers, footers and captions to be excluded. This in turn is useful for text and data mining algorithms, which can now be targeted, for example, at "all the main text excluding intruders" or "just the text in the figure captions". Recently, the Utopia team has released a free web service, called PDFX[73], that takes a PDF document, deconstructs it, and returns DoCO-annotated XML.

In addition, the Utopia team is currently developing an Open Citations plugin that pulls bibliographic citation data live from the Open Citations Corpus and uses it to display the citation network for the paper manifested by the PDF, or for any of the articles references in the paper's reference list.

References

Accomazzi, A., and R. Dave. 2011. Semantic interlinking of resources in the virtual observatory era. ArXiv:1103.5958. http://arxiv.org/pdf/1103.5958. Accessed 30 July 2013.

Aranguren, M. E., E. Antezana, M. Kuiper, and R. Stevens. 2008. Ontology design patterns for bio-ontologies: A case study on the cell cycle ontology. *BMC Bioinformatics* 9 (5): S1. (London, United Kingdom: BioMed Central). doi:10.1186/1471-2105-9-S5-S1.

Attwood, T. K., D. B. Kell, P. McDermott, J. Marsh, S. R. Pettifer, and D. Thorne. 2010. Utopia documents: Linking scholarly literature with research data. *Bioinformatics* 26 (18): 568–574. doi:10.1093/bioinformatics/btq383.

Barabucci, G., L. Cervone, M. Palmirani, S. Peroni, and F. Vitali. 2009. Multi-layer markup and ontological structures in Akoma Ntoso. In Proceeding of the international workshop on

[71] Utopia Documents: http://getutopia.com.

[72] http://www.biochemj.org/bj/424/3/.

[73] PDFX: http://pdfx.cs.man.ac.uk.

AI Approaches to the Complexity of Legal Systems II (AICOL-II), lecture notes in computer science 6237, ed. P. Casanovas, U. Pagallo, G. Sartor, and G. Ajani, 133–149. Berlin: Springer. doi:10.1007/978-3-642-16524-5_9.

Berjon, R., T. Leithead, E. D. Navara, E. O'Connor, and S. Pfeiffer. 2013. HTML5: A vocabulary and associated APIs for HTML and XHTML. W3C candidate recommendation 6 August 2013. World Wide Web Consortium. http://www.w3.org/TR/html5/. Accessed 30 July 2013.

Bojars, U., and J. G. Breslin. 2010. SIOC core ontology specification. 25 March 2010. http://rdfs.org/sioc/spec/. Accessed 30 July 2013.

Brickley, D., and L. Miller. 2010. FOAF vocabulary specification 0.98. Namespace document, 9 August 2010-Marco Polo Edition. http://xmlns.com/foaf/spec/. Accessed 30 July 2013.

Casanovas, P., N. Casellas, C. Tempich, D. Vrandecic, and R. Benjamins. 2007. OPJK and DILIGENT: Ontology modeling in a distributed environment. *Artificial Intelligence and Law* 15 (2): 171–186. doi:10.1007/s10506-007-9036-2.

Ciccarese, P., and T. Groza. 2011. Ontology of Rhetorical Blocks (ORB). Editor's draft, 5 June 2011. World Wide Web Consortium. http://www.w3.org/2001/sw/hcls/notes/orb/. Accessed 30 July 2013.

Ciccarese, P., and S. Peroni. 2013. The collections ontology: Creating and handling collections in OWL 2 DL frameworks. To appear in *Semantic Web–Interoperability, Usability, Applicability*. doi:10.3233/SW-130121.

Ciccarese, P., E. Wu, J. Kinoshita, G. Wong, M. Ocana, A. Ruttenberg, and T. Clark. 2008. The SWAN biomedical discourse ontology. *Journal of Biomedical Informatics* 41 (5): 739–751. doi:10.1016/j.jbi.2008.04.010.

Ciccarese, P., D. Shotton, S. Peroni, and T. Clark. 2011. CiTO + SWAN: The web semantics of bibliographic records, citations, evidence and discourse relationships. To appear in *Semantic Web–Interoperability, Usability, Applicability*. doi:10.3233/SW-130098.

Cimiano, P., and J. Volker. 2005. Text2Onto—A framework for ontology learning and data-driven change discovery. In Proceedings of the 10th international conference on applications of natural language to information systems (NLDB05), lecture notes in computer science 3513, ed. A. Montoyo, R. Munoz, and E. Metais, 227–238. Berlin: Springer. doi:10.1007/11428817_21.

Crofts, N., M. Doerr, T. Gill, S. Stead, and M. Stiff. 2011. Definition of the CIDOC conceptual reference model. Version 5.0.4, November 2011. ICOM/CIDOC CRM special interest group. http://www.cidoc-crm.org/docs/cidoc_crm_version_5.0.4.pdf. Accessed 30 July 2013.

D'Arcus, B., and F. Giasson. 2009. Bibliographic ontology specification. Specification document, 4 November 2009. http://bibliontology.com/specification. Accessed 30 July 2013.

Dattolo, A., A. Di Iorio, S. Duca, A. A. Feliziani, and F. Vitali. 2007. Structural patterns for descriptive documents. In Proceedings of the 7th international conference on web engineering 2007 (ICWE 2007), lecture notes in computer science 4607, ed. L. Baresi, P. Fraternali, and G. Houben, 421–426. Berlin: Springer. doi:10.1007/978-3-540-73597-7_35.

De Waard, A. 2010a. From proteins to fairytales: Directions in semantic publishing. *IEEE Intelligent Systems* 25 (2): 83–88. doi:10.1109/MIS.2010.49.

De Waard, A. 2010b. Medium-grained document structure. http://www.w3.org/wiki/HCLSIG/SWANSIOC/Actions/RhetoricalStructure/models/medium. Accessed 30 July 2013.

Di Iorio, A., D. Gubellini, and F. Vitali. 2005. Design patterns for document substructures. Proceedings of the extreme markup languages 2005. Rockville: Mulberry Technologies, Inc. http://conferences.idealliance.org/extreme/html/2005/Vitali01/EML2005Vitali01.html. Accessed 30 July 2013.

Di Iorio, A., S. Peroni, F. Poggi, and F. Vitali. 2012. A first approach to the automatic recognition of structural patterns in XML documents. Proceedings of the 2012 ACM symposium on Document Engineering (DocEng 2012), 85–94. New York: ACM. doi:10.1145/2361354.2361374.

Dublin Core Metadata Initiative. 2012. DCMI metadata terms. DCMI recommendation. http://dublincore.org/documents/dcmi-terms/. Accessed 30 July 2013.

Gangemi, A. 2010a. Submission: Participation. http://ontologydesignpatterns.org/wiki/Submissions:Participation. Accessed 30 July 2013.

Gangemi, A. 2010b. Submission: Region. http://ontologydesignpatterns.org/wiki/Submissions:Region. Accessed 30 July 2013.

Gangemi, A. 2010c. Submission: Sequence. http://ontologydesignpatterns.org/wiki/Submissions:Sequence. Accessed 30 July 2013.

Gangemi, A. 2010d. Submission: TimeIndexedSituation. http://ontologydesignpatterns.org/wiki/Submissions:TimeIndexedSituation. Accessed 30 July 2013.

Gangemi, A., S. Peroni, and F. Vitali. 2010. Literal reification. Proceedings of the Workshop on Ontology Pattern 2010 (WOP 2010), CEUR workshop proceedings 671, 65–66. Aachen: CEUR-WS.org. http://CEUR-WS.org/Vol-671/pat04.pdf. Accessed 30 July 2013.

Garlik, S. H., and A. Seaborne. 2013. SPARQL 1.1 query language. W3C recommendation 21 March 2013. World Wide Web Consortium. http://www.w3.org/TR/sparql11-query/. Accessed 30 July 2013.

Groza, T., K. Möller, S. Handschuh, D. Trif, and S. Decker. 2007. SALT: Weaving the claim web. In Proceedings of 6th International Semantic Web Conference and of the 2nd Asian Semantic Web Conference (ISWC 2007+ASWC 2007), lecture notes in computer science 4825, ed. K. Aberer, K. Choi, N. F. Noy, D. Allemang, K. Lee, L. J. B. Nixon, J. Golbeck, P. Mika, D. Maynard, R. Mizoguchi, G. Schreiber, and P. Cudré-Mauroux, 197–210. Berlin: Springer. doi:10.1007/978-3-540-76298-0_15.

Groza, T., S. Handschuh, K. Möller, and S. Decker. 2007. SALT–semantically annotated LaTeX for scientific publications. In Proceedings of the fourth European Semantic Web Conference (ESWC 2007), lecture notes in computer science 4519, ed. E. Franconi, M. Kifer, and W. May, 518–532. Berlin: Springer. doi:10.1007/978-3-540-72667-8_37.

Groza, T., S. Handschuh, and S. Decker. 2011. Capturing rhetoric and argumentation aspects within scientific publications. *Journal on Data Semantics* 15: 1–36. doi:10.1007/978-3-642-22630-4_1.

Gruber, T. R. 1995. Toward principles for the design of ontologies used for knowledge sharing. *International Journal of Human Computer Studies* 43 (5–6): 907–928. doi:10.1006/ijhc.1995.1081.

Guarino, N., and C. Welty. 2002. Evaluating ontological decisions with OntoClean. *Communications of the ACM* 45 (2): 61–65. doi:10.1145/503124.503150.

Hammond, T. 2008. RDF site summary 1.0 modules: PRISM. http://nurture.nature.com/rss/modules/mod_prism.html. Accessed 30 July 2013.

Hayes, P., and C. Welty. 2006. Defining N-ary relations on the semantic web. W3C working group note 12 April 2006. World Wide Web Consortium. http://www.w3.org/TR/swbp-n-aryRelations/. Accessed 30 July 2013.

Hobbs, J. R., and F. Pan. 2006. Time ontology in OWL. W3C working draft, 27 September 2006. World Wide Web Consortium. http://www.w3.org/TR/owl-time/. Accessed 30 July 2013.

Horridge, M., and P. Patel-Schneider. 2012. OWL 2 web ontology language Manchester syntax. 2nd ed. W3C working group note 11 December 2012. World Wide Web Consortium. http://www.w3.org/TR/owl2-manchester-syntax/. Accessed 30 July 2013.

Horrocks, I., P. F. Patel-Schneider, H. Boley, S. Tabet, B. Grosof, and M. Dean. 2004. SWRL: A semantic web rule language combining OWL and RuleML. W3C Member Submission 21 May 2004. World Wide Web Consortium. http://www.w3.org/Submission/SWRL/. Accessed 30 July 2013.

Iannella, R. 2013. vCard ontology: For describing people and organisations. W3C working draft 24 September 2013. World Wide Web Consortium. http://www.w3.org/TR/vcard-rdf/. Accessed 30 July 2013.

International Federation of Library Associations and Institutions Study Group on the Functional Requirements for Bibliographic Records. 2009. Functional requirements for bibliographic records final report. International federation of library associations and institutions. http://www.ifla.org/files/cataloguing/frbr/frbr_2008.pdf. Accessed 30 July 2013.

Kircz, J. G. 1991. Rhetorical structure of scientific articles: The case for argumentational analysis in information retrieval. *Journal of Documentation* 47 (4): 354–372. doi:10.1108/eb026884.

Masolo, C., L. Vieu, E. Bottazzi, C. Catenacci, R. Ferrario, A. Gangemi, and N. Guarino. 2004. Social roles and their descriptions. Proceedings of the 9th international conference on the principles of knowledge representation and reasoning (KR2004), 267–277. https://www.aaai.org/Papers/KR/2004/KR04-029.pdf. Accessed 30 July 2013.

Miles, A., and S. Bechhofer. 2009. SKOS simple knowledge organization system reference. W3C recommendation 18 August 2009. World Wide Web Consortium. http://www.w3.org/TR/skos-reference/. Accessed 30 July 2013.

Moller, K., S. Bechhofer, and T. Heath. 2009. Semantic web conference ontology. http://data.semanticweb.org/ns/swc/swc_2009-05-09.html. Accessed 30 July 2013.

Peroni, S., and D. Shotton. 2012. FaBiO and CiTO: Ontologies for describing bibliographic resources and citations. *Journal of Web Semantics: Science, Services and Agents on the World Wide Web* 17:33–43. doi:10.1016/j.websem.2012.08.001.

Peroni, S., E. Motta, and M. d'Aquin. 2008. Identifying key concepts in an ontology, through the integration of cognitive principles with statistical and topological measures. In Proceedings of the 3rd Asian Semantic Web Conference (ASWC 2008), ed. J. Domingue and C. Anutariya. Berlin: Springer.

Picca, D., A. Gliozzo, and A. Gangemi. 2008. LMM: An OWL-DL MetaModel to represent heterogeneous lexical knowledge. Proceedings of the 6th Language Resource and Evaluation Conference (LREC 2008). Luxembourg: European Language Resources Association. http://www.lrec-conf.org/proceedings/lrec2008/pdf/608_paper.pdf. Accessed 30 July 2013.

Presutti, V., and A. Gangemi. 2008. Content ontology design patterns as practical building blocks for web ontologies. In Proceedings of the 27th international conference on conceptual modeling (ER 2008), lecture notes in computer science 5231, ed. Q. Li, S. Spaccapietra, E. S. K. Yu, and A. Olivé, 128–141. Berlin: Springer. doi:10.1007/978-3-540-87877-3_11.

Prud'hommeaux, E., and G. Carothers. 2013. Turtle, Terse RDF triple language. W3C candidate recommendation 19 February 2013. World Wide Web Consortium. http://www.w3.org/TR/turtle/. Accessed 30 July 2013.

Rector, A. 2003. Modularisation of domain ontologies implemented in description logics and related formalisms including OWL. In Proceedings of the 2nd international conference on Knowledge Capture (K-CAP 2003), ed. J. H. Gennari, B. W. Porter, and Y. Gil. New York: ACM.

Schneider, J., T. Groza, and A. Passant. 2011. A review of argumentation for the social semantic web. *Semantic Web–Interoperability, Usability, Applicability* 4 (2): 159–218. doi:10.3233/SW-2012-0073.

Shotton, D. 2009. Semantic publishing: The coming revolution in scientific journal publishing. *Learned Publishing* 22 (2): 85–94. doi:10.1087/2009202.

Shotton, D. 2010. CiTO, the citation typing ontology. *Journal of Biomedical Semantics* 1 (1): S6. doi:10.1186/2041-1480-1-S1-S6.

Shotton, D., C. Caton, and G. Klyne. 2010. Ontologies for sharing, ontologies for use. http://ontogenesis.knowledgeblog.org/2010/01/22/ontologies-for-sharing/. Accessed 12 March 2012.

Toulmin, S. 1959. *The uses of argument*. Cambridge: Cambridge University Press. (ISBN 0521827485).

Varma, P. 2010. Project documents ontology. http://vocab.deri.ie/pdo. Accessed 30 July 2013.

Walsh, N. (2010). DocBook 5: *The definitive guide*. Sebastopol: O'Really Media. Version 1.0.3. (ISBN: 0596805029).

Wan, S., C. Paris, and R. Dale. 2010. Supporting browsing-specific information needs: Introducing the citation-sensitive in-browser summariser. *Journal of Web Semantics: Science, Services and Agents on the World Wide Web* 8 (2–3): 196–202. doi:10.1016/j.websem.2010.03.002.

Chapter 6
Semantic Data Interfaces for the Masses

Abstract Extensive research has been done on models, theoretical approaches and development of tools to infer new information from data and ontologies. However, the Semantic Web will only be fully integrated with the everyday-Web only when it will be easily available and fully accessible to every Web users and not only to Semantic Web practitioners. The Semantic Publishing community urgently needs specific tools to assist non-experts in dealing with and publishing semantic data. In this chapter, I describe influential work and my personal contribution to this area. In addition, I discuss possible next steps to extend existing legislative editor by means of Semantic Web technologies, and highlight the key characteristics of semantically-enhanced legislative editors of the future.

Any policy that guarantees the wide adoption of Semantic Web technologies, such as those introduced in the previous chapters, must be concerned with the development of applications for improving the human interaction with semantic models and data. Extensive research has been done on models, theoretical approaches and development of tools to infer new information from data and ontologies. However, the Semantic Web will only be fully integrated with the everyday-Web only when it will be easily available and fully accessible to every Web-users and not only to Semantic Web practitioners. This issue is even more crucial for Semantic Publishing and, in particular, for the legal domain since their end-users, publishers, researchers, librarians readers and legal experts are generally not competent on semantic technologies. These communities need to invest time and efforts in the development of proper user-friendly interfaces that act as intermediate between semantic models and end-users.

A good amount of work has been done in the past in this direction. For instance, ontology development editors were implemented (e.g., Protégé[1] (Knublauch et al. 2005) and the NeOn Toolkit (Suárez-ueroa et al. 2012)), Web search engines to look for semantic resources were launched (e.g., Sindice[2] (Oren et al. 2008) and Watson[3] (d'Aquin and Motta 2011)), and semantic desktop applications were released (e.g., SemNotes[4] (Dragan et al. 2011)). However, what the Semantic Publishing

[1] Protégé: http://protege.stanford.edu.

[2] Sindice: http://sindice.com.

[3] Watson: http://watson.kmi.open.ac.uk.

[4] SemNotes: http://smile.deri.ie/projects/semn.

S. Peroni, *Semantic Web Technologies and Legal Scholarly Publishing*,
Law, Governance and Technology Series 15, DOI 10.1007/978-3-319-04777-5_6,

community urgently needs specific tools to assist non-experts in semantic technologies in dealing with and publishing semantic data.

Generally, the process entails the following steps:

1. once ontologies suitable for a particular domain of interest have been found, the user needs (or wants) to *understand* these models with the minimum amount of effort;
2. then, the user will *develop* new models when existing vocabularies/ontologies are not able to fully describe the domain in consideration. The development process will require the interaction with domain experts and end-users so that a model that addresses the domain in consideration as close as possible can be produced;
3. finally, once agreed on the model to use, the user will *add* data accordingly and, furthermore, they might need to *modify* those data in the future.

Each of these four operations—understanding, developing, adding and modifying—should be supported by proper interfaces that simplify the work of users who are not expert in ontology-related formalisms and Semantic Web technologies.

In this chapter, I will describe influential work and my personal contribution in this area. I will introduce four different tools I developed—*LODE*, *KC-Viz*, *Graffoo* and *Gaffe*—so as to help users in dealing with semantic data and models, such as those described in the previous chapters. In addition, I will also discuss possible next steps to extend existing legislative editor by means of Semantic Web technologies and applications presented herein, and highlight the key characteristics of semantically-enhanced legislative editors of the future.

6.1 How to Help Users: Tools and Applications for Semantic Data

Semantic publishing end-users must be supported when choosing which ontology to adopt according to their needs. Obviously, *understanding* which ontology fits better within a particular domain is not so straightforward, in particular when users are not experts in ontology formalisms; the ontology has not a human-comprehensible *documentation*, or it is so large that it becomes difficult to quickly *make sense* of it. An additional complication is introduced when we need/want to develop new ontologies or to add/modify semantic data according to specific models. To this end, it is crucial to have functional interfaces that support the *creation* of an ontology and the *addition* of semantic data according to it.

In this section, I will introduce a series of works that try to address all the issues I listed above, namely: ontology documentation; ontology sense-making; visual modelling, and authoring tools for ontologies.

6.1.1 Ontology Documentation

The production of the natural language documentation of ontologies is an important and crucial part of any ontology development process. Such a documentation enable users to comprehend the extent of an ontology without being concern about the particular formal language used to define its axioms. At the same time, writing the documentation is an activity that requires an important amount of effort. Thus, in order to help authors of ontologies to document them, applications have been developed which create a first draft of the documentation starting from labels (i.e., *rdfs:label*); comments (i.e., *rdfs:comment*); different kinds of annotations (e.g., *dc:description*, *dc:creator*, *dc:date*), and the logical structure of the ontology itself.

SpecGen[5] is a Python tool for the generation of ontology specifications, released under the MIT license[6]. It is available as a standalone application and it has been used to prepare the HTML documentation of well-known ontologies, such as SIOC[7] (Bojars and Breslin 2010). SpecGen generates the documentation by processing an HTML template and adding the list of ontological classes and properties in specifiable positions which can be specified within that template. As result, we obtain a new HTML document where the natural language description of the ontology come entirely from the template made by authors, while the software takes care of adding all the information related to the logical structure of the ontology.

Contrarily to SpenGen that needs a base HTML template to work, *VocDoc*[8] is a (rather short) Ruby script that allows one to produce documentation starting from RDFS vocabularies and OWL ontologies and it is able to produce both HTML documents and LaTeX files containing the description of the ontology/vocabulary.

Like VocDoc, *OWLDoc*[9] is a fully-automatic generator of a set of HTML pages describing the target ontology. It organises the documentation of each ontological entity in different parts: the taxonomy involving the entity; the usage of this entity in the context of the ontology, and all the formal logical axioms related to the entity (in Manchester Syntax (Horridge and Patel-Schneider 2012)). OWLDoc has been developed as plugin of *Protégé*[10] (Knublauch et al. 2005) and as a Web application[11].

Oriented to Linked Data applications rather than to ontology documentation, *Paget*[12] is a PHP framework that, by getting an input URL through a browser, is able to dispatch the request according to the particular mime type specified by the client. Paget returns RDF entities in four different formats: RDF; HTML; Turtle, and JSON.

[5] SpecGen: http://forge.morfeo-project.org/wiki_en/index.php/SpecGen.

[6] MIT license: http://www.opensource.org/licenses/mit-license.php.

[7] The Semantically-Interlinked Online Communities (SIOC) project: http://sioc-project.org.

[8] VocDoc: http://kantenwerk.org/vocdoc/.

[9] OWLDoc: http://code.google.com/p/co-ode-owl-plugins/wiki/OWLDoc.

[10] Protégé: http://protege.stanford.edu/.

[11] Ontology browser: http://code.google.com/p/ontology-browser/.

[12] Paget: http://code.google.com/p/paget.

It can be used to describe a set of pure RDF statements (*subject-predicate-object*)[13] and, to some extents, to produce an HTML human-comprehensible description from the axioms of an OWL ontology[14].

Neologism[15] (Basca et al. 2008) is a Web-based editor for the creation of RDFS vocabularies and (very simple) OWL ontologies. Moreover, it implements a publishing system that allows the publication of vocabularies and ontologies on the Web, rendered into natural language HTML pages. Basca et al.'s main objective is to reduce the time needed to create, publish and modify vocabularies for the Semantic Web.

Finally, *Parrot*[16] (Tejo-Alonso et al. 2011) is a Web service for the generation of HTML + Javascript documentation of OWL ontologies and RIF rules (Boley et al. 2013). This service allows one to specify multiple URLs identifying ontologies in order to produce an HTML summary "on the fly", starting from their logical structure and annotations.

6.1.2 Ontology Sense-Making

The issue of how best to support visualisation and navigation of ontologies has attracted much attention in the research community. As Wang and Parsia (2006) emphasise, "effective presentation of the hierarchies can be a big win for the users", in particular, but not exclusively, during the early stages of a sense-making process, when a user is trying to build an initial mental model of an ontology and focuses less on the specific representational details than on the understanding of the overall organisation of the ontology. In particular, as discussed in Shneiderman (1996), there are a number of functionalities that an effective visualisation system needs to support, including (but not limited to) the ability to provide high level overviews of the data, to zoom in on specific parts of the data efficiently, and to filter out irrelevant details and/or irrelevant parts of the data.

One approach which allows high level overviews of hierarchical structures focuses on maximising the amount of information on display, through space-filling solutions, such as those provided by *treemaps* (Shneiderman 1992). Treemaps have proved to be a very successful and influential visualisation method, used not just to represent conceptual hierarchies but also to visualise information in several mainstream sectors, including news, politics, stock market, sport, etc. However, while treemaps define a clever way to provide concise overviews of very large hierarchical spaces, they are mostly effective when the focus is on leaf nodes and on a particular dimension of visualisation, in particular if colour-coding can be used to express different values for the dimension in question.

---

[13] Ian Davis' Linked Data profile, rendered through Paget: http://iandavis.com/id/me.html.

[14] A vocabulary for describing whisky varieties, rendered through Paget:http://vocab.org/whisky/terms.html.

[15] Neologism: http://neologism.deri.ie.

[16] Parrot: http://ontorule-project.eu/parrot/parrot.

However, as pointed out in Wang and Parsia (2006), treemaps are not very effective in supporting an understanding of topological structures, which is what is primarily needed in the ontology sense-making context. State of the art ontology engineering toolkits, such as *Protégé* (Knublauch et al. 2005) and *TopBraid Composer*[17], include visualisation systems that use the familiar node-link diagram paradigm to represent entities in an ontology and their taxonomic or domain relationships. In particular, both the *OwlViz visualizer* in Protégé and the "*Graph View*" in TopBraid, make it possible for users to navigate the ontology hierarchy by selecting, expanding and hiding nodes. However, OwlViz arguably provides more flexibility, by allowing the user to customise the expansion radius and supporting different modalities of use, including the option of automatically visualizing in OwlViz the current selection shown in the Protégé Class Browser.

SpaceTree (Plaisant et al. 2002), which also follows the node-link diagram paradigm, is able to maximise the number of nodes on display, by assessing how much empty space is available. At the same time, it also avoids clutter by utilising informative preview icons. These include miniatures of a branch, which are able to give the user an idea of the size and shape of an un-expanded subtree at a very high level of abstraction, while minimising the use of the available area.

Like treemaps, *CropCircles* (Wang and Parsia 2006) also uses geometric containment as an alternative to classic node-link displays. However, it tries to address the key weakness of treemaps, by sacrificing space in order to make it easier for users to understand the topological relations in an ontology, including both parent-child and sibling relations. The empirical evaluation comparing the performance of users on topological tasks using treemaps, CropCircles and SpaceTree introduced in Wang and Parsia (2006) showed that, at least for some tasks, users of CropCircles performed significantly better than those using treemaps. However, SpaceTree appears to perform significantly better than either treemaps or CropCircles on node finding tasks.

A number of hybrid solutions also exist, such as Jambalaya (Storey et al. 2001) and Knoocks (Kriglstein and Motschnig-Pitrik 2008), which attempt to combine the different strengths of containment-based and node-link approaches in an integrated framework, by providing both alternative visualisations and hybrid, integrated views of the two paradigms.

The group of techniques categorised in Katifori et al. (2007) as "context + focus and distortion" are based on "the notion of distorting the view of the presented graph in order to combine context and focus. The node on focus is usually the central one and the rest of the nodes are presented around it, reduced in size until they reach a point that they are no longer visible" (Katifori et al. 2007). These techniques are normally based on hyperbolic views of the data and offer a good trade-off—a part of the ontology is shown in detailed view, while the rest is depicted in the background. A good exemplar of this class of approaches is HyperTree (Souza et al. 2003).

Finally, I should also consider the most ubiquitous and least visual class of tools, exemplified by plugins such as the *Class Browser* in Protégé and the *Ontology*

[17] TopBraid Composer: http://www.topbraidcomposer.com.

Navigator in the *NeOn Toolkit*[18] (Suárez-ueroa et al. 2012). These follow the classic file system navigation metaphor, where clicking on a folder opens up its sub-folders. This approach is common in both file system interfaces and ontology engineering tools and, in the case of ontologies, it allows the user to navigate the ontology hierarchy simply by clicking on the identifier of a class, to display its subclasses, and so on. While superficially a rather basic solution, especially when compared to some of the sophisticated visual metaphors that can be found in the literature, this approach can be surprisingly effective for two reasons:

- it is very familiar to users;
- it makes it possible to display quite a lot of information in a rather small amount of space, in contrast with node-link displays, which can be space-hungry.

As a result it is not surprising that these interfaces often perform better in evaluation scenarios than the graphical alternatives. For instance, the evaluation reported in Katifori et al. (2006) shows that subjects using the Protégé Class Browser fared better than those using alternative visualisation plugins in a number of ontology engineering tasks.

6.1.3 *Visual Modelling of Ontologies*

Usually, people who want to model ontologies have to be experts in formal languages (e.g., description logic) that are expressive enough to enable the definition of all the semantic constraints required by the particular needs of conceptualisation of a domain. As consequence of that, few years ago a new professional role arose to deal specifically with the development of ontologies: the *ontology engineer*.

Nowadays an increasing number of people in several fields (e.g., biology, medicine, literature, software engineering) are beginning to develop ontologies for their own needs. To this end, they usually adopt visual approaches that enable the development of complex ontologies while hiding the intrinsic complexity of the formal language they use. Moreover, as side effect, these visual approaches help when *presenting* ontologies to an audience that is not expert in formal languages.

One of the most common of these approaches is the *semantic networks* (Woods 1975). A semantic network is a "graphic notation for representing knowledge in patterns of interconnected nodes and arcs" (Sowa 1987). Ontology classes and individuals are defined as nodes of a graph (i.e., the visual representation of a semantic network). At the same time, direct and labelled arcs can interlink nodes to represent predicates between them: sub-class relations; belongingness to a class; individual assertions, etc. Although this tool is commonly used for representing OWL ontologies, it had been developed within the Artificial Intelligence field, years before the development of the Semantic Web.

[18] NeOn Toolkit: http://www.neon-toolkit.org.

Another interesting approach coming from software engineering fields is that of using modified versions of UML (Object Management Group 2011), opportunely adapted to describe OWL ontologies. Gasevic et al. (2004) propose a new UML profile for the definition of OWL ontologies that is entirely based on the UML class notation. Moreover, they illustrate a process that allows one to produce OWL ontologies by applying an XSLT transformation to the XMI version of an UML document made through an UML editor (such as Poseidon[19]).

Brockmans et al. (2004, 2006) propose another UML profile that enables one to define OWL entities using an extended set of UML-based graphic notations. In particular, the UML class notation is used for the representation of classes and, when opportunely appointed with dedicated stereotypes, class restrictions. Properties are represented as UML n-ary associations, and they might have stereotypes specified according to property characteristics (e.g., functional, symmetric, reflexive). Individuals belonging to particular OWL classes are represented by using the UML "object:Class" notation, while OWL data types are represented as UML classes.

In 2009, the industry consortium responsible of UML, i.e., the Object Management Group, released an official UML profile (Object Management Group 2009) for defining OWL ontologies, called *Ontology Definition Metamodel* (*ODM*), which incorporates and harmonises works done previously on this topic. All these UML-like proposals appear to be less intuitive than the semantic network approach, since they ask users to learn at least some basic principles of the UML notations. Of course, the UML-like approach has been very successful in software engineering communities, because it introduced, with a relatively low cost, software engineers to ontology modelling.

6.1.4 Authoring Tools for Ontologies

Decorating resources (e.g., documents) with semantic data is usually a tedious task unless one has the support of appropriate applications that make this activity practicable, intuitive and relatively quick. Nowadays there exist many tools that help users to deal with metadata enrichment, such as metadata editors and automatic content processing mechanisms.

For instance, *DC-dot*[20] retrieves Web pages and automatically proposes related metadata according to Dublin Core Metadata Elements (Dublin Core Metadata Initiative 2012b) and Terms (Dublin Core Metadata Initiative 2012a). Metadata can be edited using the form provided by the system, which is also accompanied by a context-sensitive help. However, DC-dot only provides text areas for Dublin Core resources, and does not allow domain-specific constraints and any other kinds of customisations to the Dublin Core standard.

[19] Poseidon for UML: http://www.gentleware.com/products.html.

[20] DC-dot: http://www.ukoln.ac.uk/metadata/dcdot.

Another tool specifically designed for Dublin Core data is *Metamaker*[21]. This editor allows the creation of metadata from scratch through simple web forms. Metadata can be saved in different formats, e.g., HTML, XHTML, XML, RDF or AGRIS AP[22]. Unlike DC-dot, Metamarker allows one to use terms from external sources, such as the AGROVOC thesaurus[23].

TKME[24] is an application that allows the creation and modification of metadata, and organises them according to hierarchical structures (i.e., trees). Since TKME does not require the use of a particular metadata schema, it allows one to customise its interface according to alternative semantic models.

In contrast to TKME, *Metasaur* (Kay and Lum 2003) provides a general visualisation tool for ontologies describing a particular domain. Through Metasaur, users can create lightweight ontologies according to existing metadata schemas as well as change existing ontologies by adding new constraints and restrictions. As a drawback, however, Metasaur has not a flexible user interface. In fact, although it creates automatically a form starting from the ontology in consideration, it does not allow users to customise and personalise it in any way.

Some other approaches address metadata editing through Web applications, such as Wikis. Several approaches to semantic wikis have been developed to bring together the benefits of the free editing philosophy of wikis and ontological data. Semantic wikis can be organised into two main categories according to their connections with the ontologies: "wikis for ontologies" and "ontologies for wikis" (Buffa et al. 2008). In the first case, the wiki is used as a serialisation of the ontology: each concept is mapped into a page and typed links are used to represent object properties.

Such a model—initially proposed in the ontology for MediaWiki articles, called WikiOnt (Harth et al. 2005)—has been adopted by most semantic wikis. SemanticMediaWiki (Všlkel et al. 2006) is undoubtedly the most relevant one. It provides users with an intuitive syntax to embed semantics, i.e., RDF statements, within the markup of a page. *SemanticMediaWiki* allows users to edit the content freely without any limitation. The more the information is correctly encoded the more semantic data are available, but no constraint is imposed over the authoring process. SemanticMediaWiki has been developed with the idea of creating a machine-readable version of Wikipedia, to make full use of the huge amount of information and the competencies and enthusiasm of its community.

The original term *Wikitology* (Klein et al. 2005) summarises very well the potentialities of such approach. The DBPedia project (Auer et al. 2007) is also worth mentioning, being the most recent effort in translating the Wikipedia content into RDF. One of the main obstacles to the realisation of Wikitology and similar projects is without doubt the difficulty in creating semantic content. Although the syntax is very simple, in fact, authors still have to learn some new markup and above all they must

---

[21] Metamarker: http://www.fao.org/aims/tools/metamaker.jsp.

[22] AGRIS Application Profiles: http://aims.fao.org/standards/agmes/application-profiles/agris.

[23] AGROVOS thesaurus: http://aims.fao.org/website/AGROVOC-Thesaurus/sub.

[24] TKME: http://geology.usgs.gov/tools/metadata/tools/doc/tkme.html.

manually write each statement and the statements must be correct. *SemanticForms*[25] is an extension of SemanticMediaWiki that addresses such issue by allowing users to create semantic content via pre-defined forms. SemanticForms generates forms from templates, whose fragments and data have been previously typed. This process employs an embedded mapping between each datatype and each type of field (radio-buttons, checkboxes, textareas, etc.). Users do not need to write the statements manually anymore as they are only required to fill HTML forms.

The difficulties in generating SemanticMediaWiki data have been mitigated by an ad-hoc importer that allows the creation of multiple articles from an input OWL ontology (Vrandecic and Krötzsch 2006). This tool uses a PHP API for managing OWL and automatically creating wiki content according to the basic MediaWiki model: each concept is mapped into a page and each property into a typed link. The tool also carries out tests on the consistency of the ontology and any duplication of non-relevant data are also performed.

Other wikis provide users with mixed interfaces for creating semantic data. *MaknaWiki* (Dello et al. 2006), for example, is a JSP wiki-clone that allows users to embed semantic statements or to fill HTML forms for querying and adding data to the ontology represented by the wiki. These forms provide general tools for aided navigation of the semantic data, do not depend on the domain of the wiki and their structure is hard-coded in the system.

Rhizome (Souzis 2005) provides friendly interfaces and textareas where users can write statements directly. It relies on ZML (a textual syntax serialisable into XML), a generic language to express semi-structured data, and an engine to apply rules for intermixing semantics and free texts.

An original solution is provided by *AceWiki* (Bao et al. 2009) and *CNL-approach* (De Coi et al. 2009). AceWiki is a semantic wiki that allows users to write ontological statements by simply writing sentences in the ACE (Attempo Controlled English) language. The system includes a predictive authoring tool that suggests options to the users and autocompletes fields consistently to the ontology represented by the wiki. The same editor can be used to extend the ontology by creating new classes, instances and relations. In De Coi et al. (2009) De Coi *et al.* proposed a similar approach for SemanticMediaWiki, through a CNL (Controlled Natural Language) interface able to convert sentences written in multiple languages into semantic data.

The second category of semantic wikis, based on the principle of "ontologies for wikis", includes all those wikis that are built on top of ontological foundations. The idea is to exploit ontologies to create and maintain consistent semantic data within a wiki so that sophisticated analysis, queries and classifications can be performed on its content. *IkeWiki* (Schaffert 2006) was one of the first wikis to adopt this approach. This tool works by loading an OWL ontology into the system which is then automatically translated into a set of wiki pages and typed links. Multiple interfaces are provided to the users for editing the plain wiki content, adding new metadata or tagging pages. IkeWiki strongly relies on Semantic Web technologies: it

[25] SemanticForms: http://www.mediawiki.org/wiki/Extension:Semantic_Forms.

even includes a Jena OWL[26] (Carroll et al. 2004) repository and a SPARQL (Garlik and Seaborne 2013) engine used for navigation, queries and display of the semantic content of the wiki.

Similarly, OntOWiki (Auer et al. 2006) is a complete ontology editor. It relies on a strong distinction between the ontological back-end of the system and a user-friendly interface. Data are stored as OWL/RDF statements that are dynamically rendered into the final HTML wiki pages. OntOWiki provides users with multiple views of the same content: (1) ontological data can be navigated by listing classes, individuals, properties, etc.; (2) domain-specific views can be added as plugins (for instance, a MapView of geographical data can be dynamically mashed-up form GoogleMaps), and (3) editing-views are available in the system.

SweetWiki (Buffa et al. 2008) implements a user-friendly ontology tool designed for both expert and non-expert users. Two aspects characterise the system: the strong connection with the ontologies and the provision of Ajax-based interfaces for editing content and metadata. SweetWiki defines a "Wiki Object Model", i.e., an ontology describing the wiki structure. Concepts like "document", "page", "link", "version", "attachment" are all codified in an OWL file that is accessed and manipulated through the wiki itself. These concepts are made explicit in SweetWiki, although they are usually hard-coded in most semantic wikis. SweetWiki also allows users to import external ontologies and to access and manipulate those ontologies through ad-hoc interfaces (similar to those provided by the above mentioned full ontology editors). Finally, the system provides "assisted social tagging" facilities: users can add metadata to any page and can put pages in relation. These metadata values form a folksonomy that, on the one hand, is freely editable by users and, on the other, is built on top of ontological data. The interface for tagging, in fact, suggests consistent metadata by exploiting SPARQL queries and autocompletion features.

Finally, UFOWiki (Passant and Laublet 2008) is another project that aims at integrating wikis, ontologies and forms. UFOWiki is a wiki farm, i.e., a server that allows users to set up and deploy semantic wikis. The overall content is stored in a centralised repository as RDF triples that express both the actual content of each page and its metadata. The same farm deploys multiple wikis, so that they can share (ontological) data in a distributed environment.

6.2 LODE: Generating HTML Documentation from Ontologies

Usually, when someone wants to understand the extent of a particular ontology, the first thing to do is to look for the ontology's human-readable documentation. A large number of ontologies, especially those used in the Linked Data, have a very good and comprehensive Web page describing theoretical backgrounds and developed entities.

Problems arise in relation to underdeveloped models, since natural language documentation is usually published only when an ontology becomes stable. This

[26] Jena: http://jena.sourceforge.net.

approach is justifiable: writing a proper documentation requires a big effort and changing it every time the ontology is modified can be problematic.

An additional difficulty is given by the availability of several "stable" ontologies that do not have any document describing them. Thus, the only way to understand them is to use an ontology editor to explore their logical axioms. This approach may however create problems to people approaching the ontology world for the very first time. Firstly, they would have to download and install the ontology editor, if not already present on their machine. Secondly, they would have to learn how to use the editor. And finally, they will be able to get a sense of the ontology by loading it onto the editor.

Obviously, this process can be very time-consuming. In order to address this issue, standalone tools and Web applications have been developed, as illustrated in Sect. 6.1.1. However they lack a proper and quick mechanism for the conversion of all the ontology axioms into a human-readable documentation.

To address this issue, I developed the *Live OWL Documentation Environment*[27] (*LODE*) (Peroni et al. 2012). It is a service that automatically extracts classes, object properties, data properties, named individuals, annotation properties, meta-modelling (punning), general axioms, SWRL rules and namespace declarations from any well-formed OWL or OWL 2 ontology, and returns them as ordered lists, together with their textual definitions, in a human-readable HTML page designed for browsing and navigation by means of embedded links.

LODE is basically based on an XSLT stylesheet that takes RDF/XML linearisation of an ontology (Beckett 2004), produced through the OWLAPI[28] (Horridge and Bechhofer 2011), as input and converts it into an HTML representation. If the target ontology is already linearised in that format, it is then possible to call the service specifying directly its URL (i.e., "http://www.essepuntato.it/lode/") followed by the complete URL of the ontology. For instance:

```
http://www.essepuntato.it/lode/http://www.essepuntato.it/2008/12/earmark
```

In the following subsections I will introduce the most important features of LODE.

6.2.1 What Axioms are Used to Create the Documentation

Primarily, LODE interprets the most common annotation properties used for the description of entities, in particular[29]: *dc:contributor*; *dc:creator*; *dc:date*; *dc:description*; *dc:rights*; *dc:title*; *dcterms:contributor*; *dcterms:creator*; *dcterms:date*; *dcterms:description*; *dcterms:rights*; *dcterms:title*; *owl:versionInfo*;

---

[27] LODE, the Live OWL Documentation Environment: http://lode.sourceforge.net.

[28] OWLAPI: http://owlapi.sourceforge.net.

[29] The prefixes *dc*, *dcterms*, *owl* and *rdfs* in the following list respectively refers to "http://purl.org/dc/elements/1.1/", "http://purl.org/dc/terms/", "http://www.w3.org/2002/07/owl#" and "http://www.w3.org/2000/01/rdf-schema#".

rdfs:comment; *rdfs:isDefinedBy*, and *rdfs:label*. LODE adopts the following rules when transforming those annotations into HTML documentation:

- in the presence of Dublin Core annotations defined according to both DC Metadata Elements (Dublin Core Metadata Initiative 2012b) and DC Metadata Terms (Dublin Core Metadata Initiative 2012a), the former have precedence;
- dates (i.e., *dc:date* and *dcterms:date*) written according to the XML Schema datatype (i.e., *yyyy-mm-dd*) are automatically transformed into *dd/mm/yyyy*;
- agents (i.e., *dc:creator*, *dc:contributor*, *dcterms:creator* and *dcterms:contributor*) are rendered either as strings or as clickable URLs according to their types, i.e., literals or resources, respectively;
- descriptions (i.e., *dc:description* and *dcterms:description*) are rendered either as strings or as media objects according to their types, i.e., literals or resources, respectively;
- comments (i.e., *rdfs:comment*) and descriptions (i.e., *dc:description* and *dcterms:description*) are represented, respectively, as abstracts and as detailed descriptions of entities;
- labels (i.e., *rdfs:label*) and QNames (when labels are not specified) are used to refer to all the entities of the ontology, instead of using their URLs;
- the nature of each entity is identified by a descriptive abbreviation, according to its type: "c", "op", "dp", "ap" and "ni" are used to identify class, object property, data property, annotation property and named individual, respectively.

Figures 6.1 and 6.2 on page 207–208 show how these annotations are rendered for an example ontology, EARMARK (Di Iorio et al. 2011b), an ontology that defines entities which describe document markup (such as elements, attributes, comments and text nodes).

LODE converts all the other axioms of the ontology into Manchester Syntax definitions (Horridge and Patel-Schneider 2012), as shown in Fig. 6.3 on page 208. I prefer to use this syntax rather than any other because it is the most human-comprehensible syntax for ontological axioms, and thus the most helpful for non-specialists.

Ontological axioms are rendered in grey boxes, one for each entity declared in the ontology. The axioms taken into account by LODE refer to: super-class and super-property; equivalent class and property; disjoint class and property; property domain and range; property chain; keys; object/data property assertion; type; imported ontology; generic axiom, and SWRL rule. Moreover, LODE automatically enriches those definitions, by adding information about sub-classes, domain/range properties of classes, sub-properties and entity meta-modelling.

6.2.2 *Special Parameters to Call the Service*

LODE can be invoked with a number of optional parameters in order to limit or extend the final documentation that is produced. For instance, it is possible to take

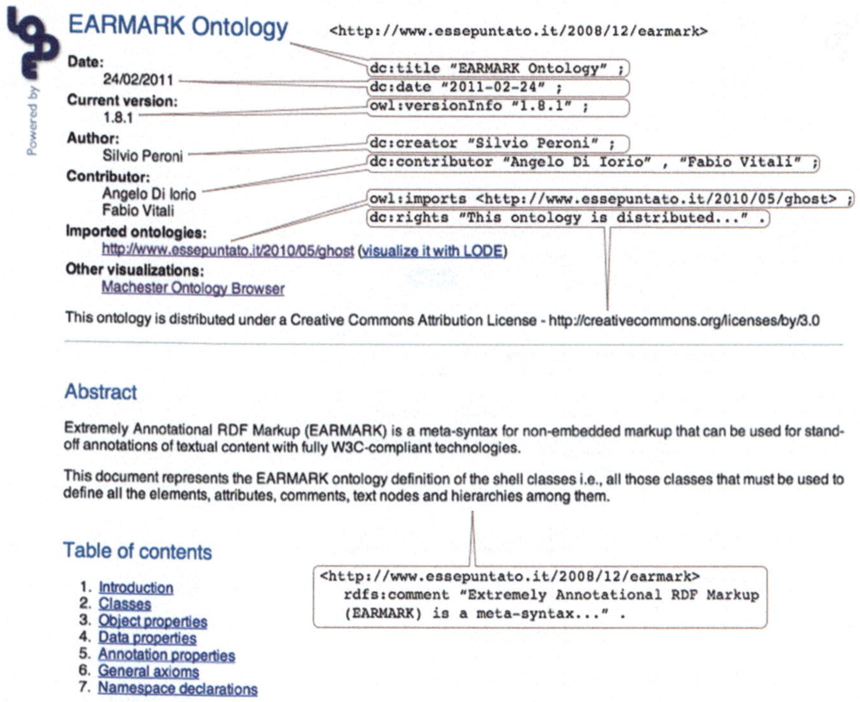

Fig. 6.1 The beginning of the Web page generated by LODE for the EARMARK Ontology, annotated with OWL assertions in Turtle (not present in the normal LODE web page) illustrating how these assertions are rendered in HTML

into account all the entities in the ontology closure and/or the inferred axioms. The following pseudo-URL describes how to call LODE:

http://*www.essepuntato.it/lode/optional-parameters/ontology-url*

In particular:

- *www.essepuntato.it/lode* is the URL to call the service;
- *ontology-url* is the full "http:// ... " URL of the OWL ontology that will be processed by the service. It must be always the last item of the pseudo-URL, and may be preceded by one or more (slash-separated) parameters.

Figure 6.4 on page 209 illustrates the alternative ways to build the URL to call LODE and the related modules used. The optional slash-separated parameters are described in the following sub-sections.

6.2.2.1 Parameter "Owlapi"

When this optional parameter is specified, the ontology defined in *ontology-url* will be pre-processed via OWLAPI (Horridge and Bechhofer 2011), in order to linearise it in the RDF/XML format accepted by LODE. The use of this parameter is strongly

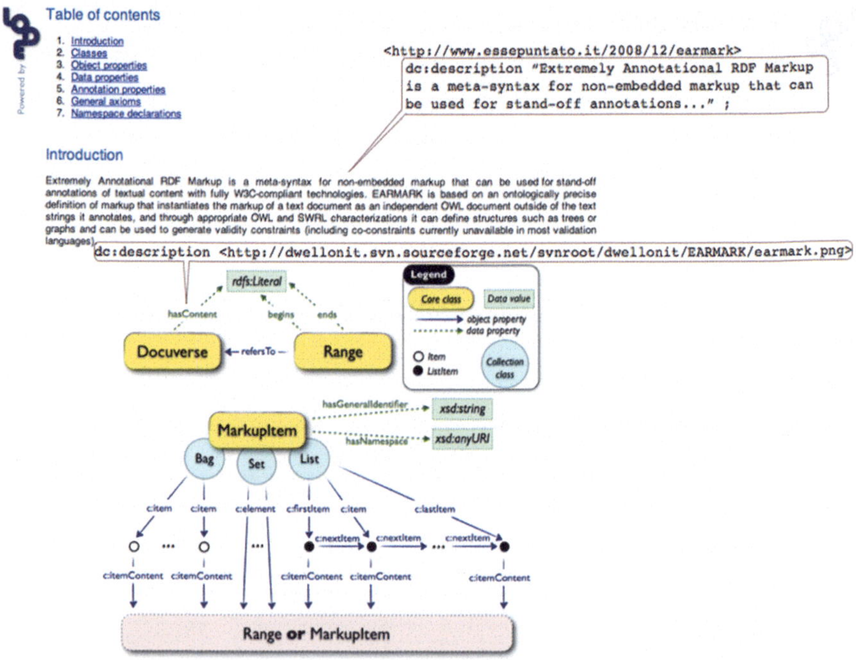

Fig. 6.2 Two possible kinds of descriptions: pure string (for literals) and media object (for resources).

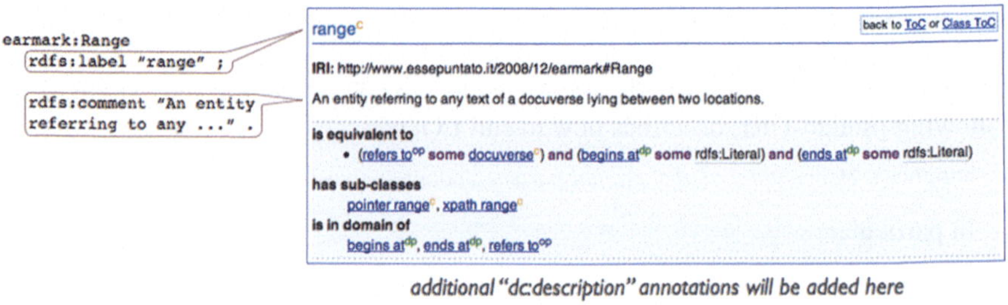

Fig. 6.3 How entities (classes, properties and individuals) are rendered by LODE

recommended: it allows LODE to process ontologies implemented in all the formats supported by the OWLAPI.

6.2.2.2 Parameter "Imported"

When this optional parameter is specified, the axioms in the imported ontologies of *ontology-url* are added to the HTML description of the ontology. This parameter implicitly specifies the *owlapi* parameter.

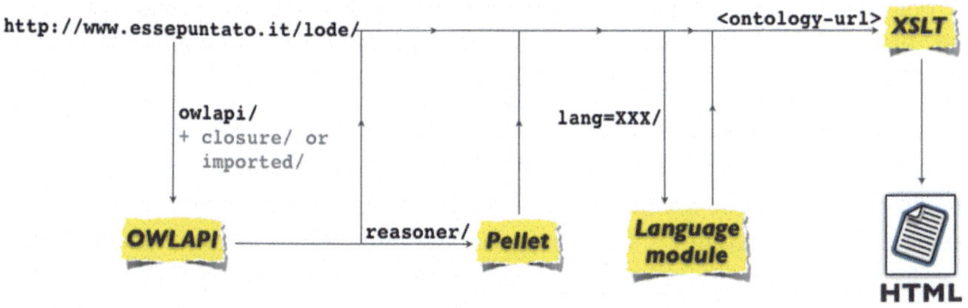

Fig. 6.4 All the possible ways, according to specific needs, for making a request to LODE

6.2.2.3 Parameter "Closure"

When this optional parameter is specified, the transitive closure given by considering the imported ontologies of *ontology-url* is added to the HTML description of the ontology. This parameter implicitly specifies the *owlapi* parameter. If both the parameters *closure* and *imported* are specified (in any order), *imported* will be preferred.

6.2.2.4 Parameter "Reasoner"

When this optional parameter is specified, the inferred axioms of *ontology-url* (through the Pellet reasoner (Sirin et al. 2007)) will be added to the HTML description of the ontology. This parameter implicitly specifies the *owlapi* parameter. Note that, depending on the nature of the ontology to process, this computationally intensive function can be very time-consuming.

6.2.2.5 Parameter "lang"

When this optional parameter is specified, the selected language will be used as preferred language instead of English when showing annotations of *ontology-url*. It must be followed by an "–" and the abbreviation of the language to use. e.g.,: "lang = en" for English, "lang = it" for Italian, "lang = fr" for French, etc.

6.2.3 URI Fragments

LODE offers intuitive mechanisms to refer to particular ontological entities within the HTML documentation, according to the URL of the entity in consideration. The following extension of the pseudo-URL introduced in Sect. 6.2.2 defines how to refer to a particular entity of an ontology:

http://www.essepuntato.it/lode/optional-parameters/ontology-url *#entity*

For instance, to generate the documentation of FaBiO (Sect. 5.1) and then jumping directly to the point where the resource "http://purl.org/spar/fabio/Article" is described, I need to invoke LODE as follows:

```
http://www.essepuntato.it/lode/http://purl.org/spar/
   fabio#http://purl.org/spar/fabio/Article
```

This request can be simplified by looking for descriptions of entities defined as *fragment* of the ontology's URL, such as the entity *Element* of the EARMARK ontology—i.e., "http://www.essepuntato.it/2008/12/earmark#Element". In this particular case, I can use either the entire entity URL as illustrated previously or the entity's local name only, as shown here below:

```
http://www.essepuntato.it/lode/http://www.essepuntato.it
   /2008/12/earmark#Element
```

6.2.4 Content Negotiation via .htaccess

LODE can be freely used by third parties, as described in its documentation. In particular, it can be very useful if used in conjunction with content negotiation mechanisms to display a human-readable version of an OWL ontology when the user accesses the ontology using a web browser, or to deliver the OWL ontology file itself when the user accesses the ontology using an ontology development tool such as *Protégé* (Knublauch et al. 2005) or the *NeOn Toolkit* (Suárez-ueroa et al. 2012). For instance, an implementation of such a content negotiation is given in Berrueta and Phipps (2008) by using the *.htaccess* file:

```
AddType application/rdf+xml .rdf

# Rewrite engine setup
RewriteEngine On

# Rewrite rule to serve HTML content
RewriteCond %{HTTP_ACCEPT} !application/rdf\+xml.*(text/
   html|application/xhtml\+xml)
RewriteCond %{HTTP_ACCEPT} text/html [OR]
RewriteCond %{HTTP_ACCEPT} application/xhtml\+xml [OR]
RewriteCond %{HTTP_USER_AGENT} ^Mozilla/.*
RewriteRule ^ontology$ http://www.essepuntato.it/lode/
   http://www.mydomain.com/ontology [R=303,L]

# Rewrite rule to serve RDF/XML content if requested
RewriteCond %{HTTP_ACCEPT} application/rdf\+xml
RewriteRule ^ontology$ ontology.owl [R=303]

# Choose the default response
RewriteRule ^ontology$ ontology.owl [R=303]
```

LODE can be seen in action by opening, in a Web browser, any of ontologies presented in this book. For instance, the URL "http://purl.org/spar/fabio" resolves,

Table 6.1 The five tasks subjects performed in the user testing session

Task 1	Describe the main aim of the ontology
Task 2	Describe what the class doctoral thesis defines
Task 3	Describe what the object property has subject term describes, and record its domain and range classes
Task 4	Record the class having the largest number of direct individuals (i.e., individuals that belongs explicitly to that class and that are not inferable from its subclasses)
Task 5	Record all the subclasses and properties involving the class item

by content negotiation, to display the LODE HTML version of the FaBiO ontology with the URL "http://www.essepuntato.it/lode/http://purl.org/spar/fabio". As shown previously, a similar syntax can be used to display the LODE visualisation of any other OWL ontology.

6.2.5 *Test and Evaluation*

In order to gather data about the usability of LODE, I carried out user testing. I asked 13 subjects to perform five unsupervised tasks (max. 5 min/task), involving ontology navigation through LODE documentation. There were no "administrators" observing the subjects while they were undertaking these tasks. All the subjects were volunteers who responded to personal e-mails or to an invitation sent to the semantic-web@w3.org and public-lod@w3.org mailing lists.

For the tasks, I used a *medium-size* ontology, namely FaBiO, the *FRBR-aligned Bibliographic Ontology* (see Sect. 5.1), which, at the time of the test, was composed by 214 classes, 69 object properties, 45 data properties and 15 individuals. FaBiO was chosen because we expected most people involved in the experiments (primarily Semantic Web researchers and practitioners) to have familiarity with the domain it describes, i.e., bibliographic entities such as research papers, journal articles and books. In addition, FaBiO was also chosen because using an ontology larger than FaBiO would have required more time to complete the tasks, potentially reducing the number of users willing to complete the test, and thus reducing the number of useful data for the evaluation.

The tasks given to the subjects are shown in Table 6.1. This set of tasks was designed to exploring the LODE capabilities in creating a human-readable documentation and in browsing ontologies.

Task 1 is a pure descriptive activity that involves only the documentation produced by LODE, without using any navigational features such as Web links. Tasks 2 and 3 are similar to Task 1, but in addition, they typically require the user to use some navigational facilities to reach the class *doctoral thesis* and the object property *has subject term*. Finally, Tasks 4 and 5 further assess how easily LODE enables users to browse the ontology and understand its structure.

My aim was to assess how well LODE would help users, by producing human-readable documentation of an OWL ontology, which would enable them to browse and make sense of it easily.

Table 6.2 System usability scale values and related sub-measures

Measure	Mean	Max. value	Min. value	Standard deviation
SUS value	77.7	92.5	57.5	12.5
Usability	76.4	90.6	56.3	12.8
Learnability	82.7	100	62.5	14.9

The test session was structured as follows. I first asked the subjects to complete a short multiple-choice questionnaire about their background knowledge and skills in OWL, ontology engineering, and ontology documentation (max. 2 min). Then, as a warm-up task, I asked the subjects to use LODE to explore the FOAF ontology[30], a relatively simple ontology, in order to become familiar with the structure of the documentation it produced, and with its navigation mechanisms (primarily, internal hypertext links) (max. 5 min). Then, for the test proper, I asked the subjects to complete the five tasks listed in Table 6.1, by using the documentation of the FaBiO ontology created by LODE (ideally 2, max. 5 min/task). Finally, I asked the subjects to fill in two short questionnaires, one multiple choice and the other textual, to report their experience of using LODE in completing these tasks (max. 5 min). All the questionnaires and all the outcomes of the experiments are available online[31].

Out of the 65 tasks in total (5 tasks given to each of 13 subjects), 58 were completed successfully (i.e., the right answer was given), while 7 had incorrect answers or were not completed at all, giving an overall success rate of 89 %. The 58 successes were distributed as follows: 13 (out of 13) in Task 1, 13 in Task 2, 13 in Task 3, 10 in Tasks 4 and 9 in Task 5.

The usability score for LODE was computed using the *System Usability Scale* (*SUS*) (Brooke 1996), a well-known methodology used for the perception of the usability of a system. It has the advantage of being technology independent (it has been tested on hardware, software, Web sites, etc.) and it is reliable even with a very small sample size (Sauro 2011). In addition to the main SUS scale, we were also interested in examining the sub-scales of pure *Usability* and pure *Learnability* of the system, as proposed by Lewis and Sauro (2009). As shown in Table 6.2, the mean SUS score for LODE was 77.69 (in a 0–100 range), abundantly surpassing the target score of 68 which indicates a good level of usability (Sauro 2011). The mean values for the SUS sub-scales Usability and Learnability were 76.4 and 82.7, respectively. In addition, two sub-scores were calculated for each of the subjects by considering the values of the answers they had given in the background questionnaire, which was composed of ten questions about the subject's experience with ontologies and two questions about their experience with ontology documentation tools. We then compared these sub-scores with the SUS values and the other sub-scales using the Pearson's r, and found weak negative correlation (between -0.34 and -0.14) between the experience sub-scores and the SUS values. This may show that the perceived usability of LODE does not depend upon any particular experience of

[30] FOAF ontology: http://xmlns.com/foaf/spec/index.rdf.

[31] http://www.essepuntato.it/2012/04/lodeusertesting.

Table 6.3 Terms—three positive (+) and two negative (−)—mentioned by more than one individual in the final questionnaire responses

Term	Description	Frequency
Search (−)	No search function was provided to directly look for and access entities of the ontology. Users acknowledge that since the ontology is on a single web page, they could use (and in fact did use) the search function of the browser, but many still found it a missing feature	7 out of 11
Readability (+)	High praise was given to the clarity of the presentation, the intuitiveness of the organisation, and the immediacy of identifying the sought information. The good typographical style of the output is clearly among the best qualities of LODE	5 out of 11
Links within the document (+)	The systematic use of internal links to the various features of the ontology was considered useful and immediately usable	4 out of 11
Scalability (−)	The LODE interface provides no links to entities provided by external, but linked ontologies. A highly modular ontology composed of a multiplicity of independent sub-ontologies is hard to navigate, and similarly the structure on a single page could make really large ontologies quite hard to access	3 out of 11
Single page (+)	Praises were given to the idea of placing all the content on a single Web page, which allows a multiplicity of approaches to accessing and reading the ontology, including visual transitions and scrolling that would not be possible if the ontologies had been presented in separate web pages	2 out of 11

the subjects in the use of ontologies and ontology documentation tools, rather the opposite. However, each correlation measure appears to be not statistically significant and we need to enrich our dataset to come to a more definite conclusion.

Axial coding of the personal comments expressed in the final questionnaires (Strauss and Corbin 1998) revealed only a small number of commonly perceived issues. Out of 13 which participated to the test, 11 subjects had comments that were meaningful for the study, and, of the 15 terms that were identified as significant, only 5 (3 positive and 2 negative) were mentioned by more than one individual (albeit sometimes with different words), as shown in Table 6.3.

Additional comparative testing sessions, which involved LODE and other Web-available ontology documentation (i.e., *Parrot* and *Ontology Browser*) and ontology engineering tools (*WebProtégé*), confirm these results. As described in Peroni et al. (2013), these latter sessions showed that LODE was perceived more usable than other tools by users when carrying out tasks involving the understanding and browsing of OWL ontologies.

6.3 KC-Viz, a Tool for Visualising and Navigating Ontologies

Sometimes, the HTML documentation may not be enough to understand an ontology properly. This is particularly true for very large ontologies that make it difficult for a person to try to understand their overall structure. Having a clear natural language documentation may not adequately support the users. In this case, using abstraction mechanisms that try to take a first meaningful snap-shot of the overall organisation of the ontology can be extremely useful. Starting from this summary, that may contain for instance the most representative concepts of the ontology, one can start to *make sense* of the ontology itself.

When I speak about "making sense" of an ontology, I refer to a specific ontology engineering task, where the user is primarily concerned with understanding the contents and overall structure of the ontology, i.e., acquiring an overview of the concepts covered by the ontology and the way they are organised in a taxonomy. Thus, the sense-making process includes:

- understanding the overall size[32] and shape[33] of the ontology;
- identifying the main components of the ontology and the typical exemplars of these components. Informative exemplars can also help the user to predict the siblings of the class (i.e., the exemplar) in question, thus playing a summarisation role not just with respect to its subtree, but also with respect to its siblings.

Of course, users need to be supported by interfaces and effective summarisation techniques when trying to make sense of large ontologies. That is because, once an ontology is large enough, it is not possible to show its entire structure in the limited space provided by a computer screen and therefore a difficult decision needs to be addressed. On the other hand the information on display needs to be coarse-grained enough to provide an overview of the ontology, thus ensuring the user can maintain an overall mental model of the ontology.

In this scenario, an exploration process needs to be supported, where the user can effectively home in on parts of the ontology, thus changing the level of analysis, while at the same time not losing track of the overall organisation of the ontology.

However, a problem affecting all the approaches discussed in Sect. 6.1.2 is that they all essentially use geometric techniques to providing abstraction. In contrast with these approaches, human experts are able to provide effective overviews of an ontology, simply by highlighting the key areas covered by the ontology and the classes that best describe these areas. In particular, the work reported in (Peroni et al. 2008), that I briefly introduce in Sect. 6.3.1, provides empirical evidence that there is a significant degree of agreement among experts in identifying the main concepts in an ontology. It also shows that the algorithm presented for *key concept extraction (KCE)* is able to retrieve a summarisation of the ontology maintaining the same level of agreement with the experts (Peroni et al. 2008).

[32] Given a node in the ontology, its *size* is the total number of its direct and indirect subclasses.

[33] Given a node in the ontology, its *shape* is an indication of the organisation of the subclasses. For instance, an ontology (or part of it) can have a horizontal (i.e., many subclasses and few levels of depth), or a vertical (i.e., many inheritance levels and only a few subclasses at each level) shape (Tartir et al. 2006). Understanding the shape of an ontology (or part of it) also means to understand whether it is balanced, indicating that all parts of the (sub-)ontology in question have been developed to a similar extent, or unbalanced, possibly indicating that some parts of the (sub-)ontology are less developed than others.

In this section, I will introduce KC-Viz, the *key concept visualiser* (Motta et al. 2010, 2011a, b, 2012), a tool for ontology visualisation and browsing I developed in collaboration with professor Enrico Motta and his research group (Open University, UK). Building on its ability to abstract out from large ontologies through the KCE algorithm, KC-Viz provides a rich set of navigation and visualisation mechanisms, including flexible zooming into and hiding of specific parts of an ontology, history browsing, saving and loading of customised ontology views, as well as essential interface customisation support, such as graphical zooming, font manipulation, tree layout customisation, and other functionalities. KC-Viz is a core plugin of the NeOn Toolkit (Suárez-ueroa et al. 2012).

In the following sections I will give a general view of the KCE algorithm principles and of the main features implemented in KC-Viz. Moreover, I will also report on additional findings gathered through questionnaires, which offer a number of other insights.

6.3.1 Key Concept Extraction

Informally, *key concepts* can be seen as the best descriptors of an ontology, i.e., information-rich concepts, which are most effective in summarising what an ontology is about. In Peroni et al. (2008) a number of criteria are considered to identify the key concepts in an ontology, which are introduced as follows.

Natural Category KCE uses the notion of *natural category* (Rosch 1978)[34], to identify concepts that are information-rich in a psycho-linguistic sense. This notion is approximated by means of two operational measures: *name simplicity*, which favours concepts that are labelled with simple names, and *basic level*, which measures how "central" a concept is in the taxonomy of an ontology.

Density The notion of *density* highlights concepts that are information-rich in a formal knowledge representation sense, i.e., they have been richly characterised with properties and taxonomic relationships. The density is decomposed in two sub-criteria, *global* and *local* density. While the global measures are normalised with respect to all the concepts in the ontology, the local ones consider the relative density of a concept with respect to its surrounding concepts. The aim here is to ensure that "locally significant" concepts get a high score, even though they may not rank too highly with respect to global measures.

[34] Eleanor Rosch has been one of the pioneers of the *prototype theory*, i.e., a cognitive approach for categorisation where some members of a particular category are considered more "central" than others. Rosch's works on categorisation have been the basis of significant subsequent research, such as the notion of *conceptual spaces* by Gardenfors (2000) and of *conceptual metaphors* by Lakoff (1987), Lakoff and Johnson (1980). In this work I have used an operative definition of Rosch's *natural category* derived from her notion of *basic level*.

Coverage The notion of *coverage* is used to ensure that no important part of the ontology is neglected, by maximising the coverage of the ontology with respect to its taxonomic relationships (*rdfs:subClassOf*).

Popularity The notion of *popularity*, drawn from lexical statistics, is introduced as a criterion to identify concepts that are likely to be most familiar to users. Similarly to the density criterion, the popularity is decomposed in two sub-criteria, global and local popularity.

Each of these seven criteria produces a score for each concept in the ontology and the final score assigned to a concept is a weighted sum of the scores resulting from individual criteria. As described in Peroni et al. (2008), which provides a detailed account of our algorithm and a formal definition of the criteria it employs, the approach has been shown to produce ontology summaries that correlate significantly with those produced by human experts.

It is important to emphasise that in the current online version of KCE[35] and in KC-Viz, the popularity criterion is not longer used, because of its computational cost on large ontologies. However, on the basis of the analytical studies described in Li et al. (2010), the weights associated with the other criteria has been parameterised, to produce a vastly more efficient version, while at the same time maintaining the same level of compliance with respect to the available human-generated benchmarks as the version of the algorithm presented in Peroni et al. (2008).

6.3.2 KC-Viz Main Features

Running KC-Viz on an ontology (e.g., FaBiO) for the first time produce an initial visualisation of the network of classes, which includes concepts at different levels in the class hierarchy. The visualisation in Fig. 6.5 includes 26 concepts because I set the size of our ontology summary to 25 and the algorithm has automatically added the most generic concept, *owl:Thing*, to ensure that the visualisation displays a connected graph.

If we wish to display more or less succinct graphs, we can do so by changing the size of the ontology summary. The solid grey arrows in Fig. 6.5 indicate direct *rdfs:subClassOf* links, while the dotted green arrows indicate indirect *rdfs:subClassOf* links.

Nevertheless, starting from the first visualisation, KC-Viz provides the size of the tree under a particular class, which is indicated by a pair of integers, referring to the number of direct and indirect subclasses. For instance, Fig. 6.5 tells us that class *Endeavour* has 4 direct subclasses and 191 total subclasses (direct + indirect). Although more exploration is obviously needed to get a thorough understanding of the content of the FaBiO ontology, it can be argued that as a first step, the visualisation

[35] KCE Live: http://www.essepuntato.it/kce.

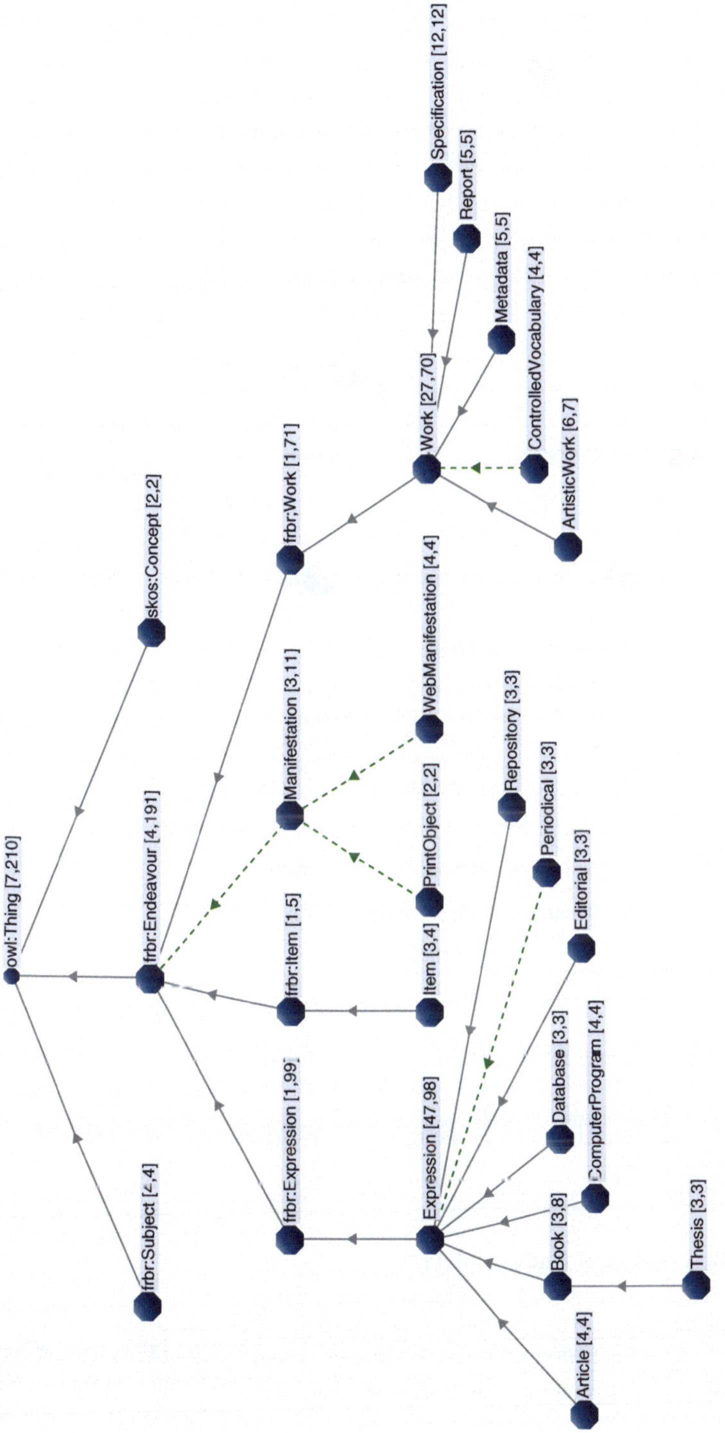

Fig. 6.5 The summarisation made by KC-Viz after its first application on an ontology

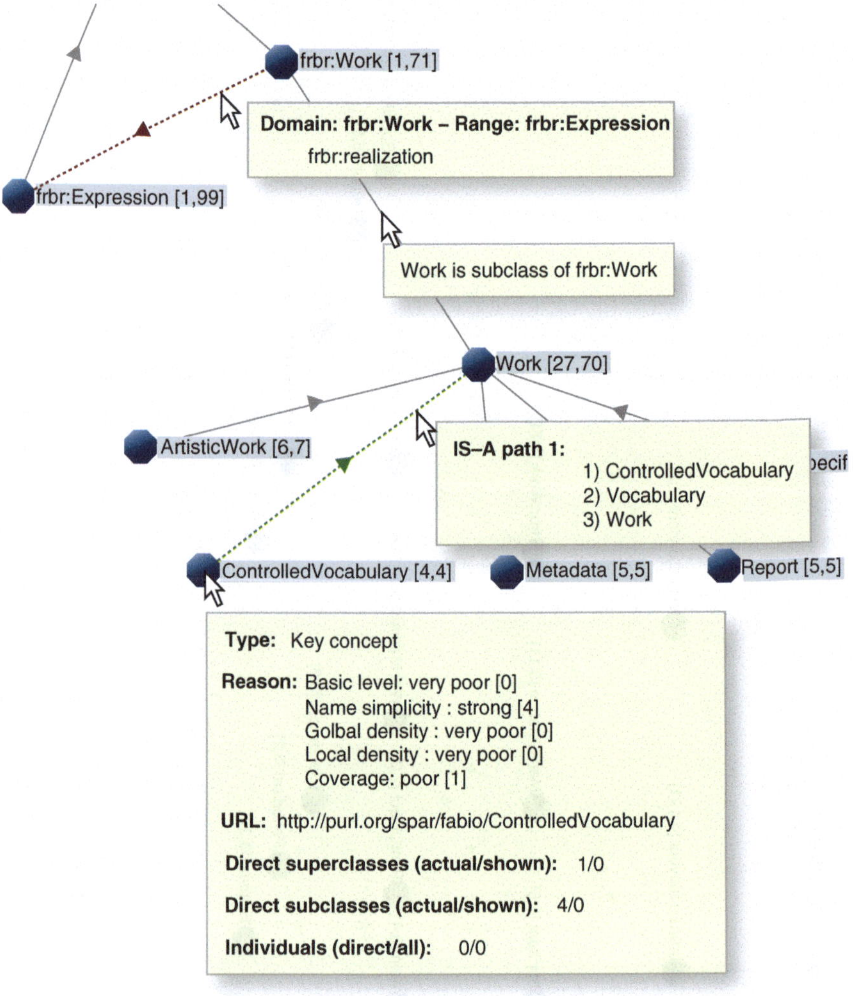

Fig. 6.6 Tooltips that appear hovering nodes and edges

shown in Fig. 6.5 already provides a rather effective starting point for the ontology sense-making process.

6.3.2.1 Description of Nodes and Arcs

By hovering the mouse over an element (node or edge) of the tree, as shown in Fig. 6.6 on page 218, a tooltip is popped up with some information about the element itself: the chain of *rdfs:subClassOf* relations or of domain/range links for edges, as well as information about number of (shown and total) sub- or super- classes for nodes. For

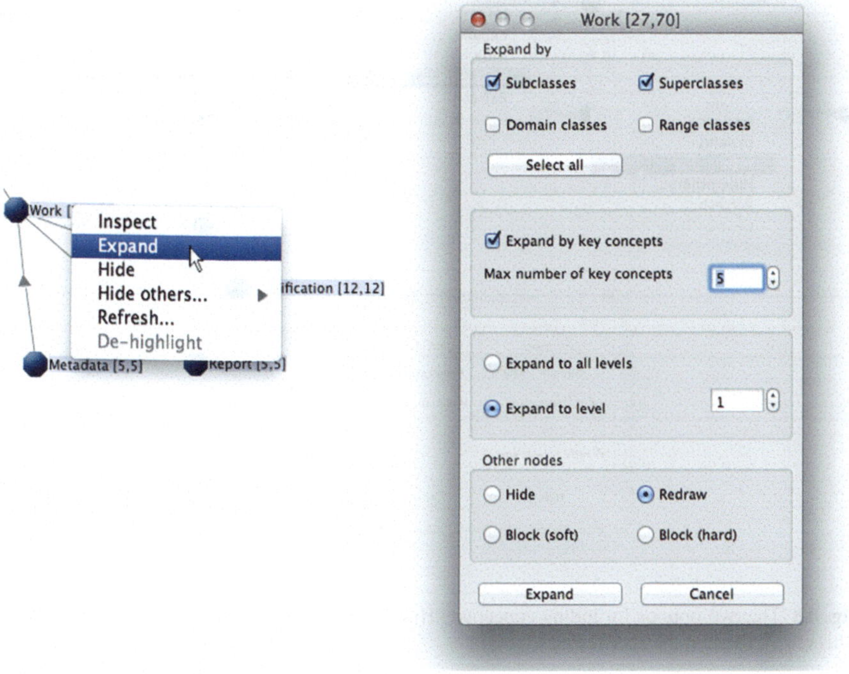

Fig. 6.7 The menu popped up after clicking on the "Expand" option

the latter elements, there exists also a section, called "Reason", which indicates how a node (i.e., a class) fares with respect to the criteria used to determine key concepts. KC-Viz uses a 0–5 scale of labelled values (0 very poor, 1 poor, 2 fair, 3 good, 4 strong, 5 very strong). Moreover, when hovering simultaneously on different arcs, all their descriptions are merged in a single tooltip.

6.3.2.2 Expansion

If we click right on a class displayed in KC-Viz, in this case *Work*, we obtain a menu that includes options for inspecting, expanding, and hiding a class. If we select "Expand", a menu pops up, which provides a rich set of options for exploring the subtree under class *Work*, as shown in Fig. 6.7. In particular, the following four options for customising the expansion algorithm are presented to the user:

- whether to explore following taxonomic relations, other relations (through domain and range), or any combination of these;
- whether or not to make use of the KCE algorithm, which in this case will be applied only to the subtree of class *Work*;
- whether or not to limit the range of the expansion—e.g., by expanding only to one or two levels;

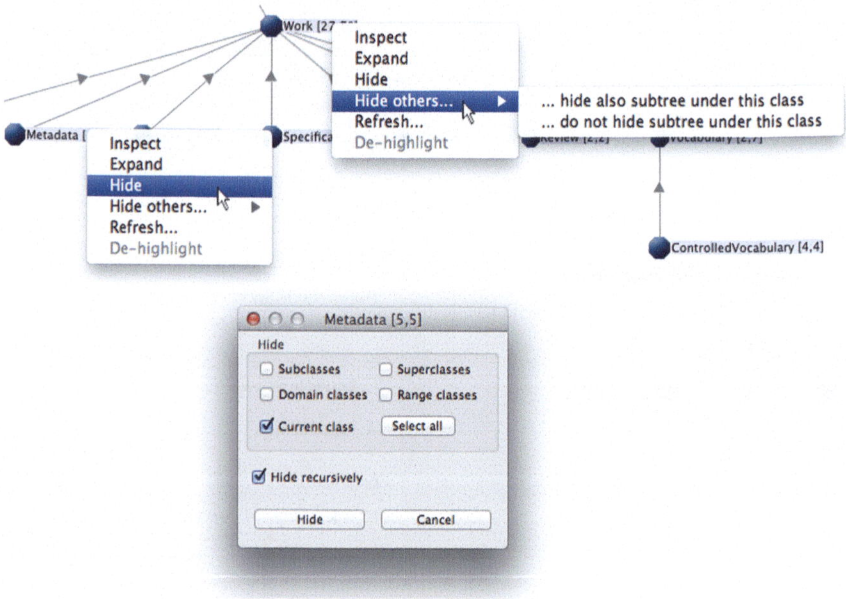

Fig. 6.8 The two options for hiding concepts: "Hide", applied on the class *Metadata*, and "Hide others . . . " used on the class *Work*

- whether to display the resulting visualisation in a new window ("Hide"), or whether to add the resulting nodes to the current windows[36].

6.3.2.3 Hiding

After right-clicking on a node, two options, "Hide" and "Hide others" implement a flexible mechanism for hiding nodes, as shown in Fig. 6.8 on page 220. If we select "Hide", a menu pops up, which provides a rich set of options for hiding the class selected and its subtree. By selecting "Hide others", one can choose to hide all the classes but the selected one and, optionally, its subclasses.

[36] In the latter case, some degree of control is given to the users with respect to the redrawing algorithm, by allowing them to decide whether or not to limit the freedom of the graph layout algorithm to rearrange existing nodes. This is particularly useful in those situations where the expansion is meant to add only a few nodes, and the users do not want the layout to be unnecessarily modified—e.g., because they have already manually rearranged the nodes according to their own preferences.

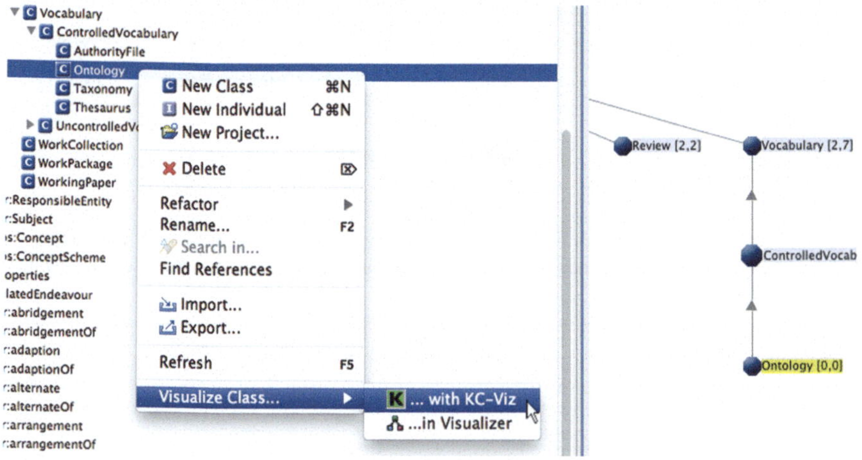

Fig. 6.9 The option "Visualize Class with KC-Viz" to highlight (and eventually add) the class in the current KC-Viz panel

6.3.2.4 Refresh Visualisation

The pop-up obtained after right-clicking inside the KC-Viz view has a new option called "Refresh", which allows the user to re-sync the visualisation with respect to changes in the model, which may have occurred since the visualisation was produced.

6.3.2.5 Integration with NeOn

KC-Viz is integrated within the core components of the NeOn Toolkit, including the Entity Properties View and Ontology Navigator. This means that it is possible to click on nodes in KC-Viz and highlight them in these components (option "Inspect"), as well as click on items shown in the Ontology Navigator and adding them to the visualisation in KC-Viz, as shown in Fig. 6.9.

6.3.2.6 Dashboard

A dashboard containing buttons for acting on the current KC-Viz panel is positioned immediately above the visualisation panel, as shown in Fig. 6.10 on page 222.

In the dashboard there are history buttons that allow the user to move back and forth through the history of KC-Viz operations. Each operation, or move, can be distinguished in macro (extraction and hiding) and micro (re-layout, axis adjustment, node movement) moves. It is important to notice that micro moves can be cancelled/re-applied only if they are not preceded/followed by macro moves in the operation history. For instance, let us consider the sequence "Mac1 mic1 mic2 Mac2 mic3 . . . " and let us suppose to be visualising in KC-Viz the window after mic2 and before Mac2. A user can decide:

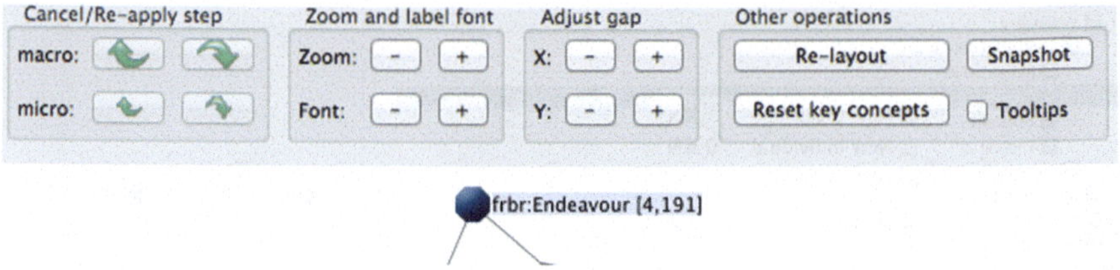

Fig. 6.10 The dashboard which allows the user to move back and forth through the history of KC-Viz operations, to modify the formatting of the layout, and to save the current display to a file, among other things

- to cancel mic2;
- to cancel Mac1;
- to re-apply Mac2.

Moreover, KC-Viz provides an essential interface customisation support, such as graphical zooming, font manipulation and tree layout customisation. For the latter, after clicking on the button "Re-layout" in the KC-Viz toolbar, a sub-menu is opened, which asks the users whether they want to redraw the current visualisation using a top-bottom orientation or a left-right orientation.

Finally, through the button "Snapshot" inside the dashboard, it is possible to save the current display to a file or to load/delete a previously stored one.

6.3.2.7 Preferences

KC-Viz has a preferences panel, shown in Fig. 6.11, which allows the user to set defaults for the most common operations and also enables them to switch to a more efficient (but sub-optimal[37]) algorithm when dealing with very large ontologies. Moreover, all the weights of the formulae used in the KCE algorithm are customisable by the user. In particular, the preference panel allows users to change the relative weights of the different criteria used to calculate the overall score for each class of an ontology. Customisation options are also provided for all the criteria.

6.3.3 *Empirical Evaluation*

In order to gather initial data about the performance of KC-Viz, Motta et al. (2011a), introduce a preliminary empirical evaluation, which required 21 subjects to perform four ontology engineering tasks (max. 15 min/task), involving ontology exploration. The tasks given to the subjects are shown in Table 6.4. This set of tasks was designed to ensure coverage of different exploration strategies, which are typically required in the context of a sense-making activity.

[37] When this preference is enabled the set of key concepts returned by the algorithm may not guarantee the best possible *coverage* of the ontology.

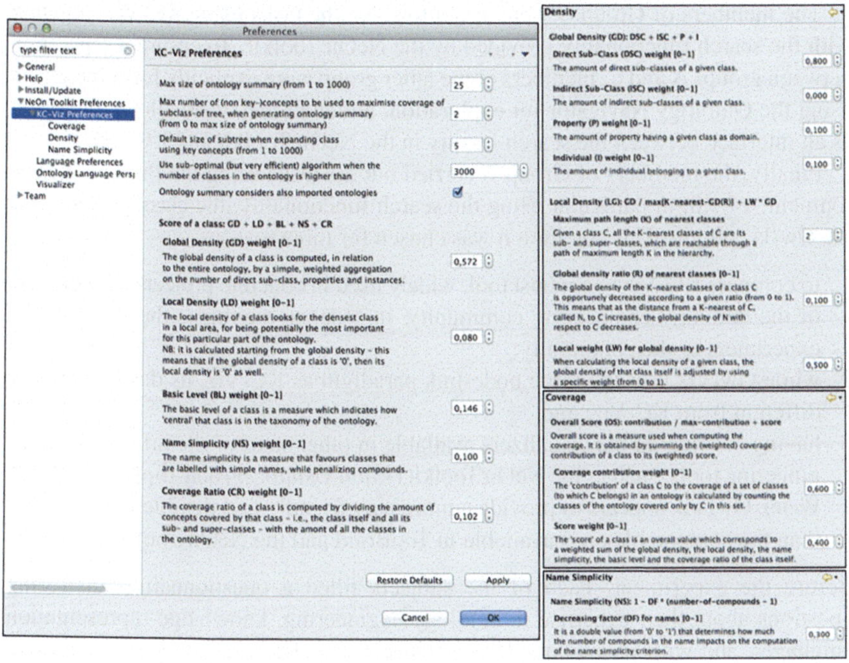

Fig. 6.11 The preference panel of KC-Viz

Table 6.4 Ontology engineering tasks

T1	Which class has the highest number of direct subclasses in the ontology?
T2	What is the most developed (i.e., has the biggest subtree) subclass of class Quantity found in the ontology at a concrete level of granularity (i.e., do not consider abstract classes which have the term 'quantity' in their id)?
T3	Find three subclasses of Agent, at the most abstract level possible (under Agent of course), which are situated at the same level in the hierarchy as each other, and are also subclasses of CorpuscularObject
T4	We have two individual entities (a particular copy of the book War & Peace and a particular 5 p coin). Find the most specific classes in the ontology, to which they belong, say P1 and P2, and then identify the most specific class in the ontology, say C1, which is a superclass of both P1 and P2—i.e., the lowest common superclass of both P1 and P2

The 21 subjects were randomly allocated to three different groups, labelled A, B, and C, where each group used a particular conuration of ontology engineering tools. In particular, members of group A carried out the tasks using the NeOn Toolkit v2.5, without any visualisation support, and they were only allowed to use the search functionality, the *Ontology Navigator* and the *Entity Properties View*. The role of this group was to provide a baseline to the experiment, providing us with some data on how effectively people can tackle ontology exploration tasks, without any visualisation support.

The members of Group C were asked to solve the tasks using KC-Viz, together with the search functionality provided by the NeOn Toolkit. To ensure a separation between groups A and C, members of the latter group were explicitly forbidden from using the Ontology Navigator for exploration, although they were allowed to use it as an interface between the search facility in the NeOn Toolkit and KC-Viz.

Finally, the members of Group B carried out the tasks using the Protégé 4 environment, v4.1.0, in particular using the search functionality, the class browser and the *OwlViz* plugin. This conuration was chosen for three reasons:

1. to compare KC-Viz to a robust tool, widely used in concrete projects by members of the ontology engineering community, in order to maximise the value of the experiment to the community;
2. while OwlViz uses the same node-link paradigm as KC-Viz, its design is rather different from KC-Viz; and
3. having considered the visualizers available in other state-of-the-art ontology engineering tools, such as the NeOn Toolkit (*Kaon Visualizer*) and TopBraid (*Graph View*), OwlViz appears to provide a more user friendly and flexible functionality than the comparable ones available in TopBraid and the NeOn Toolkit.

Before the experiment, each of the subjects filled a questionnaire, answering questions about their expertise in ontology engineering, knowledge representation languages, and with various ontology engineering tools, including (but not limited to) NeOn and Protégé. At the end of the experiment, every subject filled free text questions on the post-task questionnaire to provide views on the perceived strengths and weaknesses of the tool used during the experiment. Additionally, subjects who did not use KC-Viz provided feedback following a demo. Note that none of the subjects had much direct experience with the ontology used for the tasks (i.e., the SUMO ontology[38]).

Out of 84 tasks in total (4 times 21), 71 were completed within the 15 min time limit, while 13 tasks were not completed, a 15.47 % percentage failure. The 13 failures were distributed as follows: 5 in group A (NTK), 6 in group B (OwlViz), and 2 in group C (KC-Viz).

Figure 6.12 shows the average time (in seconds) taken by each group in each task, as well as the total averages across groups and tasks[39]. As shown in the table, on each of the four tasks the fastest mean performance was with KC-Viz, whose overall mean performance was about 13 min faster than OwlViz, which in turn was about two minutes faster than NTK. Although not significant, the difference in total time taken across the four tasks with the three different tools appeared to be approaching significance, $F(2, 20) = 2.655$, $p = 0.098$.

---

[38] The SUMO ontology: http://www.ontologyportal.org/SUMO.owl.

[39] For tasks not completed within the time limit, we consider a 15 min performance. This could be modified to consider 'penalties', such as a 5 min penalty for a non-completed task. However, adding the penalty does not lead to meaningful changes in the interpretation of the data, other than increasing the performance gap between the KC-Viz group and the others.

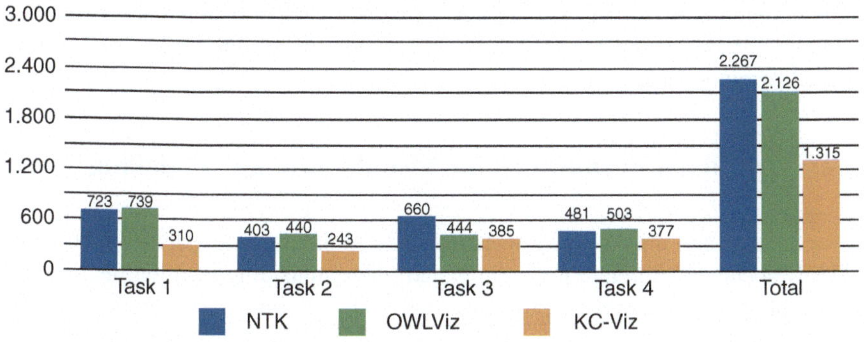

Fig. 6.12 Performances (in seconds) for each task

Table 6.5 Usability scores

NTK mean	OWLViz mean	KC-Viz mean
26.9	25.7	27.1

The difference in performance across the three tools on Task 1, was statistically significant $F(2, 20) = 9.568$, $p < 0.01$. A Tukey HSD pairwise comparison revealed a significant difference between both KC-Viz and NTK ($p < 0.01$) and KC-Viz and OwlViz ($p < 0.01$). Although mean performance was faster for KC-Viz across the board, performance differences on the other three tasks did not reach statistical significance. Nevertheless, these results suggest advantages for KC-Viz in supporting users in such realistic browsing and visualisation tasks.

From the questionnaire data, usability scores were calculated using the SUS formula (Brooke 1996) for each of the three conditions—see Table 6.5. The mean usability score was slightly higher for KC-Viz, though very similar across the three tools and not statistically significant.

The free text questions on the post-task questionnaire were analysed using a grounded theory approach (Birks and Mills 2011). This approach was used to build categories of comments that either expressed positive feedback, offered criticism, or suggested improvements. A category was discarded when it only contained comments from a single subject.

The three main categories of positive comments concerned:

- the flexible support provided by KC-Viz to manipulate the visual displays;
- the abstraction power enabled by the KCE algorithm;
- the value of the subtree summaries provided by KC-Viz.

These results are encouraging in the sense that they provide some initial indication that there is probably a direct causal link between the use of key concepts as an abstraction mechanism and the good performance of KC-Viz on the evaluation tasks, even though these were not designed specifically to map directly to KC-Viz features.

Of the three main categories of negative comments described in Motta et al. (2011a), only one still remains unsolved in the current version of KC-Viz: the lack of integration between KC-Viz and reasoning/query support in the NeOn Toolkit. Obviously, future versions of the tool will be opportunely extended to address this and other minor issues.

6.4 Graffoo, a Framework for Visual Ontology Modelling

Twenty years ago the only way Web users had to publish Web pages was to write HTML documents through text editors and, then, uploading them on the Web by means of appropriate transfer protocols (e.g., FTP). Obviously people might not be self-sufficient to accomplish this task. A first step forward was done in 1997 ca., when WYSIWYG editors for HTML documents were introduced (e.g., *Microsoft Frontpage*). However, although these editors solved the issue of writing HTML pages through the adoption of user-friendly interfaces, a problem still persisted: where and how to upload the documents.

The situation dramatically improved when the paradigm of creating and publishing HTML documents started to involve Web-based application rather than desktop applications. The introduction of blog platforms, wikis, CMSs and other social tools has generated an exponential increase of people writing for and publishing on the Web. The winning strategy has been characterised by two main points:

- to hide the complexity of the HTML markup behind Web interfaces;
- to reduce the entire publishing process to pressing a button.

Currently, some aspects of the Semantic Web, such as the creation of OWL ontologies and RDFS vocabularies, still continue to be discussed within specific research communities, e.g., the Semantic Web and the Ontology Engineering. This precludes a broad adoption of these technologies by non-expert Web users, since people cannot deal with some important semantic technologies unless having proper skills. Like the above-mentioned example about the creation and publication of HTML documents, Web users would start to write and publish OWL ontologies for/on the Web only when:

- there will exist proper interfaces that hide the intrinsic complexity of the OWL framework behind user-friendly GUI;
- the publication process of OWL ontologies will be automatised and reduced to the pressing of a button.

In this section I will describe a work that deals with the first of the above points. Similarly to what I presented in Sect. 6.1.3, here I will introduce the *Graphic framework for OWL ontologies*[40] (*Graffoo*). It is a tool that can be used to present OWL ontologies, or sub-parts of them, through clear and easy-to-understand diagrams.

All the objects that can be used in a Graffoo diagram are shown in Fig. 6.13. These have been developed using the standard library of *yEd*[41], a free diagram editor

[40] Graffoo, the Graphic framework for OWL ontologies: http://www.essepuntato.it/graffoo.

[41] The yEd diagram editor: http://www.yworks.com/en/products_yed_about.html.

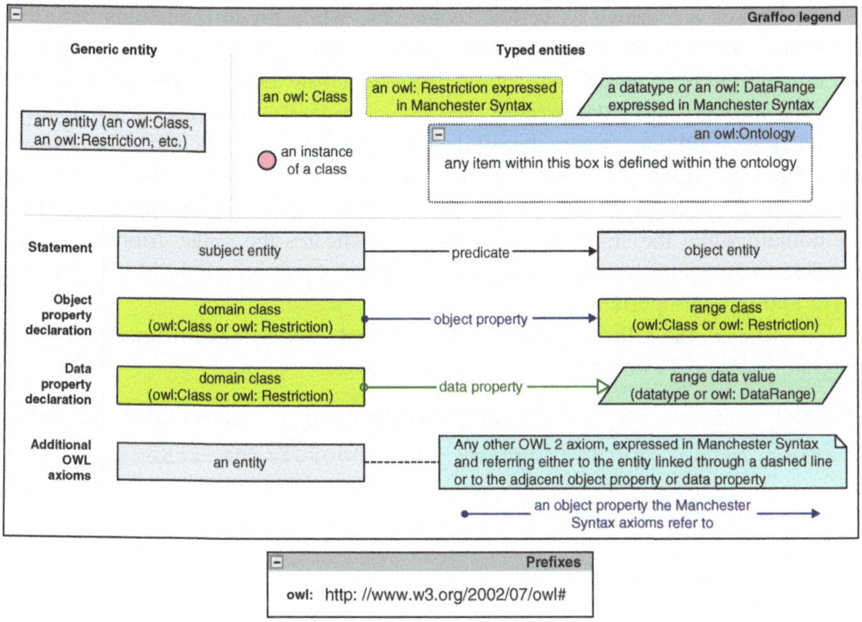

Fig. 6.13 The legend for all possible Graffoo objects

running on Windows, Mac and Linux. The *graphml* format version of these objects is also available[42] and can be loaded as proper section in the yEd palette.

From some preliminary informal studies, it seems that the Graffoo representations of OWL ontologies can be comprehended without the need to understand all the details of OWL 2 or of any of its linearisations (Turtle, RDF/XML, Manchester Syntax, OWL/XML). In particular, when I was developing the SPAR ontologies, I used Graffoo when I needed to illustrate an ontology to users who were not expert in Semantic Web technologies, but who were interested in understanding SPAR ontologies.

In the following sections, I will illustrate how to use Graffoo widgets to formalise ontologies. As example, I use some excerpts from the EARMARK ontology introduced in Sect. 3.1.

6.4.1 *Introducing Classes and Properties*

In Graffoo all the entities can be defined either as an URI surrounded by angular brackets or as a CURIE with a prefix. All the prefixes can be defined within a particular box (entitled "Prefixes") as a list of prefix-URI couples.

[42] http://www.essepuntato.it/graffoo/sources.

The classes are drawn as yellow rectangles, while green rhomboids describe datatypes, and both widgets have solid black borders. Object and data properties are created linking classes, restrictions (introduced in the following section) and datatype through particular arrows. The object property declarations are defined through blue solid lines, where the solid circle at the beginning identifies the domain while the solid arrow at the end indicates the range. The data property declarations are drawn as green solid lines, where the empty circle at the beginning identifies the domain while the empty arrow at the end indicates the range. Moreover, it is possible to associate additional axioms to properties putting a light-blue box close to (or upon) the property it refers to.

For instance, the following excerpt is the Manchester Syntax linearisation of the diagram in Fig. 6.14 on page 229:

```
Prefix: earmark: <http://www.essepuntato.it/2008/12/earmark#>
Prefix: rdfs: <http://www.w3.org/2000/01/rdf-schema#>

Class: earmark:Range

Class: earmark:Docuverse

ObjectProperty: earmark:refersTo
  Domain: earmark:Range
  Range: earmark:Docuverse
  Characteristics: Functional

DataProperty: earmark:begins
  Domain: earmark:Range
  Range: rdfs:Literal

DataProperty: earmark:ends
  Domain: earmark:Range
  Range: rdfs:Literal

DataProperty: earmark:hasContent
  Domain: earmark:Docuverse
  Range: rdfs:Literal
  Characteristics: Functional
```

6.4.2 Defining Restrictions and Additional Class Axioms

The widget that defines restrictions is a light-yellow rectangle with dotted border. Classes and restrictions can be linked to create assertions (e.g., *rdfs:subClassOf* relations) through black solid arrows, labelled according to the property involved in

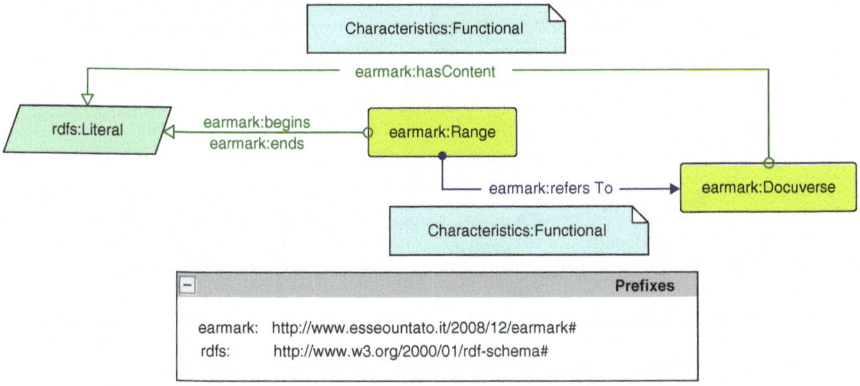

Fig. 6.14 Widgets defining prefixes, classes, object/data properties and property axioms

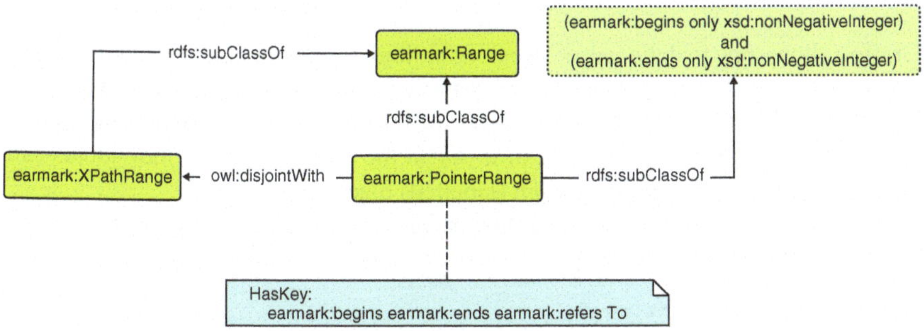

Fig. 6.15 Widgets defining restrictions and other class axioms

the assertion in consideration. Moreover, additional axioms (in Manchester Syntax) can be associated to classes using a light-blue box linked through a dashed line.

For instance, the following excerpt is the Manchester Syntax linearisation of the diagram in Fig. 6.15:

```
Class: earmark:PointerRange
  SubClassOf:

    earmark:Range ,
    (earmark:begins only xsd:nonNegativeInteger) and
      (earmark:ends only xsd:nonNegativeInteger)
  DisjointWith: earmark:XPathRange
  HasKey: earmark:begins earmark:ends earmark:refersTo

Class: earmark:XPathRange
  SubClassOf: earmark:Range
```

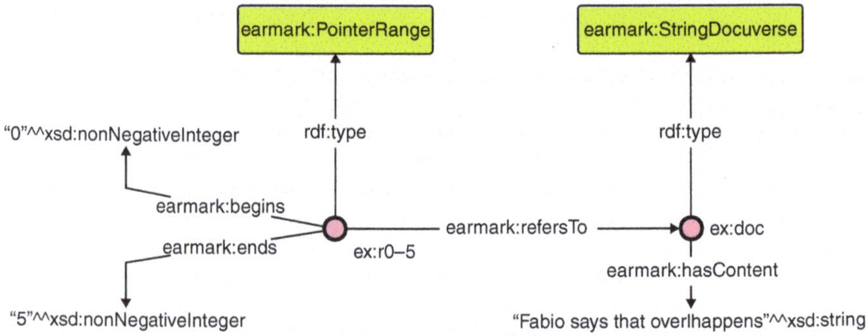

Fig. 6.16 Widgets defining individuals and related assertions

6.4.3 Linking Class Individuals

Graffoo allows one to define also ABox of ontologies, by creating individuals having a particular type. The widget used to define those individuals is a pink circle with solid black border. Note that this widget specifies the URL/CURIE of the related individual around it, rather than in the middle of it. As all the other resources, individuals can be linked to create assertions through (labelled) black solid arrows.

For instance, the following excerpt is the Manchester Syntax linearisation of the diagram in Fig. 6.16:

```
NamedIndividual: ex:r0-5
  Types: earmark:PointerRange
  Facts:
    earmark:begins "0"^^xsd:nonNegativeInteger ,
    earmark:ends "5"^^xsd:nonNegativeInteger ,
    earmark:refersTo ex:doc

NamedIndividual: ex:doc
  Types: earmark:StringDocuverse
  Facts:
    earmark:hasContent "Fabio says that overlappens"^^xsd:string
```

6.4.4 Defining Assertions Between Ontologies

Graffoo includes a specific widget—a transparent box with a light-blue heading and a dotted black border—for the specification of ontologies. The ontology URIs are put in the heading of this widget.

All the entities contained by this widget are formally defined within the related ontology. Moreover, like the other resources, ontologies can be linked to create assertions (e.g., *owl:imports*) through (labelled) black solid arrows.

For instance, the following excerpt is the Manchester Syntax linearisation of the diagram in Fig. 6.17:

```
Ontology: <http://www.essepuntato.it/2008/12/earmark>
  Import: <http://www.essepuntato.it/2010/05/ghost>

Class: earmark:PointerRange
  SubClassOf:
    earmark:Range ,
    (earmark:begins only xsd:nonNegativeInteger) and
      (earmark:ends only xsd:nonNegativeInteger)
  DisjointWith: earmark:XPathRange
  HasKey: earmark:begins earmark:ends earmark:refersTo

Class: earmark:XPathRange
  SubClassOf: earmark:Range

Class: earmark:Range
  Annotations: rdfs:isDefinedBy
    <http://www.essepuntato.it/2010/05/ghost>

Class: earmark:Docuverse
  Annotations: rdfs:isDefinedBy
    <http://www.essepuntato.it/2010/05/ghost>

ObjectProperty: earmark:refersTo
  Annotations: rdfs:isDefinedBy
    <http://www.essepuntato.it/2010/05/ghost>

DataProperty: earmark:begins
  Annotations: rdfs:isDefinedBy
    <http://www.essepuntato.it/2010/05/ghost>

DataProperty: earmark:ends
  Annotations: rdfs:isDefinedBy
    <http://www.essepuntato.it/2010/05/ghost>
```

6.5 Gaffe, a Flexible and User-Friendly Authoring Tool for Semantic Data

The process of associating semantic data to resources, such as documents, is quite complex in principle. The first issue is that several and alternative models (e.g., metadata schemas, vocabularies, ontologies) can be used to describe the same resource within a particular domain (e.g., publishing). Some of these models are almost equivalent, others are characterised by individual features. For instance, all metadata models for the description of bibliographic documents are expected to include information about the "author", "publisher" and "year". At the same time, a schema describing Ph.D. theses needs to include similar information (for instance, "author"

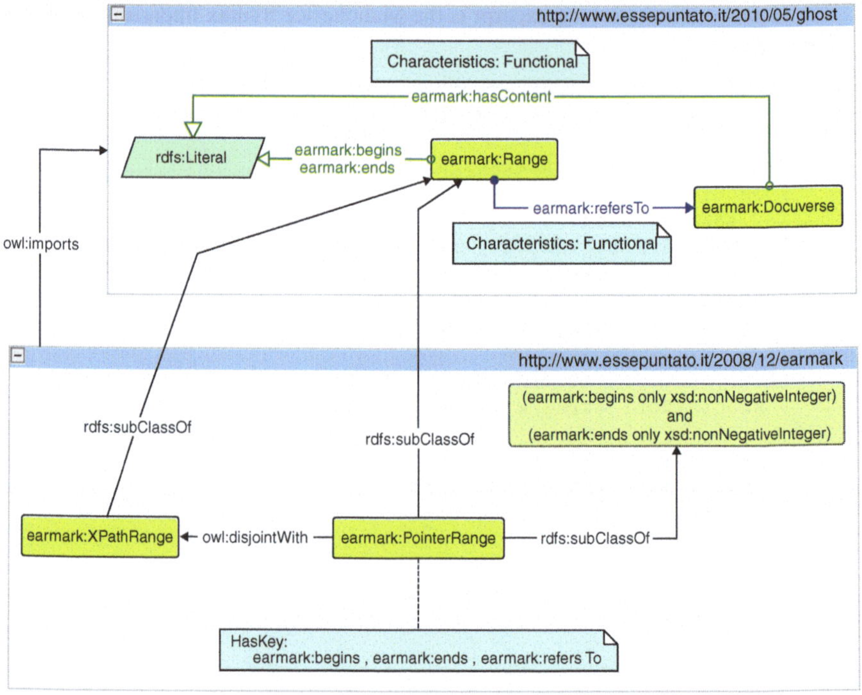

Fig. 6.17 Widgets for defining ontologies and related assertions

and "year") and more domain-specific data such as "id number", "supervisor" and "discipline". The choice of the most suitable model depends on two main factors:

- the nature of the resource (e.g., a document);
- the applications (and users) that the resource is meant to be processed by (e.g., Wikis and word processors).

Still, choosing the appropriate model is not sufficient. It is also important that an interface enables the creation of semantic data in an intuitive and usable way, thus hiding the complexity of the particular formalism or model used. A good model that is not supported by a good editing interface risks to be useless: authors would often decide not to insert data, considering it a pointless, time-consuming and deferrable task.

I have identified four main features that a flexible and user-friendly authoring tool for semantic data should have:

- *genericness*, the editor should support any model in a flexible way;
- *customisability*, instead of generating a static form—strictly dependent on a given model—the editor should be customisable for models, users' needs and preferences;

- *proactivity*, the editor should provide users with facilities that simplify the authoring process, such as pre-filled form fields, suggestions, default values, access to environment variables, and so on;
- *validation*, the editor should apply validation mechanisms to check the correctness of the inserted values.

A solid approach to flexible interfaces consists in adopting the "Model-View-Controller" (MVC) pattern (Gamma et al. 1994), as developed in the software engineering community. This pattern implements a clear separation between the *business logic* of an application and the *user interface* for visualising/editing data: it allows designers to generate applications whose interfaces can be easily modified without affecting the model and vice versa.

Discussing the benefits of MVC is out of the scope of this book, but it is important to explore how this pattern can help to design a flexible and sophisticated metadata editor. In the context of metadata editors, the three components of MVC become:

- *Model* The model corresponds to the actual semantic data as manipulated by the editor and associated to the document/resource. Changing the model describing semantic data means changing the model of MVC, and this should always be possible, in order to obtain a model-independent editor;
- *View* The view is the way semantic data are shown to the users. Usually, the view can be classified according to two different types: the *edit interface* and the *visualisation interface*. The edit interface has to be a rich graphical interface, with a large number of graphical widgets to specify semantic data values according to their type and expected values. The more widgets are sophisticated and well-structured, the more easily users can create semantic data. The visualisation interface shows the current resource-related data only, without changing the internal model. The visualisation can happen through deactivated form fields, but also with plain textual or tabular visualisation. Since model and view are separated, it is possible to assign multiple views to the same semantic model, each tailored to roles, personal preferences and local policies of the intended users;
- *Controller* The controller is the component in charge of managing the interaction between the user and the application. It has to store the values provided by user into the model. Moreover, it is expected to run a *pre-processing phase* to provide default values to relevant form fields and a *post-processing* one to validate metadata values as provided by the user. The controller thus handles all input events and notifies the model of each user's action that generates changes to the model itself.

Of course, previous solutions that combined the MVC pattern with other approaches were had been proposed to address the issue of associating semantic data to electronic documents. In particular, my research group has been working for years on an approach consisting of two steps. First, creating ontological descriptions of the domain and of the interfaces to manipulate semantic data. Second, transforming those descriptions into the actual interfaces that are shown to the users. My personal contribution in this field is the development of the new Java implementation of *Gaffe* (*Generator of Advanced Forms and Friendly Editor*; Bolognini et al. 2009). Gaffe is a MVC-based API that makes it possible to build customisable editors for semantic data, so as to allow users to annotate a resource according to any scheme as expressed through an OWL ontology. More precisely, Gaffe uses two different ontologies:

- the *domain* ontology represents the conceptual model. Since this ontology is unconstrained, users can adopt any custom model without any restriction, as long as it is expressible in OWL;
- the *GUI* ontology specifies the classes and properties of widgets and form elements of a graphical user interfaces, as well as the mapping between interface widgets and properties of the domain ontology.

The *instance* document is an instantiation of the GUI ontology to describe an actual interface, as generated by associating domain elements to graphical widgets and by customising the final appearance of each item.

In the following sections I will introduce a Gaffe-based prototypical application called OWiki, developed specifically for demonstrating the capabilities of the Gaffe principles.

6.5.1 OWiki: Ontology-Driven Generation of Templates and Forms for Semantic Wikis

OWiki (Di Iorio et al. 2010a, b, 2011a) is a Gaffe-based extension of MediaWiki that supports users in creating and editing semantic data. The basic idea of OWiki is to exploit ontologies and MediaWiki editing/viewing facilities to simplify the process of authoring semantic wiki content.

In particular, OWiki exploits MediaWiki templates, infoboxes and forms. A *template* is a set of pair *key-value,* edited as a record and usually formatted as a table in the final wiki page. Templates are particularly useful to store structured information, as they are: very easy to edit; disconnected from the final formatting of a page; very easy to search, and so on. Templates are defined in special pages that can be referenced from other pages. These pages include fragments with the same structure of the template but filled with instance data. The template-based component of a page is also called *infobox.*

OWiki exploits ontologies to represent the (semantic) knowledge base of a wiki and templates to display and add ABox assertions of the ontology through the wiki itself. The integration and interaction between ontologies and templates can be summarised in two points:

- each class of the ontology is associated to a template-page. Each property is mapped into a key of the infobox;
- each instance of that class is represented by a page associated to that template. Each line in the infobox then contains the value of a property for that instance. Data properties are displayed as simple text while object properties are displayed as links to other pages (representing other instances of the ontology).

OWiki templates are actually invisible to users. Each template is associated to a form that allows users to create and edit the relative instances. Users do not modify the templates *directly* but they only access specialised form fields.

The crucial point is that even forms are generated automatically from ontological data. Obviously, OWiki includes a *GUI ontology* describing widgets and interface elements. The concepts and relations of the *domain ontology*—that is the ontology according to which semantic data are specified—are mapped into form elements that are delivered to the final user.

During the installation phase, OWiki creates a basic set of forms by merging the domain ontology with the GUI one. At the editing phase, the system shows a very basic form and saves it as a special page (template). This page can then be organised as a new form by adding dynamic behaviours, moving buttons, changing the field order and so on.

Before describing the internal architecture of the system, it is worth spending few more words about the way OWiki uses ontologies. The extensive usage of ontologies makes it possible (1) to make OWiki independent on the domain it is used for, (2) to customise forms and templates easily, and (3) to describe the evolution of a wiki page and its semantic content fully.

6.5.1.1 The Architecture of OWiki

OWiki is an integrated framework composed of three modules, delivered with different technologies:

- a *MediaWiki extension* It is a module integrated in MediaWiki written in PHP that adds OWiki facilities;
- an *Ontology manager* It is a Java web service that processes OWL ontologies to produce forms for editing metadata. This manager uses both Jena API (Carroll et al. 2004) and OWLAPI (Horridge and Bechhofer 2011);
- an *Ajax-based interface* A client-side module that allows users to insert data directly through the forms generated by the OWiki engine.

The PHP OWiki module follows the same architecture of any MediaWiki extension: some scripts and methods are overridden to provide new features. In particular, the module implements a revised editor that initialises the OWiki environment variables, sets the communication with the client and sets the data necessary to store forms in the MediaWiki database without interfering with existing data.

To manipulate ontologies, OWiki implements a web service that uses the Jena API. Jena is integrated with the Pellet reasoner (Sirin et al. 2007), which is exploited to extract information about the instances in the ontology. Ranges of some properties, as well as their values, are in fact derived from subsumptions or other relations expressed in the ontology itself.

The web-service specifically generates templates from the ontological data, which are later sent to the PHP module and stored in the right place of the MediaWiki installation.

The connection between the modules—PHP and Java—and the core of the overall framework is the OWiki client. The client is a javascript application, based on

Mootools[43], in charge of generating and delivering forms. It is strongly based on the Model-View-Controller (MVC) pattern and its internal architecture can be divided in four layers:

- *The Connection Layer* manages the overall environment, the initialisation phase and the communication between all other layers.
- *The Model Layer* (Model of MVC) manages the data to be displayed on the page. It is composed of a factory that creates wrappers for each type of data and instantiates data from the ontology.
- *The Look And Feel* (View of MVC) manages the final representation of the form, containing atomic and complex widgets, manipulators and decorators.
- *The Interaction Layer* (Controller of MVC) implements the logic of the application, the communication with the web-service, the generation of semantic data and the end-user interaction.

6.5.1.2 Using Ontologies to Model the Domain

Since it implements the Gaffe architecture, in OWiki the entire *domain of discourse*—i.e., all the topics presented on each page—is handled by using a *domain ontology*. Two different kinds of classes exist in this ontology: those—*page-domain* classes—that strictly relate to articles and pages visualised by the wiki, and those—*data-domain* classes—that define additional data around the former ones.

Each individual of the *page-domain* classes results in a wiki page containing text content (the content is now stored in the MediaWiki internal database) and all the semantic data directly related to that individual. Figure 6.18 shows a page (about a particular type of beer[44]) that contains a textual description of it in the central page area, while in the right box there are all the metadata related to the beer.

While some metadata such as "Beer Alcoholic content" or "Beer Brewed by" are proper to any beer directly, since they are defined by OWL data or object properties having the class *Beer* as domain, that is not true for other metadata, such as "Winner Award" and "Winner Awarded on". In fact, those properties are handled using the *data-domain* class *Awarding* that represents an event concerning a particular prize occurred at a specific time. The model of such properties for the beer in consideration, shown in Fig. 6.18, is explained in the following excerpt (in Turtle syntax):

```
:carlsberg a :Beer ; :hasAwarding :awardingEuropean2007 .


:awardingEuropean2007 a :Awarding ;
  :hasAward :europeanBeerAward ;
  :hasYear "2007" .
```

[43] Mootools: http://mootools.net.

[44] The demo installation of OWiki I use in the following examples is available at http://owiki.web.cs.unibo.it.

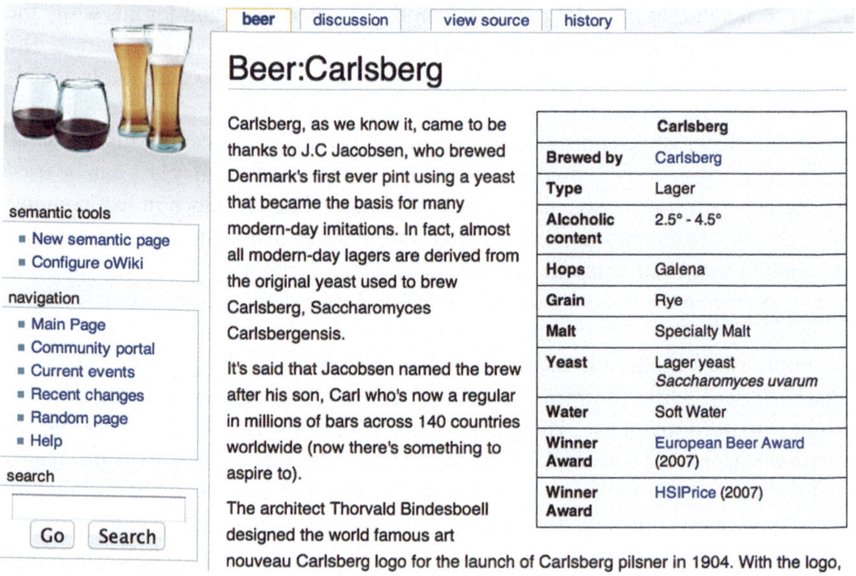

Fig. 6.18 An example page of the Beer OWiki

The values shown in the Carlsberg page are not directly extracted from the Carlsberg ontological individual: they are taken from the awarding event the Carlsberg beer participated to.

Even if they are not directly represented as wiki pages, OWiki uses *data-domain* individuals to enrich even more the metadata of *page-domain* individuals. This enrichment is achieved by retrieving related data from non-page-domain individuals making at least two steps on the RDF graph represented by the model. We call *property flattening* the visualisation of those *data-domain* property values into a *page-domain* individual.

6.5.1.3 Using Ontologies to Model the Interface

OWiki also exploits ontologies to model end-user interfaces. In particular, the system includes a preliminary version of the GUI ontology developed for Gaffe. This ontology is used for identifying all the components of web forms. The system instantiates and merges that ontology with the domain ontology in order to generate the final forms. The definitive version of the Gaffe GUI ontology is still under development but the core concepts and relations are stable and already tested in the current prototype.

The aim of separating the GUI ontology from the domain ontology is two-fold:

1. generating a declarative description of the interface widgets that can be reused across multiple domains and not being bound to specific data;
2. allowing users to customise the final interfaces by only changing the association between content and interface widgets.

It is to be noted that the GUI ontology can be designed once and for all, while the domain ontology requires different expertise for different application scenarios. The GUI ontology defines two types of graphical elements: *controllers* and *panels*. Panels are containers for other elements (that can be panels, in turn) used to organise the overall interface, while controllers are single widgets allowing users to fill metadata.

The main class of the ontology is *OWikiForm*. Instances of this class can be used to generate each form associated to each wiki page. Each instance in fact contains either graphical elements or property values from the domain ontology. *OWikiForms* can contain *simple* or *complex* types of controllers. Simple types are associated to data properties in the domain ontology, while complex types are associated to object properties.

Simple types model the basic form elements (*Textfield*, *ComboBox*, *CheckBox* e *RadioButton*) while complex types model constructs useful for mapping the GUI ontology to the domain one. There are two complex types: *ConnectField* and *ObjectContainer*. *ConnectField* model links to another wiki document. This is ultimately used to provide users with auto-completion operations on corresponding form fields: when the user fills this field, the system suggests a set of linked documents they can choose from (or create a link to a completely new resource). These links are in fact derived from the relations in the domain input ontology. *ObjectContainers* are widgets that include properties of a class which are not directly linked to the one defining a particular page, including to documents data about other (related) subjects. This class implements what I described earlier as *property flattening*.

6.5.2 *Studying OWiki Through a Use-Case*

The main goal of OWiki is to simplify the creation of semantic data *through and within* wikis. The complexity of such metadata authoring process, in fact, is hidden behind the application so that users do not need to learn new interfaces and tools. Users can therefore easily create semantic data by exploiting forms and templates that are automatically generated from ontological data.

In this section I will explain in details this generation process, making clear how ontological data are converted into (customised) interfaces. Basically, the overall OWiki process consists of three steps:

1. ontology import and forms generation;
2. forms customisation;
3. templates and data generation.

6.5.2.1 From Ontologies to Forms

The first step consists of importing the input domain ontology into the wiki. Let us consider a sample application, which we will discuss throughout the following sections: an OWiki demo installation describing beers; breweries; ingredients, etc.

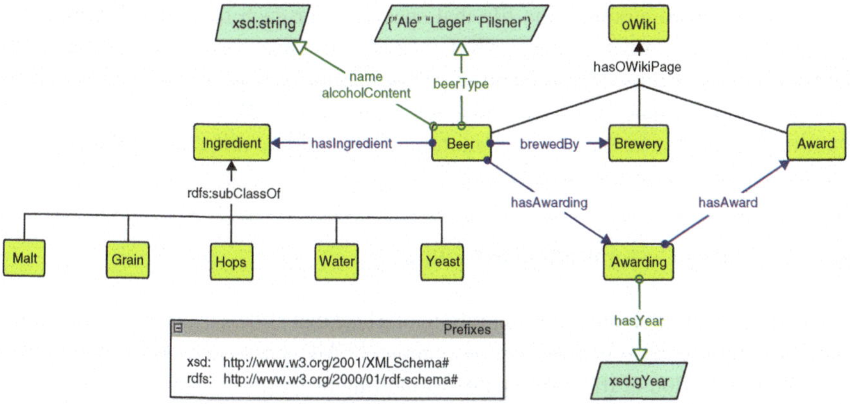

Fig. 6.19 A graphical representation of the OWiki domain ontology about beers

Figure 6.19 shows some classes and properties of a domain ontology suitable for such an application.

Classes and properties are mapped into wiki pages as follows: each concept is mapped into a page and properties are expressed through templates. In particular, data properties become lines of templates infoboxes and object properties become typed links.

Note that the overall status of the OWiki installation is consistent at this stage, assuming that the domain input ontology was consistent. The process is in fact a straightforward translation of classes and relations into pages and links.

The OWiki conversion process also produces forms to edit the ontological content. Forms are dynamically built by analysing the class properties of the imported ontology and by mapping each property in the proper element of the GUI interface.

In the example, the class *Beer* defines three properties: *name*, *beerType* and *alcoholContent*. According to the type of these properties OWiki generates text fields or radio buttons; the default element is a text field that allows any type of value. Since in the input ontology the only possible values of the property *beerType* are "Ale", "Lager" and "Pilsner", the system add to the form a RadioButton element specifying those values.

For object properties OWiki chooses between two types of widgets according to their range: if the range class is associated (through the property *hasOWikiPage*) to the class *oWiki*, the system adds a *ConnectField* to the form; otherwise it adds an *ObjectContainer*. Since the class *Beer* has the object property *brewedBy* with the class *Brewery* specified as range, the system adds to the form a widget that allows one to include a link to a corresponding brewery page. This widget will also provide auto-completion features built on top of the relations expressed in the input ontology.

It is very important to make it clear that: there is a default mapping between classes of the domain ontology and elements in the GUI ontology based on *the type of the properties*. The name of a property or its meaning in a specific domain is not relevant.

There is indeed a conuration file that specifies, for each type, which widget to use and how to conure it. In the previous case, for instance, there was an association between enumerations and radio buttons. This mapping is deployed whenever a class has a property that may only have a finite set of values, regardless of the actual domain ontology. A change in the OWiki conuration file would be reflected by the use of a different widget for the same property.

6.5.2.2 Forms Customisation and Filling

Furthermore, OWiki includes a conuration interface that allows users to set a domain-specific mapping between the input (domain and GUI) ontologies, and to conure the overall organisation of the form and its formatting properties.

The first time a user edits a page, OWiki shows a basic form. The author can then organise a new form adding dynamic behaviours, moving buttons, changing fields order and so on. Figure 6.20 shows a simple example of a customised form: while the original form only listed a set of plain text-fields, this one is organised in panels and uses radio-buttons, images and dynamic widgets.

Customisation can happen at different level. The user can change colour, font and background of the text to increase the appeal and impact of the form; they can change the position and the order of the elements to increase the importance of certain data; they can change the optionality of the elements, their default values, and so on.

The current implementation requires users to customise forms by editing an XML conuration file, through the wiki itself. Even if such an approach is not optimal, the internal architecture of the system relies on a strong distinction between the declarative description of the form (through the GUI ontology) and its actual delivery. That makes possible to implement a user-friendly and graphic environment to create and customise forms. A future development I will be working on is the implementation of such an editor within the OWiki framework.

6.5.2.3 From Semantic Data to Templates and Views

Automatically-generated forms are finally exploited by the wiki users to write the semantic data. As described in the previous section, data are stored as templates and templates are manipulated by forms *in a transparent manner*.

Let me consider again the *Beer* class of the example. OWiki generates a form to create instances of those classes showing three main components:

- a text field to insert the name of the beer;
- a radio-button to select the type of the beer. Values in the radio button are directly extracted from the domain ontology;
- a text field to insert the brewery, which suggests breweries by exploiting information in the domain ontology.

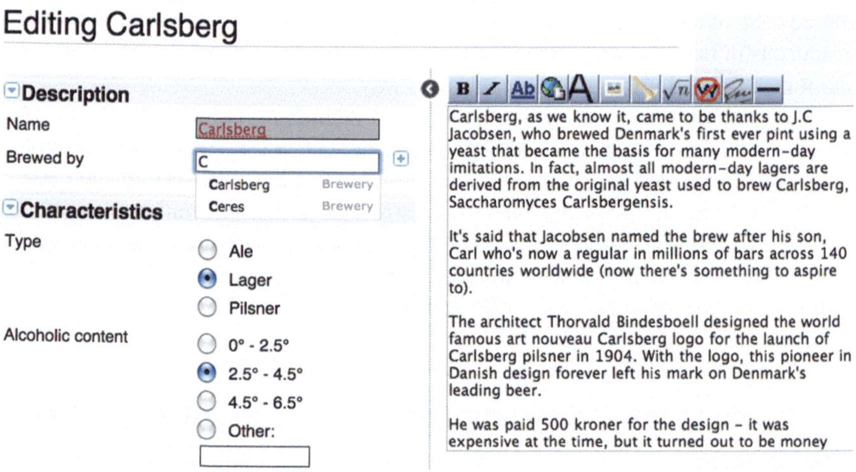

Fig. 6.20 A customised form generated by OWiki

These components can even be organised in multiple panels. Once the user has filled the form OWiki saves a template with the proper information. Infobox templates, in fact, are used to display metadata and to cluster information about the same document.

Each infobox line corresponds to a field in the form that, in turn, corresponds to a parameter and its value in the domain ontology. As expected, the data properties of a class are displayed as simple text while the object properties are displayed as links to other documents.

The page corresponding to the Carlsberg beer in the example, that is an instance of the class *Beer*, and has been edited via the corresponding form, will contain the following (partial) infobox:

```
{{Infobox Beer |
hasoWikiNamePage=Carlsberg |
Beer_brewedBy=[[Brewery:Carlsberg|Carlsberg]] |
Beer_beerType=Lager |
Beer_hasAlcoholicContent=2.5 - 4.5 |
Hops_hasName=Galena | ... }}
```

Note that the property *Beer_brewedBy* contains a link to the page *Carlsberg* that is now an instance of the *Brewery* class. Relations in the input ontology are then mapped into the links between pages. The *Carlsberg* instance follows the same approach, being described by the infobox:

```
{{Infobox Brewery |
hasoWikiNamePage=Carlsberg |
Brewery_hasAddress=Valby 11 DK - 2500, Copenhagen |
Brewery_brews=[[Beer:Carlsberg|Carlsberg]] }}
```

Some final considerations are worth here about the consistency of OWiki. First of all, note that OWiki forms only work on the instances of the underlying ontology, without any impact on the classes and relations among them. The consequence is that, assuming that users do not corrupt infoboxes (that are anyway available in the source code of a wiki page), the overall ontology keeps being consistent. The OWiki instance is in fact consistent *by construction* with the domain and the GUI ontology and it is populated via forms in a controlled way.

Thus, we can conclude—going back to the distinction between "wikis for ontologies" and "ontologies for wikis" proposed in Sect. 6.1.4—that OWiki currently belongs to the second group and does not properly use the wiki to build and update ontologies. In the future, I also plan to investigate a further integration between the wiki and the ontology—and a further integration between the textual content of a wiki page and the relative infoboxes—in order to use OWiki as a fully-fledged simplified authoring environment for ontologies as well.

6.6 From LIME to Semantically-Enhanced Legislative Editors

The legislative process is composed by two different elements: the *legal* aspect and the *documental* aspect. While the former concerns the application and evaluation of existing legislation within a particular scope, the latter, which is of particular interest for the topics of this book, addresses issues related to the documentary organisation of legislative texts, in terms of both the content (from the first draft to subsequent revisions) and the formats recording that content (from analogue to digital ones).

As introduced in Sect. 2.2, several markup languages have been developed in the past to provide robust mechanisms to define legal and legislative documents through standard digital formats such as XML. However, we still have to tackle the same point: user-friendly interfaces are needed to guarantee a broad adoption of those languages in specific contexts such as parliaments, commissions, governments, and so on. Tools enabling the creation of documents in those formats, such as editors and Web platform, are fundamental to promote the diffusion of such technologies.

One of the strategic advantages that have guaranteed the broad adoption of Akoma Ntoso (see Sects. 4.1 and 2.2.6) in real contexts is derived from the release of (standalone and Web-based) editors for Akoma Ntoso documents. These applications—namely Bungeni, AT4AM and LIME, which I will introduce in the following subsections—are thought to support domain users in structuring plain text through Akoma Ntoso markup vocabulary, even when the users are not aware of the particular technologies used to write and store legislative digital texts.

At the moment of writing this section (2013), the current implementation of such editors is quite robust for what concerns the application of XML-based markup structures upon plain text content. However, their future aim is also to enable the enhancement of documents through semantic annotations (i.e., RDF statements and OWL axioms) according to particular user-defined models, so as to let such editors evolve into fully-compliant Semantic Web applications.

In this section I will introduce briefly the aforementioned editors for Akoma Ntoso documents and then I will sketch out a list of requirements for the next generation of Semantic Web-aware legislative editors of the future[45].

6.6.1 Bungeni

Bungeni [46] (English translation: *inside Parliament*) is a collaborative software development initiative based on Akoma Ntoso and other open source applications that provides a leading solution for drafting, managing, consolidating and publishing legislative and other parliamentary documents. It aims of making Parliaments more open and accessible to citizens.

One of the outputs of Bungeni is the development of an editor for legislative documents, called *Bungeni Editor*[47], which is a markup framework for the production of XML documents that conform to the Akoma Ntoso DTD. In particular, the Bungeni Editor was developed to manage a particular kind of Akoma Ntoso document, i.e., *reports*, which are documents containing any written account of parliamentary proceedings.

The editor is an extension of OpenOffice Writer[48], and allows users to enrich documents written through the OpenOffice Writer interface by means of three particular windows: the *control panel*; the *metadata editor*, and the *markup panel*, as shown in Fig. 6.21.

The control panel is used to create and open documents. It provides several functionalities such as text boxes which allow editors to add notes to the text; metadata visualisation; document validation against Akoma Ntoso DTD, and other tools to transform documents from the ODT format into others.

The metadata editor is used to enter preliminary and/or required metadata (the latter are accompanied by an "*" in the interface) to further mark the document up. In particular, the tab "General" contains fields to specify information related to the Akoma Ntoso document, while the other tabs (e.g., "Parliament" in the example in Fig. 6.21) are specific to particular kinds of document as they are defined in the "General" tab. In addition to defining metadata for the document level, it is also possible to specify information to non-overlapping blocks of text within the same document, since it may happen that a text involves particular agents as actors (e.g., the parliament, the judge, the language used, etc.) taking part in the event it describes (e.g., a speech).

[45] Note that it is difficult to freeze a moment for a complete description of a rapidly evolving situation related to ongoing projects and applications such as those described in the following sections. Therefore, all the considerations and descriptions about such tools refers to their status in June 2013.

[46] Bungeni project homepage: http://www.bungeni.org/.

[47] Bungeni editor homepage: https://code.google.com/p/bungeni-editor/.

[48] OpenOffice Writer homepage: http://www.openoffice.org/product/writer.html.

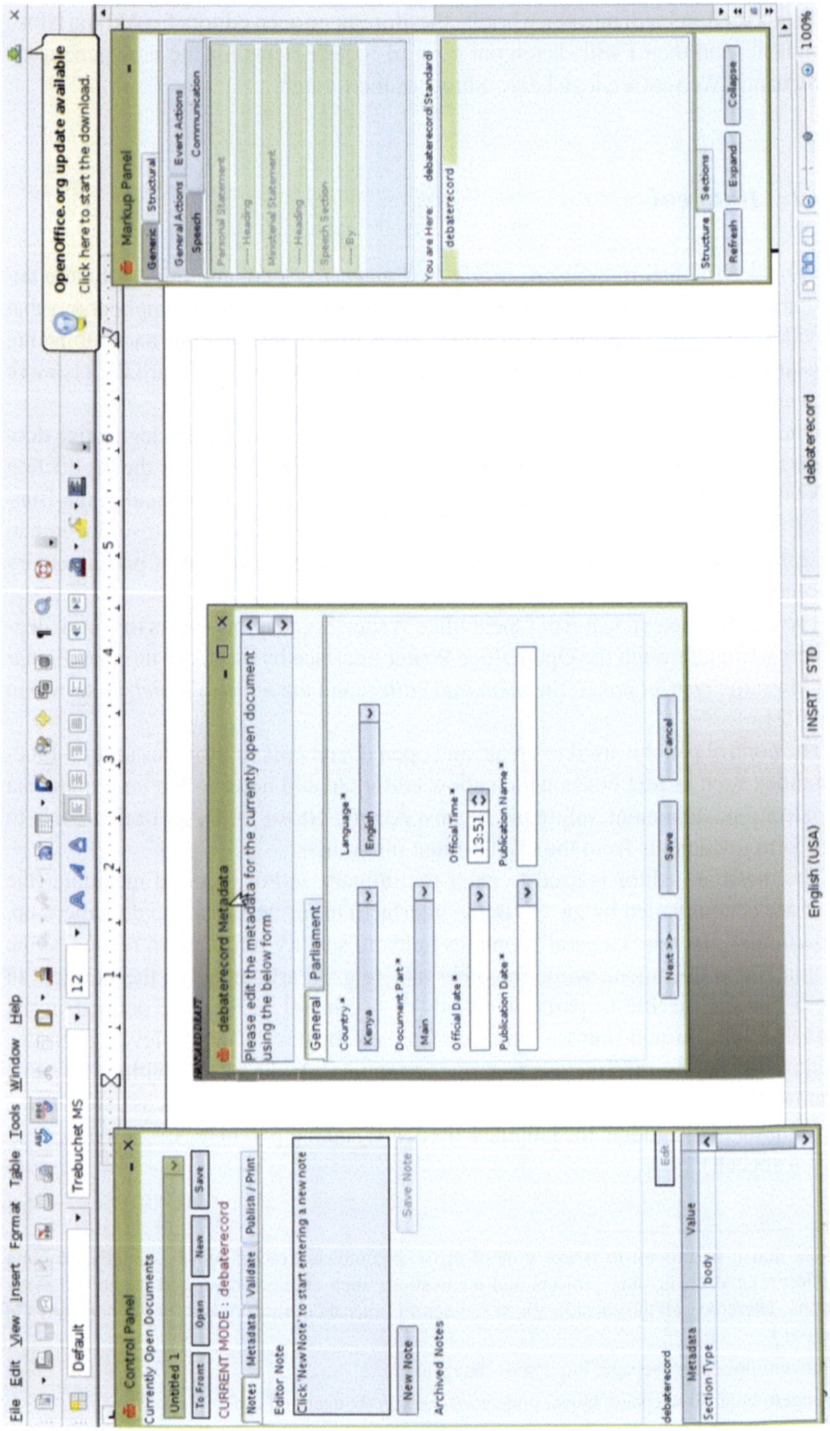

Fig. 6.21 The three additional windows Bungeni made available to enrich documents defined as OpenOffice Writer documents

Finally, the markup panel allows users to add specific markup generics and structures to text, so as to identify speeches, sections, paragraphs, prefaces, and similar. All these markup items can be applied to the textual content of the document according to appropriate contexts; certain markup entities can be specified inside others while others cannot.

6.6.2 AT4AM

AT4AM[49] is as web-based authoring tool for amendments, broadly adopted within the European Parliament since 2010. This tool allows members of the Parliament to create and table (1) amendments on proposals coming from the European Commission and the Council of the European Union, and (2) reports of the parliamentary committees.

Recently, *AT4AM for All*[50] is the free and open source release of the AT4AM Web application, which was developed in Java and uses the Google Web Toolkit (GWT). Its authors praise it as the first system of the future XML-based workflow of amendments at the European Parliament entirely based on Akoma Ntoso to take as input and store amendment documents.

As shown in Fig. 6.22, the interface available to users to suggest amendments focuses only on the content of the proposal rather than the formal layout in which it will be finally formatted and released, and makes it easy to suggest modifications (link "Amend") to a particular recital and even create new (link "New") and delete existing structures (link "Delete") such as recitals, articles, paragraphs, sections, clauses, etc.

This system is currently used by the European Parliament, the European Commission, the United Nations and the Italian Senate.

6.6.3 LIME

The *Language Independent Markup Editor* (a.k.a. *LIME*)[51] (Palmirani et al. 2013) is a Web-based and multi-language editor for Akoma Ntoso documents. It takes as input a plain TXT file containing the content of the legislative document to mark up and provides a user-friendly interface that makes available several actions on the text.

At the moment of writing this section (2013), LIME is able to define bills and acts according to the Akoma Ntoso vocabulary. However, the developers are going to extend its functionalities so as to manage the whole Akoma Ntoso specification.

---

[49] AT4AM homepage: http://www.at4am.org/.

[50] A demo of AT4AM for All is available at http://www.at4am.org/demo/.

[51] LIME homepage: http://lime.cirsfid.unibo.it.

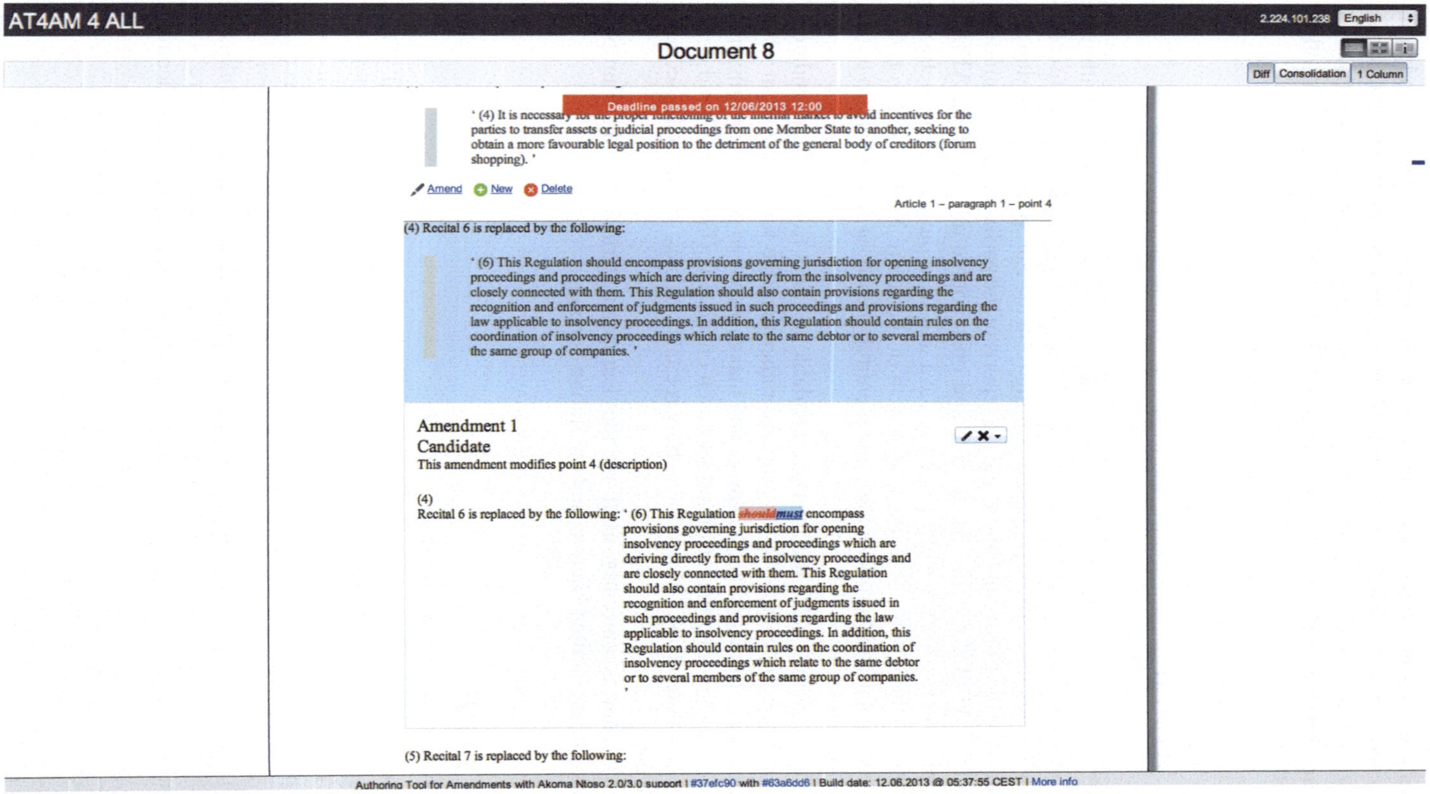

Fig. 6.22 The AT4AM for All interface available to European Parliament members to suggest amendments to proposals

The LIME interface, shown in Fig. 6.23 on page 248, is organised into three main areas. On the left hand side, the "Outline" box shows the markup structures currently associated to the document content, presenting hierarchical containments as expandable nodes when such relations exist between markup elements. In the central part of the window there is the textual content of the document and a toolbar that makes available different actions, which are: editing the document content; previewing the document in PDF, and suggesting amendments to document text by means of the AT4AM for All service presented in Sect. 6.6.2. Finally, the right hand side of the interface provides a list of markup entities that can be used to mark up the document content, which conform to Akoma Ntoso.

LIME also provides tools to export the document in several formats (i.e., Akoma Ntoso XML, HTML, PDF and EPUB) and to infer some markup structures automatically, such as references and dates. In addition, every time a user try to add markup structures within the content, LIME performs a preliminary validation of the markup against the Akoma Ntoso DTD, so as that no markup can be added within wrong contexts. For instance, considering the text in Fig. 6.23, labelling the text from "Titulo II" to the end of the document as article is denied by the editor (since that text is already part of an article) and no markup will be added in this case. These kinds of checks are performed in conformance with Akoma Ntoso DTD and, in addition, with the meta-markup organisation defined through structural patterns (see Sect. 3.3.2), to which Akoma Ntoso adheres strictly, to define the content model of its markup elements.

6.6.4 Towards the Next Generation of Legislative Editors

During the Extended Semantic Web Conference held in Montpellier in 2013, Prof. Enrico Motta and Prof. David Karger gave two interesting keynote speeches about what it means to develop Semantic Web applications. They both agreed that it is not enough to consume and/or produce RDF statements to claim that an application is a Semantic Web application; something more is actually needed (e.g. the use of statistics, inference tools and heuristics). In particular, Prof. Karger highlighted a particular requirement that any Semantic Web application must comply with (emphases added by me)[52]:

> A Semantic Web application is *one whose schema is expected to change*. [. . .] The fact that the underlying data was RDF might make it easy to change the schema in the data model, but there's no hint of how that change might easily be propagated to the user interface.

In general, this is true for any kinds of Semantic Web application and it is important to take this point into account to develop real and effective Semantic Web applications.

[52] From the Karger's blog post "Keynote at ESWC Part 3: What's Wrong with Semantic Web Research, and Some Ideas to Fix it", available at http://haystack.csail.mit.edu/blog/2013/06/10/keynote-at-eswc-part-3-whats-wrong-with-semantic-web-research-and-some-ideas-to-fix-it/.

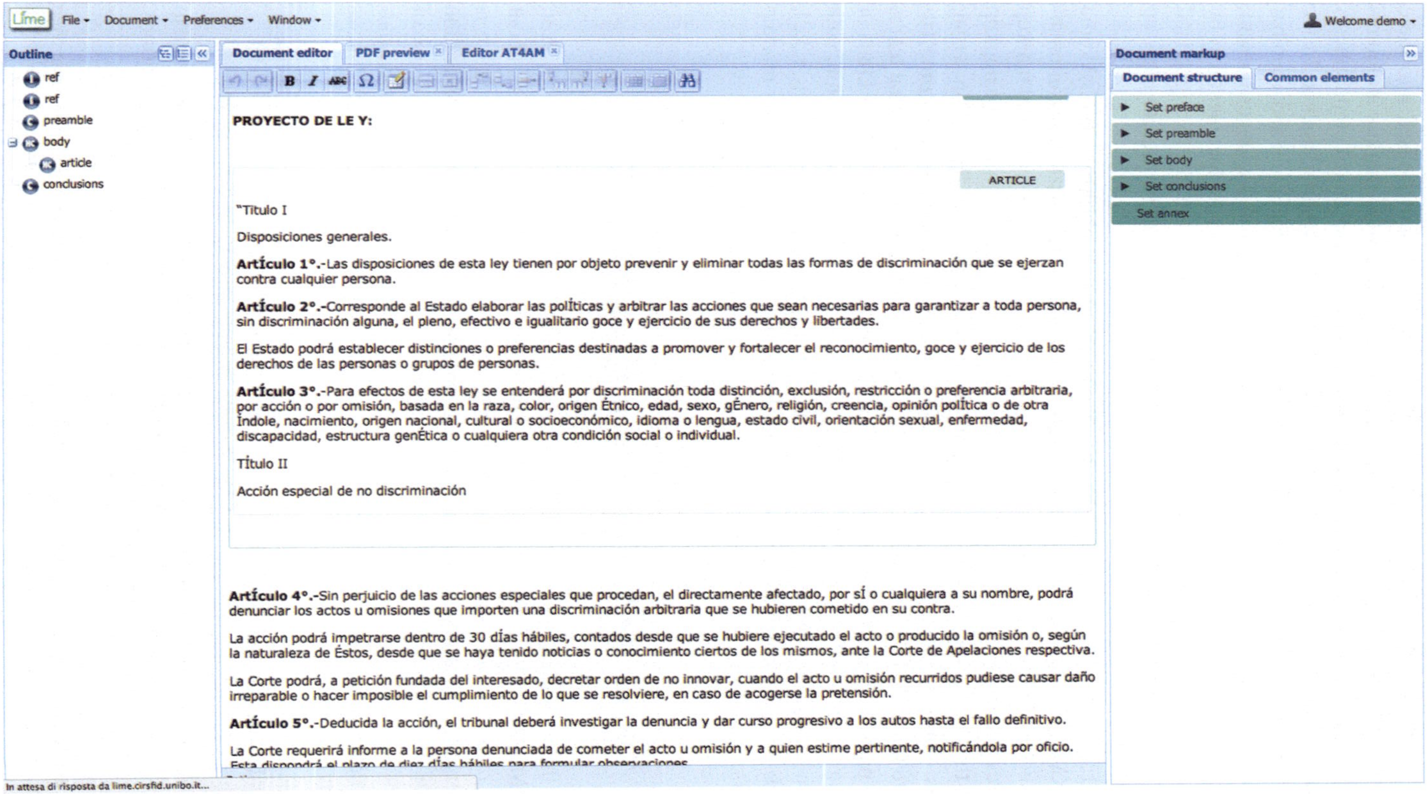

Fig. 6.23 The LIME application to create Akoma Ntoso markup documents from plain text

Karger's suggestion applies not only to particular Semantic Web languages (RDF, OWL, etc.) but refers also to all those applications that are built upon a specific model that is expected to change in the future.

Along this line, and in the context of applications and editors for legislative documents such as those described in the previous sections, I have identified three specific aspects that must be taken into account in order to develop flexible and long-lasting tools. These I will introduce in the following sections.

6.6.4.1 The Evolution of Legislative Markup Languages

XML is the most commonly used format to store and share textual documents so as to make it easy for machines to access them. Several libraries have been already developed and new tools are built on the basis of this (meta-)language. The choice to develop Akoma Ntoso as an XML-based language followed directly from these premises.

As introduced in Sects. 4.1 and 2.2.6, Akoma Ntoso is an OASIS international standard that is broadly adopted as main format to store legislative documents by different institutions and organisms, such as the European Commission; the European Parliament; the Italian Senate, and several African Parliaments, and the adoption process is set to continue.

Of course, different versions of Akoma Ntoso have been released in the past and more and will be released in the next few years to address issues and/or features deriving from particular (even new) scenarios. Since it is a live standard, Akoma Ntoso will continue to evolve during this time. In addition to that, it is also possible that, in the future, other (even new) XML languages will be preferred as standard formats for legislative documents instead of Akoma Ntoso.

The alterations required following a change of the base format for storing documents, which may happen at any point in time in the future, should be handled in an automatic manner by the legislative editors of the time. In particular, such editors should be able, automatically (or semi-automatically), to adapt their interface according to the modifications made in the particular XML language in use, without extensive effort by the developers and, in particular, the users of such editors.

The developers of LIME are currently working on enabling the editor to visualise and process automatically new versions of Akoma Ntoso. However, additional mechanisms should also be considered to enable the automatic adaptation of the user interface when users decide to adopt another markup language instead of Akoma Ntoso.

Of course it is not feasible to propose and develop an automatic approach that takes into account any possible language based on XML. A possible way around this issue could be to require that, whatever markup language is used, it will be strictly compliant with very general rules imposing only a limited but enough expressive structural organisation of document content. In practice, the idea would be to process all those "constrained" markup languages that follow some sort of general and shared design principles only. In that case, the use of such constrained markup languages should make it possible to develop an editor that adapts his interface to the new language in consideration without being concerned by its vocabulary and the particular content model of its markup elements.

A possible theory, which can be applied to XML-based languages to restrict their expressiveness to practical and circumscribed design principles, is the one about structural patterns, that I introduced in Sect. 3.3.2. As asserted that Section, a small number of patterns is sufficient to express what most users need to allow one to capture the most relevant document structures. Thus, in this case, it will be possible, in principle, to develop an editor that manages markup according to only eleven possible kinds of structures—which have precise structural and presentational semantics that act independently from the name and the content model of markup elements, as defined in the markup language in consideration. The development of an editor according to this theory will enable an easy interchange between the currently-used markup language and other languages, without being concerned about their implementation or the re-writing of pieces of programming code to adapt the editor application to a new markup format.

6.6.4.2 Use your Favourite Ontologies

The interlinking between legal and legislative content and external entities, such as those in the Linked Open Data, is an important feature that legislative editors should guarantee. As shown in Sect. 4.4, the use of external entities and ontologies to enrich document content can be very useful in real life scenarios, such as legal drafting, reference browsing, document analysis, and similar.

However, while the choice of a particular markup language for legislative documents is partially constrained by the few recognised standards already used world-wide, there are no standardised Semantic Web ontologies that are more commonly by official institutions. In addition, the ontologies developed in the past usually handle a particular subdomain of the whole legal and legislative domain, as introduced in Sect. 2.4, thus making often simultaneous use of several ontologies in order to model a legal/legislative scenario fully. For instance, in Sect. 4.4 I used ALLOT (see Sect. 2.4.4) and DBPedia (Auer et al. 2007) to model certain concepts, whereas I could have used LKIF (see Sect. 2.4.3) instead of ALLOT or both these ontologies plus DBPedia, and so on.

The choice of what ontologies to use in legislative editors, in order to open up to the semantic enrichment of legislative text, relates strictly to the users' subjective interpretations of such a text. Thus, the editor may suggest but should not impose the use of specific ontologies and particular interfaces to semantically-enhance legislative documents. Rather, it should make possible to change the ontologies and the related interface used quickly and easily to enable the users the annotation of such legislative documents with ontology entities.

The use of existing approaches and principles, such as Gaffe's (discussed in Sect. 6.5), may be very helpful in this direction by allowing one to reduce drastically the time and the complexity needed to reconure the legislative editor according to evolving users' needs.

6.6.4.3 Multilingualism as a Key Factor for a Broad Adoption

The intended audience of such legislative editors is actually very broad. They are used by people having different skills and are adopted by different countries, each with their own rules, laws and, in particular, their official language.

The multilingualism of tools and models is a very important and crucial aspect to consider when targeting a broad audience. Both Web and Semantic Web disciplines have been discussing how to use simultaneously entities (such as HTML pages and RDF resources) written in different languages, so as to facilitate their interaction with multilingual technologies and localisation processes. The interest of the academic community in this topic is confirmed by a number of recent initiatives, e.g. the W3C *MultilingualWeb-LT Working Group*[53] (which recently released a Working Draft of the *Internationalization Tag Set* (version 2; McCane et al. 2013)), the *Multilingual Semantic Web Workshop* series (Buitelaar et al. 2010, 2012; Montiel-Ponsoda et al. 2011) and the *Multilingual Web Initiative*[54].

Starting from these premises, a legislative editor should address the problem of multilingualism from different perspectives. First of all, its interface should be dynamically and automatically adaptable to the particular native language of users, and have all the menus, icons, manuals, markup elements, ontological entities, and the like, shown in the target language rather than only in English. Secondly, it should be guaranteed the interoperability between the legislative markup format in use and other formats, especially when the latter are expressed in different languages – for instance, Akoma Ntoso (see Sect. 4.1) in English and Norme in Rete (see Sect. 2.2.2) in Italian. Finally, the same degree of interoperability should be also guaranteed between the adoption of ontologies, developed in different languages according to specific purposes.

Addressing these aspects and all those introduced in the previous sections will enable legislative editors to be the flexible and broadly-adopted Semantic Web-aware applications of the future in the context of the legal domain.

References

Auer, S., S. Dietzold, and T. Riechert. 2006. OntOWiki—A tool for social, semantic collaboration. In Proceedings of the 5th international semantic web conference (ISWC 2006), eds. I. F. Cruz, S. Decker, D. Allemang, C. Preist, D. Schwabe, P. Mika, M. Uschold, and L. Aroyo, lecture notes in computer science, vol. 4273, 736–749. Berlin: Springer. doi:10.1007/11926078_53.

Auer, S., C. Bizer, J. Lehmann, G. Kobilarov, R. Cyganiak, and Z. Ives. 2007. DBpedia: A nucleus for a web of open data. In Proceedings of 6th international semantic web conference and of the 2nd Asian semantic web conference (ISWC 2007 + ASWC 2007), eds. K. Aberer, K. Choi, N. F. Noy, D. Allemang, K. Lee, L. J. B. Nixon, J. Golbeck, P. Mika, D. Maynard, R. Mizoguchi,

[53] MultilingualWeb-LT Working Group homepage: http://www.w3.org/International/multilingualweb/lt/.

[54] Multilingual Web Initiative homepage: http://www.multilingualweb.eu.

G. Schreiber, and P. Cudré-Mauroux, lecture notes in computer science, vol. 4825, 722–735. Berlin: Springer. doi:10.1007/978-3-540-76298-0_52.

Bao, J., P. R. Smart, N. Shadbolt, D. Braines, and G. Jones. 2009. A controlled natural language interface for semantic media wiki. In Proceedings of the 3rd annual conference of the International Technology Alliance (ACITA2009), 23–24 Sept 2009. Maryland, USA. http://www.usukita.org/papers/4551/SemanticWikiv7.pdf. Accessed 30 July 2013.

Basca, C., S. Corlosquet, R. Cyganiak, S. Fernández, and T. Schandl. 2008. Neologism: easy vocabulary publishing. In Proceedings of the 4th workshop on scripting for the semantic web, eds. C. Bizer, S. Auer, G. A. Grimnes, and T. Heath. CEUR workshop proceedings, vol. 368. Aachen: CEUR-WS-org. http://ceur-ws.org/Vol-368/paper10.pdf. Accessed 30 July 2013.

Beckett, D. 2004. RDF/XML syntax specification (revised). W3C recommendation, 10 Feb 2004. World Wide Web Consortium. http://www.w3.org/TR/rdf-syntax-grammar/. Accessed 30 July 2013.

Berrueta, D., and J. Phipps. 2008. Best practice recipes for publishing RDF vocabularies. W3C working group note 28 Aug 2008. World Wide Web Consortium. http://www.w3.org/TR/swbp-vocab-pub/. Accessed 30 July 2013.

Birks, M., and J. Mills. 2011. *Grounded theory: A practical guide*. Thousand Oaks: SAGE. (ISBN: 978-1848609938).

Bojars, U., and J. G. Breslin. 2010. SIOC core ontology specification. 25 March 2010. http://rdfs.org/sioc/spec/. Accessed 30 July 2013.

Boley, H., G. Hallmark, M. Kifer, A. Paschke, A. Polleres, and D. Reynolds. 2013. RIF core dialect. 2nd ed.. W3C recommendation, 5 Feb 2013. World Wide Web Consortium. http://www.w3.org/TR/rif-core/. Accessed 30 July 2013.

Bolognini, V., A. Di Iorio, S. Duca, A. Musetti, S. Peroni, and F. Vitali. 2009. Exploiting ontologies to deploy user-friendly and customized metadata editors. In Proceedings of the IADIS Internet/WWW 2009 conference, eds. B. White, P. Isaías, and M. B. Nunes. Lisbon: IADIS.

Brockmans, S., R. Volz, A. Eberhart, and P. Löffler. 2004. Visual modeling of OWL DL ontologies using UML. In Proceedings of the 3rd International Semantic Web Conference (ISWC 2004), eds. S. A. McIlraith, D. Plexousakis, and F. van Harmelen, lecture notes in computer science, vol. 3298, 198–213. Berlin: Springer. doi:10.1007/978-3-540-30475-3_15.

Brockmans, S., P. Haase, P. Hitzler, and R. Studer. 2006. A metamodel and UML profile for rule-extended OWL DL ontologies. In Proceedings of the 3rd European Semantic Web Conference (ESWC 2006), eds. Y. Sure and J. Domingue, lecture notes in computer science, vol. 4011, 303–316. Berlin: Springer. doi:10.1007/11762256_24.

Brooke, J. 1996. SUS: A "quick and dirty" usability scale. In *Usability evaluation in industry*, eds. P. W. Jordan, B. Thomas, B. A. Weerdmeester, and A. L. McClelland, 189–194. London: Taylor and Francis. (ISBN: 0748404600).

Buffa, M., F. Gandon, G. Ereteo, P. Sander, and C. Faron. 2008. SweetWiki: A semantic wiki. *Journal of Web Semantics: Science, Services and Agents on the World Wide Web* 6 (1): 84–97. doi:10.1016/j.websem.2007.11.003.

Buitelaar, P., P. Cimiano, and E. Montiel-Ponsoda, eds. 2010. Proceedings of the 1st international workshop on the Multilingual Semantic Web (MSW 2010). CEUR workshop proceedings, vol. 571. Aachen: CEUR-WS.org. http://ceur-ws.org/Vol-571/. Accessed 30 July 2013.

Buitelaar, P., P. Cimiano, D. Lewis, J. Pustejovsky, and F. Sasaki, eds. 2012. Proceedings of the 3rd international workshop on the Multilingual Semantic Web (MSW 2012). CEUR workshop proceedings 936. Aachen: CEUR-WS.org. http://ceur-ws.org/Vol-936/. Accessed 30 July 2013.

Carroll, J., I. Dickinson, C. Dollin, D. Reynolds, A. Seaborne, and K. Wilkinson. 2004. Jena: Implementing the semantic web recommendations. In Proceedings of the 13th international conference on World Wide Web—Alternate track papers & posters (WWW 2004), eds. S. I. Feldman, M. Uretsky, M. Najork, and C. E. Wills, 74–83. New York: ACM. doi:10.1145/1013367.1013381.

d'Aquin, M., and E. Motta. 2011. Watson, more than a semantic web search engine. *Semantic Web—Interoperability, Usability, Applicability* 2 (1): 55–63. doi:10.3233/SW-2011-0031.

De Coi, J. L., N. E. Fuchs, K. Kaljurand, and T. Kuhn. 2009. Controlled English for reasoning on the semantic web. In *Semantic techniques for the web—The REWERSE perspective*, eds. F. Bry and J. Maluszynski, 276–308. (ISBN: 3642045806).

Dello, K., E. B. S. Paslaru, and R. Tolksdorf. 2006. Creating and using semantic web information with makna. In Proceedings of the 1st workshop on semantic wikis—From wiki to semantics, eds. M. Völkel and S. Schaffert. CEUR workshop proceedings, vol. 206. Aachen: CEUR-WS.org. http://www.ceur-ws.org/Vol-206/paper4.pdf. Accessed 30 July 2013.

Di Iorio, A., A. Musetti, S. Peroni, and F. Vitali. 2010a. Crowdsourcing semantic content: A model and two applications. In Proceedings of the 3rd international conference on human system interaction (HSI10), ed. T. Pardela, 563–570. Washington DC: IEEE Computer Society. doi:10.1109/HSI.2010.5514513.

Di Iorio, A., A. Musetti, S. Peroni, and F. Vitali. 2010b. Ontology-driven generation of wiki content and interfaces. *New Review of Hypermedia and Multimedia* 16 (1): 9–31. doi:10.1080/13614568.2010.497194.

Di Iorio, A., A. Musetti, S. Peroni, F. Vitali. 2011a. OWiki: Enabling an ontology-led creation of semantic data. In *Human-computer systems interaction: Backgrounds and applications 2*, eds. Z. S. Hippe, J. L. Kulikowski, and T. Mroczek. Berlin: Springer. (ISBN: 3642231711).

Di Iorio, A., S. Peroni, and F. Vitali. 2011b. A semantic web approach to everyday overlapping markup. *Journal of the American Society for Information Science and Technology* 62 (9): 1696–1716. doi:10.1002/asi.21591.

Dragan, L., S. Handschuh, and S. Decker. 2011. The semantic desktop at work: Interlinking notes. In Proceedings the 7th international conference on semantic systems (I-SEMANTICS 2011), eds. C. Ghidini, A. Ngonga Ngomo, S. N. Lindstaedt, and T.Pellegrini, 17–24. New York: ACM. doi:10.1145/2063518.2063521.

Dublin Core Metadata Initiative. 2012a. DCMI metadata terms. DCMI recommendation. http://dublincore.org/documents/dcmi-terms/. Accessed 30 July 2013.

Dublin Core Metadata Initiative. 2012b. Dublin core metadata element set, version 1.1. DCMI recommendation. http://dublincore.org/documents/dces/. Accessed 30 July 2013.

Gamma, E., R. Helm, R. Johnson, and J. Vlissides. 1994. *Design patterns: Elements of reusable object-oriented software*. Boston: Addison-Wesley. (ISBN: 0201633610).

Gardenfors, P. 2000. *Conceptual spaces: The geometry of thought*. Cambridge: Bradford Books. (ISBN: 0262071991).

Garlik, S. H., and A. Seaborne. 2013. SPARQL 1.1 Query language. W3C recommendation 21 March 2013. World Wide Web Consortium. http://www.w3.org/TR/sparql11-query/. Accessed 30 July 2013.

Gasevic, D., D. Djuric, V. Devedzic, and V. Damjanovic. 2004. Converting UML to OWL ontologies. In Proceedings of the 13th international World Wide Web conference on alternate track papers & posters (WWW Alt 04), 488–489. New York: ACM. doi:10.1145/1013367.1013539.

Harth, C., H. Gassert, I. O'Murchu, J. G. Breslin, and S. Decker. 2005. WikiOnt: An ontology for describing and exchanging Wikipedia articles. In Proceedings of Wikimania 2005, eds. J. Voss, A. Lih, S. Klein, and C. Ma. http://meta.wikimedia.org/wiki/Wikimania05/Paper-IM1. Accessed 30 July 2013.

Horridge, M., and S. Bechhofer. 2011. The OWL API: A Java API for OWL ontologies. *Semantic Web—Interoperability, Usability, Applicability* 2 (1): 11–21. doi:10.3233/SW-2011-0025.

Horridge, M., and P. Patel-Schneider. 2012. OWL 2 Web ontology language Manchester syntax. 2nd ed. W3C working group note 11 Dec 2012. World Wide Web Consortium. http://www.w3.org/TR/owl2-manchester-syntax/. Accessed 30 July 2013.

Katifori, A., E. Torou, C. Halatsis, G. Lepouras, and C. Vassilakis. 2006. A comparative study of four ontology visualization techniques in Protege: Experiment setup and preliminary results. In Proceedings of the 10th international conference on information visualisation (IV 2006), eds. E. Banissi, R. A. Burkhard, A. Ursyn, J. J. Zhang, M. Bannatyne, C. Maple, A. J. Cowell, G. Y. Tian, and M. Hou, 417–423. Washington DC: IEEE Computer Society. doi:10.1109/IV.2006.3.

Katifori, A., C. Halatsis, G. Lepouras, C. Vassilakis, and E. Giannopoulou. 2007. Ontology visualization methods—A survey. ACM Computing Surveys, 39 (4): Article 10. doi:10.1145/1287620.1287621.

Kay, J., and A. Lum. 2003. An ontologically enhanced metadata editor. University of Sidney, School of Information Technologies, Technical Report 541. http://www.it.usyd.edu.au/research/tr/tr541.pdf. Accessed 30 July 2013.

Klein, B., C. Höcht, and B. Decker. 2005. Beyond capturing and maintaining software engineering knowledge—"Wikitology" as shared semantics. Presented during the workshop on Knowledge Engineering and Software Engineering (KESE 2005). 11 Sept 2005, Koblenz, Germany. http://www.dfki.uni-kl.de/~klein/papers/finalKESE05.pdf. Accessed 30 July 2013.

Knublauch, H., M. Horridge, M. A. Musen, A. L. Rector, R. Stevens, N. Drummond, P. W. Lord, N. F. Noy, J. Seidenberg, and H. Wang. 2005. The Protege OWL experience. In Proceedings of the OWLED 05 Workshop on OWL: Experiences and directions, eds. B. C. Grau, I. Horrocks, B. Parsia, P. F. Patel-Schneider. CEUR workshop proceedings, vol. 188. Aachen: CEUR-WS.org. http://ceur-ws.org/Vol-188/sub14.pdf. Accessed 30 July 2013.

Kriglstein, S., and R. Motschnig-Pitrik. 2008. Knoocks: New visualization approach for ontologies. In Proceedings of the 12th international conference on Information Visualisation (IV 2008), 163–168. Washington DC: IEEE Computer Society. doi:10.1109/IV.2008.16.

Lakoff, G. 1987. *Women, fire, and dangerous things*. Chicago: University Of Chicago Press. (ISBN: 0226468046).

Lakoff, G., and M. Johnson. 1980. *Metaphors we live by*. Chicago: University Of Chicago Press. (ISBN: 0226468011).

Lewis, J. R., and J. Sauro. 2009. The factor structure of the system usability scale. In Proceedings of the 1st international conference on human centered design (HCD 09), ed. M. Kurosu, lecture notes in computer science, vol. 5619, 94–103. Berlin: Springer. doi:10.1007/978-3-642-02806-9_12.

Li, N., E. Motta, and M. d'Aquin. 2010. Ontology summarization: An analysis and an evaluation. In Proceedings of the International Workshop on Evaluation of Semantic Technologies (IWEST 2010), eds. A. Gomez-Perez, F. Ciravegna, F. van Harmelen, and J. Hefflin. CEUR workshop proceedings, vol. 666. Aachen: CEUR-WS.org. http://ceur-ws.org/Vol-666/paper8.pdf. Accessed 30 July 2013.

McCane, S., D. Lewis, C. Lieske, A. Lommel, J. Kosek, F. Sasaki, and Y. Savourel. 2013. Internationalization tag set (ITS) version 2.0. W3C recommendation 29 Oct 2013. http://www.w3.org/TR/its20/. Accessed 30 July 2013.

Montiel-Ponsoda, E., J. McCrae, P. Buitelaar, P. Cimiano, eds. 2011. Proceedings of the 2nd international workshop on the Multilingual Semantic Web (MSW 2011). CEUR workshop proceedings, vol. 775. Aachen: CEUR-WS.org. http://ceur-ws.org/Vol-775/. Accessed 30 July 2013.

Motta, E., S. Peroni, N. Li, and M. D'Aquin. 2010. KC-Viz: A novel approach to visualizing and navigating ontologies. In Proceedings of the EKAW2010 poster and demo track, eds. J. Völker and O. Corcho. CEUR workshop proceedings, vol. 674. Aachen: CEUR-WS.org. http://ceur-ws.org/Vol-674/Paper191.pdf. Accessed 30 July 2013.

Motta, E., P. Mulholland, S. Peroni, M. D'Aquin, J. M. Gomez-Perez, V. Mendez, and F. Zablith. 2011a. A novel approach to visualizing and navigating ontologies. In Proceedings of the 10th international semantic web conference (ISWC 2011), eds. L. Aroyo, C. Welty, H. Alani, J. Taylor, A. Bernstein, L. Kagal, N. F. Noy, and E. Blomqvist, lecture notes in computer science, vol. 7031, 470–486. Berlin: Springer. doi:10.1007/978-3-642-25073-6_30.

Motta, E., S. Peroni, and M. d'Aquin. 2011b. Latest developments in KC-Viz. In Proceedings of the poster & demo track of the 10th International Semantic Web Conference (ISWC 2011). http://iswc2011.semanticweb.org/fileadmin/iswc/Papers/PostersDemos/iswc11pd_submission_22.pdf. Accessed 30 July 2013.

Motta, E., S. Peroni, J. M. Gómez-Pérez, M. d'Aquin, and N. Ning Li. 2012. Visualizing and navigating ontologies with KC-Viz. *Ontology engineering in a networked world*, eds. M.

C. Suárez-ueroa, A. Gómez-Pérez, E. Motta, and A. Gangemi, 343–362. Berlin: Springer. doi:10.1007/978-3-642-24794-1_16.

Object Management Group. 2009. Ontology Definition Metamodel (ODM) version 1.0. http://www.omg.org/spec/ODM/1.0/PDF. Accessed 30 July 2013.

Object Management Group. 2011. Unified modeling language™ (UML®). http://www.omg.org/spec/UML/2.4/. Accessed 30 July 2013.

Oren, E., R. Delbru, M. Catasta, R. Cyganiak, H. Stenzhorn, and G. Tummarello. 2008. Sindice.com: A document-oriented lookup index for open linked data. *International Journal of Metadata, Semantics and Ontologies* 3 (1): 37–52. doi:10.1504/IJMSO.2008.021204.

Palmirani, M., L. Cervone, O. Bujor, and M. Chiappetta. 2013. RAWE: An editor for rule markup of legal texts. In joint Proceedings of the 7th international rule challenge, the special track on human language technology and the 3rd RuleML doctoral consortium. CEUR workshop proceedings, vol. 1004. Aachen: CEUR-WS.org. http://ceur-ws.org/Vol-1004/paper4.pdf. Accessed 30 July 2013.

Passant, A., and P. Laublet. 2008. Towards an interlinked semantic wiki farm. In Proceedings of the 3rd semantic wiki workshop (SemWiki 2008), eds. C. Lange, S. Schaffert, H. Skaf-Molli, and M. Völkel. CEUR workshop proceedings, vol. 360, 1–14. Aachen: CEUR-WS.org. http://ceur-ws.org/Vol-360/paper-19.pdf. Accessed 30 July 2013.

Peroni, S., E. Motta, and M. d'Aquin. 2008. Identifying key concepts in an ontology, through the integration of cognitive principles with statistical and topological measures. In Proceedings of the 3rd Asian semantic web conference (ASWC 2008), eds. J. Domingue and C. Anutariya, lecture notes in computer science, vol. 5367, 242–256. Berlin: Springer. doi:10.1007/978-3-540-89704-0_17

Peroni, S., D. Shotton, and F. Vitali. 2012. The Live OWL documentation environment: A tool for the automatic generation of ontology documentation. In Proceedings of the 18th international conference on knowledge engineering and knowledge management (EKAW 2012), eds. A. ten Teije, J. Völker, S. Handschuh, H. Stuckenschmidt, M. d'Aquin, A. Nikolov, N. Aussenac-Gilles, and N. Hernandez, lecture notes in computer science, vol. 7603, 398–412. Berlin: Springer. doi:10.1007/978-3-642-33876-2_35.

Peroni, S., D. Shotton, and F. Vitali. 2013. Tools for the automatic generation of ontology documentation: A task-based evaluation. *International Journal on Semantic Web and Information Systems* 9 (1): 21–44. doi:10.4018/jswis.2013010102.

Plaisant, C., J. Grosjean, and B. B. Bederson. 2002. Spacetree: Supporting exploration in large node link tree, design evolution and empirical evaluation. In Proceedings of the IEEE symposium on Information Visualization (InfoVis 2002), 57–64. Washington DC: IEEE Computer Society. doi:10.1109/INFVIS.2002.1173148.

Rosch, E. 1978. Principles of categorization. In *Cognition and categorisation,* eds. E. Rosch and B. Lloyd. Hillsdale: Lawrence Erlbaum. (ISBN: 0470263778).

Sauro, J. 2011. A practical guide to the system usability scale: Background, benchmarks & best practices. (ISBN: 978-1461062707).

Schaffert, S. 2006. IkeWiki: A semantic wiki for collaborative knowledge management. In Proceedings of 15th IEEE International Workshops on Enabling Technologies: Infrastructures for Collaborative Enterprises (WETICE 2006), 388–396. Washington DC: IEEE Computer Society. doi:10.1109/WETICE.2006.46.

Shneiderman, B. 1992. Tree visualization with tree-Maps: A 2-d space-filling approach. *ACM Transactions on Graphics* 11 (1): 92–99. doi:10.1145/102377.115768.

Shneiderman, B. 1996. The eyes have it: A task by data type taxonomy for information visualizations. In Proceedings of the 1996 IEEE symposium on visual languages (VL 96), 336–343. Washington DC: IEEE Computer Society. doi:10.1109/VL.1996.545307.

Sirin, E., B. Parsia, B. C. Grau, A. Kalyanpur, and Y. Katz. 2007. Pellet: A practical OWL-DL reasoner. *Journal of Web Semantics: Science, Services and Agents on the World Wide Web* 5 (2): 51–53. doi:10.1016/j.websem.2007.03.004.

Souza, K., A. Dos Santos, and S. Evangelista. 2003. Visualization of ontologies through hypertrees. In Proceedings of the Latin American conference on human-computer interaction (CLIHC 03), 251–255. New York: ACM.

Souzis, A. 2005. Building a semantic wiki. *IEEE Intelligent Systems* 20 (5): 87–91. doi:10.1109/MIS.2005.83.

Sowa, J. F. 1987. Semantic networks. In *Encyclopedia of artificial intelligence,* ed. S. C. Shapiro. New York: Wiley. (ISBN: 0471503053).

Storey, M. A., M. A. Musen, J. Silva, C. Best, N. Ernst, R. Fergerson, and N. F. Noy. 2001. Jambalaya: Interactive visualization to enhance ontology authoring and knowledge acquisition in Protege. Presented during the K-CAP 2001 workshop on interactive tools for knowledge capture, 20 Oct 2001, Victoria, Canada. http://www.isi.edu/b̃lythe/kcap-interaction/papers/storey.pdf. Accessed 30 July 2013.

Strauss, A., and J. Corbin. 1998. *Basics of qualitative research techniques and procedures for developing grounded theory*. 2nd ed. London: Sage. (ISBN: 978-0803959408).

Suárez-ueroa, M. C., A. Gómez-Pérez, E. Motta, and A. Gangemi. 2012. *Ontology engineering in a networked world.* Berlin: Springer. ISBN: 3642247934.

Tartir, S., I. B. Arpinar, M. Moore, A. P. Sheth, and B. Aleman-Meza. 2006. OntoQA: Metric-based ontology quality analysis. Presented at the workshop on knowledge acquisition from distributed, autonomous, semantically heterogeneous data and knowledge sources, 27 Nov 2005, Houston, Texas, USA. http://lsdis.cs.uga.edu/library/download/OntoQA.pdf. Accessed 30 July 2013.

Tejo-Alonso, C., D. Berrueta, L. Polo, and S. Fernandez. 2011. Metadata for web ontologies and rules: Current practices and perspectives. In Proceeding of the 5th interational conference on Metadata and Semantic Research (MTSR 2011), eds. E. García-Barriocanal, Z. Cebeci, M. C. Okur, and A. Öztürk. Berlin: Springer.

Vrandecic, D., and M. Krötzsch. 2006. Reusing ontological background knowledge in semantic wikis. In Proceedings of the 1st semantic wiki workshop—From wiki to semantics (SemWiki 2008), eds. M. Völkel and S. Schaffert. CEUR workshop proceedings, vol. 206. Aachen: CEUR-WS.org. http://www.ceur-ws.org/Vol-206/paper2.pdf. Accessed 30 July 2013.

Všlkel, M., M. Krštzsch, D. Vrandecic, H. Haller, and R. Studer. 2006. Semantic wikipedia. In Proceedings of the 15th international conference on World Wide Web (WWW 2006), eds. L. Carr, D. De Roure, A. Iyengar, C. A. Goble, and M. Dahlin, 585–594. New York: ACM. doi:10.1145/1135777.1135863.

Wang, T. D., and B. Parsia. 2006. Cropcircles: Topology sensitive visualization of Owl class hierarchies. In Proceedings of the 5th International Semantic Web Conference (ISWC 2006), eds. I. F. Cruz, S. Decker, D. Allemang, C. Preist, D. Schwabe, P. Mika, M. Uschold, and L. Aroyo, lecture notes in computer science, vol. 4273, 695–708. Berlin: Springer. doi:10.1007/11926078_50.

Woods, W. A. 1975. What's in a link: Foundations for semantic networks. In *Representation and understanding: Studies in cognitive science,* eds. D. Bobrow and A. Collins. New York: Academic. (ISBN: 0121085503).

Chapter 7
Conclusions

Abstract In this chapter, I conclude the discussion of my work on Semantic Publishing. In particular, I summarise my own personal contributions in order to address one of the main issues of this field, i.e., the linking of a text to the formal representation of its meaning and thus the representation of its structure and of its argumentative discourse. In addition, I summarise my own contribution on the development of interfaces to hide the complexity of markup and ontology formalisms behind user-friendly views in order to help users of Semantic Publishing (e.g., scholars, publishers, archivists, librarians, etc.) that may have difficulties in interacting with Semantic Publishing technologies. Finally, I conclude the chapter introducing planned future works for all the languages, models and tools presented.

In the early days of the Web, the intrinsic meaning of the content of a document such as a Web page was accessible only to human readers, using their capabilities to conceptualise the particular semantics starting from natural language descriptions. The Semantic Web was born from a desire to develop mechanisms for machine understanding of that same content that would be as effective as that of humans. Its final goal was to "bring structure to the meaningful content of Web pages" and to provide "a new class of tools by which we can live, work and learn together" (Berners-Lee et al. 2001). In other words, it tried to link authored text (i.e., Web pages) to its formal semantics in a way that "intelligent" applications can be developed so as to significantly assist people in their everyday life.

To this end, the Semantic Web communities initially started to develop standards and technologies with the aim of giving a theoretical and practical background to enable the creation of intelligent applications and enhanced Web resources. Starting from these bases, recently some research and institutional domains are trying to make a further step towards the final aspirations of Semantic Web, putting people and documents back into the roles as first actors and supporting them with Semantic Web technologies and standards. This is the case for *Semantic Publishing*.

Semantic Publishing concerns "anything that enhances the meaning of a published journal article [more generally, a document], facilitates its automated discovery, enables its linking to semantically related articles, provides access to data within the article in actionable form, or facilitates integration of data between papers" (Shotton 2009). The Semantic Publishing approach goes beyond the current interest of recognising relevant entities in the text and/or transforming natural language statements into formal assertions. In fact, Semantic Publishing aims at describing the

S. Peroni, *Semantic Web Technologies and Legal Scholarly Publishing*,
Law, Governance and Technology Series 15, DOI 10.1007/978-3-319-04777-5_7,

entire discourse and argumentation of (bibliographic) documents through formal tools and semantic technologies. The final aim is to increase the *users' comprehension* of documents through software and applications that work "intelligently" on the formal conceptualisation of the narrative of the documents themselves.

To realise this vision, the actors involved—i.e., publishers, authors, readers, archivists, legal experts, technologists and developers—must be part of an organised cooperative community. Given the intrinsic heterogeneity of the actors involved, Semantic Publishing must be addressed from different perspectives.

Rather than explore the social and economical aspects of Semantic Publishing, I have in this book focussed on its technological environment, presenting examples from the legal scholarly publishing. In order to link a text to the formal representation of its meaning and thus to represent its argumentative discourse, Semantic Publishing needs at least two distinct resources: on the one hand, a powerful and expressive document markup language that allows semantic characterisations of its elements and content. On the other hand, shared models (ontologies) that allow the formal description of all the aspects of a document, from its structure to its argumentative discourse.

My contributions in this direction are shown in two projects: *EARMARK* and *SPAR*. As illustrated in Chaps. 3 and 4 EARMARK is a markup metalanguage that allows one to create markup documents as sets of OWL assertions, without the structural and semantic limits imposed by meta-markup languages such as XML. EARMARK is a platform to link the content layer of a document with its intended formal semantics. Having EARMARK as a solid base for defining the content of documents and its syntactical organisation, I then developed the *Semantic Publishing And Referencing* (*SPAR*) ontologies (Chap. 5), a collection of formal models providing an upper semantic layer for describing the publishing domain. SPAR is a set of eight modular and interoperable ontologies that precisely describe the whole publishing domain using terms from publishers' vocabulary: ranging from bibliographic, structural and rhetorical descriptions of documents to specification of publishing workflows. Thus, using EARMARK as a foundation for SPAR descriptions opens up to a semantic characterisation of all the aspects of a document and of its parts.

Of course, these two aspects—the *markup* and the *semantics*—must be understood, discussed, developed and used within an heterogeneous community that includes people who do not care about the technologies, but who are extremely competent in their own specific domains. Being domain experts, they know the needs and constraints of their own communities. Thus, their contributions to the development of sophisticated Semantic Publishing technologies are crucial.

However, such people may have difficulties in interacting with the Semantic Publishing technologies. Thus, we need user-friendly interfaces that shield such users from the underlying formalisms and semantic models of such technologies.

This is the reason why a good half of my research has concerned the development of interfaces that hide the complexity of markup and ontology formalisms behind user-friendly views. The tools I presented in Chap. 6—*LODE*, *KC-Viz*, *Graffoo* and *Gaffe*—will hopefully find extensively use for presenting ontologies to publishers, for developing new ontologies to meet particular needs, and for allowing authors to add semantic data to their own documents. These tools have had a crucial role in the development of the SPAR ontologies themselves. Without doubt, they have facilitated the frequent and productive interactions I had with publishers and domain experts, and have provided one of the main reasons for the early adoption of SPAR in the publishing domain, as described in Sect. 5.7. LODE and KC-Viz are currently being used in even broader domains and they have been flagged as important contributions in the Semantic Web community[1].

My future research will cover further aspects of Semantic Publishing. In the following sections I introduce the planned future works for all the languages, models and tools presented in this book.

7.1 EARMARK: Future Works

The main and urgent future development of my work on EARMARK, concerns a study of the applicability of this approach to markup in different research domains. In particular, my aim is to investigate real use-case scenarios that involve researchers of different disciplines, such as Humanities or Law. For instance, a relevant issue in Humanities is the use of overlapping markup structures to represent differences among different copies of the same manuscript as a unique digital document. This particular branch of Philology, called *textual criticism*, aims at reconstructing the original text of a manuscript starting from an analysis held on multiple copies of it written by different scribes. Although TEI (Text Encoding Initiative Consortium 2013) enables one to store all the overlapping fragments of a *critical edition* via XML workarounds (introduced in Sect. 2.1.1), my interest is to investigate how different approaches to overlapping markup such as EARMARK can address this problem. Since an interaction with humanists and other researchers that may not be expert in markup technologies is needed, I plan to develop a user interface that facilitates the specification of overlapping markup in EARMARK.

Although I have already carried out a first comparison between XML approaches to overlap and EARMARK (introduced in Sect. 3.2.3), it may be interesting to develop a complexity-based comparison as well, using a richer and more heterogeneous set of input documents. Moreover, this set of documents will be useful for the evaluation of a conversion framework, called the *EARMARK framework*, I am currently developing with my research group. The main aim of the EARMARK framework is to enable the automatic conversion of XML documents with overlapping markup from a format (e.g., ODT) into another (e.g., OpenXML). The framework has been developed so as to use EARMARK as intermediate format to apply the conversion. Part of this work has been already done and introduced in Barabucci et al. (2012).

[1] For instance, LODE is listed in the W3C wiki page about tools for semantic data, available at http://www.w3.org/2001/sw/wiki/LLDtools. Moreover, KC-Viz is now part of the core components of the NeOn Toolkit.

7.2 SPAR: Future Works

Although the SPAR ontologies are already being used within different communities (Sect. 5.7), my prior interest is to empirically evaluate the goodness of all the eight ontological modules to assess the quality of their vocabulary and their ease of use. I also plan to carry out other formal evaluations to understand the quality of those ontologies according to their logical organisation (e.g., through OntoClean (Guarino and Welty 2002) and similar frameworks).

Moreover, I am currently working on the release of triplestores of bibliographic information compliant with SPAR. In particular, in addition to the work already done with the JISC OpenCitation project (Sect. 2.5.1), my research group and I are collaborating with the publishing house *Società Editrice il Mulino*. Our aim is to study a way to enhance its bibliographic objects through SPAR-based semantic assertions and then to publish them as open linked data. Along the lines of the work with the above publishing house, David Shotton (University of Oxford) and I are now managing with Mulberry Technologies Inc.[2] an alignment strategy between their *Journal Article Tag Sets* (*JATS*)[3]—i.e., a set of XML DTDs to store journal articles—and SPAR entities (Peroni et al. 2012).

Another interesting aspect of my proposed research will be the study and development of algorithms for the automatic or semi-automatic identification of structural and rhetoric characteristics of document parts, such as citations (Di Iorio et al. 2013a, b) and other components. Starting from a pattern-based description of a markup document (as introduced in Sect. 5.4.1), it should be possible to deduce the structural roles of its components (sections, chapters, paragraphs, figures, etc., as sketch out in Di Iorio et al. (2013c) as well as their rhetoric functions (introduction, background, experiment, results, etc.) without having an *a priori* knowledge of the intended meaning of such markup elements. My aim is to develop automatic mechanisms that assign structural patterns and DoCO characterisations (Sect. 5.4) to markup elements of XML and EARMARK documents.

7.3 LODE: Future Works

I plan to extend the functionalities of the tool with new features. In particular, future versions of LODE will support full multi-language documentation and the explicit handling of the OWL 2 DL meta-modelling capabilities (i.e., OWL punning) in entity descriptions. Moreover I plan to use the KC-Viz abstraction capabilities, introduced in Sect. 6.3.1, to highlight the most important classes of an ontology in its HTML documentation as rendered through LODE and to develop two plugins, one for the NeOn Toolkit and the other for Protégé, to use LODE within ontology development applications.

[2] Mulberry Technologies Inc.: http://www.mulberrytech.com.

[3] Journal Article Tag Sets: http://www.mulberrytech.com/JATS/.

7.4 KC-Viz: Future Works

From the study of the user questionnaires discussed in Sect. 6.3.3 interesting ideas for future works arose. Although KC-Viz is already integrated within the NeOn Toolkit, some criticisms came up with its integration with other plugins, in particular with those supporting the reasoning and query infrastructure of the NeOn Toolkit. I plan to work on extending KC-Viz in order to enable the key-concept extraction mechanism and navigation according to both the declared and inferred ontological axioms.

Moreover, I plan to increase the interface behaviours of KC-Viz by adding layout mechanisms for coarse-grained views (or sky views) to show the entire ontology, by extending the snapshot feature to handle multiple loaded snapshots at the same time, and by highlighting connected links for a class when it is selected.

7.5 Graffoo: Future Works

There are several planned future developments of Graffoo, but the main priority will be given to its empirical evaluation. In particular, I am interested in understanding whether and how much Graffoo diagrams enable users to understand and develop ontologies. To this end, I plan to carry out a user-testing session that involves people of different fields (Semantic Web practitioners, computer scientists, humanists, etc.) interested in ontologies. The aim is to understand whether Graffoo widget are enough to make sense of a first informal presentation of an ontology.

Besides that, I also plan to work on possible prototypical applications based on the Graffoo widget. First of all, I want to develop a set of XSLT stylesheets to extend DiTTO (Gangemi and Peroni 2013), so as to enable the automatic conversion of a set of *yEd* documents specifying Graffoo diagrams into OWL 2 DL ontologies. The next step will be to develop and implementing a pure Web-based editors for the development and publication of Graffoo diagrams as OWL 2 DL ontologies.

7.6 Gaffe: Future Works

I plan to carry out several evaluation studies to assess the advantages of using Gaffe as authoring tool and form editor according to different kinds of users (ontologists, publishers, semantic data publishers, etc.). In particular, I am now developing a first user-testing session that aims at investigating the benefits introduced by Gaffe when ontologists use it to develop Web forms through the specification of instance documents that link domain ontologies to ontological descriptions of the forms. My aim is to demonstrate how experts in ontology development can make real and usable Web forms despite their inexperience in the development of Web interfaces.

Moreover, I plan to extend the Gaffe API in order to use the systems in different environment such as word processor. In particular I am now designing an integrated system to support users when enriching documents through SPAR. The idea is to use Gaffe as the main interface by which users can associate semantic metadata to markup documents defined through EARMARK, keeping track of provenance information (e.g., through the W3C Provenance Ontology (Sahoo and McGuinness 2013) of both the author(s) of the formal semantic statements about the text and the author(s) of the text itself.

References

Barabucci, G., S. Peroni, F. Poggi, and F. Vitali. 2012. Embedding semantic annotations within texts: The FRETTA approach. In Proceedings of the 27th symposium on applied computing (SAC 2012), 658–663. New York: ACM. doi:10.1145/2245276.2245403.

Berners-Lee, T., J. Hendler, and O. Lassila. 2001. The semantic web. In Scientific American, 17 May 2001. http://www.scientificamerican.com/article.cfm?id=the-semantic-web. Accessed 30 July 2013.

Di Iorio, A., A. Nuzzolese, and S. Peroni. 2013a. Characterising citations in scholarly documents: The CiTalO framework. In *ESWC 2013 satellite events—Revised selected papers*, eds. P. Cimiano, M. Fernàndez, V. Lopez, S. Schlobach, and J. Völker, lecture notes in computer science, vol. 7955, 66–77. Berlin: Springer. doi:10.1007/978-3-642-41242-4_6.

Di Iorio, A., A. Nuzzolese, and S. Peroni. 2013b. Towards the automatic identification of the nature of citations. In Proceedings of 3rd workshop on semantic publishing (SePublica 2013), CEUR workshop proceedings, vol. 994, eds. A. García Castro, C. Lange, P. Lord, and R. Stevens, 63–74. Aachen: CEUR-WS.org. http://ceur-ws.org/Vol-994/paper-06.pdf. Accessed 30 July 2013.

Di Iorio, A., S. Peroni, F. Poggi, D. Shotton, and F. Vitali. 2013c. Recognising document components in XML-based academic articles. Proceedings of the 2013 ACM symposium on document engineering (DocEng 2013), 181–184. New York: ACM. doi:10.1145/2494266.2494319.

Gangemi, A., and S. Peroni. 2013. DiTTO: Diagrams transformation into OWL. In Proceedings of the ISWC 2013 posters & demonstrations track, CEUR workshop proceedings, vol. 1035, eds. E. Blomqvist and T. Groza, 5–8. Aachen: CEUR-WS.org. http://ceur-ws.org/Vol-1035/iswc2013_demo_2.pdf. Accessed 30 July 2013.

Guarino, N., and C. Welty. 2002. Evaluating ontological decisions with OntoClean. *Communications of the ACM* 45 (2): 61–65. doi:10.1145/503124.503150.

Peroni, S., D. A. Lapeyre, and D. Shotton. 2012. Mapping JATS to RDF using the SPAR (semantic publishing and referencing) ontologies. Proceedings of the Journal Article Tag Suite Conference 2012 (JATS-Con 2012). Bethesda: National Center for Biotechnology Information. http://www.ncbi.nlm.nih.gov/books/NBK100491/. Accessed 30 July 2013.

Sahoo, S., and D. McGuinness. 2013. The PROV ontology. W3C recommendation 30 April 2013. World Wide Web Consortium. http://ceur-ws.org/Vol-1035/iswc2013_demo_2.pdf. Accessed 30 July 2013.

Shotton, D. 2009. Semantic publishing: The coming revolution in scientific journal publishing. *Learned Publishing* 22 (2): 85–94. doi:10.1087/2009202.

Text Encoding Initiative Consortium. 2013. TEI P5: Guidelines for electronic text encoding and interchange. Charlottesville: TEI Consortium. http://www.tei-c.org/Guidelines/P5. Accessed 30 July 2013.

Appendices

Appendix 1: EARMARK Java API

I designed and implemented a framework (Barabucci et al. 2013) for the creation, validation and manipulation of EARMARK documents. The API is hosted by GitHub[1] under the Apache 2.0 license and fully implements the current model of EARMARK.

All the code is written in Java™ and uses well-known libraries from the Semantic Web community such as Jena (Carroll et al. 2004). The implementation of the EARMARK data structure follows exactly what is defined in the EARMARK ontology and uses ghost and shell classes, encoding OWL properties as methods of these classes.

The Java™ classes *EARMARKDocument* , *Range* and *MarkupItem* have been written taking into consideration a particular interface, *EARMARKNode*, directly inspired by the *Node* interface of the Java™ DOM implementation[2]. This choice has been made to maintain the EARMARK data structure as close as possible to a well-known and widely used model of XML documents.

The API makes it simple to create/load/store/modify EARMARK documents directly in a Java™ framework.Considering again the simple example previously introduced, in the following fragments I illustrate how to build it using the API.

In order to understand how EARMARK API can be used to describe markup hierarchies, I introduce again the XML fragment shown in Sect. 3.1.3, using TEI fragmentation (Text Encoding Initiative Consortium 2013) to express overlapping elements upon the string "Fabio says that overlhappens":

[1] EARMARK API: http://www.github.com/essepuntato/EarmarkDataStructure.

[2] http://java.sun.com/xml

S. Peroni, *Semantic Web Technologies and Legal Scholarly Publishing*,
Law, Governance and Technology Series 15, DOI 10.1007/978-3-319-04777-5,

```
<p>
  <agent>Fabio</agent> says that
  <noun xml:id="e1" next="e2">overl</noun>
  <verb>
    h<noun xml:id="e2">ap</noun>pens
  </verb>
</p>
```

Let me start creating a new EARMARK document and a docuverse, containing all the text content of the above document:

```
EARMARKDocument ed =
  new EARMARKDocument(URI.create("http://www.example.com"));


String ex = "http://www.example.com/";

Docuverse doc = ed.createStringDocuverse(ex+"doc",
  "Fabio says that overlhappens");
```

The next excerpt shows how to create ranges starting from the above docuverse:

```
Range r0_5 = ed.createPointerRange(ex+"r0_5", doc, 0, 5);
...
```

Finally, I define all the markup items we need to build the structure of the document. Usually, a markup item needs three different values in order to be created: a string representing its general identifier, an identifier for the item and the type for the collection it defines (either a set, a bag or a list). In the following fragment I show the creation of three different elements, composed so as to define hierarchical relations among them by using the method *appendChild*:

```
Element p = ed.createElement(
  "p", ex+"p", Collection.Type.List);
Element agent = ed.createElement(
  "agent", ex+"agent", Collection.Type.List);

ed.appendChild(p); p.appendChild(agent);
agent.appendChild(r0_5);
...
```

As seen, the API allows one to create EARMARK documents with very simple and straightforward methods. Even rather complicated structures can be created with a few lines of Java code.

Appendix 2: Full Example of EARMARK Document

In this section I introduce a full example of an EARMARK document expressed in Turtle (Prud'hommeaux and Carothers 2013). The original source of such a document is the article by Biagioli and Francesconi entitled "A Semantics-based Visual Framework for Planning a New Bill" (Biagioli and Francesconi 2005). In addition to EARMARK markup items introduced in Chap. 3 (i.e. elements, attributes and text nodes, expressed according to the DocBook schema (Walsh 2010)), the example also includes annotations that relate to the ontologies presented in two other chapters, i.e., the *Linguistic Act Ontology* (introduced in Chap. 4) and the *SPAR Ontologies* (introduced in Chap. 5). The whole example is also available online at http://www.essepuntato.it/2013/11/earmark-example.

```
@prefix : <http://www.essepuntato.it/2013/11/earmark-example/> .
@prefix co: <http://swan.mindinformatics.org/ontologies/1.2/collections/> .
@prefix earmark: <http://www.essepuntato.it/2008/12/earmark#> .
@prefix owl: <http://www.w3.org/2002/07/owl#> .
@prefix rdf: <http://www.w3.org/1999/02/22-rdf-syntax-ns#> .
@prefix rdfs: <http://www.w3.org/2000/01/rdf-schema#> .
@prefix xml: <http://www.w3.org/XML/1998/namespace> .
@prefix xsd: <http://www.w3.org/2001/XMLSchema#> .
@prefix doco: <http://purl.org/spar/doco/> .
@prefix deo: <http://purl.org/spar/deo/> .
@prefix c4o: <http://purl.org/spar/c4o/> .
@prefix biro: <http://purl.org/spar/biro/> .
@prefix fabio: <http://purl.org/spar/fabio/> .
@prefix cito: <http://purl.org/spar/cito/> .
@prefix pro: <http://purl.org/spar/pro/> .
@prefix pso: <http://purl.org/spar/pso/> .
@prefix pwo: <http://purl.org/spar/pwo/> .
@prefix salt: <http://salt.semanticauthoring.org/ontologies/sro#> .
@prefix la: <http://www.ontologydesignpatterns.org/cp/owl/semiotics.owl#> .
@prefix dcterms: <http://purl.org/dc/terms/> .
@prefix prism: <http://prismstandard.org/namespaces/basic/2.0/> .
@prefix foaf: <http://xmlns.com/foaf/0.1/> .
@prefix frbr: <http://purl.org/vocab/frbr/core#> .
@prefix part: <http://www.ontologydesignpatterns.org/cp/owl/participation.
    owl#> .

<http://www.essepuntato.it/2013/11/earmark-example> a owl:Ontology .

:e_article_1 a earmark:Element ;
```

```
  co:firstItem [ co:itemContent :a_version_1 ;
  co:nextItem [ co:itemContent :a_lang_1 ;
  co:nextItem [ co:itemContent :e_info_1 ;
  co:nextItem [ co:itemContent :e_section_1 ;
  co:nextItem [ co:itemContent :e_section_2 ;
  co:nextItem [ co:itemContent :e_section_3 ;
  co:nextItem [ co:itemContent :e_section_4 ;
  co:nextItem [ co:itemContent :e_bibliography_1 ] ] ] ] ] ] ] ] ;
  earmark:hasGeneralIdentifier "article"^^xsd:string ;
  earmark:hasNamespace "http://docbook.org/ns/docbook"^^xsd:anyURI .

:a_id_1 a co:Set,
    earmark:Attribute ;
  co:element :a_id_1_r ;
  earmark:hasGeneralIdentifier "id"^^xsd:string ;
  earmark:hasNamespace "http://www.w3.org/XML/1998/namespace"^^xsd:anyURI .

:a_id_1_r a earmark:PointerRange ;
  earmark:begins "53"^^xsd:nonNegativeInteger ;
  earmark:ends "57"^^xsd:nonNegativeInteger ;
  earmark:refersTo :a_text .

:a_id_2 a co:Set,
    earmark:Attribute ;
  co:element :a_id_2_r ;
  earmark:hasGeneralIdentifier "id"^^xsd:string ;
  earmark:hasNamespace "http://www.w3.org/XML/1998/namespace"^^xsd:anyURI .

:a_id_2_r a earmark:PointerRange ;
  earmark:begins "102"^^xsd:nonNegativeInteger ;
  earmark:ends "106"^^xsd:nonNegativeInteger ;
  earmark:refersTo :a_text .

:a_id_3 a co:Set,
    earmark:Attribute ;
  co:element :a_id_3_r ;
  earmark:hasGeneralIdentifier "id"^^xsd:string ;
  earmark:hasNamespace "http://www.w3.org/XML/1998/namespace"^^xsd:anyURI .

:a_id_3_r a earmark:PointerRange ;
  earmark:begins "151"^^xsd:nonNegativeInteger ;
  earmark:ends "155"^^xsd:nonNegativeInteger ;
  earmark:refersTo :a_text .

:a_lang_1 a co:Set,
    earmark:Attribute ;
  co:element :a_lang_1_r ;
  earmark:hasGeneralIdentifier "lang"^^xsd:string ;
  earmark:hasNamespace "http://www.w3.org/XML/1998/namespace"^^xsd:anyURI .

:a_lang_1_r a earmark:PointerRange ;
  earmark:begins "4"^^xsd:nonNegativeInteger ;
  earmark:ends "6"^^xsd:nonNegativeInteger ;
  earmark:refersTo :a_text .

:a_linkend_1 a co:Set,
    earmark:Attribute ;
  co:element :a_linkend_1_r ;
  earmark:hasGeneralIdentifier "linkend"^^xsd:string .

:a_linkend_1_r a earmark:PointerRange ;
  earmark:begins "38"^^xsd:nonNegativeInteger ;
```

```
  earmark:ends "42"^^xsd:nonNegativeInteger ;
  earmark:refersTo :a_text .

:a_linkend_2 a co:Set,
    earmark:Attribute ;
  co:element :a_linkend_2_r ;
  earmark:hasGeneralIdentifier "linkend"^^xsd:string .

:a_linkend_2_r a earmark:PointerRange ;
  earmark:begins "43"^^xsd:nonNegativeInteger ;
  earmark:ends "47"^^xsd:nonNegativeInteger ;
  earmark:refersTo :a_text .

:a_linkend_3 a co:Set,
    earmark:Attribute ;
  co:element :a_linkend_3_r ;
  earmark:hasGeneralIdentifier "linkend"^^xsd:string .

:a_linkend_3_r a earmark:PointerRange ;
  earmark:begins "48"^^xsd:nonNegativeInteger ;
  earmark:ends "52"^^xsd:nonNegativeInteger ;
  earmark:refersTo :a_text .

:a_relation_1 a co:Set,
    earmark:Attribute ;
  co:element :a_relation_1_r ;
  earmark:hasGeneralIdentifier "relation"^^xsd:string .

:a_relation_1_r a earmark:PointerRange ;
  earmark:begins "62"^^xsd:nonNegativeInteger ;
  earmark:ends "78"^^xsd:nonNegativeInteger ;
  earmark:refersTo :a_text .

:a_relation_2 a co:Set,
    earmark:Attribute ;
  co:element :a_relation_2_r ;
  earmark:hasGeneralIdentifier "relation"^^xsd:string .

:a_relation_2_r a earmark:PointerRange ;
  earmark:begins "79"^^xsd:nonNegativeInteger ;
  earmark:ends "101"^^xsd:nonNegativeInteger ;
  earmark:refersTo :a_text .

:a_relation_3 a co:Set,
    earmark:Attribute ;
  co:element :a_relation_3_r ;
  earmark:hasGeneralIdentifier "relation"^^xsd:string .

:a_relation_3_r a earmark:PointerRange ;
  earmark:begins "111"^^xsd:nonNegativeInteger ;
  earmark:ends "127"^^xsd:nonNegativeInteger ;
  earmark:refersTo :a_text .

:a_relation_4 a co:Set,
    earmark:Attribute ;
  co:element :a_relation_4_r ;
  earmark:hasGeneralIdentifier "relation"^^xsd:string .

:a_relation_4_r a earmark:PointerRange ;
  earmark:begins "128"^^xsd:nonNegativeInteger ;
  earmark:ends "150"^^xsd:nonNegativeInteger ;
  earmark:refersTo :a_text .
```

```
:a_relation_5 a co:Set,
    earmark:Attribute ;
  co:element :a_relation_5_r ;
  earmark:hasGeneralIdentifier "relation"^^xsd:string .

:a_relation_5_r a earmark:PointerRange ;
  earmark:begins "160"^^xsd:nonNegativeInteger ;
  earmark:ends "174"^^xsd:nonNegativeInteger ;
  earmark:refersTo :a_text .

:a_relation_6 a co:Set,
    earmark:Attribute ;
  co:element :a_relation_6_r ;
  earmark:hasGeneralIdentifier "relation"^^xsd:string .

:a_relation_6_r a earmark:PointerRange ;
  earmark:begins "175"^^xsd:nonNegativeInteger ;
  earmark:ends "195"^^xsd:nonNegativeInteger ;
  earmark:refersTo :a_text .

:a_role_1 a co:Set,
    earmark:Attribute ;
  co:element :a_role_1_r ;
  earmark:hasGeneralIdentifier "role"^^xsd:string .

:a_role_1_r a earmark:PointerRange ;
  earmark:begins "7"^^xsd:nonNegativeInteger ;
  earmark:ends "27"^^xsd:nonNegativeInteger ;
  earmark:refersTo :a_text .

:a_role_2 a co:Set,
    earmark:Attribute ;
  co:element :a_role_2_r ;
  earmark:hasGeneralIdentifier "role"^^xsd:string .

:a_role_2_r a earmark:PointerRange ;
  earmark:begins "28"^^xsd:nonNegativeInteger ;
  earmark:ends "37"^^xsd:nonNegativeInteger ;
  earmark:refersTo :a_text .

:a_version_1 a co:Set,
    earmark:Attribute ;
  co:element :a_version_1_r ;
  earmark:hasGeneralIdentifier "version"^^xsd:string .

:a_version_1_r a earmark:PointerRange ;
  earmark:begins "0"^^xsd:nonNegativeInteger ;
  earmark:ends "3"^^xsd:nonNegativeInteger ;
  earmark:refersTo :a_text .

:a_xreflabel_1 a co:Set,
    earmark:Attribute ;
  co:element :a_xreflabel_1_r ;
  earmark:hasGeneralIdentifier "xreflabel"^^xsd:string .

:a_xreflabel_1_r a earmark:PointerRange ;
  earmark:begins "58"^^xsd:nonNegativeInteger ;
  earmark:ends "61"^^xsd:nonNegativeInteger ;
  earmark:refersTo :a_text .

:a_xreflabel_2 a co:Set,
```

```
    earmark:Attribute ;
  co:element :a_xreflabel_2_r ;
  earmark:hasGeneralIdentifier "xreflabel"^^xsd:string .

:a_xreflabel_2_r a earmark:PointerRange ;
  earmark:begins "107"^^xsd:nonNegativeInteger ;
  earmark:ends "110"^^xsd:nonNegativeInteger ;
  earmark:refersTo :a_text .

:a_xreflabel_3 a co:Set,
    earmark:Attribute ;
  co:element :a_xreflabel_3_r ;
  earmark:hasGeneralIdentifier "xreflabel"^^xsd:string .

:a_xreflabel_3_r a earmark:PointerRange ;
  earmark:begins "156"^^xsd:nonNegativeInteger ;
  earmark:ends "159"^^xsd:nonNegativeInteger ;
  earmark:refersTo :a_text .

:e_abstract_1 a earmark:Element ;
  la:expresses salt:Abstract ;
  co:firstItem [ co:itemContent :e_para_1 ] ;
  earmark:hasGeneralIdentifier "abstract"^^xsd:string ;
  earmark:hasNamespace "http://docbook.org/ns/docbook"^^xsd:anyURI .

:e_address_1 a earmark:Element ;
  co:firstItem [ co:itemContent :e_street_1 ;
  co:nextItem [ co:itemContent :e_postcode_1 ;
  co:nextItem [ co:itemContent :e_city_1 ;
  co:nextItem [ co:itemContent :e_country_1 ] ] ] ] ;
  earmark:hasGeneralIdentifier "address"^^xsd:string ;
  earmark:hasNamespace "http://docbook.org/ns/docbook"^^xsd:anyURI .

:e_address_2 a earmark:Element ;
  co:firstItem [ co:itemContent :e_phrase_1 ;
  co:nextItem [ co:itemContent :e_street_2 ;
  co:nextItem [ co:itemContent :e_postcode_2 ;
  co:nextItem [ co:itemContent :e_city_2 ;
  co:nextItem [ co:itemContent :e_country_2 ;
  co:nextItem [ co:itemContent :e_phone_1 ;
  co:nextItem [ co:itemContent :e_fax_1 ] ] ] ] ] ] ] ;
  earmark:hasGeneralIdentifier "address"^^xsd:string ;
  earmark:hasNamespace "http://docbook.org/ns/docbook"^^xsd:anyURI .

:e_address_3 a earmark:Element ;
  co:firstItem [ co:itemContent :e_street_3 ;
  co:nextItem [ co:itemContent :e_postcode_3 ;
  co:nextItem [ co:itemContent :e_city_3 ;
  co:nextItem [ co:itemContent :e_country_3 ] ] ] ] ;
  earmark:hasGeneralIdentifier "address"^^xsd:string ;
  earmark:hasNamespace "http://docbook.org/ns/docbook"^^xsd:anyURI .

:e_affiliation_1 a earmark:Element ;
  co:firstItem [ co:itemContent :e_org_1 ] ;
  earmark:hasGeneralIdentifier "affiliation"^^xsd:string ;
  earmark:hasNamespace "http://docbook.org/ns/docbook"^^xsd:anyURI .

:e_affiliation_2 a earmark:Element ;
  co:firstItem [ co:itemContent :e_org_2 ] ;
  earmark:hasGeneralIdentifier "affiliation"^^xsd:string ;
  earmark:hasNamespace "http://docbook.org/ns/docbook"^^xsd:anyURI .
```

```
:e_author_1 a earmark:Element ;
  co:firstItem [ co:itemContent :e_personname_1 ;
  co:nextItem [ co:itemContent :e_affiliation_1 ] ] ;
  earmark:hasGeneralIdentifier "author"^^xsd:string ;
  earmark:hasNamespace "http://docbook.org/ns/docbook"^^xsd:anyURI .

:e_author_10 a earmark:Element ;
  co:firstItem [ co:itemContent :e_personname_10 ] ;
  earmark:hasGeneralIdentifier "author"^^xsd:string ;
  earmark:hasNamespace "http://docbook.org/ns/docbook"^^xsd:anyURI .

:e_author_11 a earmark:Element ;
  co:firstItem [ co:itemContent :e_personname_11 ] ;
  earmark:hasGeneralIdentifier "author"^^xsd:string ;
  earmark:hasNamespace "http://docbook.org/ns/docbook"^^xsd:anyURI .

:e_author_2 a earmark:Element ;
  co:firstItem [ co:itemContent :a_role_1 ;
  co:nextItem [ co:itemContent :e_personname_2 ;
  co:nextItem [ co:itemContent :e_email_1 ;
  co:nextItem [ co:itemContent :e_address_2 ;
  co:nextItem [ co:itemContent :e_affiliation_2 ] ] ] ] ] ;
  earmark:hasGeneralIdentifier "author"^^xsd:string ;
  earmark:hasNamespace "http://docbook.org/ns/docbook"^^xsd:anyURI .

:e_author_3 a earmark:Element ;
  co:firstItem [ co:itemContent :e_personname_3 ] ;
  earmark:hasGeneralIdentifier "author"^^xsd:string ;
  earmark:hasNamespace "http://docbook.org/ns/docbook"^^xsd:anyURI .

:e_author_4 a earmark:Element ;
  co:firstItem [ co:itemContent :e_personname_4 ] ;
  earmark:hasGeneralIdentifier "author"^^xsd:string ;
  earmark:hasNamespace "http://docbook.org/ns/docbook"^^xsd:anyURI .

:e_author_5 a earmark:Element ;
  co:firstItem [ co:itemContent :e_personname_5 ] ;
  earmark:hasGeneralIdentifier "author"^^xsd:string ;
  earmark:hasNamespace "http://docbook.org/ns/docbook"^^xsd:anyURI .

:e_author_6 a earmark:Element ;
  co:firstItem [ co:itemContent :e_personname_6 ] ;
  earmark:hasGeneralIdentifier "author"^^xsd:string ;
  earmark:hasNamespace "http://docbook.org/ns/docbook"^^xsd:anyURI .

:e_author_7 a earmark:Element ;
  co:firstItem [ co:itemContent :e_personname_7 ] ;
  earmark:hasGeneralIdentifier "author"^^xsd:string ;
  earmark:hasNamespace "http://docbook.org/ns/docbook"^^xsd:anyURI .

:e_author_8 a earmark:Element ;
  co:firstItem [ co:itemContent :e_personname_8 ] ;
  earmark:hasGeneralIdentifier "author"^^xsd:string ;
  earmark:hasNamespace "http://docbook.org/ns/docbook"^^xsd:anyURI .

:e_author_9 a earmark:Element ;
  co:firstItem [ co:itemContent :e_personname_9 ] ;
  earmark:hasGeneralIdentifier "author"^^xsd:string ;
  earmark:hasNamespace "http://docbook.org/ns/docbook"^^xsd:anyURI .

:e_authorgroup_1 a earmark:Element ;
  la:expresses doco:ListOfAuthors ;
```

```
    co:firstItem [ co:itemContent :e_author_1 ;
    co:nextItem [ co:itemContent :e_author_2 ] ] ;
    earmark:hasGeneralIdentifier "authorgroup"^^xsd:string ;
    earmark:hasNamespace "http://docbook.org/ns/docbook"^^xsd:anyURI .

  :e_authorgroup_2 a earmark:Element ;
    la:expresses doco:ListOfAuthors ;
    co:firstItem [ co:itemContent :e_author_3 ;
    co:nextItem [ co:itemContent :e_author_4 ;
    co:nextItem [ co:itemContent :e_author_5 ;
    co:nextItem [ co:itemContent :e_author_6 ] ] ] ] ;
    earmark:hasGeneralIdentifier "authorgroup"^^xsd:string ;
    earmark:hasNamespace "http://docbook.org/ns/docbook"^^xsd:anyURI .

  :e_authorgroup_3 a earmark:Element ;
    la:expresses doco:ListOfAuthors ;
    co:firstItem [ co:itemContent :e_author_7 ;
    co:nextItem [ co:itemContent :e_author_8 ;
    co:nextItem [ co:itemContent :e_author_9 ] ] ] ;
    earmark:hasGeneralIdentifier "authorgroup"^^xsd:string ;
    earmark:hasNamespace "http://docbook.org/ns/docbook"^^xsd:anyURI .

  :e_authorgroup_4 a earmark:Element ;
    la:expresses doco:ListOfAuthors ;
    co:firstItem [ co:itemContent :e_author_10 ;
    co:nextItem [ co:itemContent :e_author_11 ] ] ;
    earmark:hasGeneralIdentifier "authorgroup"^^xsd:string ;
    earmark:hasNamespace "http://docbook.org/ns/docbook"^^xsd:anyURI .

  :e_bibliography_1 a earmark:Element ;
    la:expresses doco:Bibliography ;
    co:firstItem [ co:itemContent :e_title_6 ;
    co:nextItem [ co:itemContent :ref1 ;
    co:nextItem [ co:itemContent :ref2 ;
    co:nextItem [ co:itemContent :ref3 ] ] ] ] ;
    earmark:hasGeneralIdentifier "bibliography"^^xsd:string ;
    earmark:hasNamespace "http://docbook.org/ns/docbook"^^xsd:anyURI .

  :e_bibliomset_1 a earmark:Element ;
    co:firstItem [ co:itemContent :a_relation_1 ;
    co:nextItem [ co:itemContent :e_authorgroup_2 ;
    co:nextItem [ co:itemContent :e_title_7 ] ] ] ;
    earmark:hasGeneralIdentifier "bibliomset"^^xsd:string ;
    earmark:hasNamespace "http://docbook.org/ns/docbook"^^xsd:anyURI .

  :e_bibliomset_2 a earmark:Element ;
    co:firstItem [ co:itemContent :a_relation_2 ;
    co:nextItem [ co:itemContent :e_title_8 ;
    co:nextItem [ co:itemContent :e_pagenums_1 ;
    co:nextItem [ co:itemContent :e_pubdate_1 ] ] ] ] ;
    earmark:hasGeneralIdentifier "bibliomset"^^xsd:string ;
    earmark:hasNamespace "http://docbook.org/ns/docbook"^^xsd:anyURI .

  :e_bibliomset_3 a earmark:Element ;
    co:firstItem [ co:itemContent :a_relation_3 ;
    co:nextItem [ co:itemContent :e_authorgroup_3 ;
    co:nextItem [ co:itemContent :e_title_9 ] ] ] ;
    earmark:hasGeneralIdentifier "bibliomset"^^xsd:string ;
    earmark:hasNamespace "http://docbook.org/ns/docbook"^^xsd:anyURI .

  :e_bibliomset_4 a earmark:Element ;
    co:firstItem [ co:itemContent :a_relation_4 ;
```

```
  co:nextItem [ co:itemContent :e_title_10 ;
  co:nextItem [ co:itemContent :e_pagenums_2 ;
  co:nextItem [ co:itemContent :e_pubdate_2 ] ] ] ] ;
  earmark:hasGeneralIdentifier "bibliomset"^^xsd:string ;
  earmark:hasNamespace "http://docbook.org/ns/docbook"^^xsd:anyURI .

:e_bibliomset_5 a earmark:Element ;
  co:firstItem [ co:itemContent :a_relation_5 ;
  co:nextItem [ co:itemContent :e_authorgroup_4 ;
  co:nextItem [ co:itemContent :e_title_11 ] ] ] ;
  earmark:hasGeneralIdentifier "bibliomset"^^xsd:string ;
  earmark:hasNamespace "http://docbook.org/ns/docbook"^^xsd:anyURI .

:e_bibliomset_6 a earmark:Element ;
  co:firstItem [ co:itemContent :a_relation_6 ;
  co:nextItem [ co:itemContent :e_title_12 ;
  co:nextItem [ co:itemContent :e_pagenums_3 ;
  co:nextItem [ co:itemContent :e_pubdate_3 ] ] ] ] ;
  earmark:hasGeneralIdentifier "bibliomset"^^xsd:string ;
  earmark:hasNamespace "http://docbook.org/ns/docbook"^^xsd:anyURI .

:e_city_1 a earmark:Element ;
  co:firstItem [ co:itemContent :r_112-120 ] ;
  earmark:hasGeneralIdentifier "city"^^xsd:string ;
  earmark:hasNamespace "http://docbook.org/ns/docbook"^^xsd:anyURI .

:e_city_2 a earmark:Element ;
  co:firstItem [ co:itemContent :r_209-217 ] ;
  earmark:hasGeneralIdentifier "city"^^xsd:string ;
  earmark:hasNamespace "http://docbook.org/ns/docbook"^^xsd:anyURI .

:e_city_3 a earmark:Element ;
  co:firstItem [ co:itemContent :r_287-295 ] ;
  earmark:hasGeneralIdentifier "city"^^xsd:string ;
  earmark:hasNamespace "http://docbook.org/ns/docbook"^^xsd:anyURI .

:e_country_1 a earmark:Element ;
  co:firstItem [ co:itemContent :r_121-126 ] ;
  earmark:hasGeneralIdentifier "country"^^xsd:string ;
  earmark:hasNamespace "http://docbook.org/ns/docbook"^^xsd:anyURI .

:e_country_2 a earmark:Element ;
  co:firstItem [ co:itemContent :r_218-223 ] ;
  earmark:hasGeneralIdentifier "country"^^xsd:string ;
  earmark:hasNamespace "http://docbook.org/ns/docbook"^^xsd:anyURI .

:e_country_3 a earmark:Element ;
  co:firstItem [ co:itemContent :r_296-301 ] ;
  earmark:hasGeneralIdentifier "country"^^xsd:string ;
  earmark:hasNamespace "http://docbook.org/ns/docbook"^^xsd:anyURI .

:e_email_1 a earmark:Element ;
  co:firstItem [ co:itemContent :r_146-170 ] ;
  earmark:hasGeneralIdentifier "email"^^xsd:string ;
  earmark:hasNamespace "http://docbook.org/ns/docbook"^^xsd:anyURI .

:e_emphasis_1 a earmark:Element ;
  co:firstItem [ co:itemContent :r_1252-1262 ] ;
  earmark:hasGeneralIdentifier "emphasis"^^xsd:string ;
  earmark:hasNamespace "http://docbook.org/ns/docbook"^^xsd:anyURI .

:e_emphasis_10 a earmark:Element ;
```

```
  co:firstItem [ co:itemContent :r_4452-4463 ] ;
  earmark:hasGeneralIdentifier "emphasis"^^xsd:string ;
  earmark:hasNamespace "http://docbook.org/ns/docbook"^^xsd:anyURI .

:e_emphasis_2 a earmark:Element ;
  co:firstItem [ co:itemContent :r_1268-1278 ] ;
  earmark:hasGeneralIdentifier "emphasis"^^xsd:string ;
  earmark:hasNamespace "http://docbook.org/ns/docbook"^^xsd:anyURI .

:e_emphasis_3 a earmark:Element ;
  co:firstItem [ co:itemContent :r_1281-1291 ] ;
  earmark:hasGeneralIdentifier "emphasis"^^xsd:string ;
  earmark:hasNamespace "http://docbook.org/ns/docbook"^^xsd:anyURI .

:e_emphasis_4 a earmark:Element ;
  co:firstItem [ co:itemContent :r_1294-1302 ] ;
  earmark:hasGeneralIdentifier "emphasis"^^xsd:string ;
  earmark:hasNamespace "http://docbook.org/ns/docbook"^^xsd:anyURI .

:e_emphasis_5 a earmark:Element ;
  co:firstItem [ co:itemContent :r_1305-1315 ] ;
  earmark:hasGeneralIdentifier "emphasis"^^xsd:string ;
  earmark:hasNamespace "http://docbook.org/ns/docbook"^^xsd:anyURI .

:e_emphasis_6 a earmark:Element ;
  co:firstItem [ co:itemContent :r_1334-1343 ] ;
  earmark:hasGeneralIdentifier "emphasis"^^xsd:string ;
  earmark:hasNamespace "http://docbook.org/ns/docbook"^^xsd:anyURI .

:e_emphasis_7 a earmark:Element ;
  co:firstItem [ co:itemContent :r_1353-1362 ] ;
  earmark:hasGeneralIdentifier "emphasis"^^xsd:string ;
  earmark:hasNamespace "http://docbook.org/ns/docbook"^^xsd:anyURI .

:e_emphasis_8 a earmark:Element ;
  co:firstItem [ co:itemContent :r_2803-2813 ] ;
  earmark:hasGeneralIdentifier "emphasis"^^xsd:string ;
  earmark:hasNamespace "http://docbook.org/ns/docbook"^^xsd:anyURI .

:e_emphasis_9 a earmark:Element ;
  co:firstItem [ co:itemContent :r_2818-2827 ] ;
  earmark:hasGeneralIdentifier "emphasis"^^xsd:string ;
  earmark:hasNamespace "http://docbook.org/ns/docbook"^^xsd:anyURI .

:e_fax_1 a earmark:Element ;
  co:firstItem [ co:itemContent :r_236-248 ] ;
  earmark:hasGeneralIdentifier "fax"^^xsd:string ;
  earmark:hasNamespace "http://docbook.org/ns/docbook"^^xsd:anyURI .

:e_firstname_1 a earmark:Element ;
  co:firstItem [ co:itemContent :r_59-64 ] ;
  earmark:hasGeneralIdentifier "firstname"^^xsd:string ;
  earmark:hasNamespace "http://docbook.org/ns/docbook"^^xsd:anyURI .

:e_firstname_10 a earmark:Element ;
  co:firstItem [ co:itemContent :r_6159-6161 ] ;
  earmark:hasGeneralIdentifier "firstname"^^xsd:string ;
  earmark:hasNamespace "http://docbook.org/ns/docbook"^^xsd:anyURI .

:e_firstname_11 a earmark:Element ;
  co:firstItem [ co:itemContent :r_6172-6174 ] ;
  earmark:hasGeneralIdentifier "firstname"^^xsd:string ;
```

```
  earmark:hasNamespace "http://docbook.org/ns/docbook"^^xsd:anyURI .

:e_firstname_2 a earmark:Element ;
  co:firstItem [ co:itemContent :r_127-133 ] ;
  earmark:hasGeneralIdentifier "firstname"^^xsd:string ;
  earmark:hasNamespace "http://docbook.org/ns/docbook"^^xsd:anyURI .

:e_firstname_3 a earmark:Element ;
  co:firstItem [ co:itemContent :r_5764-5766 ] ;
  earmark:hasGeneralIdentifier "firstname"^^xsd:string ;
  earmark:hasNamespace "http://docbook.org/ns/docbook"^^xsd:anyURI .

:e_firstname_4 a earmark:Element ;
  co:firstItem [ co:itemContent :r_5776-5778 ] ;
  earmark:hasGeneralIdentifier "firstname"^^xsd:string ;
  earmark:hasNamespace "http://docbook.org/ns/docbook"^^xsd:anyURI .

:e_firstname_5 a earmark:Element ;
  co:firstItem [ co:itemContent :r_5791-5793 ] ;
  earmark:hasGeneralIdentifier "firstname"^^xsd:string ;
  earmark:hasNamespace "http://docbook.org/ns/docbook"^^xsd:anyURI .

:e_firstname_6 a earmark:Element ;
  co:firstItem [ co:itemContent :r_5802-5804 ] ;
  earmark:hasGeneralIdentifier "firstname"^^xsd:string ;
  earmark:hasNamespace "http://docbook.org/ns/docbook"^^xsd:anyURI .

:e_firstname_7 a earmark:Element ;
  co:firstItem [ co:itemContent :r_5982-5984 ] ;
  earmark:hasGeneralIdentifier "firstname"^^xsd:string ;
  earmark:hasNamespace "http://docbook.org/ns/docbook"^^xsd:anyURI .

:e_firstname_8 a earmark:Element ;
  co:firstItem [ co:itemContent :r_5994-5996 ] ;
  earmark:hasGeneralIdentifier "firstname"^^xsd:string ;
  earmark:hasNamespace "http://docbook.org/ns/docbook"^^xsd:anyURI .

:e_firstname_9 a earmark:Element ;
  co:firstItem [ co:itemContent :r_6004-6006 ] ;
  earmark:hasGeneralIdentifier "firstname"^^xsd:string ;
  earmark:hasNamespace "http://docbook.org/ns/docbook"^^xsd:anyURI .

:e_info_1 a earmark:Element ;
  la:expresses doco:FrontMatter ;
  co:firstItem [ co:itemContent :e_title_1 ;
  co:nextItem [ co:itemContent :e_authorgroup_1 ;
  co:nextItem [ co:itemContent :e_abstract_1 ;
  co:nextItem [ co:itemContent :e_keywordset_1 ] ] ] ] ;
  earmark:hasGeneralIdentifier "info"^^xsd:string ;
  earmark:hasNamespace "http://docbook.org/ns/docbook"^^xsd:anyURI .

:e_keyword_1 a earmark:Element ;
  co:firstItem [ co:itemContent :r_636-651 ] ;
  earmark:hasGeneralIdentifier "keyword"^^xsd:string ;
  earmark:hasNamespace "http://docbook.org/ns/docbook"^^xsd:anyURI .

:e_keyword_2 a earmark:Element ;
  co:firstItem [ co:itemContent :r_652-655 ] ;
  earmark:hasGeneralIdentifier "keyword"^^xsd:string ;
  earmark:hasNamespace "http://docbook.org/ns/docbook"^^xsd:anyURI .

:e_keyword_3 a earmark:Element ;
```

```
    co:firstItem [ co:itemContent :r_656-664 ] ;
    earmark:hasGeneralIdentifier "keyword"^^xsd:string ;
    earmark:hasNamespace "http://docbook.org/ns/docbook"^^xsd:anyURI .

  :e_keyword_4 a earmark:Element ;
    co:firstItem [ co:itemContent :r_665-688 ] ;
    earmark:hasGeneralIdentifier "keyword"^^xsd:string ;
    earmark:hasNamespace "http://docbook.org/ns/docbook"^^xsd:anyURI .

  :e_keywordset_1 a earmark:Element ;
    co:firstItem [ co:itemContent :e_keyword_1 ;
    co:nextItem [ co:itemContent :e_keyword_2 ;
    co:nextItem [ co:itemContent :e_keyword_3 ;
    co:nextItem [ co:itemContent :e_keyword_4 ] ] ] ] ;
    earmark:hasGeneralIdentifier "keywordset"^^xsd:string ;
    earmark:hasNamespace "http://docbook.org/ns/docbook"^^xsd:anyURI .

  :e_org_1 a earmark:Element ;
    co:firstItem [ co:itemContent :e_orgname_1 ;
    co:nextItem [ co:itemContent :e_orgdiv_1 ;
    co:nextItem [ co:itemContent :e_address_1 ] ] ] ;
    earmark:hasGeneralIdentifier "org"^^xsd:string ;
    earmark:hasNamespace "http://docbook.org/ns/docbook"^^xsd:anyURI .

  :e_org_2 a earmark:Element ;
    co:firstItem [ co:itemContent :e_orgname_2 ;
    co:nextItem [ co:itemContent :e_orgdiv_2 ;
    co:nextItem [ co:itemContent :e_address_3 ] ] ] ;
    earmark:hasGeneralIdentifier "org"^^xsd:string ;
    earmark:hasNamespace "http://docbook.org/ns/docbook"^^xsd:anyURI .

  :e_orgdiv_1 a earmark:Element ;
    co:firstItem [ co:itemContent :r_78-83 ] ;
    earmark:hasGeneralIdentifier "orgdiv"^^xsd:string ;
    earmark:hasNamespace "http://docbook.org/ns/docbook"^^xsd:anyURI .

  :e_orgdiv_2 a earmark:Element ;
    co:firstItem [ co:itemContent :r_253-258 ] ;
    earmark:hasGeneralIdentifier "orgdiv"^^xsd:string ;
    earmark:hasNamespace "http://docbook.org/ns/docbook"^^xsd:anyURI .

  :e_orgname_1 a earmark:Element ;
    co:firstItem [ co:itemContent :r_74-77 ] ;
    earmark:hasGeneralIdentifier "orgname"^^xsd:string ;
    earmark:hasNamespace "http://docbook.org/ns/docbook"^^xsd:anyURI .

  :e_orgname_2 a earmark:Element ;
    co:firstItem [ co:itemContent :r_249-252 ] ;
    earmark:hasGeneralIdentifier "orgname"^^xsd:string ;
    earmark:hasNamespace "http://docbook.org/ns/docbook"^^xsd:anyURI .

  :e_pagenums_1 a earmark:Element ;
    co:firstItem [ co:itemContent :r_5969-5976 ] ;
    earmark:hasGeneralIdentifier "pagenums"^^xsd:string ;
    earmark:hasNamespace "http://docbook.org/ns/docbook"^^xsd:anyURI .

  :e_pagenums_2 a earmark:Element ;
    co:firstItem [ co:itemContent :r_6148-6153 ] ;
    earmark:hasGeneralIdentifier "pagenums"^^xsd:string ;
    earmark:hasNamespace "http://docbook.org/ns/docbook"^^xsd:anyURI .

  :e_pagenums_3 a earmark:Element ;
```

```
  co:firstItem [ co:itemContent :r_6318-6323 ] ;
  earmark:hasGeneralIdentifier "pagenums"^^xsd:string ;
  earmark:hasNamespace "http://docbook.org/ns/docbook"^^xsd:anyURI .

:e_para_1 a earmark:Element ;
  la:expresses doco:Paragraph ;
  co:firstItem [ co:itemContent :r_302-635 ] ;
  earmark:hasGeneralIdentifier "para"^^xsd:string ;
  earmark:hasNamespace "http://docbook.org/ns/docbook"^^xsd:anyURI .

:e_para_2 a earmark:Element ;
  la:expresses doco:Paragraph ;
  co:firstItem [ co:itemContent :r_702-818 ;
  co:nextItem [ co:itemContent :e_quote_1 ;
  co:nextItem [ co:itemContent :r_842-904 ;
  co:nextItem [ co:itemContent :e_xref_1 ;
  co:nextItem [ co:itemContent :r_905-1048 ;
  co:nextItem [ co:itemContent :e_quote_2 ;
  co:nextItem [ co:itemContent :r_1063-1155 ;
  co:nextItem [ co:itemContent :e_xref_2 ;
  co:nextItem [ co:itemContent :r_1156-1251 ;
  co:nextItem [ co:itemContent :e_emphasis_1 ;
  co:nextItem [ co:itemContent :r_1263-1267 ;
  co:nextItem [ co:itemContent :e_emphasis_2 ;
  co:nextItem [ co:itemContent :r_1279-1280 ;
  co:nextItem [ co:itemContent :e_emphasis_3 ;
  co:nextItem [ co:itemContent :r_1292-1293 ;
  co:nextItem [ co:itemContent :e_emphasis_4 ;
  co:nextItem [ co:itemContent :r_1303-1304 ;
  co:nextItem [ co:itemContent :e_emphasis_5 ;
  co:nextItem [ co:itemContent :r_1316-1333 ;
  co:nextItem [ co:itemContent :e_emphasis_6 ;
  co:nextItem [ co:itemContent :r_1344-1352 ;
  co:nextItem [ co:itemContent :e_emphasis_7 ;
  co:nextItem [ co:itemContent :r_1363-1647 ] ] ] ] ] ] ] ] ] ] ] ] ] ] ]
      ] ] ] ] ] ] ] ;
  earmark:hasGeneralIdentifier "para"^^xsd:string ;
  earmark:hasNamespace "http://docbook.org/ns/docbook"^^xsd:anyURI .

:e_para_3 a earmark:Element ;
  la:expresses doco:Paragraph ;
  co:firstItem [ co:itemContent :r_1668-2284 ;
  co:nextItem [ co:itemContent :e_xref_3 ;
  co:nextItem [ co:itemContent :r_2285-2376 ] ] ] ;
  earmark:hasGeneralIdentifier "para"^^xsd:string ;
  earmark:hasNamespace "http://docbook.org/ns/docbook"^^xsd:anyURI .

:e_para_4 a earmark:Element ;
  la:expresses doco:Paragraph ;
  co:firstItem [ co:itemContent :r_2377-2802 ;
  co:nextItem [ co:itemContent :e_emphasis_8 ;
  co:nextItem [ co:itemContent :r_2814-2817 ;
  co:nextItem [ co:itemContent :e_emphasis_9 ;
  co:nextItem [ co:itemContent :r_2828-3500 ] ] ] ] ] ;
  earmark:hasGeneralIdentifier "para"^^xsd:string ;
  earmark:hasNamespace "http://docbook.org/ns/docbook"^^xsd:anyURI .

:e_para_5 a earmark:Element ;
  la:expresses doco:Paragraph ;
  co:firstItem [ co:itemContent :r_3543-3778 ] ;
  earmark:hasGeneralIdentifier "para"^^xsd:string ;
  earmark:hasNamespace "http://docbook.org/ns/docbook"^^xsd:anyURI .
```

```
:e_para_6 a earmark:Element ;
  la:expresses doco:Paragraph ;
  co:firstItem [ co:itemContent :r_3779-4451 ;
  co:nextItem [ co:itemContent :e_emphasis_10 ;
  co:nextItem [ co:itemContent :r_4464-4818 ;
  co:nextItem [ co:itemContent :e_quote_3 ;
  co:nextItem [ co:itemContent :r_4830-4904 ;
  co:nextItem [ co:itemContent :e_quote_4 ;
  co:nextItem [ co:itemContent :r_4916-5039 ;
  co:nextItem [ co:itemContent :e_quote_5 ;
  co:nextItem [ co:itemContent :r_5049-5293 ] ] ] ] ] ] ] ] ] ;
  earmark:hasGeneralIdentifier "para"^^xsd:string ;
  earmark:hasNamespace "http://docbook.org/ns/docbook"^^xsd:anyURI .

:e_para_7 a earmark:Element ;
  la:expresses doco:Paragraph ;
  co:firstItem [ co:itemContent :r_5306-5752 ] ;
  earmark:hasGeneralIdentifier "para"^^xsd:string ;
  earmark:hasNamespace "http://docbook.org/ns/docbook"^^xsd:anyURI .

:e_personname_1 a earmark:Element ;
  co:firstItem [ co:itemContent :e_firstname_1 ;
  co:nextItem [ co:itemContent :e_surname_1 ] ] ;
  earmark:hasGeneralIdentifier "personname"^^xsd:string ;
  earmark:hasNamespace "http://docbook.org/ns/docbook"^^xsd:anyURI .

:e_personname_10 a earmark:Element ;
  co:firstItem [ co:itemContent :e_firstname_10 ;
  co:nextItem [ co:itemContent :e_surname_10 ] ] ;
  earmark:hasGeneralIdentifier "personname"^^xsd:string ;
  earmark:hasNamespace "http://docbook.org/ns/docbook"^^xsd:anyURI .

:e_personname_11 a earmark:Element ;
  co:firstItem [ co:itemContent :e_firstname_11 ;
  co:nextItem [ co:itemContent :e_surname_11 ] ] ;
  earmark:hasGeneralIdentifier "personname"^^xsd:string ;
  earmark:hasNamespace "http://docbook.org/ns/docbook"^^xsd:anyURI .

:e_personname_2 a earmark:Element ;
  co:firstItem [ co:itemContent :e_firstname_2 ;
  co:nextItem [ co:itemContent :e_surname_2 ] ] ;
  earmark:hasGeneralIdentifier "personname"^^xsd:string ;
  earmark:hasNamespace "http://docbook.org/ns/docbook"^^xsd:anyURI .

:e_personname_3 a earmark:Element ;
  co:firstItem [ co:itemContent :e_firstname_3 ;
  co:nextItem [ co:itemContent :e_surname_3 ] ] ;
  earmark:hasGeneralIdentifier "personname"^^xsd:string ;
  earmark:hasNamespace "http://docbook.org/ns/docbook"^^xsd:anyURI .

:e_personname_4 a earmark:Element ;
  co:firstItem [ co:itemContent :e_firstname_4 ;
  co:nextItem [ co:itemContent :e_surname_4 ] ] ;
  earmark:hasGeneralIdentifier "personname"^^xsd:string ;
  earmark:hasNamespace "http://docbook.org/ns/docbook"^^xsd:anyURI .

:e_personname_5 a earmark:Element ;
  co:firstItem [ co:itemContent :e_firstname_5 ;
  co:nextItem [ co:itemContent :e_surname_5 ] ] ;
  earmark:hasGeneralIdentifier "personname"^^xsd:string ;
  earmark:hasNamespace "http://docbook.org/ns/docbook"^^xsd:anyURI .
```

```
:e_personname_6 a earmark:Element ;
  co:firstItem [ co:itemContent :e_firstname_6 ;
  co:nextItem [ co:itemContent :e_surname_6 ] ] ;
  earmark:hasGeneralIdentifier "personname"^^xsd:string ;
  earmark:hasNamespace "http://docbook.org/ns/docbook"^^xsd:anyURI .

:e_personname_7 a earmark:Element ;
  co:firstItem [ co:itemContent :e_firstname_7 ;
  co:nextItem [ co:itemContent :e_surname_7 ] ] ;
  earmark:hasGeneralIdentifier "personname"^^xsd:string ;
  earmark:hasNamespace "http://docbook.org/ns/docbook"^^xsd:anyURI .

:e_personname_8 a earmark:Element ;
  co:firstItem [ co:itemContent :e_firstname_8 ;
  co:nextItem [ co:itemContent :e_surname_8 ] ] ;
  earmark:hasGeneralIdentifier "personname"^^xsd:string ;
  earmark:hasNamespace "http://docbook.org/ns/docbook"^^xsd:anyURI .

:e_personname_9 a earmark:Element ;
  co:firstItem [ co:itemContent :e_firstname_9 ;
  co:nextItem [ co:itemContent :e_surname_9 ] ] ;
  earmark:hasGeneralIdentifier "personname"^^xsd:string ;
  earmark:hasNamespace "http://docbook.org/ns/docbook"^^xsd:anyURI .

:e_phone_1 a earmark:Element ;
  co:firstItem [ co:itemContent :r_224-235 ] ;
  earmark:hasGeneralIdentifier "phone"^^xsd:string ;
  earmark:hasNamespace "http://docbook.org/ns/docbook"^^xsd:anyURI .

:e_phrase_1 a earmark:Element ;
  co:firstItem [ co:itemContent :a_role_2 ;
  co:nextItem [ co:itemContent :r_171-180 ] ] ;
  earmark:hasGeneralIdentifier "phrase"^^xsd:string ;
  earmark:hasNamespace "http://docbook.org/ns/docbook"^^xsd:anyURI .

:e_postcode_1 a earmark:Element ;
  co:firstItem [ co:itemContent :r_106-111 ] ;
  earmark:hasGeneralIdentifier "postcode"^^xsd:string ;
  earmark:hasNamespace "http://docbook.org/ns/docbook"^^xsd:anyURI .

:e_postcode_2 a earmark:Element ;
  co:firstItem [ co:itemContent :r_203-208 ] ;
  earmark:hasGeneralIdentifier "postcode"^^xsd:string ;
  earmark:hasNamespace "http://docbook.org/ns/docbook"^^xsd:anyURI .

:e_postcode_3 a earmark:Element ;
  co:firstItem [ co:itemContent :r_281-286 ] ;
  earmark:hasGeneralIdentifier "postcode"^^xsd:string ;
  earmark:hasNamespace "http://docbook.org/ns/docbook"^^xsd:anyURI .

:e_pubdate_1 a earmark:Element ;
  co:firstItem [ co:itemContent :r_5977-5981 ] ;
  earmark:hasGeneralIdentifier "pubdate"^^xsd:string ;
  earmark:hasNamespace "http://docbook.org/ns/docbook"^^xsd:anyURI .

:e_pubdate_2 a earmark:Element ;
  co:firstItem [ co:itemContent :r_6154-6158 ] ;
  earmark:hasGeneralIdentifier "pubdate"^^xsd:string ;
  earmark:hasNamespace "http://docbook.org/ns/docbook"^^xsd:anyURI .

:e_pubdate_3 a earmark:Element ;
```

```
    co:firstItem [ co:itemContent :r_6324-6328 ] ;
    earmark:hasGeneralIdentifier "pubdate"^^xsd:string ;
    earmark:hasNamespace "http://docbook.org/ns/docbook"^^xsd:anyURI .

  :e_quote_1 a earmark:Element ;
    la:expresses doco:SimpleRunInQuotation ;
    co:firstItem [ co:itemContent :r_819-841 ] ;
    earmark:hasGeneralIdentifier "quote"^^xsd:string ;
    earmark:hasNamespace "http://docbook.org/ns/docbook"^^xsd:anyURI .

  :e_quote_2 a earmark:Element ;
    la:expresses doco:SimpleRunInQuotation ;
    co:firstItem [ co:itemContent :r_1049-1062 ] ;
    earmark:hasGeneralIdentifier "quote"^^xsd:string ;
    earmark:hasNamespace "http://docbook.org/ns/docbook"^^xsd:anyURI .

  :e_quote_3 a earmark:Element ;
    la:expresses doco:SimpleRunInQuotation ;
    co:firstItem [ co:itemContent :r_4819-4829 ] ;
    earmark:hasGeneralIdentifier "quote"^^xsd:string ;
    earmark:hasNamespace "http://docbook.org/ns/docbook"^^xsd:anyURI .

  :e_quote_4 a earmark:Element ;
    la:expresses doco:SimpleRunInQuotation ;
    co:firstItem [ co:itemContent :r_4905-4915 ] ;
    earmark:hasGeneralIdentifier "quote"^^xsd:string ;
    earmark:hasNamespace "http://docbook.org/ns/docbook"^^xsd:anyURI .

  :e_quote_5 a earmark:Element ;
    la:expresses doco:SimpleRunInQuotation ;
    co:firstItem [ co:itemContent :r_5040-5048 ] ;
    earmark:hasGeneralIdentifier "quote"^^xsd:string ;
    earmark:hasNamespace "http://docbook.org/ns/docbook"^^xsd:anyURI .

  :e_section_1 a earmark:Element ;
    la:expresses doco:Section , deo:Introduction ;
    co:firstItem [ co:itemContent :e_title_2 ;
    co:nextItem [ co:itemContent :e_para_2 ] ] ;
    earmark:hasGeneralIdentifier "section"^^xsd:string ;
    earmark:hasNamespace "http://docbook.org/ns/docbook"^^xsd:anyURI .

  :e_section_2 a earmark:Element ;
    la:expresses doco:Section , salt:Scenario ;
    co:firstItem [ co:itemContent :e_title_3 ;
    co:nextItem [ co:itemContent :e_para_3 ;
    co:nextItem [ co:itemContent :e_para_4 ] ] ] ;
    earmark:hasGeneralIdentifier "section"^^xsd:string ;
    earmark:hasNamespace "http://docbook.org/ns/docbook"^^xsd:anyURI .

  :e_section_3 a earmark:Element ;
    la:expresses doco:Section , deo:Model ;
    co:firstItem [ co:itemContent :e_title_4 ;
    co:nextItem [ co:itemContent :e_para_5 ;
    co:nextItem [ co:itemContent :e_para_6 ] ] ] ;
    earmark:hasGeneralIdentifier "section"^^xsd:string ;
    earmark:hasNamespace "http://docbook.org/ns/docbook"^^xsd:anyURI .

  :e_section_4 a earmark:Element ;
    la:expresses doco:Section , salt:Conclusion ;
    co:firstItem [ co:itemContent :e_title_5 ;
    co:nextItem [ co:itemContent :e_para_7 ] ] ;
    earmark:hasGeneralIdentifier "section"^^xsd:string ;
```

```
  earmark:hasNamespace "http://docbook.org/ns/docbook"^^xsd:anyURI .

:e_street_1 a earmark:Element ;
  co:firstItem [ co:itemContent :r_84-105 ] ;
  earmark:hasGeneralIdentifier "street"^^xsd:string ;
  earmark:hasNamespace "http://docbook.org/ns/docbook"^^xsd:anyURI .

:e_street_2 a earmark:Element ;
  co:firstItem [ co:itemContent :r_181-202 ] ;
  earmark:hasGeneralIdentifier "street"^^xsd:string ;
  earmark:hasNamespace "http://docbook.org/ns/docbook"^^xsd:anyURI .

:e_street_3 a earmark:Element ;
  co:firstItem [ co:itemContent :r_259-280 ] ;
  earmark:hasGeneralIdentifier "street"^^xsd:string ;
  earmark:hasNamespace "http://docbook.org/ns/docbook"^^xsd:anyURI .

:e_surname_1 a earmark:Element ;
  co:firstItem [ co:itemContent :r_65-73 ] ;
  earmark:hasGeneralIdentifier "surname"^^xsd:string ;
  earmark:hasNamespace "http://docbook.org/ns/docbook"^^xsd:anyURI .

:e_surname_10 a earmark:Element ;
  co:firstItem [ co:itemContent :r_6162-6171 ] ;
  earmark:hasGeneralIdentifier "surname"^^xsd:string ;
  earmark:hasNamespace "http://docbook.org/ns/docbook"^^xsd:anyURI .

:e_surname_11 a earmark:Element ;
  co:firstItem [ co:itemContent :r_6175-6183 ] ;
  earmark:hasGeneralIdentifier "surname"^^xsd:string ;
  earmark:hasNamespace "http://docbook.org/ns/docbook"^^xsd:anyURI .

:e_surname_2 a earmark:Element ;
  co:firstItem [ co:itemContent :r_134-145 ] ;
  earmark:hasGeneralIdentifier "surname"^^xsd:string ;
  earmark:hasNamespace "http://docbook.org/ns/docbook"^^xsd:anyURI .

:e_surname_3 a earmark:Element ;
  co:firstItem [ co:itemContent :r_5767-5775 ] ;
  earmark:hasGeneralIdentifier "surname"^^xsd:string ;
  earmark:hasNamespace "http://docbook.org/ns/docbook"^^xsd:anyURI .

:e_surname_4 a earmark:Element ;
  co:firstItem [ co:itemContent :r_5779-5790 ] ;
  earmark:hasGeneralIdentifier "surname"^^xsd:string ;
  earmark:hasNamespace "http://docbook.org/ns/docbook"^^xsd:anyURI .

:e_surname_5 a earmark:Element ;
  co:firstItem [ co:itemContent :r_5794-5801 ] ;
  earmark:hasGeneralIdentifier "surname"^^xsd:string ;
  earmark:hasNamespace "http://docbook.org/ns/docbook"^^xsd:anyURI .

:e_surname_6 a earmark:Element ;
  co:firstItem [ co:itemContent :r_5805-5811 ] ;
  earmark:hasGeneralIdentifier "surname"^^xsd:string ;
  earmark:hasNamespace "http://docbook.org/ns/docbook"^^xsd:anyURI .

:e_surname_7 a earmark:Element ;
  co:firstItem [ co:itemContent :r_5985-5993 ] ;
  earmark:hasGeneralIdentifier "surname"^^xsd:string ;
  earmark:hasNamespace "http://docbook.org/ns/docbook"^^xsd:anyURI .
```

```
:e_surname_8 a earmark:Element ;
  co:firstItem [ co:itemContent :r_5997-6003 ] ;
  earmark:hasGeneralIdentifier "surname"^^xsd:string ;
  earmark:hasNamespace "http://docbook.org/ns/docbook"^^xsd:anyURI .

:e_surname_9 a earmark:Element ;
  co:firstItem [ co:itemContent :r_6007-6015 ] ;
  earmark:hasGeneralIdentifier "surname"^^xsd:string ;
  earmark:hasNamespace "http://docbook.org/ns/docbook"^^xsd:anyURI .

:e_title_1 a earmark:Element ;
  la:expresses doco:Title ;
  co:firstItem [ co:itemContent :r_0-58 ] ;
  earmark:hasGeneralIdentifier "title"^^xsd:string ;
  earmark:hasNamespace "http://docbook.org/ns/docbook"^^xsd:anyURI .

:e_title_10 a earmark:Element ;
  co:firstItem [ co:itemContent :r_6063-6147 ] ;
  earmark:hasGeneralIdentifier "title"^^xsd:string ;
  earmark:hasNamespace "http://docbook.org/ns/docbook"^^xsd:anyURI .

:e_title_11 a earmark:Element ;
  co:firstItem [ co:itemContent :r_6184-6230 ] ;
  earmark:hasGeneralIdentifier "title"^^xsd:string ;
  earmark:hasNamespace "http://docbook.org/ns/docbook"^^xsd:anyURI .

:e_title_12 a earmark:Element ;
  co:firstItem [ co:itemContent :r_6231-6317 ] ;
  earmark:hasGeneralIdentifier "title"^^xsd:string ;
  earmark:hasNamespace "http://docbook.org/ns/docbook"^^xsd:anyURI .

:e_title_2 a earmark:Element ;
  la:expresses doco:SectionTitle ;
  co:firstItem [ co:itemContent :r_689-701 ] ;
  earmark:hasGeneralIdentifier "title"^^xsd:string ;
  earmark:hasNamespace "http://docbook.org/ns/docbook"^^xsd:anyURI .

:e_title_3 a earmark:Element ;
  la:expresses doco:SectionTitle ;
  co:firstItem [ co:itemContent :r_1648-1667 ] ;
  earmark:hasGeneralIdentifier "title"^^xsd:string ;
  earmark:hasNamespace "http://docbook.org/ns/docbook"^^xsd:anyURI .

:e_title_4 a earmark:Element ;
  la:expresses doco:SectionTitle ;
  co:firstItem [ co:itemContent :r_3501-3542 ] ;
  earmark:hasGeneralIdentifier "title"^^xsd:string ;
  earmark:hasNamespace "http://docbook.org/ns/docbook"^^xsd:anyURI .

:e_title_5 a earmark:Element ;
  la:expresses doco:SectionTitle ;
  co:firstItem [ co:itemContent :r_5294-5305 ] ;
  earmark:hasGeneralIdentifier "title"^^xsd:string ;
  earmark:hasNamespace "http://docbook.org/ns/docbook"^^xsd:anyURI .

:e_title_6 a earmark:Element ;
  co:firstItem [ co:itemContent :r_5753-5763 ] ;
  earmark:hasGeneralIdentifier "title"^^xsd:string ;
  earmark:hasNamespace "http://docbook.org/ns/docbook"^^xsd:anyURI .

:e_title_7 a earmark:Element ;
  co:firstItem [ co:itemContent :r_5812-5883 ] ;
```

```
  earmark:hasGeneralIdentifier "title"^^xsd:string ;
  earmark:hasNamespace "http://docbook.org/ns/docbook"^^xsd:anyURI .

:e_title_8 a earmark:Element ;
  co:firstItem [ co:itemContent :r_5884-5968 ] ;
  earmark:hasGeneralIdentifier "title"^^xsd:string ;
  earmark:hasNamespace "http://docbook.org/ns/docbook"^^xsd:anyURI .

:e_title_9 a earmark:Element ;
  co:firstItem [ co:itemContent :r_6016-6062 ] ;
  earmark:hasGeneralIdentifier "title"^^xsd:string ;
  earmark:hasNamespace "http://docbook.org/ns/docbook"^^xsd:anyURI .

:e_xref_1 a earmark:Element ;
  la:expresses [
    a owl:Class ;
    owl:intersectionOf (
      c4o:InTextReferencePointer
      [
        a owl:Restriction ;
        owl:onProperty c4o:denotes ;
        owl:hasValue :r5764-5981 ] ) ] ;
  co:firstItem [ co:itemContent :a_linkend_1 ] ;
  earmark:hasGeneralIdentifier "xref"^^xsd:string ;
  earmark:hasNamespace "http://docbook.org/ns/docbook"^^xsd:anyURI .

:r5764-5981 a earmark:PointerRange ;
  earmark:begins "5764"^^xsd:nonNegativeInteger ;
  earmark:ends "5981"^^xsd:nonNegativeInteger ;
  earmark:refersTo :d_text .

:e_xref_2 a earmark:Element ;
  la:expresses [
    a owl:Class ;
    owl:intersectionOf (
      c4o:InTextReferencePointer
      [
        a owl:Restriction ;
        owl:onProperty c4o:denotes ;
        owl:hasValue :r5982-6158 ] ) ] ;
  co:firstItem [ co:itemContent :a_linkend_2 ] ;
  earmark:hasGeneralIdentifier "xref"^^xsd:string ;
  earmark:hasNamespace "http://docbook.org/ns/docbook"^^xsd:anyURI .

:r5982-6158 a earmark:PointerRange ;
  earmark:begins "5982"^^xsd:nonNegativeInteger ;
  earmark:ends "6158"^^xsd:nonNegativeInteger ;
  earmark:refersTo :d_text .

:e_xref_3 a earmark:Element ;
  la:expresses [
    a owl:Class ;
    owl:intersectionOf (
      c4o:InTextReferencePointer
      [
        a owl:Restriction ;
        owl:onProperty c4o:denotes ;
        owl:hasValue :r6159-6328 ] ) ] ;
  co:firstItem [ co:itemContent :a_linkend_3 ] ;
  earmark:hasGeneralIdentifier "xref"^^xsd:string ;
  earmark:hasNamespace "http://docbook.org/ns/docbook"^^xsd:anyURI .
```

```
:r6159-6328 a earmark:PointerRange ;
  earmark:begins "6159"^^xsd:nonNegativeInteger ;
  earmark:ends "6328"^^xsd:nonNegativeInteger ;
  earmark:refersTo :d_text .

:r_0-58 a earmark:PointerRange ;
  earmark:begins "0"^^xsd:nonNegativeInteger ;
  earmark:ends "58"^^xsd:nonNegativeInteger ;
  earmark:refersTo :d_text .

:r_1049-1062 a earmark:PointerRange ;
  earmark:begins "1049"^^xsd:nonNegativeInteger ;
  earmark:ends "1062"^^xsd:nonNegativeInteger ;
  earmark:refersTo :d_text .

:r_106-111 a earmark:PointerRange ;
  earmark:begins "106"^^xsd:nonNegativeInteger ;
  earmark:ends "111"^^xsd:nonNegativeInteger ;
  earmark:refersTo :d_text .

:r_1063-1155 a earmark:PointerRange ;
  earmark:begins "1063"^^xsd:nonNegativeInteger ;
  earmark:ends "1155"^^xsd:nonNegativeInteger ;
  earmark:refersTo :d_text .

:r_112-120 a earmark:PointerRange ;
  earmark:begins "112"^^xsd:nonNegativeInteger ;
  earmark:ends "120"^^xsd:nonNegativeInteger ;
  earmark:refersTo :d_text .

:r_1156-1251 a earmark:PointerRange ;
  earmark:begins "1156"^^xsd:nonNegativeInteger ;
  earmark:ends "1251"^^xsd:nonNegativeInteger ;
  earmark:refersTo :d_text .

:r_121-126 a earmark:PointerRange ;
  earmark:begins "121"^^xsd:nonNegativeInteger ;
  earmark:ends "126"^^xsd:nonNegativeInteger ;
  earmark:refersTo :d_text .

:r_1252-1262 a earmark:PointerRange ;
  earmark:begins "1252"^^xsd:nonNegativeInteger ;
  earmark:ends "1262"^^xsd:nonNegativeInteger ;
  earmark:refersTo :d_text .

:r_1263-1267 a earmark:PointerRange ;
  earmark:begins "1263"^^xsd:nonNegativeInteger ;
  earmark:ends "1267"^^xsd:nonNegativeInteger ;
  earmark:refersTo :d_text .

:r_1268-1278 a earmark:PointerRange ;
  earmark:begins "1268"^^xsd:nonNegativeInteger ;
  earmark:ends "1278"^^xsd:nonNegativeInteger ;
  earmark:refersTo :d_text .

:r_127-133 a earmark:PointerRange ;
  earmark:begins "127"^^xsd:nonNegativeInteger ;
  earmark:ends "133"^^xsd:nonNegativeInteger ;
  earmark:refersTo :d_text .

:r_1279-1280 a earmark:PointerRange ;
  earmark:begins "1279"^^xsd:nonNegativeInteger ;
```

```
  earmark:ends "1280"^^xsd:nonNegativeInteger ;
  earmark:refersTo :d_text .

:r_1281-1291 a earmark:PointerRange ;
  earmark:begins "1281"^^xsd:nonNegativeInteger ;
  earmark:ends "1291"^^xsd:nonNegativeInteger ;
  earmark:refersTo :d_text .

:r_1292-1293 a earmark:PointerRange ;
  earmark:begins "1292"^^xsd:nonNegativeInteger ;
  earmark:ends "1293"^^xsd:nonNegativeInteger ;
  earmark:refersTo :d_text .

:r_1294-1302 a earmark:PointerRange ;
  earmark:begins "1294"^^xsd:nonNegativeInteger ;
  earmark:ends "1302"^^xsd:nonNegativeInteger ;
  earmark:refersTo :d_text .

:r_1303-1304 a earmark:PointerRange ;
  earmark:begins "1303"^^xsd:nonNegativeInteger ;
  earmark:ends "1304"^^xsd:nonNegativeInteger ;
  earmark:refersTo :d_text .

:r_1305-1315 a earmark:PointerRange ;
  earmark:begins "1305"^^xsd:nonNegativeInteger ;
  earmark:ends "1315"^^xsd:nonNegativeInteger ;
  earmark:refersTo :d_text .

:r_1316-1333 a earmark:PointerRange ;
  earmark:begins "1316"^^xsd:nonNegativeInteger ;
  earmark:ends "1333"^^xsd:nonNegativeInteger ;
  earmark:refersTo :d_text .

:r_1334-1343 a earmark:PointerRange ;
  earmark:begins "1334"^^xsd:nonNegativeInteger ;
  earmark:ends "1343"^^xsd:nonNegativeInteger ;
  earmark:refersTo :d_text .

:r_134-145 a earmark:PointerRange ;
  earmark:begins "134"^^xsd:nonNegativeInteger ;
  earmark:ends "145"^^xsd:nonNegativeInteger ;
  earmark:refersTo :d_text .

:r_1344-1352 a earmark:PointerRange ;
  earmark:begins "1344"^^xsd:nonNegativeInteger ;
  earmark:ends "1352"^^xsd:nonNegativeInteger ;
  earmark:refersTo :d_text .

:r_1353-1362 a earmark:PointerRange ;
  earmark:begins "1353"^^xsd:nonNegativeInteger ;
  earmark:ends "1362"^^xsd:nonNegativeInteger ;
  earmark:refersTo :d_text .

:r_1363-1647 a earmark:PointerRange ;
  earmark:begins "1363"^^xsd:nonNegativeInteger ;
  earmark:ends "1647"^^xsd:nonNegativeInteger ;
  earmark:refersTo :d_text .

:r_146-170 a earmark:PointerRange ;
  earmark:begins "146"^^xsd:nonNegativeInteger ;
  earmark:ends "170"^^xsd:nonNegativeInteger ;
  earmark:refersTo :d_text .
```

```
:r_1648-1667 a earmark:PointerRange ;
  earmark:begins "1648"^^xsd:nonNegativeInteger ;
  earmark:ends "1667"^^xsd:nonNegativeInteger ;
  earmark:refersTo :d_text .

:r_1668-2284 a earmark:PointerRange ;
  earmark:begins "1668"^^xsd:nonNegativeInteger ;
  earmark:ends "2284"^^xsd:nonNegativeInteger ;
  earmark:refersTo :d_text .

:r_171-180 a earmark:PointerRange ;
  earmark:begins "171"^^xsd:nonNegativeInteger ;
  earmark:ends "180"^^xsd:nonNegativeInteger ;
  earmark:refersTo :d_text .

:r_181-202 a earmark:PointerRange ;
  earmark:begins "181"^^xsd:nonNegativeInteger ;
  earmark:ends "202"^^xsd:nonNegativeInteger ;
  earmark:refersTo :d_text .

:r_203-208 a earmark:PointerRange ;
  earmark:begins "203"^^xsd:nonNegativeInteger ;
  earmark:ends "208"^^xsd:nonNegativeInteger ;
  earmark:refersTo :d_text .

:r_209-217 a earmark:PointerRange ;
  earmark:begins "209"^^xsd:nonNegativeInteger ;
  earmark:ends "217"^^xsd:nonNegativeInteger ;
  earmark:refersTo :d_text .

:r_218-223 a earmark:PointerRange ;
  earmark:begins "218"^^xsd:nonNegativeInteger ;
  earmark:ends "223"^^xsd:nonNegativeInteger ;
  earmark:refersTo :d_text .

:r_224-235 a earmark:PointerRange ;
  earmark:begins "224"^^xsd:nonNegativeInteger ;
  earmark:ends "235"^^xsd:nonNegativeInteger ;
  earmark:refersTo :d_text .

:r_2285-2376 a earmark:PointerRange ;
  earmark:begins "2285"^^xsd:nonNegativeInteger ;
  earmark:ends "2376"^^xsd:nonNegativeInteger ;
  earmark:refersTo :d_text .

:r_236-248 a earmark:PointerRange ;
  earmark:begins "236"^^xsd:nonNegativeInteger ;
  earmark:ends "248"^^xsd:nonNegativeInteger ;
  earmark:refersTo :d_text .

:r_2377-2802 a earmark:PointerRange ;
  earmark:begins "2377"^^xsd:nonNegativeInteger ;
  earmark:ends "2802"^^xsd:nonNegativeInteger ;
  earmark:refersTo :d_text .

:r_249-252 a earmark:PointerRange ;
  earmark:begins "249"^^xsd:nonNegativeInteger ;
  earmark:ends "252"^^xsd:nonNegativeInteger ;
  earmark:refersTo :d_text .

:r_253-258 a earmark:PointerRange ;
```

```
  earmark:begins "253"^^xsd:nonNegativeInteger ;
  earmark:ends "258"^^xsd:nonNegativeInteger ;
  earmark:refersTo :d_text .

:r_259-280 a earmark:PointerRange ;
  earmark:begins "259"^^xsd:nonNegativeInteger ;
  earmark:ends "280"^^xsd:nonNegativeInteger ;
  earmark:refersTo :d_text .

:r_2803-2813 a earmark:PointerRange ;
  earmark:begins "2803"^^xsd:nonNegativeInteger ;
  earmark:ends "2813"^^xsd:nonNegativeInteger ;
  earmark:refersTo :d_text .

:r_281-286 a earmark:PointerRange ;
  earmark:begins "281"^^xsd:nonNegativeInteger ;
  earmark:ends "286"^^xsd:nonNegativeInteger ;
  earmark:refersTo :d_text .

:r_2814-2817 a earmark:PointerRange ;
  earmark:begins "2814"^^xsd:nonNegativeInteger ;
  earmark:ends "2817"^^xsd:nonNegativeInteger ;
  earmark:refersTo :d_text .

:r_2818-2827 a earmark:PointerRange ;
  earmark:begins "2818"^^xsd:nonNegativeInteger ;
  earmark:ends "2827"^^xsd:nonNegativeInteger ;
  earmark:refersTo :d_text .

:r_2828-3500 a earmark:PointerRange ;
  earmark:begins "2828"^^xsd:nonNegativeInteger ;
  earmark:ends "3500"^^xsd:nonNegativeInteger ;
  earmark:refersTo :d_text .

:r_287-295 a earmark:PointerRange ;
  earmark:begins "287"^^xsd:nonNegativeInteger ;
  earmark:ends "295"^^xsd:nonNegativeInteger ;
  earmark:refersTo :d_text .

:r_296-301 a earmark:PointerRange ;
  earmark:begins "296"^^xsd:nonNegativeInteger ;
  earmark:ends "301"^^xsd:nonNegativeInteger ;
  earmark:refersTo :d_text .

:r_302-635 a earmark:PointerRange ;
  earmark:begins "302"^^xsd:nonNegativeInteger ;
  earmark:ends "635"^^xsd:nonNegativeInteger ;
  earmark:refersTo :d_text .

:r_3501-3542 a earmark:PointerRange ;
  earmark:begins "3501"^^xsd:nonNegativeInteger ;
  earmark:ends "3542"^^xsd:nonNegativeInteger ;
  earmark:refersTo :d_text .

:r_3543-3778 a earmark:PointerRange ;
  earmark:begins "3543"^^xsd:nonNegativeInteger ;
  earmark:ends "3778"^^xsd:nonNegativeInteger ;
  earmark:refersTo :d_text .

:r_3779-4451 a earmark:PointerRange ;
  earmark:begins "3779"^^xsd:nonNegativeInteger ;
  earmark:ends "4451"^^xsd:nonNegativeInteger ;
```

```
  earmark:refersTo :d_text .

:r_4452-4463 a earmark:PointerRange ;
  earmark:begins "4452"^^xsd:nonNegativeInteger ;
  earmark:ends "4463"^^xsd:nonNegativeInteger ;
  earmark:refersTo :d_text .

:r_4464-4818 a earmark:PointerRange ;
  earmark:begins "4464"^^xsd:nonNegativeInteger ;
  earmark:ends "4818"^^xsd:nonNegativeInteger ;
  earmark:refersTo :d_text .

:r_4819-4829 a earmark:PointerRange ;
  earmark:begins "4819"^^xsd:nonNegativeInteger ;
  earmark:ends "4829"^^xsd:nonNegativeInteger ;
  earmark:refersTo :d_text .

:r_4830-4904 a earmark:PointerRange ;
  earmark:begins "4830"^^xsd:nonNegativeInteger ;
  earmark:ends "4904"^^xsd:nonNegativeInteger ;
  earmark:refersTo :d_text .

:r_4905-4915 a earmark:PointerRange ;
  earmark:begins "4905"^^xsd:nonNegativeInteger ;
  earmark:ends "4915"^^xsd:nonNegativeInteger ;
  earmark:refersTo :d_text .

:r_4916-5039 a earmark:PointerRange ;
  earmark:begins "4916"^^xsd:nonNegativeInteger ;
  earmark:ends "5039"^^xsd:nonNegativeInteger ;
  earmark:refersTo :d_text .

:r_5040-5048 a earmark:PointerRange ;
  earmark:begins "5040"^^xsd:nonNegativeInteger ;
  earmark:ends "5048"^^xsd:nonNegativeInteger ;
  earmark:refersTo :d_text .

:r_5049-5293 a earmark:PointerRange ;
  earmark:begins "5049"^^xsd:nonNegativeInteger ;
  earmark:ends "5293"^^xsd:nonNegativeInteger ;
  earmark:refersTo :d_text .

:r_5294-5305 a earmark:PointerRange ;
  earmark:begins "5294"^^xsd:nonNegativeInteger ;
  earmark:ends "5305"^^xsd:nonNegativeInteger ;
  earmark:refersTo :d_text .

:r_5306-5752 a earmark:PointerRange ;
  earmark:begins "5306"^^xsd:nonNegativeInteger ;
  earmark:ends "5752"^^xsd:nonNegativeInteger ;
  earmark:refersTo :d_text .

:r_5753-5763 a earmark:PointerRange ;
  earmark:begins "5753"^^xsd:nonNegativeInteger ;
  earmark:ends "5763"^^xsd:nonNegativeInteger ;
  earmark:refersTo :d_text .

:r_5764-5766 a earmark:PointerRange ;
  earmark:begins "5764"^^xsd:nonNegativeInteger ;
  earmark:ends "5766"^^xsd:nonNegativeInteger ;
  earmark:refersTo :d_text .
```

```
:r_5767-5775 a earmark:PointerRange ;
  earmark:begins "5767"^^xsd:nonNegativeInteger ;
  earmark:ends "5775"^^xsd:nonNegativeInteger ;
  earmark:refersTo :d_text .

:r_5776-5778 a earmark:PointerRange ;
  earmark:begins "5776"^^xsd:nonNegativeInteger ;
  earmark:ends "5778"^^xsd:nonNegativeInteger ;
  earmark:refersTo :d_text .

:r_5779-5790 a earmark:PointerRange ;
  earmark:begins "5779"^^xsd:nonNegativeInteger ;
  earmark:ends "5790"^^xsd:nonNegativeInteger ;
  earmark:refersTo :d_text .

:r_5791-5793 a earmark:PointerRange ;
  earmark:begins "5791"^^xsd:nonNegativeInteger ;
  earmark:ends "5793"^^xsd:nonNegativeInteger ;
  earmark:refersTo :d_text .

:r_5794-5801 a earmark:PointerRange ;
  earmark:begins "5794"^^xsd:nonNegativeInteger ;
  earmark:ends "5801"^^xsd:nonNegativeInteger ;
  earmark:refersTo :d_text .

:r_5802-5804 a earmark:PointerRange ;
  earmark:begins "5802"^^xsd:nonNegativeInteger ;
  earmark:ends "5804"^^xsd:nonNegativeInteger ;
  earmark:refersTo :d_text .

:r_5805-5811 a earmark:PointerRange ;
  earmark:begins "5805"^^xsd:nonNegativeInteger ;
  earmark:ends "5811"^^xsd:nonNegativeInteger ;
  earmark:refersTo :d_text .

:r_5812-5883 a earmark:PointerRange ;
  earmark:begins "5812"^^xsd:nonNegativeInteger ;
  earmark:ends "5883"^^xsd:nonNegativeInteger ;
  earmark:refersTo :d_text .

:r_5884-5968 a earmark:PointerRange ;
  earmark:begins "5884"^^xsd:nonNegativeInteger ;
  earmark:ends "5968"^^xsd:nonNegativeInteger ;
  earmark:refersTo :d_text .

:r_59-64 a earmark:PointerRange ;
  earmark:begins "59"^^xsd:nonNegativeInteger ;
  earmark:ends "64"^^xsd:nonNegativeInteger ;
  earmark:refersTo :d_text .

:r_5969-5976 a earmark:PointerRange ;
  earmark:begins "5969"^^xsd:nonNegativeInteger ;
  earmark:ends "5976"^^xsd:nonNegativeInteger ;
  earmark:refersTo :d_text .

:r_5977-5981 a earmark:PointerRange ;
  earmark:begins "5977"^^xsd:nonNegativeInteger ;
  earmark:ends "5981"^^xsd:nonNegativeInteger ;
  earmark:refersTo :d_text .

:r_5982-5984 a earmark:PointerRange ;
  earmark:begins "5982"^^xsd:nonNegativeInteger ;
```

```
  earmark:ends "5984"^^xsd:nonNegativeInteger ;
  earmark:refersTo :d_text .

:r_5985-5993 a earmark:PointerRange ;
  earmark:begins "5985"^^xsd:nonNegativeInteger ;
  earmark:ends "5993"^^xsd:nonNegativeInteger ;
  earmark:refersTo :d_text .

:r_5994-5996 a earmark:PointerRange ;
  earmark:begins "5994"^^xsd:nonNegativeInteger ;
  earmark:ends "5996"^^xsd:nonNegativeInteger ;
  earmark:refersTo :d_text .

:r_5997-6003 a earmark:PointerRange ;
  earmark:begins "5997"^^xsd:nonNegativeInteger ;
  earmark:ends "6003"^^xsd:nonNegativeInteger ;
  earmark:refersTo :d_text .

:r_6004-6006 a earmark:PointerRange ;
  earmark:begins "6004"^^xsd:nonNegativeInteger ;
  earmark:ends "6006"^^xsd:nonNegativeInteger ;
  earmark:refersTo :d_text .

:r_6007-6015 a earmark:PointerRange ;
  earmark:begins "6007"^^xsd:nonNegativeInteger ;
  earmark:ends "6015"^^xsd:nonNegativeInteger ;
  earmark:refersTo :d_text .

:r_6016-6062 a earmark:PointerRange ;
  earmark:begins "6016"^^xsd:nonNegativeInteger ;
  earmark:ends "6062"^^xsd:nonNegativeInteger ;
  earmark:refersTo :d_text .

:r_6063-6147 a earmark:PointerRange ;
  earmark:begins "6063"^^xsd:nonNegativeInteger ;
  earmark:ends "6147"^^xsd:nonNegativeInteger ;
  earmark:refersTo :d_text .

:r_6148-6153 a earmark:PointerRange ;
  earmark:begins "6148"^^xsd:nonNegativeInteger ;
  earmark:ends "6153"^^xsd:nonNegativeInteger ;
  earmark:refersTo :d_text .

:r_6154-6158 a earmark:PointerRange ;
  earmark:begins "6154"^^xsd:nonNegativeInteger ;
  earmark:ends "6158"^^xsd:nonNegativeInteger ;
  earmark:refersTo :d_text .

:r_6159-6161 a earmark:PointerRange ;
  earmark:begins "6159"^^xsd:nonNegativeInteger ;
  earmark:ends "6161"^^xsd:nonNegativeInteger ;
  earmark:refersTo :d_text .

:r_6162-6171 a earmark:PointerRange ;
  earmark:begins "6162"^^xsd:nonNegativeInteger ;
  earmark:ends "6171"^^xsd:nonNegativeInteger ;
  earmark:refersTo :d_text .

:r_6172-6174 a earmark:PointerRange ;
  earmark:begins "6172"^^xsd:nonNegativeInteger ;
  earmark:ends "6174"^^xsd:nonNegativeInteger ;
  earmark:refersTo :d_text .
```

```
:r_6175-6183 a earmark:PointerRange ;
  earmark:begins "6175"^^xsd:nonNegativeInteger ;
  earmark:ends "6183"^^xsd:nonNegativeInteger ;
  earmark:refersTo :d_text .

:r_6184-6230 a earmark:PointerRange ;
  earmark:begins "6184"^^xsd:nonNegativeInteger ;
  earmark:ends "6230"^^xsd:nonNegativeInteger ;
  earmark:refersTo :d_text .

:r_6231-6317 a earmark:PointerRange ;
  earmark:begins "6231"^^xsd:nonNegativeInteger ;
  earmark:ends "6317"^^xsd:nonNegativeInteger ;
  earmark:refersTo :d_text .

:r_6318-6323 a earmark:PointerRange ;
  earmark:begins "6318"^^xsd:nonNegativeInteger ;
  earmark:ends "6323"^^xsd:nonNegativeInteger ;
  earmark:refersTo :d_text .

:r_6324-6328 a earmark:PointerRange ;
  earmark:begins "6324"^^xsd:nonNegativeInteger ;
  earmark:ends "6328"^^xsd:nonNegativeInteger ;
  earmark:refersTo :d_text .

:r_636-651 a earmark:PointerRange ;
  earmark:begins "636"^^xsd:nonNegativeInteger ;
  earmark:ends "651"^^xsd:nonNegativeInteger ;
  earmark:refersTo :d_text .

:r_65-73 a earmark:PointerRange ;
  earmark:begins "65"^^xsd:nonNegativeInteger ;
  earmark:ends "73"^^xsd:nonNegativeInteger ;
  earmark:refersTo :d_text .

:r_652-655 a earmark:PointerRange ;
  earmark:begins "652"^^xsd:nonNegativeInteger ;
  earmark:ends "655"^^xsd:nonNegativeInteger ;
  earmark:refersTo :d_text .

:r_656-664 a earmark:PointerRange ;
  earmark:begins "656"^^xsd:nonNegativeInteger ;
  earmark:ends "664"^^xsd:nonNegativeInteger ;
  earmark:refersTo :d_text .

:r_665-688 a earmark:PointerRange ;
  earmark:begins "665"^^xsd:nonNegativeInteger ;
  earmark:ends "688"^^xsd:nonNegativeInteger ;
  earmark:refersTo :d_text .

:r_689-701 a earmark:PointerRange ;
  earmark:begins "689"^^xsd:nonNegativeInteger ;
  earmark:ends "701"^^xsd:nonNegativeInteger ;
  earmark:refersTo :d_text .

:r_702-818 a earmark:PointerRange ;
  earmark:begins "702"^^xsd:nonNegativeInteger ;
  earmark:ends "818"^^xsd:nonNegativeInteger ;
  earmark:refersTo :d_text .

:r_74-77 a earmark:PointerRange ;
```

```
    earmark:begins "74"^^xsd:nonNegativeInteger ;
    earmark:ends "77"^^xsd:nonNegativeInteger ;
    earmark:refersTo :d_text .

  :r_78-83 a earmark:PointerRange ;
    earmark:begins "78"^^xsd:nonNegativeInteger ;
    earmark:ends "83"^^xsd:nonNegativeInteger ;
    earmark:refersTo :d_text .

  :r_819-841 a earmark:PointerRange ;
    earmark:begins "819"^^xsd:nonNegativeInteger ;
    earmark:ends "841"^^xsd:nonNegativeInteger ;
    earmark:refersTo :d_text .

  :r_84-105 a earmark:PointerRange ;
    earmark:begins "84"^^xsd:nonNegativeInteger ;
    earmark:ends "105"^^xsd:nonNegativeInteger ;
    earmark:refersTo :d_text .

  :r_842-904 a earmark:PointerRange ;
    earmark:begins "842"^^xsd:nonNegativeInteger ;
    earmark:ends "904"^^xsd:nonNegativeInteger ;
    earmark:refersTo :d_text .

  :r_905-1048 a earmark:PointerRange ;
    earmark:begins "905"^^xsd:nonNegativeInteger ;
    earmark:ends "1048"^^xsd:nonNegativeInteger ;
    earmark:refersTo :d_text .

  :ref1 a earmark:Element ;
    la:expresses [
      a owl:Class ;
      owl:intersectionOf (
        biro:BibliographicReference
        [
          a owl:Restriction ;
          owl:onProperty biro:references ;
          owl:hasValue :cited-document-1 ] ) ] ;
    co:firstItem [ co:itemContent :a_id_1 ;
    co:nextItem [ co:itemContent :a_xreflabel_1 ;
    co:nextItem [ co:itemContent :e_bibliomset_1 ;
    co:nextItem [ co:itemContent :e_bibliomset_2 ] ] ] ] ;
    earmark:hasGeneralIdentifier "biblioentry"^^xsd:string ;
    earmark:hasNamespace "http://docbook.org/ns/docbook"^^xsd:anyURI .

  :ref2 a earmark:Element ;
    la:expresses [
      a owl:Class ;
      owl:intersectionOf (
        biro:BibliographicReference
        [
          a owl:Restriction ;
          owl:onProperty biro:references ;
          owl:hasValue :cited-document-2 ] ) ] ;
    co:firstItem [ co:itemContent :a_id_2 ;
    co:nextItem [ co:itemContent :a_xreflabel_2 ;
    co:nextItem [ co:itemContent :e_bibliomset_3 ;
    co:nextItem [ co:itemContent :e_bibliomset_4 ] ] ] ] ;
    earmark:hasGeneralIdentifier "biblioentry"^^xsd:string ;
    earmark:hasNamespace "http://docbook.org/ns/docbook"^^xsd:anyURI .

  :ref3 a earmark:Element ;
```

```
  la:expresses [
    a owl:Class ;
    owl:intersectionOf (
      biro:BibliographicReference
      [
        a owl:Restriction ;
        owl:onProperty biro:references ;
        owl:hasValue :cited-document-1 ] ) ] ;
  co:firstItem [ co:itemContent :a_id_3 ;
  co:nextItem [ co:itemContent :a_xreflabel_3 ;
  co:nextItem [ co:itemContent :e_bibliomset_5 ;
  co:nextItem [ co:itemContent :e_bibliomset_6 ] ] ] ] ;
  earmark:hasGeneralIdentifier "biblioentry"^^xsd:string ;
  earmark:hasNamespace "http://docbook.org/ns/docbook"^^xsd:anyURI .

:paper-work a a fabio:ResearchPaper ;
  frbr:creator :biagioli , :francesconi ;
  frbr:realization :paper-expression .

:paper-expression a fabio:ConferencePaper;
  dcterms:title
    "A Semantics-based Visual Framework for Planning a New Bill" ;
  cito:obtainsBackgroundFrom :cited-document-1 , :cited-document-2 ;
  cito:citesForInformation :cited-document-3 ;
  frbr:embodiment :paper-manifestation .

:paper-manifestation a fabio:DigitalManifestation ;
  dcterms:format <http://mediatypes.appspot.com/text/turtle> ;
  frbr:exemplar <http://www.essepuntato.it/2013/11/earmark-example> .

<http://www.essepuntato.it/2013/11/earmark-example> a fabio:ComputerFile ;
  fabio:isStoredOn fabio:web .

:biagioli a foaf:Person ;
  foaf:givenName "Carlo" ;
  foaf:familyName "Biagioli" ;
  pro:holdsRoleInTime [
    a pro:RoleInTime ;
    pro:withRole pro:author ;
    pro:relatesToDocument :paper-work , :cited-document-1-work ] .

:francesconi a foaf:Person ;
  foaf:givenName "Enrico" ;
  foaf:familyName "Francesconi" ;
  pro:holdsRoleInTime [
    a pro:RoleInTime ;
    pro:withRole pro:author ;
    pro:relatesToDocument :paper-work , :cited-document-1-work ] .

:cited-document-1-work a fabio:ResearchPaper ;
    frbr:creator :biagioli , :francesconi , :spinosa , :taddei ;
    frbr:realization :cited-document-1-expression .

:cited-document-1-expression a fabio:ConferencePaper ;
  dcterms:title "A legal drafting environment based on formal and semantic
      XML standards" ;
  frbr:partOf [
    a fabio:ConferenceProceedings ;
    dcterms:title "Proceedings of the Tenth International Conference on
        Artificial Intelligence and Law" ] ;
  frbr:embodiment :cited-document-1-manifestation ;
  pso:holdsStatusInTime :published-cited-document-1 ;
```

```
  frbr:revisionOf :cited-document-1-preprint .

:cited-document-1-preprint a fabio:Preprint ;
  pso:holdsStatusInTime :accepted-cited-document-1 .

:cited-document-1-manifestation a fabio:Manifestation ;
  prism:publicationDate "2005"^^xsd:gYear ;
  prims:startingPage "244" ;
  prims:endingPage "245" .

:spinosa a foaf:Person ;
  foaf:givenName "P." ;
  foaf:familyName "Spinosa" ;
  pro:holdsRoleInTime [
    a pro:RoleInTime ;
    pro:withRole pro:author ;
    pro:relatesToDocument :cited-document-1-work ] .

:taddei a foaf:Person ;
  foaf:givenName "M." ;
  foaf:familyName "Taddei" ;
  pro:holdsRoleInTime [
    a pro:RoleInTime ;
    pro:withRole pro:author ;
    pro:relatesToDocument :cited-document-1-work ] .

:accepted-cited-document-1 a pso:StatusInTime ;
  pso:withStatus pro:accepted-for-publication ;
  pso:isAquiredAsConsequenceOf :decision-process-of-cited-document-1 .

:published-cited-document-1 a pso:StatusInTime ;
  pso:withStatus pro:published ;
  pso:isAquiredAsConsequenceOf :publishing-process-of-cited-document-1 ;
  tvc:atTime [
    a ti:TimeInterval ;
    ti:hasStartingTime "2005-01-01T00:00:00"^^xsd:dateTime ] .

:decision-process-of-cited-document-1 a part:Event ;
  dcterms:description "The decision process of the chairs for the paper
      entitled 'A legal drafting environment based on formal and semantic
      XML standards'." .

:publishing-process-of-cited-document-1 a part:Event ;
  dcterms:description "The publisher produces the version of record of the
      paper entitled 'A legal drafting environment based on formal and
      semantic XML standards'." .

:workflow-cited-document-1 a pwo:Workflow ;
  pwo:hasStep [
    a pwo:Step ;
    pwo:involvesEvent :decision-process-of-cited-document-1 ;
    pwo:needs :cited-document-1-preprint ;
    pwo:produces :accepted-cited-document-1 ;
    pwo:hasNextStep [
      a pwo:Step ;
      pwo:involvesEvent :publishing-process-of-cited-document-1 ;
      pwo:needs
        :accepted-cited-document-1 ,
        :cited-document-1-expression ;
      pwo:produces :published-cited-document-1 ] ] .

:cited-document-2-work a fabio:ResearchPaper ;
```

```
  frbr:creator :branting , :lester , :callaway ;
  frbr:realization :cited-document-2-expression .

:cited-document-2-expression a fabio:ConferencePaper ;
  dcterms:title "Automated Drafting of Self-Explainig Documents" ;
  frbr:partOf [
    a fabio:ConferenceProceedings ;
    dcterms:title "Proceedings of the Sixth International Conference on
        Artificial Intelligence and Law" ] ;
  frbr:embodiment :cited-document-2-manifestation ;
  pso:holdsStatusInTime :published-cited-document-2 ;
  frbr:revisionOf :cited-document-2-preprint .

:cited-document-2-preprint a fabio:Preprint ;
  pso:holdsStatusInTime :accepted-cited-document-2 .

:cited-document-2-manifestation a fabio:Manifestation ;
  prism:publicationDate "2005"^^xsd:gYear ;
  prims:startingPage "72" ;
  prims:endingPage "81" .

:branting a foaf:Person ;
  foaf:givenName "L." ;
  foaf:familyName "Branting" ;
  pro:holdsRoleInTime [
    a pro:RoleInTime ;
    pro:withRole pro:author ;
    pro:relatesToDocument :cited-document-2-work ] .

:lester a foaf:Person ;
  foaf:givenName "J." ;
  foaf:familyName "Lester" ;
  pro:holdsRoleInTime [
    a pro:RoleInTime ;
    pro:withRole pro:author ;
    pro:relatesToDocument :cited-document-2-work ] .

:callaway a foaf:Person ;
  foaf:givenName "C." ;
  foaf:familyName "Callaway" ;
  pro:holdsRoleInTime [
    a pro:RoleInTime ;
    pro:withRole pro:author ;
    pro:relatesToDocument :cited-document-2-work ] .

:accepted-cited-document-2 a pso:StatusInTime ;
  pso:withStatus pro:accepted-for-publication ;
  pso:isAquiredAsConsequenceOf :decision-process-of-cited-document-2 .

:published-cited-document-2 a pso:StatusInTime ;
  pso:withStatus pro:published ;
  pso:isAquiredAsConsequenceOf :publishing-process-of-cited-document-2 ;
  tvc:atTime [
    a ti:TimeInterval ;
    ti:hasStartingTime "1997-01-01T00:00:00"^^xsd:dateTime ] .

:decision-process-of-cited-document-2 a part:Event ;
  dcterms:description "The decision process of the chairs for the paper
      entitled 'Automated Drafting of Self-Explainig Documents'." .

:publishing-process-of-cited-document-2 a part:Event ;
```

```
  dcterms:description "The publisher produces the version of record of the
      paper entitled 'Automated Drafting of Self-Explainig Documents'." .

:workflow-cited-document-2 a pwo:Workflow ;
  pwo:hasStep [
    a pwo:Step ;
    pwo:involvesEvent :decision-process-of-cited-document-2 ;
    pwo:needs :cited-document-2-preprint ;
    pwo:produces :accepted-cited-document-2 ;
    pwo:hasNextStep [
      a pwo:Step ;
      pwo:involvesEvent :publishing-process-of-cited-document-2 ;
      pwo:needs
        :accepted-cited-document-2 ,
        :cited-document-2-expression ;
      pwo:produces :published-cited-document-2 ] ] .

:cited-document-3-work a fabio:ResearchPaper ;
  frbr:creator :lachmayer , :hoffmann ;
  frbr:realization :cited-document-3-expression .

:cited-document-3-expression a fabio:WorkshopPaper ;
  dcterms:title "From legal categories towards legal ontologies" ;
  frbr:partOf [
    a fabio:WorkshopProceedings ;
    dcterms:title "Proceedings of the Workshop on Legal Ontologies and
        Artificial Intelligence Techniques" ] ;
  frbr:embodiment :cited-document-3-manifestation ;
  pso:holdsStatusInTime :published-cited-document-3 ;
  frbr:revisionOf :cited-document-3-preprint .

:cited-document-3-preprint a fabio:Preprint ;
  pso:holdsStatusInTime :accepted-cited-document-3 .

:cited-document-3-manifestation a fabio:Manifestation ;
  prism:publicationDate "2005"^^xsd:gYear ;
  prims:startingPage "63" ;
  prims:endingPage "69" .

:lachmayer a foaf:Person ;
  foaf:givenName "F." ;
  foaf:familyName "Lachmayer" ;
  pro:holdsRoleInTime [
    a pro:RoleInTime ;
    pro:withRole pro:author ;
    pro:relatesToDocument :cited-document-3-work ] .

:hoffmann a foaf:Person ;
  foaf:givenName "H." ;
  foaf:familyName "Hoffmann" ;
  pro:holdsRoleInTime [
    a pro:RoleInTime ;
    pro:withRole pro:author ;
    pro:relatesToDocument :cited-document-3-work ] .

:accepted-cited-document-3 a pso:StatusInTime ;
  pso:withStatus pro:accepted-for-publication ;
  pso:isAquiredAsConsequenceOf :decision-process-of-cited-document-3 .

:published-cited-document-3 a pso:StatusInTime ;
  pso:withStatus pro:published ;
  pso:isAquiredAsConsequenceOf :publishing-process-of-cited-document-3 ;
```

```
  tvc:atTime [
    a ti:TimeInterval ;
    ti:hasStartingTime "2005-01-01T00:00:00"^^xsd:dateTime ] .

:decision-process-of-cited-document-3 a part:Event ;
  dcterms:description "The decision process of the chairs for the paper
      entitled 'From legal categories towards legal ontologies'." .

:publishing-process-of-cited-document-3 a part:Event ;
  dcterms:description "The publisher produces the version of record of the
      paper entitled 'From legal categories towards legal ontologies'." .

:workflow-cited-document-3 a pwo:Workflow ;
  pwo:hasStep [
    a pwo:Step ;
    pwo:involvesEvent :decision-process-of-cited-document-3 ;
    pwo:needs :cited-document-3-preprint ;
    pwo:produces :accepted-cited-document-3 ;
    pwo:hasNextStep [
      a pwo:Step ;
      pwo:involvesEvent :publishing-process-of-cited-document-3 ;
      pwo:needs
        :accepted-cited-document-3 ,
        :cited-document-3-expression ;
      pwo:produces :published-cited-document-3 ] ] .

:a_text a earmark:StringDocuverse ;
  earmark:hasContent "5.0 en corresponding author workplace ref1 ref2 ref3
      ref1 [1] conference paper conference proceedings ref2 [2] conference
      paper conference proceedings ref3 [3] workshop paper workshop
      proceedings"^^xsd:string .

:d_text a earmark:StringDocuverse ;
  earmark:hasContent "A Semantics-based Visual Framework
  for Planning a New Bill Carlo Biagioli CNR ITTIG via
    Panciatichi 56/16 50127 Florence Italy Enrico Francesconi
    francesconi@ittig.cnr.it ITTIG-CNR via Panciatichi
    56/16 50127 Florence Italy +3905543995 +39055410644
    CNR ITTIG via Panciatichi 56/16 50127 Florence Italy In
    this paper a module able to guide the legislative drafter in
    planning a new bill is presented. This module aims at
    helping the legislative drafter to build a new act from a
    conceptual point of view. Using this module the classical
    drafting process is inverted: the structure of a bill is constructed
    on the basis of its semantics. Provision Model OWL
    Planning Semantic Legal Drafting Introduction This project
    aims at building a module for planning new bills. It is
    conceived as a part of a project to implement a law making
    environment for the production and reviews of
    legislative texts. NIREditor is the central element of this
    environment, being a law drafting module able to produce
    law texts according to the standards established by the
    Norme in Rete (NIR) project. It is based on a double vision
    of the legislative text: formal and functional . Articles,
    paragraphs, etc., are entities of the formal profile, while
    functional entities are provisions (ex. definition , obligation ,
    sanction , amendments , etc.) and their arguments (ex.
    the addressee of an obligation) represented as metadata
    in the DTD NIR. The planning module presented in this
    paper aims at providing the legislative drafter with facilities
    for the construction of a new bill starting from the
    definition of its semantics in terms of provisions and their
```

arguments. The Planning Module This project aims at providing users with facilities to help the organization of a new legislative text according to a semantic point of view. In the traditional legal drafting the formal structure of a document may not be the best one to express the semantics of the text. The Planning module aims at turning over the traditional legal drafting process, providing facilities to firstly express the semantics (functional profile), then to organize the semantic components in a well-suited formal structure. In this process metadata are chosen by the legislative drafter himself: therefore they are authentic metadata , as chosen by the legislative drafter, and they are used also to guide the drafting phase. The planning activity basically consists in describing how the domain of interest of the human activities (a scenario) will be regulated by the new act. The formalization of this can rely on a model of the scenario to be regulated (terms and concepts drawn from or organized into term hierarchies (thesauri) and concept taxonomies (ontologies)) and on a model of the possible ways the act will regulate the scenario (model of provisions and arguments). The established relations and the instances of these models will represent the semantics (the functional profile) of the bill under construction. Facilities will be provided helping the organization of the semantic components (provisions) into formal partitions of the constructing act. At the end of this process, the formal partitions of the act will contain semantically correlated components (provisions), and the semantically qualified formal structure skeleton of the new act can be obtained. Partition wording can rely upon the user, or proposals of partitions wording can be generated on the basis of the semantics of the provision associated to each partition. The Planning Module Software Architecture The Planning module is conceived as a visual editor of provisions and it is composed by four main elements: a Model of Provisions and Arguments, a Model of the scenario to be regulated, a Definition manager, a Visual Provision Manager. The Model of Provisions and Arguments is represented using OWL, since it guarantees interoperability among applications relying on it and a well-grounded framework for reasoning on provisions. The Model of the scenario is described by legal concepts or terms drawn from JurWordNet or from ontologies and lexicons of the domain of interest: usually they are the description of the involved actors (norm addressees), the main activities, the regulated actions, and in general the entities of the domain regulated by the law. Along with possible new terms, they can be collected in a Definition Manager. They will be used mainly as provision argument values (ex: arguments of Definitions). The Visual Provision Manager is a visual panel where provisions types and their arguments can be inserted and handled as visual objects, thus defining the functional profile of the new act. In a second phase the user will be able to provide the best structural organization (formal profile) of the text, with the advantage to see the building blocks (paragraphs) of the bill under construction from the point of view of their meaning (provisions). Provision instances can be grouped, through queries on provisions and arguments, into semantically correlated clusters (articles , from the formal point of view). This process can be recursively repeated, obtaining a tree representing the

```
semantically annotated document formal profile, to be
worded (manually or semi-automatically) being guided
by the semantic annotation. Conclusions A module able to
guide the legislative drafter in planning a new bill from a
conceptual point of view has been presented. The
traditional drafting process is inverted: the structure of a
bill (formal profile) is constructed on the basis of its
semantics (functional profile), so to obtain a well-structured
text, where the chosen formal structure fits well the
functional profile. A prototype is currently under
implementation on a Java platform. References C. Biagioli E.
Francesconi P. Spinosa M. Taddei A legal drafting
environment based on formal and semantic XML standards
Proceedings of the Tenth International Conference on
Artificial Intelligence and Law 244-245 2005 L. Branting J.
Lester C. Callaway Automated Drafting of Self-Explainig
Documents Proceedings of the Sixth International
Conference on Artificial Intelligence and Law 72-81 1997
F. Lachmayer H. Hoffmann From legal categories
towards legal ontologies Proceedings of the Workshop on
Legal Ontologies and Artificial Intelligence Techniques
63-69 2005"^^xsd:string .
```

Appendix 3: Software and Ontology Sources

In this appendix I list the software and the ontologies that I developed and that I used for the purpose of this book.

EARMARK Java API The *Extremely Annotational RDF Markup* (*EARMARK*) is a meta-syntax for non-embedded markup that can be used for stand-off annotations of textual content with fully Semantic Web W3C-compliant technologies. EARMARK is based on an ontologically precise definition of markup that instantiates the markup of a text document as an independent OWL document outside of the text strings it annotates, and through appropriate OWL characterisations it can define structures such as trees or graphs and can be used to generate validity constraints (including co-constraints currently unavailable in most validation languages). This ontology was implemented as a Java API for the creation, validation and manipulation of EARMARK documents, such as the above one. The API is hosted by GitHub at the URL `http://www.github.com/essepuntato/EarmarkDataStructure` under the Apache 2.0 license, and uses Jena (`http://jena.apache.org`), a well-known library that allows one to load, manipulate and store RDF graphs.

XML2EARMARK *XML2EARMARK* is a Web application, available at `http://www.essepuntato.it/xml2earmark`, that allows one to convert an XML document into an EARMARK one (linearised in RDF/XML). The Java source code of the application is hosted by GitHub at the URL `http://www.github.com/essepuntato/XML2EARMARK` under the Internet Systems Consortium (ISC) license, and uses Saxon9 Home Edition (`http://saxon.sourceforge.net`) to perform XSLT transformations.

LODE The *Live OWL Documentation Environment* (*LODE*) is a service, available at `http://www.essepuntato.it/lode`, that extracts classes, object properties, data properties, named individuals, annotation properties, general axioms and namespace declarations from an OWL and OWL2 ontology automatically, and renders them as ordered lists, together with their textual definitions, in a human-readable HTML page designed for browsing and navigation by means of embedded links. The Java source code of the application is hosted by GitHub at the URL `http://www.github.com/essepuntato/LODE` under the Internet Systems Consortium (ISC) license. LODE uses Saxon9 Home Edition (`http://saxon.sourceforge.net`) to perform XSLT transformations, and the OWLAPI (`http://owlapi.sourceforge.net`) to convert OWL ontologies and RDF(S) vocabularies into RDF/XML sources.

KC-Viz The *Key Concept Visualiser* (*KC-Viz*) is a tool for visualising and navigating ontologies, which exploits an innovative ontology summarisation method to support a *middle-out* ontology browsing approach, where it becomes possible to navigate ontologies starting from the most information-rich nodes (i.e., key concepts). KC-Viz is one of the core component of the NeOn Toolkit, which can be downloaded at `http://neon-toolkit.org/wiki/Download`.

KCE The *Key Concepts Extraction* (KCE) algorithm, available online at `http://www.essepuntato.it/kce`, defines a novel approach to identifying the concepts in an ontology, which best summarise what the ontology is about. KCE makes use of a number of criteria, drawn from cognitive science, network topology, and lexical statistics to try and produce the kind of ontology summaries which human experts would come up with. While the generation of automatic methods for ontology summarisation is an interesting research area in itself, KCE also provides a basis for novel approaches to a variety of ontology engineering tasks, including ontology matching, automatic classification, ontology modularisation, and ontology. The Java source code of the algorithm is hosted by GitHub at the URL `http://www.github.com/essepuntato/KCE` under the Internet Systems Consortium (ISC) license.

Graffoo *Graffoo*, the *Graphical Framework for OWL Ontologies*, is an open source set of widgets, available online at `http://www.essepuntato.it/graffoo`, that can be used to present the classes, properties and restrictions within OWL ontologies, or sub-sections of them, as clear and easy-to-understand diagrams. Several Graffoo diagrams have been developed to explain, e.g., SPAR ontologies – that are included in the documentation of the ontology available at `http://purl.org/spar`.

Ontologies All the ontologies developed and presented in this book are available online. In particular, the *Semantic Publishing and Referencing* (*SPAR*)*Ontologies* are introduced in several blog posts of the blog *Semantic Publishing* (`http://semanticpublishing.wordpress.com`), while the whole set of pages documenting such ontologies is available at `http://purl.org/spar`. The rest of the ontologies introduced herein – e.g., *EARMARK*, the *Literal Reification* ontology pattern, the *Error Ontology* – are available at `http://www.essepuntato.it` (i.e., my personal homepage).

References

Barabucci, G., A. Di Iorio, S. Peroni, F. Poggi, F. Vitali. 2013. Annotations with EARMARK in practice: A fairy tale. Proceedings of the 2013 workshop on collaborative annotations in shared environments: Metadata, vocabularies and techniques in the Digital Humanities (DH-CASE 2013). New York: ACM. doi:10.1145/2517978.2517990

Carroll, J., I. Dickinson, C. Dollin, D. Reynolds, A. Seaborne, K. Wilkinson. 2004. Jena: implementing the semantic web recommendations. In Proceedings of the 13th international conference on World Wide Web - Alternate Track Papers & Posters (WWW 2004), ed. S. I. Feldman, M. Uretsky, M. Najork, and C. E. Wills, 74–83. New York: ACM. doi:10.1145/1013367.1013381

Text Encoding Initiative Consortium. 2013. TEI P5: Guidelines for electronic text encoding and interchange. Charlottesville: TEI Consortium. http://www.tei-c.org/Guidelines/P5. Accessed 30 July 2013.

Biagioli, C., E. Francesconi. 2005. A semantics-based visual framework for planning a new bill. In Proceedings of the 18th annual conference on legal knowledge and information systems (JURIX 2005), ed. M.-F. Moens and P. Spyns, 103–104. Amsterdam: IOS Press.

Prud'hommeaux, E., and G. Carothers. 2013. Turtle, terse RDF triple language. W3C Candidate Recommendation 19 February 2013. World Wide Web Consortium. http://www.w3.org/TR/turtle/. Accessed 30 July 2013.

Walsh, N. 2010. DocBook 5: The definitive guide. Sebastopol: O'Really Media. Version 1.0.3. (ISBN: 0596805029).

Index

S. Peroni, *Semantic Web Technologies and Legal Scholarly Publishing*,
Law, Governance and Technology Series 15, DOI 10.1007/978-3-319-04777-5,

The manufacturer's authorised representative in the EU is Springer Nature Customer Service Centre GmbH, Europaplatz 3, 69115 Heidelberg, Germany. If you have any concerns regarding our products, please contact ProductSafety@springernature.com

Printed and bound by CPI Group (UK) Ltd, Croydon, CR0 4YY
30/09/2026
02225651-0009